BRITISH T
COMPANIES: 1965–1979

In the same series from Bloomsbury Methuen Drama:

BRITISH THEATRE COMPANIES: 1980–1994
by Graham Saunders
ISBN 978-1-4081-7548-4
Joint Stock, Gay Sweatshop, Théâtre de Complicité, Forced
Entertainment, Women's Theatre Group, and Talawa

BRITISH THEATRE COMPANIES: 1995–2014
by Liz Tomlin
ISBN 978-1-4081-7727-3
Mind the Gap, Blast Theory, Suspect Culture,
Punchdrunk, Kneehigh, and Stan's Cafe

Related titles:

MODERN BRITISH PLAYWRITING: THE 1950s
by David Pattie
Detailed studies of works by T. S. Eliot, Terence
Rattigan, John Osborne and Arnold Wesker

MODERN BRITISH PLAYWRITING: THE 1960s
by Steve Nicholson
Detailed studies of works by John Arden, Edward
Bond, Harold Pinter and Alan Ayckbourn

MODERN BRITISH PLAYWRITING: THE 1970s
by Chris Megson
Detailed studies of works by Caryl Churchill, David
Edgar, Howard Brenton and David Hare

MODERN BRITISH PLAYWRITING: THE 1980s
by Jane Milling
Detailed studies of works by Howard Barker, Jim Cartwright,
Sarah Daniels and Timberlake Wertenbaker

MODERN BRITISH PLAYWRITING: THE 1990s
by Aleks Sierz
Detailed studies of works by Philip Ridley, Sarah
Kane, Anthony Neilson and Mark Ravenhill

MODERN BRITISH PLAYWRITING: 2000–2009
edited by Dan Rebellato
Detailed studies of works by David Greig, Simon Stephens,
Tim Crouch, Roy Williams and debbie tucker green

BRITISH THEATRE
COMPANIES: 1965–1979

CAST, The People Show, Portable Theatre, Pip Simmons Theatre Group, Welfare State International, 7:84 Theatre Companies

John Bull

Series Editors: John Bull and Graham Saunders

Bloomsbury Methuen Drama
An imprint of Bloomsbury Publishing Plc

B L O O M S B U R Y
LONDON · OXFORD · NEW YORK · NEW DELHI · SYDNEY

Bloomsbury Methuen Drama

An imprint of Bloomsbury Publishing Plc

Imprint previously known as Methuen Drama

50 Bedford Square	1385 Broadway
London	New York
WC1B 3DP	NY 10018
UK	USA

www.bloomsbury.com

BLOOMSBURY, METHUEN DRAMA and the Diana logo are trademarks of Bloomsbury Publishing Plc

First published 2017

British Library Cataloguing-in-Publication Data
A catalogue record for this book is available from the British Library.

ISBN: HB: 978-1-4081-7544-6
PB: 978-1-4081-7543-9
ePDF: 978-1-4081-7546-0
ePub: 978-1-4081-7545-3

Library of Congress Cataloging-in-Publication Data
A catalog record for this book is available from the Library of Congress.

Series: British Theatre Companies: From Fringe to Mainstream
Cover design: Louise Dugdale
Cover image © Shutterstock

Typeset by Fakenham Prepress Solutions, Fakenham, Norfolk NR21 8NN
Printed and bound in India

CONTENTS

ACKNOWLEDGEMENTS

The groundwork for this volume came from my involvement with the Arts and Humanities Research Council (AHRC)-funded five-year project, 'Giving Voice to the Nation: The Arts Council of Great Britain and the Development of Theatre and Performance in Britain 1945–1995', and I am very grateful to the Council for giving me the opportunity of digging into the seemingly bottomless, and hitherto essentially unexcavated, pit that is the Arts Council archive. Research on these papers was greatly aided by the always helpful and always patient members of staff in the Blythe House Reading Room of the Victoria and Albert Museum's Theatre and Performance Collection, which is where the Arts Council archive is held. I would also like to thank in the warmest possible terms all my fellow members of Team GV, Jackie Bolton, Tony Coult, Kate Dorney, Taryn Storey and of course my fellow series editor, Graham Saunders. Your help, advice and the not infrequent archival tit-bit has been invaluable. I have been much helped also by Mark Dudgeon, a fine editor and a gent. In addition, I wish to gratefully acknowledge Tony Coult as the author of the section on Theatre-in-Education in the second chapter of this book.

And finally I would like to dedicate this book to Carole, to Lydia and to Philip. How would I have survived those long days in Blythe House without knowing that you were always willing to be wined, dined and theatred in the evening?

John Bull
London, 2016

SERIES EDITORS' PREFACE

In the first major study of John McGrath's theatre company 7:84 Scotland, published in 1996, Maria DiCenzo notes a curious omission in scholarship: 'While it is not unusual to find book-length studies of the work of playwrights (often an analysis of plays with a bit of socio-political context thrown in), alternative theatre *companies* in the same period have received comparatively little detailed coverage' (DiCenzo, 1996, 6). Despite the remarkable proliferation of companies that emerged from the late 1960s until the end of the 1980s, a phenomenon that undoubtedly reshaped the ecology of British theatre, the area has only ever partially been addressed in edited collections such as Catherine Itzin's *Stages in the Revolution* (1980) and Sandy Craig's *Dreams and Deconstructions: Alternative Theatre in Britain* (1980), or in monographs, principally Andrew Davies's *Other Theatres: The Development of Alternative and Experimental Theatre in Britain* (1987) and Baz Kershaw's *The Politics of Performance: Radical Theatre as Cultural Intervention* (1992). However, in all these cases, the companies themselves are rarely considered collectively, comprising instead one strand of an alternative theatre culture that included arts labs/centres, individual practitioners and dramatists.

In recent years, this situation has changed through the endeavours of Susan Croft's exhaustive online project Unfinished Histories, which concentrates on the work of companies operating between 1968 and 1988. The project seeks to archive and document materials relating to these companies including posters and photographs of productions as well as interviews with former company members. However, being a website, Unfinished Histories, despite providing both valuable focus and scope, cannot provide a clear chronological and contextual account of the overall development of these groups, how they related to each other or how funding policies and shifts in cultural agendas changed their evolution in the course of over forty years.

This three-volume series aims to address this lacuna. Individually, each volume charts the progress – and sometimes demise – of small- to medium-scale touring companies, who from the late 1960s took to the road in a fleet of transit vans and established a network of performance venues for themselves throughout the British Isles. These included theatres, community centres, youth clubs and arts centres as well as urban and rural outdoor spaces.

These companies have been variously described as 'alternative' or 'fringe', yet over the years both their work and more significantly much of their influence have been assimilated into mainstream British theatre culture. For some groups, including Complicité (originally Théâtre de Complicité), Cheek by Jowl and Punchdrunk, their move from the margins to international status has been easy to identify. However, more often than not, the process has been more subtle, and so consequently unrecognized and unacknowledged. A good example of this has been the gradual absorption of black and Asian work into the repertoires of many major subsidized London and regional theatres since the late 1990s. This did not happen by accident: rather it came about through a long succession of gruelling one-night stands by pioneering companies including Tara Arts, Temba and the Black Theatre Co-operative during the 1970s and 1980s.

Each volume covers a distinct historical era. The first discusses the period 1965–79; volume two 1980–94, while volume three covers 1995–2014. The format for all three includes an opening chapter written by each editor that provides a contextual political and cultural background to the period in which the companies operated. The second chapter gives a broad outline and discussion of the many types of companies operating within the given period. Here, the editors have endeavoured not only to include familiar names, but other lesser-known documented groups. The final section of each volume includes a series of case studies from chosen contributors on the work of a particular theatre company active in the period covered.

Archival sources, both from holdings dedicated to a specific company and from the Arts Council of Great Britain, largely inform the choice of companies and approach taken in volumes one and two. This has come out of a larger five-year AHRC-funded project, *Giving Voice to the Nation: The Arts Council of Great Britain and the Development of Theatre and Performance in Britain 1945–1995*, that the editors Bull and Saunders have been engaged on since 2009. It soon became clear that, for the period covered, between 1965 and 1994, the Arts Council archive would provide a unique and, up until recently, unexplored resource for the study of theatre companies active in those years: materials include minutes of company meetings, funding proposals for projects, records of tour dates, statistics on box-office takings and audience attendance, newspaper and magazine reviews and publicity materials, as well as Arts Council memos, letters and records of meetings. These frequently reveal much about the Arts Council's often cryptic assessment methods and more tellingly their attitudes towards particular companies, or the types of work they produced. The archive also offers insights into wider questions relating to changing priorities in policy towards alternative/fringe theatre in Britain from the late 1960s to the mid-1990s. Contributors, where possible (and where relevant), have made use of this resource as well as individual company archives in assessing their work.

As editors, we are mindful of what we have left out. We also fully recognize that some of our decisions will be highly contentious. For instance, with hindsight, the first two volumes could perhaps have been retitled *English Theatre Companies*, as relatively little space is accorded to Scottish, Welsh or Northern Irish companies. This has been influenced by a number of factors: for one thing, we wanted each of the volumes to look at the *kinds* of work produced, rather than the geographical location they came out of. While it also might be assumed that the Arts Council archive would have provided a detailed national survey of British companies, in reality the archive resembles more of a Domesday Book on English theatre. The reasons for this are both historical and administrative, in that the Welsh, Scottish and Northern Ireland offices of the Arts Council, while answerable to London, were in effect autonomous bodies with their own allocated budgets and set of policies. This meant (with the often-made exception for the annual Edinburgh Festival) that a company such as 7:84 Scotland would be funded on the proviso that they tour exclusively within Scotland, unless prior arrangements had been made between other regional offices, or the company had secured necessary funds to tour within England. The third volume begins as the Arts Council of Great Britain devolved into three distinct Arts Councils for England, Scotland and Wales, and so looks at how arts policy develops in each and the impact of this on the independent theatre ecology that emerges across the UK (with the exception of Northern Ireland) in this period.

The editors have also endeavoured to provide as comprehensive an insight as possible into the types of work produced in any given period; yet this will always mean that certain companies will be privileged over others. Sometimes this is reflected in the priorities operating in a given period: in volume one, the second chapter places more emphasis on the relationship between the Arts Council of Great Britain and the theatre/performance companies, because this was the period when public sponsorship in these areas was at its height, and had a significant role to play in developments; in volume two, the second chapter places more emphasis on black, Asian and women's companies simply because these were areas that experienced the largest growth and afforded greater priority in terms of funding allocation than companies specializing in Live Art or Theatre-in-Education; whereas volume three takes particular account of the participation and access agenda that supported a growth in theatre for children and young people, as well as more widespread experimentation with audience involvement.

The editors are also aware of the problems of adopting a chronological approach. While the majority of companies only enjoyed a comparatively short life span, others such as CAST, The Women's Theatre Group and Temba continued to work over several decades. While each editor's second chapter concentrates on the work of groups who were formed within the period covered by their respective volumes (with some leeway given between companies who formed on the cusp), the contributors' chapters on particular companies assess the work on the basis of what they consider to be their most significant or celebrated of the period.

John Bull and Graham Saunders
Series Editors

PREFACE TO THE VOLUME

The period, 1965–79, considered in this volume was a truly remarkable one for the British theatre. For not only did it see the emergence of a new generation of playwrights, but these were the years when for the first time a widespread alternative theatre circuit was developed: a circuit that grew to serve an increasing host of new theatre companies largely intent on avoiding the traditional venues of theatrical performance, with the aim of locating new audiences – ones that would prove to be as varied in their constituencies as were the companies that courted their attendance. It was a period of 'hopes for great happenings', to borrow Albert Hunt's famous words: and these hopes were mostly seen as being in opposition to the practices and mores of straight bourgeois society, and associated with what became labelled the 'alternative society', an exciting mash-up of politics, culture and art, in which everything was up for questioning, everything subject to challenge.

It was also a period, initially at least, of unprecedented amounts of public subsidy for the arts being made available: and many of the new theatrical companies made good use of the opportunities. Indeed, the 'movement' – and I use the word for convenience as much as anything else, being aware that in many ways its formlessness was its point – could not have developed at the speed with which it did without the availability of such public funding. There were, however, individuals and companies who felt that the very fact of being in receipt of subsidy was a move towards being assimilated into mainstream culture – particularly politically committed groups set on changing the world, or at least aspects of it.

A great deal of the research for the second chapter of this book derives from the opportunity given to colleagues from the 'Giving Voice' AHRC-funded project and other authors in this volume, myself included, to delve properly for the first-time into the archives of the Arts Council of Great Britain (ACGB), the body responsible for dispensing most of that subsidy. As well as information about funding decisions, touring schedules, future production plans, minutes of company meetings, manifestos, correspondence and internal memos, accounts of internal General Council, Drama Panel and associated committee meetings, there are invaluable Show Reports prepared as an aid to making funding decisions on individual companies. The last often provides effectively the only way of recalling past performances for which no other records exist.

This series of three volumes, covering the years between 1965 and 2014, has a subtitle of 'From Fringe to Mainstream'. Given that this was the last time in post-war British theatre history that was almost entirely free of the increasing move (from 1980 on) towards private and corporate sponsorship 'encouraged' by successive governments, this is the volume that is most concerned with the Fringe end of that arc. It is, by the same token, the one in which the public support is most important and, for that reason, a major theme of my second chapter will be a concern with the relationship between the companies and the ACGB.

John Bull

Professor of Drama at the University of Lincoln, UK, and Emeritus Professor in Film and Theatre at the University of Reading, UK

Chapter 1

HISTORICAL, POLITICAL AND CULTURAL CONTEXT

John Bull

In the Beginning

'To begin at the beginning' – the famous opening words of Dylan Thomas's 1954 radio play, *Under Milk Wood*, have a total relevance to a story or a piece of theatre, but are less helpful with an introduction that is seeking to contextualize a particular historical period. For history – despite the best efforts of historians – does not divide itself neatly into a series of narratives that have an easily identifiable beginning, middle and end. So, while the starting point of 1965 for most of this volume is largely determined by the fact that the first material embodiments of what we can now see as a modern 'alternative theatre' movement can be dated from this year, its roots – politically, historically and culturally – are to be found rather earlier. These could, theoretically, be traced back to the pre-Second World War years, to Unity Theatre, for example, and to the various ventures that led eventually to Joan Littlewood's Theatre Workshop finding a London base at the Theatre Royal, Stratford East, in 1953 – and there are, indeed, important connections to be made (see Davies, 1987, for instance). However, the particular circumstances, which led to the formation of the many groups whose work forms the subject of this volume, can be found in the years immediately preceding 1965. Thus, this will be about a series of frequently and fascinatingly related narratives that belong to Britain from the late 1950s to the late 1970s.

For most of the generation growing up after 1945, the Second World War was far more removed from their lives than it was for their parents and, for the most part, it will be the activities of that younger generation with which we will be concerned in this book. The mid-1950s' cinema was dominated by British-made reconstructions of the war, as seen in *The Colditz Story* (1954), *The Dambusters* and *Cockleshell Heroes* (both 1955), and, most famously, *Reach for the Sky* (1957). These films provided glorified and, for the younger cinema-goers, in particular, second-hand memories of the conflict that their parents had experienced first-hand, in a country in which the last connections with that war were beginning to disappear. Clothes rationing had been halted in 1949; four years later, confectionary and then sugar rationing followed – thus enabling John Osborne's Jimmy Porter to run a street-market sweet stall by the time that *Look Back in Anger* opened in 1956. And in 1954, all restrictions on the sale of meat and other food were finally lifted. Similarly, in December 1960, National Service was abolished and the last conscripts embarked on their two years of conscription into the Armed Forces and the final servicemen were demobbed in 1963, the same year in which Arnold Wesker's most successful play, *Chips With Everything*, based on the playwright's own experiences of National Service in the Royal Air Force (RAF) in the early 1950s, was playing in London's West End.

The generation growing up after 1945 would be the first to have the generic label 'teenagers' attached to them as they passed through their adolescent years. This was a process of labelling that acknowledged the significance of two related factors: the increasing economic significance of adolescents as consumers, and also the steady development of what came to be known as 'mass' or 'popular' culture. This culture of the young defined itself – sometimes aggressively – in terms of such things as clothes style and tastes in popular music. And in 1958 there were a million more 'teens' than there had been a decade earlier and a million more potential consumers in a market that was increasingly catering to their tastes.

Whose History are we Talking About?

This chapter, while it will essentially be concerned with alternative theatrical/performance activity created and witnessed by a post-war generation, will also seek to define more narrowly the constituency of these creators and witnesses. They were regarded as being largely on the margins by what came to be known as 'straight society'. A comparison with a more traditional approach to cultural and social history – one less concerned with a world of alternative visions – will make the point much more clear. In a remarkable series of books, the historian Dominic Sandbrook has provided a narrative that melds together the party political with the cultural in the period between 1956 and 1979.

However, as fascinating and instructive as Sandbrook's work is, it cannot provide in itself an adequate introduction to the context in which the development of an alternative theatre movement can be traced. For, the protagonists of this new wave did not perceive their contemporary world through the lens of 'normality', which is Sandbrook's central criterion in developing his argument, but with reference to events that he largely refers to as peripheral, as not engaging the attention of the majority of the great British public.

To take but one of Sandbrook's examples by way of amplification, in *White Heat: A History of Britain in the Swinging Sixties,* he discusses the famous free concert that the Rolling Stones performed at in Hyde Park on 5 July 1969. Following the death of former group member Brian Jones, the event became more of a memorial for him at which Mick Jagger read from *Adonais,* the poet Shelley's elegy on the death of Keats, after which hundreds of white butterflies were released. Sandbrook's account of the event is, however, prefaced by an attempt to 'put the event in context':

> the estimated 250,000 people who crowded into the park on that searing afternoon might have amounted to a vast crowd by the standards of pop concerts, but they looked pretty puny when set alongside the 20 million or so who preferred entertainment like *The Black and White Minstrel Show'.* (Sandbrook, 2007, 566)

Leaving the absurdity of the terms of Sandbrook's comparison aside – the comparison of the audience of a nationwide television show against that of a concert in a park – what Sandbrook totally fails to acknowledge is the fact that these two events would not only fail to share a common audience constituency, but also that those two constituencies would have been positively hostile to each other's choice of entertainment. Another example of this might be when Prime Minister Harold Wilson recommended to the Queen that the Beatles be made MBEs (Members of the Most Honourable Order of the British Empire) in 1965. Whereas many of his '20-million-or so' TV viewers may possibly have wondered why Wilson had given them MBEs in the first place, others (some of them the people who would crowd into Hyde Park to watch the Stones four years later) would more likely be wondering why the Beatles had actually accepted them. My narrative will be more concerned with the latter, and certainly not with a Saturday night television audience settled down cosily to watch a show in which white singers blacked up to sing minstrel songs. The alternative society simply did not stay in on a Saturday night.

A Musical Interlude

These two examples are indicative of the way in which a popular music culture developed – from the birth of rock 'n' roll in the mid-1950s onwards – providing not just the soundtrack to subsequent cultural events, but also helping to define the many socio-cultural schisms and groupings that occurred in the post-war period. In 1960, a young teenage boy, urged on by his somewhat older friends, attended his very first pop concert, at the Elephant and Castle Trocadero in London. He had gone principally to see the American Duane Eddy, accompanied by the Rebel Rousers. Later that same year, Eddy would be voted the 'World's Number One Musical Personality' by the readers of the *New Musical Express*, an honour previously accorded to Elvis Presley in the year before. The only snag was that Eddy was not the star of the show, as events would show.

Pride of place went to another American act, Bobby Darin, who had started UK chart life as a somewhat ambivalent rock 'n' roller, before turning his talents to ballads. This culminated in the release of 'Beyond the Sea', just before the British tour got under way, a 'back-to-the-crooners' version of the French song 'La Mer'. Darin's UK chart success was a surprise and caused the tour management to rethink their strategy: Eddy's pre-announced slot as the finale act instead went to Darin, a move that did not please everyone, especially Eddy's Teddy Boy following.

Eddy closed the first half with a suitably rousing set, which was received with great enthusiasm all round. Darin was met with a very different air of expectancy from the audience. Once on stage, he was jeered and whistled at by the group of Teddy Boys at the back of the balcony seats. However, it was when the singer launched into 'Beyond the Sea' that they started to throw old (and heavy) pennies at the stage, directly at Darin. It was at this point, as the shower of coins passed just over our heads, that my friends and I took shelter on the floor of our seats in the front of the balcony.

Where Darin was self-consciously and nostalgically looking back to the previous generation of crooners and, in particular, to Frank Sinatra, rock 'n' roll was perceived – for better or worse – as 'of the moment' and was associated with a spirit of adolescent rebellion. In fact, the record that first announced the birth of rock 'n' roll to a wider public, Bill Haley's 'Rock Around the Clock', only cracked the US music charts after it aired in *Blackboard Jungle* (1955), a movie about a troubled inner-city high school in the States.

Perhaps ironically, shortly after the aforementioned concert at which Darin got slated for crooning, Eddy had his biggest UK hit, 'Because They're Young', a lush ballad complete with strings: it wasn't exactly rock 'n' roll. His song was adopted by Jimmy Savile as the theme music for his weekly DJ slot on Radio Luxemburg, the only real point of public access for this new teenage audience. Apart from the BBC Light Programme's 'Saturday Club', the corporation was almost entirely rock-free until post 1967, when offshore pirate radio stations were prohibited from broadcasting and the BBC belatedly acknowledged public demand for the genre with the creation of Radio 1.

Popular music, and in particular rock 'n' roll and its various offsprings, most reliably furnishes evidence of the development of a modern Britain that did not rise from establishment culture. As music historian Clive Martin notes:

> There are two histories of modern Britain, running concurrently and only occasionally touching. The first is the one of parliaments, politicians, royal babies, military interventions, prosperity, austerity and all the rest of it. The other is surely the history of the streets, sounds and styles that inform not only our culture, but also how we are seen across the world. (Martin, 2015)

By 1960, Teddy Boys, influenced by American rock 'n' roll and the fashions of the Edwardian era, and the first of many subcultural formations arising in Britain post 1945, were an increasingly less common phenomenon. From the early to mid-1960s, the Mods became identifiable, not just by their choice of fashion style, but also by the music that they listened to – largely R&B and Jamaican ska. For many, this group is brought to mind through their 1964 seaside rumbles with the Rockers, whose music of choice was basic rock 'n' roll – and also as the scooter boys versus motorbike boys, as defined in the 1979 film *Quadrophenia*, based on the 1973 album by one of the most quintessentially Mod groups, the Who. The Mods, who were never really a single unified entity, evolved into various offshoot groups, among them 'rude boys' (influenced by the music favoured by young West Indian immigrants) and, by the end of the 1960s, a more aggressive wing, the embryonic 'skinheads', although that group did not initially have the racist overtones with which it would become linked later.

There is not space here to describe the complicated evolution of these various groups and their musical, cultural and class affiliations (for this, see Hebdige, 1979, 1993): but the clash between old and new musical cultures would be central to the continual remapping of the counterculture – for a common factor in the early development of all these groups was the conscious desire for separation from mainstream popular culture. At the other end of the period covered in this volume, the punk movement defined itself in opposition to a whole catalogue of mainstream phenomena. But there was always a dichotomy present. In 1956, even as Elvis Presley was enjoying his first US Number One on the Billboard singles chart with 'Heartbreak Hotel', the doyen of the pre-rock generation, Frank Sinatra, was firmly ensconced at the top of the album charts with his most successful LP, *Songs for Swinging Lovers*. It is an instructive model and provides a direct and related parallel to much of the avant-garde theatrical movement, which, too, sought to distance itself from the conventional theatrical mainstream, from what was seen as culturally associated with the establishment. And, of course, Presley would himself become rapidly assimilated into the mainstream. For, as this and subsequent volumes in this series will reveal, the lure of the mainstream is always there: in this case the desire to move from small non-theatrical venues to the big stages pulling like a magnet – from fringe to mainstream, indeed.

The Establishment and its Discontents

In 1974, the poet Philip Larkin published his final collection of poetry, *High Windows*. It contains one poem, in particular, that is often quoted as if it offered some kind of way-in to the preceding decade. The poem, 'Annus Mirabilis', opens with a somewhat sad and actually erroneous expression of Larkin having essentially missed the boat. Here, he states 'sexual intercourse' (or sexual permissiveness, as Larkin means it) begins in 'nineteen sixty three', a year falling between the attempt to ban the Penguin paperback edition of D. H. Lawrence's contentious *Lady Chatterley's Lover* and the release of the Beatles' 'first LP'. Larkin is referring to the unsuccessful prosecution of Penguin Books under the aegis of the 1959 Obscene Publications Act, an event that has come to be seen as a prelude to what became known as the 'swinging sixties'. Sixty years later, the Queen's Councillor, Geoffrey Robertson, stated why the case was so important:

> The verdict was a crucial step towards the freedom of the written
> word, at least for works of literary merit [...] [The] trial marked
> the first symbolic moral battle between the humanitarian force of

English liberalism and the dead hand of those described by George Orwell as 'the striped-trousered ones who rule', a battle joined in the 1960s on issues crucial to human rights, including the legalisation of homosexuality and abortion, abolition of the death penalty and of theatre censorship, and reform of the divorce laws. The acquittal of *Lady Chatterley* was the first sign that victory was achievable. (Robertson, 2010)

In 1960, just one year after the case, the contraceptive pill was made available on the National Health Service (NHS), enabling women – and men – greater sexual freedom. Fifty years later, the journalist Rebecca Café evaluated its significance: 'In 1961, women's lives were very different. Often married at an early age, most women were expected to stay at home and raise an expanding family while men went out to work. Nowadays, women can choose to have children, further education and a career on their own terms [because of the pill]' (Café, 2011).

Initially, the new pill was seen firstly as a means of helping older women who felt that they had completed their families still enjoy a sex life; and certainly, and above all, it was to be prescribed exclusively to married women. The authorities were clear that they did not want it to encourage non-marital sexual relationships and promiscuity. As the 1960s progressed, however, it was not uncommon to see unmarried women sporting wedding rings in unfamiliar doctors' surgeries, although it was not actually until 1974 that Family Planning Clinics received government approval to prescribe the pill to single women: and, even then, demands were made in Parliament and elsewhere that parents should be informed if their young daughters were in possession of it. So, throughout a good part of the 1960s, gentlemen's barbers continued to ask rather significantly if 'Sir requires *anything* for the weekend?' and nervous young men were seen waiting anxiously at the dispensing counter of the chemists, until a male assistant was in attendance and no one else was in the queue. As late as 1972, the British movie *Carry on Matron* featured actor Sid James as a petty crook intent on stealing contraceptive pills from a maternity hospital to sell abroad. The placement of the pills as a central part of the narrative structure of a *Carry On* film is indicative of the fact that they were still a slightly risqué topic in the popular imagination.

The year 1963 also saw the release of what Larkin references in his poem as 'The Beatles' first LP', *Please Please Me*. The group's Top 20 singles' career had started with 'Love Me Do' and 'Please Please Me' in the previous year – they achieved the first of their seventeen

UK Number Ones with 'From Me to You' in 1963, the year in which 'Beatlemania' really took off. Credited with changing the course of rock/pop history, the Beatles were originally reliant – as were their supposed rivals, the Rolling Stones – on the US back catalogue of songs. Thus, arguably if they pointed a way forward to their fans, then they also looked back. This can be best illustrated with reference to the Beatles' first LP that Larkin refers to. The front cover is dominated by a photograph taken by Angus McBean. Shot from below, it shows the four Beatles, John Lennon, Paul McCartney, George Harrison and Ringo Starr, all looking down from a stairwell bannister inside the London Headquarters of EMI records. However, while John, Paul and George are already sporting the mop-cut hairstyle that would soon become iconic, Ringo – who had recently replaced Pete Best as drummer and was poached from another Liverpool act, Rory Storm and the Hurricanes – still has a Teddy Boy quiff. At this point, he looks as though he belongs to an entirely different group to the other three.

Beatlemania was not the only thing to engage public and media attention in 1963, however. Not referenced by Larkin, but impossible all the same to ignore at the time, that year also saw the unravelling of the Profumo Affair, the most notorious scandal to rock the post-war British establishment and Prime Minister Harold MacMillan's government, one in which the significance of 'sexual intercourse' was certainly recognized.

MacMillan had taken office following the Suez fiasco of 1957 – when the United States had failed to support a military project to recover the Suez Canal after it had been 'nationalized' by Egypt's Colonel Nasser. Born in 1894, MacMillan grew up in the Edwardian period, and everything about his presence and his style proclaimed his allegiance to it. He was, in a very different sense, a 'Teddy' boy, and rather an anachronism in the Britain of the 1960s, something that was much played upon by the 'other Harold' (Harold Wilson), who had been elected as the new leader of the Labour Party in 1963. In any event, MacMillan was simply too ill-equipped to fully understand, let alone deal with, the implications of what was about to unfold.

On 21 March 1963, in the House of Commons questions were raised for the first-time about rumours that had been circulating for several months pertaining to events 'involving a member of the Government front bench [...] Miss Christine Keeler, and Miss [Mandy Rice-]Davies and a shooting by a West Indian [Johnny Edgecombe]' (*Hansard*, 1963). The following day, John Profumo, the minister in question, issued a statement in Parliament, saying that 'there was no impropriety whatsoever in my relationship with Miss Keeler', and threatening to sue if such allegations were repeated outside the House (Denning, 1963, 113–15).

It was open season for the British press as details emerged that linked the activities of a London osteopath, Stephen Ward, as 'sponsor' of a number of young girls (including Keeler and Rice-Davies), with boisterous house parties held at Clivedon, Lord Astor's country house in Berkshire. Profumo had first encountered Christine Keeler naked, after a late night swim in the pool, at one such event. And, as if this wasn't salacious enough, other party attendees included Russian agent Eugene Ivanov (who also shared Keeler's favours with Profumo), the infamous slum landlord Peter Rachman, a former lover of Rice-Davies, along with a West Indian rival for Keeler's affection. There were also reported illegal 'shebeens', drugs, knives and guns.

Eventually, and perhaps inevitably, Profumo apologized for lying to the House and resigned – events recalled in Hugh Whitemore's 1997 play, *A Letter of Resignation*. In July 1963, Stephen Ward was tried for living off the immoral earnings of prostitutes and, after having been found guilty on what now looks like very weak evidence, died of a self-inflicted overdose of Nembutal. In July, MacMillan asked the Master of the Rolls, Lord Denning, to prepare a report, subsequently published in September of that year. Its investigation of the truths about an alleged 'bizarre world of sado-masochism, sex slaves and general debauchery' resulted in unprecedented sales of the paperback of *Lord Denning's Report* – 100,000 copies on the first day of sale alone – figures unrivalled since the sale of the Penguin edition of *Lady Chatterley's Lover* in 1960 (Sandbrook, 2006, 671, 677).

The scandal and the opportunity to air the related stories of a corrupt ruling class and its connections with an underworld of vice and crime came at an opportune time – and not just for the traditional press. The early 1960s had seen an opening up of debate about public issues in all areas of the media. This sense of a newly acquired freedom to take aim at the sacred cows of a passing world was perhaps best typified by the Cambridge Footlights revue, *Beyond the Fringe*, which, as its name suggests, started life at the Edinburgh Fringe Festival, before opening in London in August 1960. Written and performed by Peter Cook, Dudley Moore, Alan Bennett and Jonathan Miller – names that would find international recognition in the years to come – it transferred to New York's Broadway, but continued to play with new casts in London's Mayfair Theatre until 1966. Its mixture of undergraduate humour and political satire struck a sympathetic note with audiences more used to the conventional fare of revues such as *Pieces of Eight*, which had been a great success the previous year and had featured a sketch by Harold Pinter, as well as work by Peter Cook.

Cook was to become involved in two further ventures in the following year. In October 1961 the Establishment Club, owned by Cook and Nicholas Luard, opened its doors in London's Greek Street, taking advantage of its club status to avoid the attentions of the Lord Chamberlain's office. Although it only lasted until 1964, it was for a short period the single most important venue for 'alternative comedy' – a term that meant nothing at the time – in Britain, offering a showcase for, among others, the notorious US comedian Lenny Bruce and Barry Humphries' Edna Everage. In addition, Cook and Luard were very much involved with the satirical magazine *Private Eye* which had also started life in 1961. After a somewhat slow start in circulation terms, sales had begun to pick up as it acquired a more professional look – the Prufumo affair came gift-wrapped for the paper and it took every possible advantage to stick it to the 'establishment'. Contributors included Barry Humphries, whose comic strip, 'The Wonderful World of Barry McKenzie', featuring the adventures of Bazza, a beer-swilling and thoroughly politically incorrect (many years before the term was first coined) Australian at large in Earls Court and elsewhere in London, helps to illustrate the essentially anarchic format of the early issues. Its radicalism was then more wayward than political.

One of the other regular contributors to *Private Eye* was Willie Rushton who was very much a part of the ground-breaking BBC Television programme, *That Was The Week That Was* – affectionately known as *TW3* – a weekly Saturday night 'must-see' that was first broadcast on 24 November 1962. Itself a product of the 'satire boom' of the early 1960s, its launch just as the Profumo scandal was about to break could not have been better timed. Produced by Ned Sherrin and hosted by David Frost, its irreverent and provocative tone was something quite new for British television and it did not always go down well with those public figures that it attacked and lampooned.

Never Had It So Good

Harold MacMillan had been Prime Minister during the years of post-war adjustment in Britain. Under his leadership, Britain had started to get rid of its imperialist legacy. In 1960, he had delivered a clear message to the African nations seeking independence from British rule: 'The wind of change is blowing through this continent and, whether we like it or not, this growth of national consciousness is a political fact. We must all accept it as a fact, and our national policies must take account of it' (Levin, 1970, 203). MacMillan also oversaw the beginnings of a new affluence in Britain, at least in comparative terms. His most frequently recalled words sought to underline the point: 'Indeed, let us be frank about it – most of our people have never had it so good' (see *Daily Telegraph*, 19 November 2010; the text of the 1957 Tory rally speech is quoted in full): but it was not a feeling that was shared by all.

In 1958, the doors were opened on the first new theatre to be built in Britain since the war, The Belgrade in Coventry, a venue that would pioneer Theatre-in-Education (TiE) in the 1960s. For its very first production, it commissioned Joan Littlewood's Theatre Workshop: the resulting *Never Had It So Good* recalled Macmillan's words ironically, and presented a very different picture of life in Britain. However, Macmillan stuck with his theme, securing a substantially increased majority in the 1959 General Election for a Conservative Party campaigning under the slogan 'Life's better under the Conservatives'. One later analyst was to claim that Macmillan's assertion and the accompanying slogan 'reflected a new reality of working-class affluence', and that 'the key factor in the Conservative victory was that average real pay for industrial workers had risen since Churchill's 1951 victory by over twenty per cent' (Lamb, 1995, 62).

However, there were also fundamental economic problems and, in particular, a worsening balance of payments situation. It was a somewhat paradoxical nation that saw in the new decade: By late 1960, the gap between revenue from exports and expenditure from imports was widening still further, and a crisis seemed imminent, with strikes in the key areas of the docks and the car and construction industries (Lamb, 1995, 69). In July of the following year, attempts by Macmillan's Chancellor of the Exchequer, Selwyn Lloyd, to address the problem with an emergency austerity budget were accompanied by a freeze on public sector wage rises: a move that was not only ineffectual but proved extremely unpopular, and resulted in a series of by-election losses. In 1962, in desperation and alarmed about his own position as prime minister, Macmillan, in an operation immediately labelled the 'Night of the Long Knives', sacked one-third of his cabinet ministers in the hope that a reshuffle might somehow stave off disaster. It was a strategy wonderfully memorialized by a politician, later to become the ill-fated

Liberal Party leader, Jeremy Thorpe: 'Greater love hath no man than this, than to lay down his friends for his life' (Thomas, 1998, 17).

For Macmillan, the writing was on the wall. In 1963, he resigned and was succeeded by Lord Alec Douglas-Home, a man who was, in his own way, as much an anachronism as Macmillan had come to seem as Britain entered the 1960s: the fourteenth Earl of Home, he was forced to relinquish his peerage, but not his Scottish estate, in order to qualify for office by successfully standing for election to the House of Commons. In any event, he would be prime minister for less than a year before the 1964 General Election was held.

The 1964 General Election and Extra-Parliamentary Activity

The election came at a particularly traumatic time for both leaders of the two major parties. Home's aristocratic roots seemed to many – including even staunch party members – an embarrassment in the 1960s; and the Labour Party was going through a considerable crisis of identity following the death of its leader, Hugh Gaitskell, also in 1963. Gaitskell had been a popular figure, but his political views did not meet with accord from the left-of-centre members of his party and the last three years of his leadership had seen the possibility of an imminent Labour triumph in the polls threatened by internal wranglings about two major issues. The first, which was to continue to be a thorn in the side until the mid-1980s, was the Labour Party's long-held commitment – under Clause IV of its constitution, dating from 1918:

> To secure for the workers by hand or by brain the full fruits of their industry and the most equitable distribution thereof that may be possible upon the basis of the common ownership of the means of production, distribution and exchange, and the best obtainable system of popular administration and control of each industry or service.

Gaitskell's attempts to rid the party of a basic ideological tenet was based pragmatically on his belief that it made it unelectable. His support of the possession of a nuclear deterrent by Britain was an even more contentious issue; and when – at the 1960 Labour Party conference – he unsuccessfully opposed a motion proposing unilateral nuclear disarmament, he gave the impassioned speech for which he is best known to this day, concluding, 'We will fight, and fight, and fight again, to bring back sanity and honesty and dignity, so that our party – with its great past – may retain its glory and its greatness (Macintyre, 2013).

This speech, with its conscious echoing of Winston Churchill's famous wartime declaration, 'We shall fight them on the beaches', may have been greeted with rapturous applause by his parliamentary allies, but it was not only on the radical fringes of his party that Gaitskell's words seemed like a betrayal. In 1958, the Campaign for Nuclear Disarmament (CND) had organized an Easter weekend march from London to the Aldermaston Atomic Weapons Establishment in Berkshire. Among the many marchers was a solid phalanx of writers and directors associated with the recently established English Stage Company at the Royal Court Theatre in London: and one of them, Lindsay Anderson, made a film about the event, *March to Aldermaston*. In 1959, and in subsequent years, the protest march left from Aldermaston and finished in London's Trafalgar Square. By 1961, an estimated one-hundred-and-fifty thousand people participated (Carter, 1986, 110). That same year, a more militant branch of the organization, the Committee of 100, was formed – promising, and delivering, direct civil disobedience, and declaring in its handouts 'you must fill the jails'. Among its original members could be found the playwrights John Osborne and Arnold Wesker, the latter of whom received a prison sentence for his activities.

These two related organizations can be seen as not only the start of an organized public opposition to the deployment of nuclear weapons, but as the starting-point for the development of radical non-conventional, non-party-based extra-parliamentary opposition. CND continues to exist today, though in a very different form, but it can also lay claim as the 'only begetter' of groups such as: Greenpeace (formed 1970); the Ecology Party (formed 1975), which became the Green Party in 1985; and the Greenham Common Women's Peace Camp (1981–2000). CND's formation represents the point from which the 'alternative society' – as it came to be known – can date its birth. And, indeed, the history of the relationship between CND and the Committee of 100 through the early 1960s provided a template for subsequent divisions, schisms and rifts in the world of alternative politics (on this, see Nuttall, 1968).

Opposition to the existence of a nuclear deterrent would be given an added sense of urgency by the Cuban Missile Crisis of late 1962: brought about by the USSR's siting of USA-threatening missiles on Fidel Castro's Cuba, supposedly in response to the farcical attempt at invasion of the island, and the overthrow of Castro by Cuban exiles, in the 'Bay of Pigs' fiasco of 1961. In retaliation, President John F. Kennedy ordered a blockade to prevent further missiles arriving: and for thirteen anxious days, the two super powers were locked in a terrifying face-off. Nor was Britain unprepared for war, as a later RAF chief subsequently revealed:

> While Macmillan played down the British involvement in the affair, what people didn't realise was that we had the entire force of 100 V-bombers standing at 15 minutes' readiness, bombs loaded and with the crews kitted up and ready to go, to drop nuclear bombs on Russia. (Beetham, 2015)

Eventually, the USSR backed down, the two countries signed an accord, the missiles were removed from Cuba and the nearest the world had yet come to an all-out nuclear war was over.

By 1963, the crisis had begun to fade in public memory, and attention generally on the left was more focused on the specifically parliamentary struggle, since there was the strong possibility of the formation of the first Labour Party administration since 1951. For, the Labour Party chose to follow Gaitskell with a man who was then regarded as being on the left of the party. Harold Wilson promised to usher in a new world of consensus and class mobility made possible by a new technological revolution. He presented himself – at a time when the full impact of the Profumo affair as an essentially Tory Party scandal was still very much present – as an ordinary 'man of the people', a construction aided by him being photographed publicly drinking beer and smoking a pipe when, privately, he preferred spirits and cigars.

The basis for the campaign for the 1964 General Election was laid out in a series of carefully orchestrated public meetings following on from Wilson's famous speech to the Labour Party Conference on October 1963:

> We are redefining and we are restating our socialism in terms of the scientific revolution [...] The Britain that is going to be forged in the white heat of this revolution will be no place for restrictive practices or outdated methods on either side of industry. (Wilson, 1963)

In this key speech, Wilson presented a vision of a new society, in which merit and not rank would predominate: a society that would look forward to a future of technological advancement in the context of a more egalitarian state. In the fiercely fought campaign, he appeared to have united both the centre-left and middle-ground, and the result of the election looked for a long time like a foregone conclusion, with the bright new man wiping the floor with the hopeless old landed buffer. Although *That Was the Week* did not have a third series in 1964 – the BBC explaining that because it was an election year, the corporation could not be seen to be taking sides – *Private Eye* had the most important year of its short life. However, Home did have the advantage of being in office as Macmillan's successor before the Election Campaign proper got under way. A 'giveaway' budget from his Chancellor of the Exchequer, Reginald Maulding, proved popular in 1963 and the opinion polls, which had spelt disaster for the Tory Party on Home's succession, began to change. By the eve of the election, the two parties were neck and neck and towards the end of the vote-counting exercises, Wilson thought that he had lost. He was right to be worried, for records would show that the Labour vote had dropped from that of the last Election: but not so disastrously as for the Tories, a lot of whose traditional supporters deserted to Jo Grimond's Liberal Party – at this point a minor player but, in its various alliances and reconfigurations, to become far more important in the 1980s. In any event, Wilson did win, but with a tiny majority of five that was to prove to be the albatross around the prime minister's neck in the years to come.

Harold Wilson was above, all a pragmatic politician, and his was a pragmatism that was to become the stronger as a result, first of all, of the slimness of his parliamentary majority, and then, after he had increased it to 96 seats in a snap election in 1966, by steadily worsening economic circumstances. He had inherited an enormous balance of payments deficit – caused in great part by the previous government's belated spending-spree – and this impacted on his attempts to introduce any of the sweeping reforms he had promised in an election campaign that had consciously drawn on that of John F. Kennedy, the US President who had been assassinated in November 1963.

Wilson and his team encouraged such parallels. The week that the Labour Party Manifesto, *Let's Go With Labour For The New Britain*, was published, Wilson had echoed the late president in predicting a 'programme of a hundred days of dynamic action'. To be associated with Kennedy was to be associated with visions of a new – and 'new' was a key word in the manifesto – and optimistic future, where science and the new technology would be united with enterprise and new educational initiatives. In his conference speech, Wilson had placed great stress on the need to greatly enlarge the number of young people who would be able to go to University, in order to create all the new scientists and new technologists that his new society would need; and in 1969 one of his key promises was realized with the opening of the Open University, allowing students to accumulate degrees from home, via distance learning programmes involving both the radio and television. It was an innovation that ticked every one of Wilson's 1964 boxes: the widening of higher education and the broadening of the social/class base of its potential students in social terms; an emphasis on an equality of opportunity, including in gender terms (with what was still for many women in the early sixties a role as non-employed stay-at-home mothers); and the deployment of technology – the newly introduced computer technology joining television and radio as part of the educational package.

One of the chief government instigators of the Open University was Jennie Lee, the widow of the Labour MP Aneurin Bevan. In 1964, she was appointed Minister for the Arts by Wilson and Lee was to play a key role in the development of the Arts in Britain, assuring the renewal of the Arts Council of Great Britain's (ACGB) charter in 1967 and – of particular significance for the new theatre/performance groups that are the subject of this volume – significantly increasing public patronage of the Arts, and helping to bring about a greater emphasis on ACGB's support for regional activity.

Although Wilson is now remembered more for the length of his time in power than for his achievements, his two successive administrations in the 1960s did achieve some notable goals of social reform in the United Kingdom: the abolition of the death penalty in 1965, the decriminalization of homosexuality and the legalization of abortion in 1967, as well as a general freeing-up of divorce procedures, for example. However, there was always a feeling that Wilson's celebrated pragmatism owed more to his desire to cling on to power than to any attempt to achieve a real public consensus.

His problems were at least double-edged, in what was to become a familiar trope in Labour Party politics until the invention of 'New Labour' under Tony Blair in the 1990s. On one hand the prime minister wished to appeal not only to the economic interests of business and capital, but, on the other – and this was in the face of attempting to hold on to the middle-ground of politics – retaining a degree of credibility as the leader of a leftward-looking socialist party, committed to the nationalization of public resources, the full institution of the welfare state, and so on. In his 1974 television play, *All Good Men*, Trevor

Griffiths uses this tension between past and present alternative left strategies as the basis for his dramatization of the conflict between a father who had been an active party member at the time of the 1926 General Strike and his son, a committed activist who sees the Labour Party's gradualist tactics as a betrayal that has prevented real socialist change from ever occurring.

One of the most significant ways in which this tension manifested itself for politically involved members of, in particular but by no means exclusively, the younger generation concerned the issue of nuclear disarmament. Following the abandonment of the Blue Streak missile programme in 1960, the final attempt at an independent British nuclear deterrent, the country has been dependent on the provision of delivery missiles by the United States. The Trades Union Congress (TUC) supported the call by CND for nuclear disarmament, but this was over-ruled by the then Labour leader, Hugh Gaitskill, also in 1960. Macmillan had been a vocal supporter of the deployment of nuclear weapons on British soil, but it was hoped by CND, the trade unions and others that Wilson would institute a change in policy. This he resolutely failed to do. This, coupled with an increasing realization that any hopes for a programme of socialist reform that would build on the achievements of the post-1945 Labour administration were in vain, began to firm up what would continue to be a confusingly organized but vociferous extra-parliamentary 'movement'. *The May Day Manifesto,* produced by prominent left-wing intellectuals in 1967, summed up well the disillusionment felt in socialist circles:

> The Labour Party, under the leadership of Harold Wilson, caught up for a while, the sense of movement, the practical urgency of a change of direction [...] After those years of shared effort, we are all, who worked for the Labour Party, in a new situation. For the sense of failure – a new kind of failure, in apparent victory – is implacably there, in every part of the Left. (Hall, Thompson and Williams, 1967, 1)

However, it was opposition to the United States' involvement in Vietnam that gave the growing 'countercultural movement' its real momentum, and its sense that it was a part of a larger global entity: ironically so, given Wilson's refusal to commit British soldiers to fight in the Vietnam War. Serious opposition to the war can be dated from 1965 in the US, when American soldiers were directly deployed in Vietnam for the first-time, and the anti-war movement soon spread across Western Europe. In Britain, the largest manifestations of this opposition were the two huge protest marches in London, on 17 March and on 27 October 1968. The second of these mass marches would be the first time a political protest had been screened live on British television. Mick Jagger, lead singer with the Rolling Stones, was on the first of these marches, and afterwards penned 'Street Fighting Man'. The lyrics were printed on the front page of the November edition of *Black Dwarf*, published by Tariq Ali, a student activist, later theatrical collaborator with Howard Brenton and founder of the left-wing group the International Marxist Group (IMG). In between these two events, however, came the momentous events of May in France, events – together with their knock-on effects in England – that would give an apparent coherence to what was in reality an extremely disparate extra-parliamentary opposition, and would also prove to have an enormous influence on the development of alternative theatre in Britain. Opposition to the US presence in Vietnam was, then, not only a cause for an ill-defined left to 'fight' for, but it was the one thing that brought together the various groups and factions: from Maoists; to such groupings as the International Socialists, IS (later the Socialists Workers' Party, SWP) and the Trotskyist Militant group; to politically complicatedly affiliated Hippies; to Anarchists.

On the weekend of 27 October 1968, the London School of Economics (LSE) was occupied by students. It was an occupation that was declaredly undertaken as a part of the Anti-Vietnam War protest, but it was equally concerned with an attempt to critique and to challenge the entire structure and *raison d'être* of the university. In both respects the LSE was not alone in the English Higher Education Sector, and it would be primarily, though by no means exclusively, through student activity that the new 'movement' would assume an identifiable face. This tactic of occupation was taken up elsewhere, at the universities of Essex and Warwick, for example. Roland Muldoon, founder of Cartoon Archetypical Slogan Theatre (CAST), the self-declared 'first British left-wing "underground" theatre group in the 60s', recalls supporting the occupations: 'A number of times we played student-occupied buildings', adding the claim that 'on one famous occasion Warwick University students waited until we were available before they occupied the campus' (Muldoon, 2013, 1, 21). That is to say that, although the counterculture existed quite independently of the Higher Education sector – many concerned would, indeed, have argued that it was just one of the many institutions that it was in opposition to – it was the militant protests that spread from the campuses of the US, to Western Europe and to England that provided the intellectual context for constructing it as more than simply a series of random occurrences. If the initial impetus derived from the United States and organized opposition to the war, then the specific match that lit the fuse was to be found in France.

May 1968 and its Aftermath

> What happened there [in France] that spring [1968] is historically without precedent – the creation of a potentially revolutionary situation within the context of a stable and securely affluent society. It was a situation that was fermented and stage-managed not by the traditional organs of political conflict – the unions and political organisations of the working class – but by a young, radical and alienated intelligensia. A movement that started in a university in the suburbs of Paris was briefly to bring France to a standstill, and to threaten even the Gaullist regime, as serious attempts were made to construct a revolutionary counter-society that would bypass the machinery of the modern state. (Bull, 1984, 10–11)

When the barricades went up in the streets of the left bank of Paris on the night of May 10, what was at least as striking as the dramatic response to the police attempt to prevent student protest spreading from the Sorbonne and across the river was the speed with which events had gathered momentum. Although the origins of the struggle can be traced back to 22 March and a comparatively small protest at Nanterre, it was only after disciplinary action had been taken against what were regarded as the ringleaders that things began to escalate. However, by the first days of May a body of students, teachers and, soon, school kids were engaged in effective warfare with the police on the streets of Paris, at first to oust the police from the Sorbonne and then to prevent it being retaken. Following the first night of the barricades, a General Strike was declared for 13 May: on the same day a Protest March was held and substantially more than one million people took to the streets.

Protest spread from the universities and schools to factories, and by mid-May more than fifty factories were occupied and a quarter of a million workers were on strike. Within a week ten million had downed tools. The situation was seen as so potentially threatening by President de Gaulle that he briefly left the capital to reassure himself of the support of the army in the event of any further escalation.

France, for a short while, was at a virtual halt in terms of production. It was a euphoric period for those involved in the struggle, and its initial success encouraged relatable activity in British and Western European Universities, as well as in the United States where opposition to the Vietnam War – one of the original touch-points for the French struggle – was already mobilizing campus as well as non-campus activity. However, with the collusion of the communist CGT union, and its agreement to settle the industrial dispute along the traditional lines of shorter working hours and increased pay, the anyway unlikely revolution gradually ran out of steam.

Much of the events of that May were intrinsically theatrical, and many of its manifestations can be seen as early exemplars of what would come to be described as performance art. For example, the National Theatre, the Odeon, was also occupied, and heated debates took place there: and as a result of the occupation, figures in chain-mail looted from the costume-collection could be seen as guards outside the doors. And, indeed, much of what was going on inside the building smacked more of performance than conventional debate. It was appropriate that, above the front doors to the Odeon, the graffiti should read, 'When the National Assembly becomes a bourgeois theatre, all the bourgeois theatres should be turned into national assemblies.' In Britain, what is generally seen as little more than a footnote to history was of fundamental importance to a generation of writers and theatre companies whose first work derives from the mid- to late 1960s, and it is impossible to exaggerate the significance of the 'evenements' in France on the development of modern British theatre.

Howard Brenton, who initially worked with two alternative theatre groups – Brighton Combination and Portable – was but one of a number of burgeoning playwrights who was greatly influenced in his early work by his time in Paris: as he later wrote:

> May 1968 was crucial. It was a great watershed and directly affected me […] And it failed. A generation dreaming of a beautiful utopia was kicked – kicked awake and not dead. I've got to believe not kicked dead. May 68 gave me a desperation I still have. (Brenton, 1975, 20)

In 1973, Trevor Griffiths' *The Party* was produced at the National Theatre at the Old Vic. It was to be the last time that Laurence Olivier would appear on the professional stage and an unlikely curtain-call it was. Griffiths' play concerns the coming together of a group of representative figures from the left – from hard-line 'Stalinist' to liber-tarian anarchist – to discuss the formation of a new revolutionary party: a heated discussion that takes place in the context of the simul-taneous explosion of protest in France. Griffiths had experienced both:

> It started with a number of images [...] and what happened to me, in 1968, in France. And the American universities, the Blacks in Detroit, Watts. It started with the experience of the Friday night meetings at Tony Garnett's where sixty or seventy people would crowd into a room to do more, to get it right, to be correct, to read the situation as a first step towards changing it utterly. (Griffiths, 1976)

John McGrath, the founder of theatre company 7:84, was embarking on a new play, which he temporarily abandoned to go to France that Spring:

> I started to write [...] and in May 68 things started happening in Paris. And I went over and spent some time there [...] And the importance of the thinking around that whole time, the excitement of that whole complex set of attitudes to life which that para-revolutionary situation threw up was incredible – the thinking about ordinary life, the freshness of approach, the urgency and the beauty of the ideas was amazing. *But* what didn't happen was the organisation [...] In the middle of all that you have this absolute contradiction. I came back and left the play, actually for about six months to a year, and then I finished it. But it was changed by that experience. (McGrath, 19, 48–9)

In the completed play *Random Happenings in the Hebrides* (1970), the tension between the urge to take direct and illegal action in support of a threatened fishing fleet and the desire to work within conventional political methods of persuasion is highlighted by the alternative title, *The Social Democrat and the Stormy Sea*. And, meanwhile, back in the world of that conventional parliamentary politics, the social democrat Prime Minister Harold Wilson was confronted with his own increas-ingly stormy sea.

1966–70: The Ups

Britain had gone to the polls on 31 March 1966. The result was an emphatic victory for the Labour Party, with a 96-seat majority over the Conservatives under the leadership of Edward Heath, who had taken over from Sir Alec Douglas-Home the previous year. The turnout was reasonably high, at about 76 per cent of the population eligible to vote, a figure of just over 27 million. However, as annual statistics go, this was dwarfed by the year's other major public event, the football World Cup which was being held in England for the first time. On 30 July 1966, a record number of television viewers, in excess of 32 million, saw England beat West Germany after extra time. Although not perhaps celebrated quite so vociferously in the rest of the UK – none of whose teams qualified for the finals – it was generally embraced as something that offered a symbolic sense that all was now beginning to feel good in England.

The phrase that was frequently used to describe and locate this new sense of national identity was the 'swinging sixties', a description that encapsulated the feeling that, in the world of popular music, the arts and fashion, England – and, in particular, London – was, in then common parlance, 'where it was at'. The American artist Roger Miller had a cross-transatlantic hit in 1965 with 'England Swings', a strange mix of contemporary reference and twee nostalgia: and the editor of the influential magazine *Vogue*, Diana Vreeland, had declared that 'London is the most swinging city in the world at the moment' (quoted in Crosby, 1965); while in 1966 *Time* magazine was probably the first publication to refer directly to 'Swinging London' (see Gilbert, 2006, 3). Musically, the net could be spread much wider: in particular, to Liverpool, which had spawned not only the Beatles but a host of other successful acts, including Gerry and the Pacemakers, who were the first act to top the UK singles charts with their first three releases. But the recognition from *Time* and *Vogue* and, indeed, more problematically from Roger Miller derived not just from the fact that the pop 'scene' in Britain was so vibrant but from the subsequent success of so many of these UK groups when they hit the shores of the United States. It was a success that came to be known as the 'British Invasion', and it is perhaps best memorialized by the extraordinary feat of the Beatles who had, on 4 April 1964, occupied all five of the top spots on the *Billboard* charts, something never seen before or since.

Other successful groups, such as the Small Faces and the Who, became more specifically associated with the Mods; and new boutiques crammed with clothes by young designers were to be found in all the major industrial cities. In London, the King's Road in Chelsea contained a host of clothes shops and bars in which to sport the new gear, including the Chelsea Drugstore, a central venue in the Rolling Stones' 'You Can't Always Get What You Want', recorded in 1968. Just round the corner from the Marquee, one of the most important clubs for the new music, situated in London's Soho, was Carnaby Street, a powerhouse of small shops catering for the new fashions, be they mod or hippy. When, in 1966, the Kinks released their tongue-in-cheek 'celebration' of the new peacocks of the fashion world – 'Dedicated Follower of Fashion' – it had a chorus that recalls the Scarlet Pimpernel – 'they seek him here, they seek him there' – before locating the new fashionistas firmly as 'the Carnabetian army'.

Nothing summed up the style of the time more than the rise of the androgynous model Twiggy who was named the 'Face of 1966' in the *Daily Express* newspaper, and whose oft-photographed Leonard of Mayfair-cropped hair and succession of mini-skirts are an abiding image of the period. She had taken over from the previous generation of fashion models, most notably Jean Shrimpton (the 'Shrimp') whose sister Chrissie had dated the young Mick Jagger. The second-half of the sixties saw both a democratization of the fashion world, as comparatively cheap designs became increasingly available, and also its opposite, the creation of the cult of pop celebrity, of a glamorous world where rock stars rubbed shoulders with artists. Indeed, when Mick Jagger and Keith Richards were briefly imprisoned for the possession of drugs in 1967, the artist Richard Hamilton, having been a co-signatory of a protest letter to the *Times*, produced a poster, savagely entitled 'Swingeing London 67', showing Jagger and Hamilton's art-dealer handcuffed in the back of a police car. It was a social world in which celebrity hairdressers, clothes designers and photographers mixed with the rock elite and the new young UK stars of the movie world, Michael Caine among them. So it was that when the Kinks issued their hymn to the superiority of South London, 'Waterloo Sunset', in 1967, many people assumed – erroneously or not – that the Terry and Julie who cross over the river every Friday night were Terence Stamp and Julie Christie, who were at the time an 'item', after having starred in *Far From the Madding Crowd*, released that same year.

The truth or otherwise of this identification between fictional characters in the narrative of a popular song and the by then out-of-reach stars of the screen is in one sense irrelevant. What it does point to is the gap between what we could call the street sense of an alternative society and a celebrity ambiance made the more heightened by the fact that many of the new super figures – Julie Christie certainly accepted – had come from essentially humble social origins. This move between two social worlds in the UK in the 1960s is well illustrated by the development of British cinema. At the beginning of the decade there was a new wave of films whose origins lay in the somewhat loosely labelled 'Angry Young Man' movement in the theatre and, in particular, novels of the 1950s. The emphasis was on the working and aspirant lower-middle-class protagonist, usually male: and it was kick-started, in 1960, with the film that set Albert Finney on the road to stardom, *Saturday Night and Sunday Morning* (Karel Reisz). It was followed by *A Kind of Loving* (John Schlesinger, 1962); *The Loneliness of the Long Distance Runner* (Tony Richardson, 1962); *Billy Liar* (Schlesinger, 1962, the film that was to prove Julie Christie's breakthrough); and finally *This Sporting Life* (Lindsay Anderson, 1963).

However, it was a brief renaissance and when British cinema began to regain some kind of momentum, it was with a very different kind of movie, one that was centred on the sometimes slightly ambiguous celebration of the swinging scene: *Georgy Girl* (Silvio Narrizano, 1966); *The Knack … And How To Get It* (1965), directed by Richard Lester in the zany style that he would bring to bear on the Beatles' first film, *Hard Day's Night*, released later that year; and *Here We Go Round the Mulberry Bush* (Clive Donner, 1967), with music from the newly formed super group Traffic, fronted by Stevie Winwood. But perhaps the most significant celebration/demolition of the swinging sixties came with Michelangelo Antonioni's *Blow-Up* of 1966, where the emphasis was solidly on the clash between the street scene and the world of celebrity photographers and the like.

By this time it was possible to talk of the existence of an alternative society, of an amorphous group of mainly, though by no means entirely, young people who held politically very diverse opinions, but who saw themselves as hostile to the values of conventional bourgeois society. In some cases this was an absolute, and not always temporarily, lifestyle choice; for others it was something you put on once let out of work on a Friday, like the much advertised Beatles wig. In its most extreme version this was different from earlier groups, such as the Mods, whose largely working-class roots meant that their activities were necessarily undertaken in their leisure time. Radical politics had its part to play, as did drugs. Cannabis use was nothing new, but in the 1960s it began to become more widespread, and it was no longer simply a property of West Indian immigrants and a bohemian subgroup. The possession of Speed (amphetamines), like that of cannabis, did not become illegal until its use had spread to the middle classes.

The most public expression of the alternative society at play came in 1967, the 'Summer of Love', a celebration of partying and excess that owed its title to contemporary events in the Haight-Ashbury district of San Francisco on America's west coast, where thousands of young people – loosely described as hippies – arrived that summer to party and to dream. And in doing the latter, they were greatly helped by the increasing availability of LSD or acid (lysergic acid diethylamide) and its hallucinatory effects. Its introduction into the British counterculture led to the development of a psychedelic rock scene, in which groups such as Pink Floyd and Soft Machine played in London at, in particular, the Middle Earth Club (formerly the Electric Garden Club) in Covent Garden, and the Roundhouse in Camden. The generic title 'flower power' came to be associated with drug-induced dreams of peace and love, but was originally derived from the practice of demonstrators presenting flowers to the armed guards present. Political and cultural 'activism' provided a heady mix.

It may have taken the ACGB until 1967 to recognize that Jazz should be supported, but in the period covered in this volume, it was learning very quickly how past assumptions about performance and audiences were increasingly under threat across the entire cultural spectrum. Alternative theatre did not grow in a vacuum: it was a part – albeit an extremely important part – of a far larger set of changes and developments that were linked politically, socially and culturally. A single example, of an infinite number of other possibilities, will have to suffice to demonstrate the way in which these links can be made.

In 1962, following in the wake of the highly successful season of *Beyond the Fringe* two years before, the latest emanation of the Cambridge Footlights appeared as a part of the Edinburgh Fringe Festival. Among the cast were Graham Chapman and John Cleese (later of *Monty Python* fame) and Trevor Nunn (later Artistic Director of both the Royal Shakespeare Company and the Royal National Theatre and director of many highly successful large-scale stage musicals, including *Cats, Starlight Express* and *Les Miserables*). The show was performed in a new, temporary venue, the Sphinx Nightclub, on which conversion into a theatre space began as soon as the annual Festival was over. The Traverse, as it would be known, was in great part the brainchild of a remarkable American, Jim Haynes, who at the time was running an independent bookshop in the city. Its first production took place in January 1962. In August 1964, Haynes became The Traverse's third Artistic Director, a post he held until June 1966, when he resigned in order to concentrate on the running of a new Traverse Theatre in London. The 1963 Edinburgh Festival, however, saw a Drama Conference organized by Haynes, together with publisher John Calder and influential theatre critic Kenneth Tynan. Although a great success in its own right at the time, it is now best remembered for the staging of the first 'happening' in the UK, when a naked girl was wheeled across the gallery on a BBC lighting trolley: brief though the event was, it created an enormous furore and, perhaps, can now be seen as a minor landmark in the history of Performance Art.

In London, Haynes had already established contact with Harold Wilson's Arts Minister, Jennie Lee, and, through her, the Chair of the Arts Council of Great Britain, Lord Goodman.

> He suggested we take over the Jeanetta Cochrane Theatre in Holborn. It was newly built but something of a white elephant. No one seemed to be able to make a go of it: he thought that we could. We would get Arts Council support. (Haynes, 1984, 124)

In 1965, Haynes and his team – including a fellow American, Charles Marowitz, co-founder of *Encore*, an influential journal on contemporary drama (1954–65) and also of the major alternative theatre venue, Open Space, in 1968 – were quickly frustrated by the limitations of the London Traverse Theatre Company's base. Haynes successfully negotiated for a more flexible space in Covent Garden: this would become the Arts Lab, a major venue for fringe and underground activity. At the same time, he became involved with the creation and publication of a new underground newspaper, the *International Times*, or *IT* as it was known.

One of the most important people behind the launch of *IT* in 1966 was a Cambridge University graduate named John 'Hoppy' Hopkins who had arrived in London in 1960 and had subsequently worked as a photographer for the *Sunday Times*, the *Observer*, *Peace News*, *Jazz Journal* and the *Melody Maker*. Hopkins was a first-hand observer of the emergence of the alternative society. His photographs provided documentation of political street activity and avant-garde events; and his work brought him into contact with many of the figures and groups of the new rock music scene, whom he recorded visually for posterity, including the Beatles and the Rolling Stones. By the time that the idea of *IT* was maturing, Hopkins had already been involved with the inception of the London Free School in Notting Hill, and as a result had helped with the organization of the first two Notting Hill Festivals. He had become a major player in the developing psychedelic music movement, associated with a drug culture spear-headed by the use of LSD. In 1966, he was joint founder of the UFO Club in London's Tottenham Court Road and then reopened in the Roundhouse. A leading but short-lived venue for the pyschedelic scene, its first two weeks hosted Soft Machine and Pink Floyd, and Procul Harum played there the same week that 'A Whiter Shade of Pale' first topped the singles charts. Hopkins also continued to be involved with the Arts Lab until its much-lamented closure in 1969. Among its many visitors was an undergraduate from Keele University, Tony Elliott, who wanted to do a complete issue of his student newspaper on events in 'Swinging London': fired by his discoveries, he soon came up with an idea for a rival to the rather staid *What's On*, a regular listings publication that continued to ignore the alternative scene. And so it was that 1968 saw the first issue of *Time Out*, a weekly listings publication that, as it grew and developed, sought to bring all aspects of the alternative culture under one roof: alternative music, alternative drama, alternative medicine, alternative plumbers and cooks, the whole alternative world was there.

In theatrical terms, the single most important piece of legislation to come from this era concerned the abolition of theatre censorship in 1968, a result brought about by several factors: the pressure that had been brought to bear by those hostile to any limitation on self-expression; the controversial plays staged in the 1960s by such divergent writers as Edward Bond and Joe Orton; and simply the changing mores of the time. One almost immediate response to the abolition was Kenneth Tynan's 'nudie' and expletive-ridden *Oh! Calcutta!*, which opened Off-Broadway in 1969 and in London in 1970, before becoming the then longest-running Broadway show. However, the real beneficiaries would prove to be the alternative theatre companies who no longer had to submit scripts and revisions to the Lord Chancellor before permission could be granted to perform. It was one of the most important elements in the development of the new theatre, allowing its participants to explore previous no-go areas, and to do so in ways that would previously have been prohibited.

1966–70: The Downs

Now, all of this may seem a somewhat incongruous background to the second Labour administration of the 1960s, if only because the concept of a 'swinging' culture implied exuberance and extravagance, albeit behaviour and expense fixed at varying social levels, whereas party politics during that same period was dominated by the demand for restraint and financial planning. And, indeed, there was, of course, another and very different narrative unfolding in contemporary Britain. On 12 November 1966, BBC television had broadcast *Cathy Come Home*, a new play in the 'Wednesday Play' slot. Written by Jeremy Sandford, produced by Tony Garnett and directed by Ken Loach, the play was a harrowing story of a young couple who, when the man loses his job, move on a downward spiral from living in a contemporary property to squats and eventual complete homelessness, at which point their baby is taken away by care workers. Watched by an estimated quarter of the British population, it created an enormous impression. Almost contemporaneously – though not as a result of the screening of and reaction to *Cathy* – the organization Shelter was formed to help the homeless and dispossessed. This was a very different Britain.

Although illegal squatting in empty flats and houses had been a fact of urban life for some time, towards the end of the decade it took on a stance that was political and organized, rather than simply personal and random. Next door to Jim Haynes's Arts Lab was an unoccupied building, the Bell Hotel, belonging to the Greater London Council (GLC) which had plans to redevelop the site. Before long, the hotel had been entered and rapidly prepared for occupation.

> Everyone wanted to live in Covent Garden. It was a very desirable area. It was booming and alive and a walkabout area, and here was this fifty-room hotel sitting there and saying 'do something about me.' And I did. I started telling the homeless and friends who needed a place to stay. And people started moving in. (Haynes, 1984, 165)

The squat was soon emptied by the police but Haynes argues that it could be seen as 'the beginning of the London squatting movement which exploded in Britain and Europe from the late sixties' (Haynes, 1984, 165). But, whether or not it actually did lead, there certainly was plenty to follow.

In late 1968, a mixed group of homeless people and anarchists, who labelled themselves the London Squatters Campaign, occupied part of a luxury block of flats in London. In September of the following year, a group calling itself the London Street Commune took over 144 Piccadilly in London (not far from the headquarters of the Arts Council), painting a slogan reminiscent of Paris '68 on the exterior: 'We are the writing on your wall'. Despite (or because of) massive publicity, they were forcibly ejected from it after six days. These were but two of the many organized squats that abounded towards the end of the 1960s, not only in London, but in all the major industrial cities. The choice was born out of necessity in many cases, but also out of political and lifestyle considerations, as a protest against the 'straight' world of bourgeois society. Squats also fulfilled an essential need for alternative art and performance groups, providing space for studios and workshops, for rehearsal and even performance areas: something that is recalled by Mary Turner, one of the founders of Action Space, the Community Arts/Performance Group, after it had moved into temporary accommodation in a derelict piano factory in Camden, North London, in 1971. The factory was made available by the local council on a short-term lease, but it rapidly became the focus for more extensive cultural and political activity:

> There was the Old Dairy which housed people from the George Street Arts Lab, John Hopkins, Hoppy's video workshop, Ed Berman's Inter-Action and many squats that doubled for studios and band rehearsal rooms. Necessity and conviction led us to claiming empty properties and putting them to use. Some we negotiated, others we opened up and squatted. We hoped to hold back the massive redevelopment plans by direct action. (Turner, 2012, 56)

And again, when the company had moved into its new Drill Hall home off the Tottenham Court Road in 1974, 'the squatters moved into Huntley Street, a stone's throw away from the Drill Hall and down the Charing Cross Road into Trentishoe Mansions. Some were our colleagues and helped to convert the new building and run the café in it' (Turner, 2012, 98). It was the same year that the neighbouring Centre Point was taken over by squatters in protest against its planned lack of occupation since its completion in 1966 – it having been built for capital accumulation rather than use.

Howard Brenton's 1973 play *Magnificence* had opened with just such a protest, though it was not presented uncritically. However, in the play, as in the many unsuccessful squats, it is the confrontation between the forces of authority – police, bailiffs, magistrates, etc. – and the protesters/squatters that is paramount in the political analysis. For a Labour administration that prioritized housing, and had a proud record for new builds, all this was an unwanted intrusion: even though, as it would prove, its policy of building high-rise buildings and estates would very quickly lead to worsening social conditions, the creation of modern slums and a number of unmanageable council estates. Public spending was inevitably spread too thin, and the people who were to be rehoused went largely unconsulted. It was not all what Wilson had in mind when he gave his official address at the annual Labour Party Conference held in Brighton in 1969: he looked forward to continuing social progress after the next election:

> First among the priorities of the seventies is to get rid of the scandal of bad housing and no-housing [...] Shelter themselves acknowledged how much has been done by this Labour Government. In a few weeks' time, in little over five years, your Labour Government will have built two million homes. This is a record contribution in rehousing the homeless and the ill-housed. (Wilson, 1971, 706)

However, the majority of this building had consisted in the construction of high-rise building: such as the (in)famous Hyde Park flats in Sheffield, officially opened in 1966. With their 'pavements in the sky', they sought to reproduce vertically the community interaction that had occurred in the horizontal homes they had replaced. Although clearly a quick-fix solution for housing the maximum amount of people, such schemes were largely a failure, not the least reason being that individuals felt that they had no control over, and therefore no responsibility for, their immediate environment.

Thus, Wilson's claim was a brave one, but even as he was boasting of the progress towards greater equality made by his government, he knew that the dream had, at least temporarily, ended, and he clearly felt that he knew why. He prefaced his account of the Labour administrations of 1964–70 by describing it as 'the record of a Government all but a year of whose life was dominated by an inherited balance of payments problem which was nearing a crisis at the moment we took office', and continued with 'we lived and governed during a period when that problem made frenetic speculative attack on Britain both easy and profitable' (Wilson, 1971, xvii). By 'speculative attack', he is referring here to the act of trading between different national currencies. His foregrounding of this particular aspect of the Wilson years correctly emphasizes the continuing pressure that his government had been under since first taking office, to devalue the pound which was held at too high a rate against, most importantly, the US dollar. This helped greatly to create an imbalance between imported and exported goods and commodities: and it thus prevented Wilson from ever being able to properly institute 'the National Plan, in which the government was to co-operate with industry and the unions to increase both private and public investment, with rises in income held to what could be justified by improvements in productivity' (Newton, 2010, 912).

The 1970 General Election

By 1967, the situation had grown desperate and on 19 November, after the Bank of England had spent some £200 million of its gold and dollar reserves in a vain attempt to support the pound, the decision to devalue was made. The prime minister addressed the nation on radio and television that evening, assuring listeners that this 'does not mean that the pound here in Britain, in your pocket or purse or in your bank, has been devalued', before adding the postscript that usually goes unforgotten that imported goods would of course now be more expensive. From the government's point of view, the situation had been made worse by a six-week unofficial strike by Britain's Dockers that had started in September. It was a strike that would result in the end of the practice of casual labour in the dockyards, by which men were paid only if there was work available, and it was celebrated in Tony Garnett and Ken Loach's BBC television 'Wednesday Play' of the same year, *The Big Flame* (written by Jim Allen).

The Wilson government was continually attempting to negotiate, via the TUC, settlements to the many industrial disputes that were a feature of the contemporary landscape, as the push for better terms and conditions met the perceived need to keep production costs (and especially wages) down. In 1969, Wilson and the Secretary of State for Employment and Productivity, Barbara Castle, published a white paper entitled *In Place of Strife*, which sought to reduce the power of the trade unions by making it more difficult to call a strike: but internal opposition and the intervention of the TUC ensured that the white paper would never successfully pass into law.

As the decade moved towards its end, the gap widened between the government's attempts to control the economy and what the right in the Labour Party and the majority of the opposition saw as militant activity. After devaluation, the situation was still perceived as grave by the establishment. In December 1967, a Conservative MP wrote to *The Times* newspaper lamenting the under-usage of factory and office space at weekends, and expressing the desire that people 'particularly in responsible positions would set an example by sacrificing say the first Saturday of every month [...] without extra pay, profits or overtime' in order to demonstrate to the world 'we were in earnest' (Boyd-Carpenter, 1967). Prompted by a memo from their boss, five secretaries in a Surrey Office 'spontaneously' decided to take up the challenge and to come in half an hour early without pay. The tabloid press rose to the occasion and, despite TUC protests, the 'I'm Backing Britain' campaign was launched, complete with badges and tea mugs. However, by mid-1968, this right-wing populist movement had collapsed under the weight of its contradictions, not the least being the revelation that a batch of T-shirts with the 'I'm Backing Britain' slogan had actually been manufactured in Portugal, because they were so much cheaper to produce there (Hawthorne, 1968).

Shortly after this, the balance of payments situation, in fact, started to improve, although it would be a full year before that would be confirmed. Over the summer of 1969, British exports grew considerably in value and by December there was a £440 million surplus in the balance of payments (*The Times*, 9 September 1969; cited in Sandbrook, 2006, 761).

A General Election was forecast for 1970: the only question was when. Buoyed by memories of the 1966 England World Cup triumph that had followed his own election, Wilson was well aware that the next World Cup would take place in Mexico and that the semi-final was due to be played on 17 June 1970. Thus, perhaps on the assumption that England would be contesting it, the date 18 June was chosen for the election. The news from the polls was good and everything seemed fair set for a victory for Labour over Heath's Conservative Party. However, not all of Wilson's cabinet were in agreement with this forecast, as Barbara Castle recalled after the event:

> As early as 13 June I was writing in my diary: 'I wish there weren't another five days before the Election! I don't believe those poll figures and although Heath is making such a pathetic showing personally and is getting such a bad press, I have a haunting feeling there is a silent majority sitting behind its lace curtains, waiting to come out and vote Tory.' (Castle, 1984, 805)

The build-up to June 18 was marred by a number of things. Firstly, what would prove to be a temporary blip in the balance of payments was announced on 15 June. Secondly, SOGAT (the Society of Graphical and Allied Trades, the Newspaper Printworkers' Union) went on strike, a strike that required all of Wilson's efforts to get it settled in four days. But then, thirdly, in the words of Wilson himself: 'On the

Friday agreement was reached, and newspapers resumed printing at the weekend – in time for the Mondays to print the depressing news of the last minute defeat of England [by West Germany] in the World Cup in Mexico' (Wilson, 1971, 789). Like the Labour Party, England had held a commanding lead, only to be defeated in extra time. Barbara Castle was right to have been worried about the 'silent majority': when the polls closed, the Labour vote was down 5 per cent: the Conservatives, in contrast, were up 4.5 per cent and were elected to office with a majority of thirty-one seats. But there was possibly another more sinister reason why those lace curtains might have been twitching, and not just because it was the first time that eighteen year olds had been given the vote.

Public worries about the extent of immigration to Britain and its effect on the composition of the country had been simmering below the surface for some time: and the plain fact is that racial prejudice was a given in almost all walks of life at that time. There were, however, particular moments that stood out, the Notting Hill Race Riots of 1958 being one. In 1964, however, a by-election was held in the Midlands constituency of Smethwick. It was, like all the post-1964 by-elections, a significant one as the Labour Party ruled with a very slim majority, but the district was confidently expected to remain in Labour control. During the course of the campaign, it was alleged that Conservative canvassers had used the slogan 'If you want a nigger for neighbour, vote Labour' to push their vote. Although the Tory candidate, Peter Griffiths, denied this, he did add, 'I should think that is a manifestation of popular feeling. I would not condemn anyone who said that' (quoted in Bleich, 2003, 48).

Griffiths went on to win the by-election. It was the first time that the deliberate incitement of racial hatred had formed any part of a mainstream political party's election campaign, and it certainly played a part in encouraging the development of extreme right-wing groups such as the National Front (NF). Formed in 1967, the NF was made up of a number of pre-existing groups, in particular the British National Party (BNP). In 1965, the Race Relations Act had been passed, the first-time that Parliament had ever been asked to consider the race issue. Later in 1967, immigration again became a major public issue as an exodus of British passport-holding Asians from Kenya, a member of the British Commonwealth since gaining independence in 1963, arrived in Britain in ever-greater numbers. Faced with the prospect of mass immigration, the government took away the automatic right of all British passport holders to enter the home country. Then in March 1968 the Commonwealth Immigrants' Bill was pushed through by the then Secretary of State for Home Affairs, James Callaghan. It was not just the left-wing that condemned it. The newspaper of the establishment, *The Times*, 'called it "the most shameful measure" that a Labour government had ever introduced, while the *Spectator* (a right-wing periodical) thought that it was "one of the most immoral pieces of legislation to have emerged from any British Parliament"' (quoted in Sandbrook, 2006, 676).

Feelings were running high, in Parliament and across the country at large. The NF organized marches and these were opposed forcibly by leftish organizations. And it was at this point that the maverick Conservative MP Enoch Powell chose to give his most (in)famous speech. On 20 April 1968, he addressed a meeting of the West Midlands Conservative Association, having thoughtfully remembered to invite representatives of the press. The timing was deliberate: the second reading of a controversial Race Relations Bill making it a legal offence to discriminate in matters of housing, employment or public service on the grounds of colour, race, ethnicity or original place of birth was about to have its second reading in the House of Commons. Powell's speech invoked Virgil's *Aeneid* in its strident declaration, 'As I look ahead, I am filled with foreboding. I seem to see the River Tiber foaming with blood' (see *Daily Telegraph*, 6 November 2007 for full speech). The 'Rivers of Blood' speech, as it soon became known, looked to a future in which 'native' Britons would be outnumbered by immigrants of foreign origin and their descendants. Powell called for an immediate end to immigration and the offer of free repatriation to those already here. It was as close to the NF line as could be imagined from a Conservative politician. Despite being removed from office by Edward Heath, Powell enjoyed enormous popular support – a Gallup Poll at the end of April found that 74 per cent of people polled agreed with what he had said in his speech (Heffer, 1999, 467).

The Troubles

The end of the 1960s also saw the beginning of the 'Troubles' in Northern Ireland, an ongoing and worsening struggle that did not begin to be resolved until the end of the century. The struggle had its origins in the tangled relationships between England and Ireland, dating back to the seventeenth century; in 1921, however, there was a formal division between Ireland and Northern Ireland (the six counties in the north). Although the newly created Northern Ireland had a population that was dominated by Protestants and Loyalists to the British crown and to an independent state, it also had a large Catholic population, which was by no means, initially or even later, all Republican (that is, seeking a united Ireland), but which rightly saw itself as being actively discriminated against in terms of parliamentary representation, public housing, education and other social issues in the new region:

It began with the disruption by the essentially Protestant Royal Ulster Constabulary (RUC) of a peaceful civil rights march from Belfast to Derry in October 1968. That event was followed by two days of rioting and continuing unrest and the scale of the violence was available to be seen by all:

> The television coverage […] changed the course of Northern Ireland history. The media gave widespread coverage to the unrestrained batoning by the RUC of demonstrators, including MPs, without 'restraint or excuse' (according to the Cameron Commission). (Bew and Gillespie, 1999, 4)

In subsequent months the violence increased. Belfast and Derry were the two main areas of contestation and parts of both cities established both Catholic and Protestant 'no-go' areas. In August 1969, Derry experienced three days of fighting between Catholics and the RUC, frequently in the company of Protestant Loyalists. The 'Battle of the Bogside' in Derry was accompanied by rioting in Belfast, where seven people were killed, hundreds wounded and mostly Catholic businesses and houses burnt to the ground.

In desperation, the Catholic minority began to look towards Britain to defend them by sending the British Army in. Then Home Office Minister James Callaghan allegedly responded: 'I can get the army in, but it's going to be a devil of a job to get it out' (quoted in Sandbrook, 2006, 754). On 14 August, the first troops were sent into Derry. Initially welcomed by the Northern Irish Catholic population as offering security, relations soon turned sour as army 'police' activity started to target Catholic parts of the cities. This was arguably made worse by the change of British government in 1970: Callaghan was succeeded by Tory Home Secretary Reginald Maudling who was less aware of the problematics of the situation and reportedly commented as he took his seat on a plane after his first visit to the province: 'Bloody awful country; give me a whisky' (quoted in Tonge, 2002, 39).

At the beginning of 1970, the Irish Republican Army (IRA), first constituted in 1917, split and the Provisional IRA (the Provos) soon took a far more aggressive lead in what was by now escalating towards civil war. The internment of suspected terrorists was introduced and it is this that is the main focus of the Portable Theatre's final production, *England's Ireland* (1972), a collaboration between Tony Bicat, Howard Brenton, Brian Clarke, David Edgar, Francis Fuchs, David Hare and Snoo Wilson. On 30 January 1972, a march protesting against internment in the Bogside area of Derry was fired on by the army, resulting in the deaths of fourteen people. It took until 2010 for the Saville Report to be published, which directly implicated British soldiers in instigating an unprovoked response. Paul McCartney recorded 'Give Ireland Back to the Irish' two days later, but the song was banned by the BBC. Brian Friel's play, *The Freedom of the City* (1973), centres on the event, though it took until 2002 for British television to dramatize it: with two docudrama re-enactments, *Bloody Sunday* and *Sunday*.

By 1972, in one academic's opinion, the terms '"ungovernability" and "Northern Ireland" had become synonymous' (Tonge, 2002, 49). For the rest of the decade, the struggle continued on, largely unabated. And from 1972, the IRA also started to target mainland Britain: a number of towns and cities were the focus of bomb attacks, including Birmingham in November 1974, where twenty-one people were killed. In 1979, the MP Airey Neave was killed by a car bomb outside the House of Commons and Lord Mountbatten was also killed at his home in Sligo. Both these figures feature as ghosts in Howard Brenton and Tony Howard's satirical drama on Margaret Thatcher's accession to power, *A Short Sharp Shock for the Government* (1980).

The Oil Crisis and the Three-Day Week

Terrorist violence was something that was not just confined to Northern Ireland at this time. The move from peaceful protest to armed struggle was mirrored elsewhere. In 1969, the Students for a Democratic Society (SDS) Convention in Chicago was invaded by an embryonic organization calling itself the Weathermen (later the Weathermen Underground Organization, WUO): they carried out a series of politically inspired robberies and bombings throughout much of the 1970s. In Italy, The Red Brigade was formed in 1970 and followed a similar path to the WUO, culminating in 1978 with the kidnap and murder of former Prime Minister Aldo Moro. In that same year, in Germany the Baader-Meinhof Group (later the Red Army Faction) first came to public attention with a series of bomb and arson attacks. In Britain, in 1970, following the London anti-Vietnam War protests, the Angry Brigade started on a bombing campaign designed to send a message rather than kill: thus, unlike their American and European counterparts their actions resulted in no deaths.

Tariq Ali remembers being approached by someone claiming to represent the Angry Brigade, who suggested planting a bomb in the American Embassy in London's Grosvenor Square. 'I told them it was a terrible idea. They were a distraction. It was difficult enough building an anti-war movement without the press linking this kind of activity to the wider left' (Bright, 2002).

In the end, the Brigade was responsible for some twenty-five bombings, including the house of then Secretary of State for Employment Robert Carr. As a result of their activities, the Bomb Squad was formed and arrests soon followed. The so-called 'Stoke Newington Eight' were brought to court in what was to prove to be the longest criminal trial in English history and four of them were given lengthy prison sentences. The reaction to their activities was out of all proportion to their actual acts, but the new prime minister was very preoccupied by their escapades including their initial ability to escape detection and especially the fact that three of their bombs had targeted the property of members of his government.

The particular target of the Angry Brigade's anger was the bill that Heath hoped would end what he perceived as the economically crippling round of industrial action, the Industrial Relations Act (1971). Introduced to parliament by Carr, it sought to curb the power of the unions, in particular banning the 'closed shop' and curbing the right to strike. It was a response to the perception that Union militancy was increasing in the teeth of government attempts to institute a threshold on wage rises. Fervently and actively opposed by the Trade Union movement – and the subject of the Agitprop Street Players' *The Big Con* (1971) – the act was eventually repealed and its failure can be seen to epitomize the entire period of Heath's brief period in office. Trade Union militancy was at its height, and there were clearly establishment fears that the succession of individual actions could escalate into a larger struggle. Thus when, in the summer of 1972, a twelve-week building workers' strike occurred, its use of the tactic of flying pickets to reinforce the withdrawal of labour was presented as a case of conspiracy, and hefty prison sentences were handed out, including to Ricky Tomlinson, who would later find fame as an actor.

Recent revelations show that the prime minister intervened directly to influence the outcome of the trials. Paul Mason, the Economics Editor of Channel 4 television, while highlighting the depth of the conflict, may have exaggerated the overall situation when he said: 'When we see the 1970s reconstructed now, in popular culture, the most commonly omitted fact is the biggest: between 1972 and 1974, Britain could easily have seen either a workers' revolution or a military coup' (Mason, 2015).

In January 1972, Britain's coalminers came out on strike for the first time since 1926. In addition to picketing the nation's power stations, they prevented coal from being delivered to all major fuel users, such as steelworkers. They were supported by dockworkers, who refused to unload imported coal, at a number of ports. Within a few weeks, the government was forced to offer pay conditions that briefly made the miners one of the highest paid group of workers within the UK. However, worse was to come for Heath's administration. In response to US support of Israel in the 1973 Yom Kippur War – when Egypt and Syria sought to reclaim by military force territory lost during the 1967 Six-Day War – the Organisation of Petroleum Exporting Countries (OPEC) embargoed the sale of oil to the West. This situation lasted for over a year and resulted in a fuel crisis that was to have a profound effect in Britain. In the face of the shortage of oil, coal prices peaked and, after a period of working-to-rule, in February 1974 the Mineworkers again came out on strike.

In part, the all-out strike was in recognition of the potential strength of union action at that time. Faced with dwindling fuel supplies, the prime minister had introduced a 'state of emergency' and, from the very beginning of 1974, instituted a three-day week to conserve energy. In response, the miners went on strike and the PM announced a General Election for 28 February, hoping that the continuation of the three-day week would persuade voters that the Conservatives were the only party that could contain Trade Union militancy: the party's election slogan was 'Who Governs Britain?' In the event, his gamble nearly paid off, with Harold Wilson only being able to form a minority government. However, in October of that same year, a second General Election was held, this time resulting in an overall majority for Labour of just three seats, essentially in the same situation it had been in 1964. Heath lost the party leadership in 1965. His chief claim to subsequent fame was that he negotiated Britain's entry into Europe, and the nation officially became part of the Common Market on 1 January 1973. A celebratory Gala Concert, 'A Fanfare for Europe', was held in London's Royal Albert Hall. Not everyone was happy about Britain joining the

Common Market, as seen by Howard Brenton and David Edgar's scathing attack, *A Fart for Europe* (1972).

The new Tory party leader was Margaret Thatcher, who had previously been appointed Secretary of State for Education and Science in 1970. Thatcher's most remembered act while in that office was the abolition of free milk for school children aged seven to eleven, for which she received the hostile soubriquet 'Maggie Thatcher, Milk Snatcher'. She was to show in the 1980s that she had learnt much from her experience of the 1972 and 1974 Miners' Strikes.

Feminism and Gay Rights

Thatcher had been the only female candidate in her constituency selection process when she first stood (unsuccessfully) for parliament in 1950 (Beckett, 2010, 23–4), just one year after the publication of Simone de Beauvoir's influential feminist classic *The Second Sex* (1949). At the time, that might not have seemed that unusual, but attitudes were about to change rapidly. As a movement, second-wave feminism came earlier to the United States than it did to Britain, and works such as Betty Friedan's *The Feminine Mystique* of 1963 did much to open up the terms and to define the parameters of the next stage of the women's movement. A defining moment had been the 1968 strike by women workers at Ford's Dagenham factory – memorialized in the film *Made in Dagenham* (2010), and the musical of the same name in 2014. That strike had led to the introduction of the Equal Pay Act of 1970.

In Britain, however, a properly organized opposition to the patriarchal status quo dates from 1970, when the first Women's Liberation movement conference took place in Oxford. In that same year, a significant triple-whammy of protests occurred at the annual Miss World Contest, held at the Royal Albert Hall in November, protests that came from different parts of the alternative movement. Before the event, members of the Angry Brigade had successfully planted a bomb under an outside BBC broadcast van to stop the event being televised. Inside the hall, Womens' Liberation activists disrupted proceedings with posters held aloft and flour, smoke, ink and stink bombs were thrown at the stage. They were joined by members of the newly formed Women's Street Theatre Group (later the Womens' Theatre Group, and later still Sphinx Theatre Company) who lined up with their nipples and crotches illuminated.

1970 saw two seminal books published: Kate Millett's *Sexual Politics* and Germaine Greer's *The Female Eunuch*. Other influential books published in the 1970s included Sheila Rowbotham's *Woman's Consciousness, Man's World* (1973) and Juliet Mitchell's *Women's Estate* (1971). The decade also saw the construction of a multi-faceted women's movement which united at certain moments, such as the first 'Reclaim the Streets' event, which began in Britain, in November 1977, in response to the activities of serial murderer Peter Sutcliffe, the Yorkshire Ripper who, between 1975 and 1980, mutilated and killed thirteen women in the Leeds/Bradford area. The co-ordinated torch-lit marches took place in Brighton, Bristol, Leeds, London, Manchester, Newcastle and York. The feminist magazine *Spare Rib* began publishing in 1972 and the feminist publishing imprint Virago in 1975. Among the less proletarian successes – but still successes – that might be listed were that women were allowed to trade on the floor of the London Stock Exchange in 1973 and in the following year five Oxford University Colleges finally allowed, after much anguished debate, the admission of women. There were also some significant legislative advances: in 1975, the Equal Pay Act and the Sexual Discrimination Act became law and in 1976, the Domestic Violence Act was passed. However, these laws were not seen as, in themselves, solutions to the real problems and the struggle continued – and continues.

The 1970s also marked other significant advances for another group of marginalized people. Following the legalization of homosexuality between consenting adults in 1967, the Gay Liberation Front (GLF) was founded in 1970. As well as reflecting concerns about the way in which gay men and lesbians struggled and were frequently victimized, GLF sought to take a more positive stance, celebrating rather than simply defending their differences. In 1972, *Gay News* was published for the first time and also in that same year the first Gay Pride Rally occurred in London. Although a modest affair initially, it would become an annual event that rapidly grew to have simultaneous rallies in cities and towns all over the nation. Throughout the rest of the 1970s, alternative theatre groups such as Gay Sweatshop, Beryl and the Perils and Cunning Stunts enthusiastically embraced the territory that the mainstream theatre was largely content to ignore.

1974–6

On retaking office in 1974, Harold Wilson experienced *déjà vu* as he explained when he wrote:

> It seems to be almost a law of British politics that when Labour becomes the Government, we inherit a record balance-of-payments deficit, and, equally, that we bequeath a record surplus when we go out of office. (Wilson, 1979, 22)

A generous wage rise offer was accepted by the miners, and the state of emergency and the three-day week immediately halted. However, economically the nation was in a very parlous state, still very much feeling the effects of the oil crisis. Even so, it was difficult for Wilson to act. One of his chief problems was that without a working majority, he had to attempt to balance the left and right factions of his cabinet. It was a difficult juggling act: Michael Foot and the newly radicalized Tony Benn had to be weighed up against more obviously right and right-of-centre ministers – and all this against the 1974 election manifesto which had promised a more socialist programme of reform. At constituency level, and particularly in the cities, there was a move towards actively embacing a more directly socialist agenda.

The 'leftward shift in the party as a whole' had come about partly as a result of the shock of the 1970 General Election result: the assumption on the left had been that Labour would remain in power. Its failure to do so gave rise to the feeling that the party could now be moved away from its centrist position and new, younger and more radical members began to dominate many of the local constituency branches of the party. The total number of traditional activists in any given constituency was likely to be quite low – and reduced anyway by disillusionment with the failure of the party to achieve real change in the 1960s – and thus more open to adopting more radical proposals. In particular, the Trotskyist group Militant abandoned its policy of total hostility towards the entire parliamentary system, recreating itself as Militant Tendency and seeking to work from within and to revive commitment to Clause Four (or Clause IV, part of the 1918 UK Labour Party's constitution) and state control of industry and resources. So seriously was this invasion taken, that an internal party enquiry was undertaken in 1975: though the issue would not be resolved until well into the 1980s.

This leftward shift – the pay-dirt for many 1960s activists who had learnt the hard way that real change can only be brought about by engagement and organization – could not have come at a worse time for the government. By the beginning of 1975, inflation was running at 25 per cent and wage rises were at an annual rate of about 37 per cent (Holmes, 1985, 19, 25). In the face of the ongoing effects of the oil crisis on Britain's economy, the government placed great faith in the future exploitation of the country's own oil and gas reserves. In December 1969, the rig *Ocean Viking* found oil in the waters off Norway. The implications were enormous.

Although North Sea oil production did not become really significant until 1977, in Scotland – off whose shores the oil was located, and where Aberdeen started very quickly to become an oil-boom town – many nationalists regarded the discovery in a very different light. The Scottish National Party (SNP) had been formed in 1934, but in the modern period it had enjoyed little electoral success, failing to win a seat in 1964 and 1966, and winning just one in the 1970 General Election. During the election campaigns for the two 1974 elections its adopted slogan was 'It's Scotland's Oil': in March seven candidates were elected, and in October eleven. But, although there was a serious parliamentary slump in the 1979 election – with the SNP losing nine of its eleven seats, largely as a result of the failure to achieve a victory in a Devolution Referendum earlier that year – overall there was a steadily rising tide of popular nationalist feeling: and it was a rising tide that provided the context for what would prove to be the breakthrough for the 7:84 Theatre Company. A socialist company, opposed to nationalism in all its forms, it toured the highlands and islands of Scotland with John McGrath's ground-breaking *The Cheviot, the Stag and the Black, Black Oil* (1973) – a play that combined historical narrative, traditional song and dance and satire in a tour through the nation's history, seeking to demonstrate that North Sea oil was but the latest stage in the exploitation of Scotland first by English landowners and latterly by international capitalist institutions.

Although the effects of North Sea oil revenue were already being felt in Scotland, it would not be until the 1980s that a real impact would be felt in terms of the whole British economy. In 1975, the government issued a white paper, *The Attack on Inflation*, that imposed a £6 wage-rise cap, with a zero rise for individuals earning above £8,500. From then until the next election, it found itself committed to a policy of compulsory wage control that was ever harder to maintain. By March 1976, Harold Wilson – just sixty years old, but over-stretched and probably already quite ill – had had enough; he resigned as prime minister – early as he had always promised he would do. He was succeeded by Foreign Secretary and erstwhile Chancellor of the Exchequer James Callaghan.

The Left against Racism

In 1972, Uganda's President Idi Amin had announced the expulsion of the entire Asian population of his country, resulting in a significant increase in the number of new immigrants to Britain. This, coupled with the steadily rising population of non-white native Britons, ensured that the fuse that had been lit by Enoch Powell continued to burn. There was an emergent concept of multiculturalism – a celebration of racial, ethnic and geographical difference – but it faced a solid wall of silent prejudice and worse. In 1965, BBC television had started to screen a new comedy series, *Till Death Us Do Part*, starring Warren Mitchell as Alf Garnett, an unrepentantly racist and homophobic working-class supporter of West Ham football club. Alf hero-worshipped Powell. His creator, the writer Johnny Speight, had intended the figure to be dammed by his own words and actions but clearly not all viewers saw the joke and Alf rapidly became a kind of folk hero in non-ironic, as well as ironic, terms. The series ran until 1975 and, by the time it was terminated, racial tensions were rising in the towns and cities of Britain – and in particular in the Midlands, where a large percentage of the new immigration population was settled – in an unprecedented manner. The following year, the NF polled one-fifth of the popular vote in the local elections in Leicester.

In that same year, while intoxicated during a concert in Birmingham, the much venerated rock musician Eric Clapton ranted, 'I think Enoch's right [...] we should send them all back. Throw the wogs out! Keep Britain white!' (Bainbridge, 2017). This was the trigger for the formation of what was at first a loose-knit organization, Rock Against Racism (RAR). Its origins could be found in a letter of protest – reminding Clapton that 'Half your music is black' – written to the popular music press and *The Socialist Worker* by Red Saunders, Roger Huddle and members of Kartoon Klowns, a performance group formed after a split in the ranks of CAST, the early agit-pop performance group. By 1978, an organized march to a free music festival in Hackney, in London's East End, attracted some one hundred thousand people from across the country. Among the acts playing that day were the Buzzcocks, Clash and the Ruts, all a part of the emergent punk movement as epitomized by the Sex Pistols' 1977 'God Save the Queen', a number one single on

the *New Musical Express* charts, but banned by the BBC in Elizabeth
II's Diamond Jubilee year. Support for the concerts and the cause grew
rapidly and active RAR groups soon developed in the major towns and
cities, such as Manchester and Sheffield.

   RAR drew its support quite widely from left-wing organizations
and individuals – and because the main focus of its activities was
on music with street credibility, it attracted a far more amorphous
constituency than other, less single-issue, groupings. But the chief
organized support came from the Anti-Nazi League (ANL), a group
that had been formed after an attempt by the NF to march through
Lewisham in South London had been prevented by a large force of
anti-racists, including local black youths. It continued to maintain a
strong presence in organized opposition to the activities of the NF
and other extreme right-wing groups. It was supposedly supported
by the Socialist Workers' Party (SWP), and thought by many to be
'the only begetter' of the ANL. Formerly the International Socialists,
the group had renamed itself in 1977, and soon became the largest
extra-parliamentary left-wing organization in the country, their characteristically emblazoned banners visually dominating many a march and
demonstration.

   David Edgar's 1976 play, *Destiny*, is concerned with an election
in the English Midlands (much like Smethwick) and the attempts of
an extreme-right racist group to achieve respectability and success
by getting into bed with the right-wing of Powell's own Tory party.
The narrative of the play begins on Independence Day in India and
then transports the four main characters – British and Indian –
to a Midlands' town on the eve of a contemporary racially heated
by-election held in the context of a strike by Asian workers at a local
factory. Given the theme, Edgar 'wanted the play to be performed in
a big rep in a multiracial city' (Edgar, 1976), but it was eventually first
staged at the Other Place in Stratford before transferring to the RSC's
London base, the Aldwych. In that year when the new National Theatre
was finally opened on London's South Bank, *Destiny* signalled not only
Edgar's move from alternative theatre venues to the mainstream, but
a larger change in the overall picture of alternative theatre. The first
newly commissioned play to be put on at the National was *Weapons
of Happiness*, written by Howard Brenton and directed by David Hare,
two of the early stalwarts of fringe theatre. Brenton's play was also
concerned with a factory strike as a central part of its narrative: its
author had talked of it 'as an armoured charabanc [sight-seeing bus]
[…] parked within the National walls' (Brenton, *The Times*, 1976).

In any event, *Destiny* was a great success, and cemented Edgar's reputation as an astute theatrical analyst of the contemporary political scene: however, as the playwright recalled, it did not go unheeded by those right-wing elements that it sought to vilify:

> [the] play was picketed by members of a small neo-fascist group, whose union flags echoed the patriotic bunting on the front of the theatre. The scuffles that broke out between the emerging audience and the National Party pickets were pretty small beer, compared with the regular confrontations between National Front marchers, the Anti-Nazi League and the police. But they were scary at the time. (Edgar, 2005)

In April 1977, the ANL organized a demonstration in Southall, Middlesex against an NF meeting in support of its candidate in the forthcoming General Election. On this occasion, there were nearly as many police present as demonstrators, and, as ever, it was not always clear where individual officers' allegiances lay. It was also the first time, outside of Northern Ireland, that the police had made use of riot shields (Mackie, 1977). In the violence that ensued, some streets away from the central action, Blair Peach, a leading member of the ANL, was struck by an unidentified weapon and died the next day in hospital. It was widely believed by members of the ANL and other sympathizers that Peach had been killed by a member of the police, a fact not officially confirmed until 2010 (Lewis, 2010). His death was publicly mourned by members of the local community and he has come to be seen almost as a martyr to the cause. In the subsequent election (in a safe Labour seat), the NF candidate polled just under 3 per cent of the votes, which was at least better than Tariq Ali who, standing for Socialist Unity – formed from his International Marxist Group (IMG) in opposition to SWP in 1977 – received less than 1 per cent. In that same year, the Greenwich Theatre staged Barrie Keeffe's *Barbarians*, a trilogy of short plays concerned with three disaffected adolescent boys. The last play, *In the City*, is set at the time of the Notting Hill Carnival and draws upon the characters' memories of the events in Lewisham and the proximity of the war in Northern Ireland; it culminates in a horrific racial attack. In 1979, a Blair Peach Memorial Event at the Royal Court Theatre in London was organized by the Belts and Braces theatre company: among the offerings was a satire by John McGrath, *If You Want to Know the Time*, its title ironically recalling the lines of a popular music song that continues 'Ask a Policeman'.

The Winter of Discontent and the 1979 General Election

By the time that Callaghan became prime minister, losing by-elections and changing parliamentary allegiances meant that he was the leader of a minority government and, consequently, in a weaker position than ever to push through hardline policies. Between 1977 and 1978, there was an uneasy pact with the Liberal Party, but this did little to help the overall economic situation. In 1976, Callaghan had almost immediately accepted a loan of £2.3 billion to ease the financial situation. Both inflation and unemployment rates were rising rapidly – although in the latter case, the rise was very much less than that in Thatcher's first administration – and, despite attempts to cap wages, the situation continued to worsen. Part of the problem was that, in as much as Callaghan had any power to exercise control, he could only do so in the public sector. The private sector could do pretty much as it wanted. And, in September 1978, the workers at Ford – one of the largest industrial employers in England – went on strike. Eventually, a settlement of a 17 per cent rise was agreed and the Labour government's desperate attempts to stem a rising tide of trade union militancy were doomed. This was reinforced by the failed attempts to impose sanctions on Ford. Suddenly the floodgates were open.

In January 1979, lorry drivers belonging to the Transport and General Workers' Union (TGWU) went on strike, and the ensuing meltdown with secondary picketing at ports and at oil refineries was the context for what seemed at the time like a nation grinding to a halt: with its prime minister contemplating declaring a state of emergency once again. Following a strike by train drivers, public sector workers held a 'day of action' on 22 January, and this was followed by the progressive withdrawal of labour by local authority workers, including gravediggers and refuse collectors. As corpses waited to be buried and rubbish piled up in the streets of towns and cities across the country, it was open season for the tabloid press, and the Shakespearean borrowing 'Winter of Discontent' was quickly adopted. Frantic efforts at resolution were made, and finally a settlement that was more than double the attempted 5 per cent cap was offered and accepted.

Although the economic situation recovered somewhat after the Winter of Discontent, Callaghan chose to go for the longer haul and a General Election was not held until 3 May 1979. It would be the first election in British history in which the kind of media campaigning associated with the US presidential races would begin to be employed: although it would be well into the twenty-first century before live television debates with the various party leaders would occur. The Conservative Party employed the American advertising agency Saatchi and Saatchi to front their campaign: the result was the now iconic poster featuring a queue of supposedly unemployed people under the heading 'Labour Isn't Working'. In reality it made use of repeated images of twenty Young Conservative volunteers (BBC News, 16 March 2001).

This essentially negative message, however, summed up well the general tenor of the campaign. It is tempting to rewrite history in the light of Thatcher's own attempts to deconstruct past history through the 1980s, but the Conservative Election Manifesto contained virtually no promises of change and was, indeed, vague to the point of blandness:

> [A]lthough the new leader knew what she wanted to achieve if she and her party won the election, she knew it only in the most general terms. She had a compass but no map [...] [and] [...] had neither the time nor the inclination – nor the political support she required – to conduct the kind of meticulous policy review that Ted Heath had superintended during his period as opposition leader. (King, 2009)

Unlike the election at the end of the 1960s, there was to be no surprise result, no kick-in-the-face for the professional pollsters. Thatcher's Conservative Party came to power with a majority of forty-four seats and would remain there until 1990. When Thatcher arrived to take up residence in 10 Downing Street, the cameras were in place to record her first message as prime minister to the British public: she memorably borrowed from a prayer of St Francis of Assisi: 'Where there is discord, may we bring harmony. Where there is error, may we bring truth. Where there is doubt, may we bring faith. And where there is despair, may we bring hope.' It may then have been thought that these words principally looked back to the immediate past and the Winter of Discontent. In the years and events that were to follow, for an ever-vocal, extra-parliamentary opposition, they came to seem increasingly, and savagely, ironic.

John McGrath reacted quickly to the situation with a play for 7:84 (Scotland), *Joe's Drum* (1979), which responded both to the failed Scottish Devolution vote and to the election of the new prime minister. In the following year, Howard Brenton and Tony Howard produced a satirical piece, *A Short Sharp Shock for the Government* (1980), the title of which was altered from the original *Ditch the Bitch* as a result of feminist opposition.

Chapter 2

FRINGE AND ALTERNATIVE THEATRE COMPANIES, 1965–79

John Bull

Fringe and Alternative

As a source of new work and new ideas, 'fringe' theatre must, of its very nature, resist definition. It might even be argued that once a 'fringe' company slots into some kind of pigeonhole, it is probably approaching moribundity. Heraclitus might well have been talking about the 'fringe' when he uttered his famous doctrine: 'You cannot step twice into the same river; for fresh waters are ever flowing in upon you'. (ACGB, 1977b, 38/9/19)

This extract from an internal memo circulated around members of the Drama Panel of the ACGB in November 1976 will serve well to introduce the notion of slippage between the terms 'fringe' and 'alternative'. During the period covered by this volume, the terms were often seen as interchangeable, but also frequently as quite different animals. The concept of 'fringe theatre' has its roots in the annual Edinburgh Festival and the creation of a Fringe Festival in 1947 – and might also reference the smash hit of the 1960 festival, *Beyond the Fringe*. It suggests a theatre ecology that is slightly off the map.

'Alternative' is a stronger word, and can be linked with more directly political activity: as, for example, in the concept of an 'alternative society', operating outside and in opposition to the mores of conventional bourgeois society. When the influential journal *Theatre Quarterly* published its first edition in 1971, it avoided the use of either label, offering instead a far more oppositional 'A Guide to Underground Theatre'. Interestingly, its editor, Simon Trussler, later revealed that the idea of the journal was actually 'conceived in May 1968 – in part, one of the more sedate sorts of British response to *les evenements* in Paris that month' – and that the choice of 'underground' was a very conscious one. 'When [...] we tried to chart [...] the turbulent progress of what was then still called "fringe" theatre, it soon became clear that the theatrical changes of 1968 were not only a response to but an organic part of a movement for social and political change which had swept the western world' (Trussler, 1981, xii).

Here are two examples of the way in which the two terms can have both separate and over-lapping existence. First, in July 1976 the socialist theatre group Red Ladder was touring Merseyside with *It Makes Yer Sick,* a play about the current state of affairs in the National Health Service (NHS). After each performance an appeal was made for 'voluntary donations to raise funds for the Company, and also [...] a petition was available for signatures to gain support for the work of "fringe" companies'. The 'Fight for the Fringe Campaign' handout opened with, 'If you see a play about the crisis of the National Health Service in a Trades Club – that's "Fringe" theatre. If you see an experimental version of Hamlet in a pub – that's "Fringe"'. Drama Director, Dick Linklater, thanked the North West Arts Promotions Manager for forwarding a copy of the leaflet, commenting in his reply, 'Whenever we refer to them as the fringe, they don't like it!' (ACGB, 1976j, 34/124/1). So, for Red Ladder, presumably, alternative theatre would be the crisis of the NHS in a Trade's Club, and Hamlet in a pub, however experimental, the fringe. Second, when the first edition of *The British Alternative Theatre Directory* was published in 1979 it had, on the inside cover, a map of 'London Fringe Theatres': so, the companies were alternative, but the venues were fringe.

Here is another binary: although, as the 1970s proceeded, the term 'alternative' came to be mostly used by the companies, the ACGB, wishing to stress their essentially non-political interest in performance – always arguing in terms of artistic quality – usually continued to favour 'fringe'. The use of the two terms as linked in this chapter is, however, not to suggest that one can or cannot be distinguished from the other: rather to emphasize the fact that the volume will be concerned with a wide range of companies with a wide range of targets, tactics and techniques. What is most relevant is that whether (or not) they individually chose to be described as fringe, alternative or, indeed, underground, the groups are all linked in the sense that they collectively constitute a theatrical moment unparalleled in previous history. It was a realization that came to the young Tony Robinson – now a well-known actor – looking back to the 1970s:

In Bristol a few of us set up the Avon Touring Theatre. Our aim was to produce progressive plays for working class audiences, an antidote to the tired West End hits performed at the Bristol Old Vic and the like [...] I don't remember when we first realised we were part of a nationwide phenomenon. But suddenly we undoubtedly were. There were Pip Simmons, Foco Novo, 7:84, Solent People's Theatre, Women's Theatre Group. M6, Belts and Braces and hundreds more, all talented radical artists struggling to make meaningful, contemporary theatre. (Croft, 2013, 1)

A nationwide phenomenon, indeed.

Susan Croft calculates that between 1968 and 1988, more than 700 alternative theatre companies were formed in London alone (Croft, 2013, 2). Of course, many of these did not last very long; many, faced with internal disputes, split up and new companies were formed instead; many lost their writers to the mainstream theatre, in a move that was seen in the 1970s by such as Howard Brenton and David Edgar as a further infiltration of that mainstream. It is, however, a rising tide. In 1992, Baz Kershaw produced a table that demonstrated the growth in numbers of the alternative theatre groups. Starting from Catherine Itzin's claim that 'in 1968 there were half a dozen "fringe" theatre groups' (Itzin, 1980, xiv), Kershaw calculates that in 1971 there were 32; 1973 40; 1975 56; 1976 133; 1977 141; and in 1979 171 (Kershaw, 1992, 48). This almost certainly underestimates the extent of growth. For instance, three years later, Andrew Sinclair argued that Arts Council's financial 'support of "fringe" drama groups had risen by 1972 to fifty-six clients, including Incubus, John Bull Puncture Repair Outfit, Landscapes and Living Spaces, Low Moan Spectacular, Sal's Meat Market, 7:84 Theatre Company and The Yorkshire Gnomes' (Sinclair, 1995, 172). While, in 1979, narrowing the field down considerably, David Edgar had argued that 'there are now at least eighteen full-time subsidised socialist groups, in addition to perhaps as many unsubsidised or local groups who propagate revolutionary socialist views' (Edgar, 1979, 24). The last part of that sentence is key to the problem of being entirely sure about the size of this loosely defined movement. We can calculate figures based on the facts of public subsidy, but this will never provide the entire picture, as even a cursory glance at the lists of rejected applications for company funding in the Arts Council's files will reveal.

However, what all these suggested figures do point to is the supreme importance of public subsidy for the arts in a period of considerable turbulence and change. Without it, what must be seen as the most important fifteen-or-so years in the history of alternative theatre simply would not have been possible. So, a major part of this chapter will be concerned with considering the interaction, and often the tension, between the aspirations of individual companies and the necessarily bureaucratic attempts to both encourage and control the activities of this new movement – attempts that saw many of the more radical members of the Drama Department, and its panellists, often at odds with their 'superiors'. But it will also attempt to offer a wide, and occasionally quite detailed, picture of some of the many branches of this alternative world, and its inhabitants. It will do so, furthermore, with more than a passing interest in the kind of day-to-day concerns identified by so many companies committed to the exhausting world of life on the road. Bryony Lavery recalls her early days as a writer and director in the 1970s:

> While I had my eyes on the ground, others were looking at the landscape. Some started Fringe Theatre. Others started The Women's Movement [...] [We] started a fringe theatre company because we were putting on a play and we were infinitely unknown and profoundly non-famous so the venue insisted we gave ourselves a collective group name, and in a devil-may-care fashion we called ourselves Les Oeufs Malades [...] which had everyone thinking we were art students who threw bad eggs at each other. We were not. We put on plays I had written [...] We toured the country in vans that broke down a lot, appeared sometimes before twelve people, argued with jobsworth caretakers and learned that 'venue has good lighting system' usually means four Anglepoise lamps. (Lavery, 1983, 27)

With problematic, sometimes rather sparsely attended venues and dodgy vans, never mind iffy overnight accommodation and the week-by-week pressure of existing on various combinations of dole money and subsidy, it is little wonder that so many companies crashed almost as soon as they took off.

Funding and Subsidy

The years 1965 to 1979 saw the development of an entirely new phenomenon, the creation and growth of an ever-increasing number of fringe/alternative theatre groups. This would not have been possible without the fact of public subsidy – indeed its denigrators would argue that it was precisely created by the existence of that. This was a period before government policy increasingly insisted on the necessity of obtaining funding from the private sector (from roughly the 1980s onwards), and in which – in a way never seen before or since in Britain – public finance actively encouraged the growth and development of an extraordinarily diverse body of new and ground-breaking theatre/ performance companies. During the period from 1965 to 1971, the Arts Council's allocation for theatre/performance subsidy virtually trebled and it was not a coincidence that this should have been paralleled by the many-coloured and many-shaped changes and developments in cultural consciousness. In Stuart Laing's words: 'late-1960s re-definitions of what constituted theatre and of where plays might be presented (streets, factories, pubs), together with the effects of Arts Council support, allowed a fast growth of new forms of theatre group' (Laing, 1972, 88). So, before examining the range of companies, it would be useful to look at how the process of subsidy was operated and to do this it is necessary to start with the most important provider of financial assistance in the period, the Arts Council of Great Britain (ACGB), its workings, the rationale of decision-making and its attempts to keep some kind of control over the monster that many of its staff thought they had helped to unleash. Oh, and, of course, its internal disagreements.

In 1972, the soon to be Drama Director at the ACGB, Dick Linklater, sent an internal memo around, following his reading of a statement of policy or intention that he had found on a programme cover of The Natural Theatre Company:

'To present to a wide range of people a social/political viewpoint different from their own.' […] This seems an admirable and simple clear definition which could, and perhaps should, be the motto of many of the experimental fringe groups that we support, and if it were, would make our task of answering criticisms much easier. It might also be, or could be, adapted to become our own policy for helping such companies.

However, a rather more worldly wise handwritten addendum from another member of staff, Dennis Andrews, reads 'I suspect that at present they tend to play to the converted' (ACGB, 1972a, 38/9/11).

Welcome, to the world of decision-making.

The Arts Council of Great Britain (ACGB)

The Arts Council has frequently been accused of elitism, both in terms of the 'high' or 'serious' art projects it appears to nurture and also in the way in which its government-funded resources are allocated. And historically there have appeared to be strong grounds for such accusations. In 1960/1, over half of the available funds were given as grant aid to the Sadler's Wells Ballet Company and the Royal Opera, Covent Garden. As Robert Hutchison points out, between 1946 and 1981, four of the Arts Council Chairmen were also Trustees or Directors of the Royal Opera House (Hutchison, 1982, 27–8), something which may help to account for a memo circulated around officers of the ACGB in October 1966:

> From time to time there have been complaints from people occupying Box 40 that occupants of Box 39 lean forward and obstruct the view of the stage. Members of the staff using the Arts Council box are asked to co-operate to avoid such complaints in future. (ACGB, 1966b, 38/19/2)

Although local councils played a significant role in the provision of funds for the support of alternative theatre companies in the period between 1965 and 1979, it was the ACGB that was easily the major provider of public subsidy. It did so initially somewhat hesitantly: for a while such companies were not formally identified in the allocation lists as 'fringe' or 'alternative', but rather were lined up separately after the details about grants to mainstream companies. And it did so in a very limited way – although this was also partly down to the relatively small number of groups applying for assistance at that time. However, as far as performance was concerned, at the start of this period, the vast majority of funding for Drama went into three subsidized companies. In the financial year 1965/6, for example, the English Stage Company (ESC) at the Royal Court received £40,000 from the ACGB, £90,000 from the Royal Shakespeare Theatre (RSC) and £160,000 from the National Theatre (NT). By 1968/9 the figures were ESC £80,000 plus £14,000 Guarantee Against Loss (GAL), RSC £240,000 and NT, which was at this time still at the Old Vic, £260,000 (ACGB, 1965a, 38/18/2).

To put this into some kind of perspective, by 1977/8 the NT was receiving £2,770,593 and the RSC £1,365,000 from the ACGB. That same year, the Arts Council provided subsidy for 63 theatre-based drama companies, 33 touring companies and 58 assorted groups (broadly termed 'fringe'), many of these also receiving some assistance from other sources such as Local Authorities (ACGB, 1979a, 98/38). The previous year, 1976/7, a total of £850,000 was allocated to Fringe and Experimental Drama Groups (ACGB, 1976a, 38/9/13). However, it is dangerous to take these figures at face value. The accompanying list reveals that 61 per cent (£521,000) of that total 'fringe' allocation relates to 'well established companies which have already been in receipt of subsidy for four years or more'. Given that this is very near the end of the period under review, it would be interesting to list the twenty-four companies in order of the size of subsidy, as it will give something of a snap portrait, as well as allowing direct comparison with the NT and RSC figures above. They are:

- Combination (47,500);
- 7:84, the Half Moon and Welfare State (40,000 each);
- Alternative Theatre (32,000);
- Pip Simmons and Red Ladder (30,000 each);
- Soho Poly, Foco Novo and Wakefield Tricycle Company (25,000 each);
- Oval House (23,500); Richmond Fringe Theatre Group (20,000);
- Kings Head Theatre Productions (17,000);
- Recreation Ground (16,500);
- The People Show (16,000);
- Triple Action (15,000);
- John Bull Puncture Repair Kit, London Theatre Group and Phantom Captain (13,000 each);
- Incubus and Natural Theatre (12,000);
- Mikron (6,000);
- Jean Pritchard Management (5,000);
- Sal's Meat Market (3,500) (ACGB, 1976b, 38/9/13)

These are the established companies. For London-based companies alone, the following can be added (at between £12 and £40,000): Common Stock; Belts and Braces; CAST; Gay Sweatshop; Incubus; Joint Stock; Major Road; Monstrous Regiment; Pip Simmons; Pirate Jenny; Shared Experience; Phantom Captain; and the Women's Theatre Group (ACGB, 1977a, 38/9/19). However, most of the newer and smaller companies – and, indeed, some of the more established companies – would only have been on GAL or on individual Project rather than Revenue funding. This was a frequent source of distress and insecurity, making it sometimes extremely difficult for forward planning of productions and tours to take place: and it resulted increasingly in the raising of the issue of company members receiving below the Equity minimum wages as a result of the low and unreliable ACGB funding.

What emerges from detailed examination of the ACGB archives is that the offers of grant aid – and the subsequent creation of specified areas of specialist panels, such as for Experimental Theatre, Community Theatre and Performance Art – did not occur as a result of internal initiatives originally, but through external pressure from the various groups for recognition of the multiplicity of performance modes, and the need for financial support across the entire sector. That is to say that, in relation to experimental theatre as a whole, although the ACGB would become the first port of call for companies, it was always firstly acted upon before it became active. Why this should have been the case is worth brief consideration.

The Workings of the Arts Council

The reason why most accounts of the activities of the ACGB are, at best, partial is because there is an almost universal assumption that it was an ideologically hegemonic institution. It was not: but the assumption has been made possible because of two related facts – virtually all of these accounts come from ex-employees, and they all have one thing in common in that their written archival sources come almost exclusively from the published annual reports of the Council, because until recently nothing else was available for perusal. This exclusion included not only the general public. By way of example, in the Preface to his 1982 book *The Politics of the Arts Council*, Robert Hutchison expresses gratitude for being allowed what was actually only partial access to files, in contrast to the time when he was employed by the ACGB, as Research and Information Officer 1973–8, when he found that his job gave him 'no entitlement to see the minutes of Arts Council meetings or many of the papers considered by the Council' (Hutchison, 1982, 9). The ACGB archive was only presented to the V&A in 1996, and it was not until the twenty-first century that the initial cataloguing was completed and it was available – after individual clearance – for general consultation. So now, access to all the files, including those concerned with individual clients and individual subpanels, allows a much more accurate picture to emerge.

The ACGB was formed of the classic bureaucratic structure of the pyramid. All power – and all publicly issued statement – comes from the very top of the model: so, although over the years power shifted from time to time between the chair and the secretary general, and although some of the holders of these posts were more autocratic than others, every 'decision' made at the various levels below this level was in reality no more than 'advice'. As early as 1968, the then chair of the ACGB, Lord Goodman, responded somewhat briskly to the Drama Department's challenge to the Council's decision not to subsidize the Arts Laboratory: 'There was a tendency for the Panels to consider themselves as independent bodies rather than as agencies to give advice which the Council was at liberty to accept or reject' – and this came in the same year that the Council minutes first actually acknowledged the existence of 'Fringe and Alternative Theatres' in an appendix of Grant allocations (ACGB, 1968a, 36/1).

Although a more democratic structure evolved in the 1970s and the Drama Panel had power to disseminate funding, following Roy Shaw's appointment as secretary general in 1975, things converted back again. Shaw reintroduced a more hierarchical structure because he wanted to disempower the myriad of panels that were making decisions about which he profoundly disagreed. So, in 1979, following attempts to question Council decisions that countermanded its recommendations, the nature of the relationship was reinforced quite bluntly as the Drama Panel became the Drama Advisory Panel (ACGB, 1979a, 38/9/21). It is not that everything was questioned as a matter of course: rather that it could be, something that has led critics from time to time to accuse the ACGB of being unduly influenced by the ruling political party of the day, the chair being a direct government appointment. For example, when the decision to cut funding from 7:84 (England) was made in 1984, during Thatcher's years in power, the theatre company responded with a massive campaign to gain public sympathy, posted on correspondence that, over the group's postal address, had the word CENSORED stamped in bold capitals.

The pyramid power structure was particularly problematic in the case of the ACGB, for not only was all the direct contact with companies, venues and individuals – and the attendant awareness of changing performance landscapes – made from the furthest points from the top, but the bottom level was continually expanding in response to developments in the alternative theatre sector. To simplify, the layer of control went down from the chair/secretary general to the directors of Art, Dance, Drama, Literature and Music and then to their various panels. However, from the mid-1960s as far as Drama was concerned, it was clear that this monolithic structure could no longer work, and that some panel members who had been recruited on the back of their knowledge of mainstream theatre proved unable or unwilling to comment on – and occasionally outrightly hostile to – the new theatre. With considerable reluctance initially, it was recognized that a further subpanel was needed; thus, on 28 November 1968, the appropriately entitled New Activities Committee (NAC) met to discuss applications for grants for the first time, deciding that, before decisions could be made, information needed to be obtained. So it allocated all that year's funds to the organization of a series of 'Regional Gatherings', to which organizations and individuals from the whole range of experimental performance in the various regions would be invited (ACGB, 1968b, 36/1).

Some of these gatherings were more successful than others. The London one appears to have used all its financial allocation trying to decide how the money should be spent, for example. There was an East Anglian gathering, but the most productive one was the Yorkshire gathering held at Hebden Bridge, bringing together a vast collection of acts that would go on to play a major part in the development of alternative forms in the years to come: including the People Show, with Mark Long, Laura Gilbert, John Darling and Roland Miller, the latter working on his own in an early emanation of People/Time/Space, and the John Bull Puncture Repair Kit, two seminal Performance Art groups; the original line-up of Welfare State, with John Fox and Roger Coleman; and Albert Hunt's Bradford College of Art Theatre Group. The last named would become a central figure in the important 1971 Bradford Festival (ACGB, 1973a, 43/42/7).

In partial response to these events, the NAC produced a 'New Activities Report' in 1970, successfully recommending its own demise and the formation of an Experimental Projects Committee (EPC). A measure of the ground it had potentially to cover can be gained by learning of the acknowledgement at its very first meeting that Moving Being, as a ballet company, was being dealt with by the Music Department (ACGB, 1971b, 43/42/6). This was despite the fact that it was in no way a ballet company, but its use of multimedia, mime and modern dance was something that the EPC could not handle at this stage, so it categorized it in terms of convenience rather than accuracy: and, naturally, shunted the problem off for another department to deal with.

The EPC in turn ceased to convene in December 1973, when Performance Art and Community Arts were identified as the two main areas of new activity to be considered, the first initially to be put under the umbrella of the Arts Department. Community Arts was seen by many from the outset as a contentious area of activity, raising as it did questions of amateur as well as professional participation (the former of which the ACGB was not anxious to embrace) and in addition leading many to think that it should be considered as a part of an Education budget, being often as much concerned with issues of social welfare as cultural creation. The issue was raised in a 1972 meeting of the Experimental Drama Committee which worried that, after their move to London, Brighton Combination was moving more into social than to theatre work (ACGB, 1972b, 43/43/7). Indeed, it was with this division very much in mind that the playwright Howard Brenton made his break with the group in 1969:

> There was this idea that theatre should be communicative work, socially and politically active. There was the idea of very aggressive theatrical experiment. And there was always that tension in the Combination – which has been resolved now that they are at Deptford – between theatre and community work. They really are a socially active group, now, not a theatre. I went the theatre way. (Brenton, 1974, 7)

All these, and other, subpanels reported back to the main Drama Panel, which made recommendations based on the recommendations it had received, which were then sent, via the Finance Office, ever upward, until they reached the full Council, where most but not all recommendations were confirmed.

At the start of the period under consideration there was, inevitably, virtually no representation on panels by figures associated with the new and experimental groups. But this did change, at first somewhat fitfully and later more frequently. So, it was perhaps slightly odd for Roy Shaw to receive a letter, as late as August 1979, from a representative of the Wakefield Tricycle Company, wanting to propose a member of the company, Di Seymour, and saying that the company had 'always been concerned about the lack of representation on the panel of people who have actually worked in the alternative theatre world' (ACGB, 1979b, 38/9/24) – for this latter claim had become increasingly less valid.

Not all those involved were willing to act for the ACGB, however. The playwright Howard Brenton, who had been involved with Portable and Brighton Combination, regretfully turned down an invitation to serve on the Experimental Drama Panel in 1972:

I feel too involved with the work of 'Experimental' Groups, and allied to their struggles for new ways of performing and just don't want to be involved in deciding who gets what share of the money cake going. For example, I'm interested in Roland Miller's work, and have worked with him on a piece. And I know Pip Simmons' work, and know him. I don't know how I'd begin, saying Roland should get or not get x, Pip y. (ACGB, 1972c, 43/43/1)

One of the most important tasks undertaken by drama officers involved attendance at the performances of existing and potential clients, and the writing up of Show Reports as a basis – along with evidence of tour dates, attendance figures and regular financial details – for making decisions about future funding. Given that the number of groups being considered was always rising, and with the demand that groups should tour all parts of the nation, getting Show Reports became increasingly difficult, and additional advisors were recruited. One such was Professor Ted Shank, a visiting American theatre academic who, as a co-opted member of NAPS (New Applications and Projects Committee), saw and reported on an extraordinary 130 performances of ACGB-funded companies between 1 July and 16 December 1977. This was far from the norm. In addition, ACGB staff members were given a series of companies that they would have special responsibility for, as an advisor and an intermediary, if necessary, and whose company board meetings they would attend, the regular occurrence of which became an ever more vital condition for support.

Direct subsidy by the ACGB was, of course, not the only route that companies could take. By the early 1970s, there were twelve Regional Arts Associations (RAAs) in England and, although the artistic programme and funding of ACGB-supported theatres was under centralized control, the RAAs had autonomous authority to support the arts. This situation inevitably caused conflict and the ACGB files offer considerable evidence of the RAAs responding somewhat huffily to questions about the number of ACGB-sponsored touring companies each had hosted, for example. Local Authorities were also potential sources of subsidy. For example, from 1966, the Greater London authority funded arts provision through the Greater London Arts Association (GLAA). However, it was only after 1972 that the cap on the amount that a Local Authority could spend on the arts was lifted. Between 1974 and 1980, Local Authorities contributed just 26 per cent of RAA income, thus leading them to be largely supported by ACGB money (Laing, 1992, 81).

Case Study: The Arts Council of Great Britain and its Clients: Pirate Jenny, 'Oh lord won't you buy me ...?'

Given the nature of the relationship between the theatre companies and their chief potential funding body in this period, the ACGB, and given the existence of strong-minded and dedicated figures on both sides of this relationship, it is inevitable that, occasionally, communications might become quite strained. The extent of these problems can often be gauged by the amount of space that a company occupies in the Arts Council's archived files. Pirate Jenny is a serious contender for top spot in that particular league. To see why this is so, is to learn a great deal both about the development of alternative theatre in this period, its twists and its changes, and about the way in which sponsorship decisions were made.

Pirate Jenny's origins date from early 1969, when an ex-Cambridge graduate, Bruce Birchall penned a desperate plea for financial help from the ACGB for himself and his Cambridge Arts Lab. Birchall explained that he had 'built up a reputation as Cambridge's leading director' and that, subsequently, he had visited the United States, 'seeing experimental theatre in New York, New England, Chicago, San Francisco, Los Angeles, finishing up by spending 3 weeks with the Living Theatre Company – from whom I have learnt most'. He goes on to point out that he had 'started street theatre in Cambridge and Norwich [...] and done a lot of theatre workshop[s], from which there are three productions in the offing', as well as a 'community-created, improvised double-bill, *Exploits*' (ACGB, 1969a, 41/46/2). His handwritten letter had the stamped heading ARTS LAB/FREE U – giving a good sense in his short form of 'Free University' of the radical routes of his company in events in Cambridge and the larger world in 1968.

Assistant Drama Director Dennis Andrews replied, telling him that a joint meeting of the new Drama and Policy Committees had recently discussed 'what should be done about the various new applications we are receiving almost daily from what we must continue to call, I suppose, fringe and experimental theatre companies'. Andrews' words give a good indication of both the way in which the new companies were beginning to mushroom towards the end of the 1960s, and also the uncertainty with which the ACGB was responding: the use of the phrase 'I suppose' is telling. Birchall was told that he should arrange to have his work seen, but to be aware that 'if any help is eventually offered it can only be pretty minimal' (ACGB, 1969b, 41/46/2). In November 1968, the New Activities Committee had met for the first time (ACGB,

1968a, 36/1), and in the new year the ACGB council gave consideration to what it regarded as breakaway groups that could be associated with the kind of work that Jim Haynes was identified with: and related that to the recent first conference on Alternative Theatre, in Cambridge, of which Birchall had been a prominent organizer (ACGB, 1969c, 36/1). There is very much the sense of an institution trying to understand something new to them, something quite outside the parameters of their usual mainstream interests.

Birchall then moved his base of operations to London. He first worked with Guerilla Theatre (ACGB, 1969d, 41/47/4), before founding the Notting Hill Theatre Workshop, which then became the West London Theatre Workshop (WLTW), developing agit-prop and community/street theatre events – the titles of both companies consciously echoing that of Joan Littlewood's Theatre Workshop at Stratford East. He was the co-ordinator for the London gathering, formed as a part of the initiative of the new Experimental Drama Committee in 1971. The company did fourteen or fifteen performances a week, and was awarded £1,650 (plus £350 capital grant towards a van) for the year 1973/74. But, he was a frequent, insistent and lengthy correspondent to the ACGB, explaining in October 1973, as a part of an application for funding for 1974/5, the need for fringe-/experimental theatre-group members to be paid the same Equity minimum wage as mainstream professional actors. 'The concept that there is such a breed as "fringe actors", a separate species, a race apart, needs to be challenged (i.e. "fringe= amateur = bad")', he wrote (ACGB, 1973c, 38/35/1).

During 1973, most of Birchall's correspondence with the ACGB was concerned with the acquisition of a van, the losing of said van and its recovery (ACGB, 1973d, 38/35/1), while he was in the course of buying Pip Simmons' old van for £350 (ACGB, 1973e, 38/35/1). In February 1974, Birchall wrote to say that the van was in a possibly terminal condition and that he must have a new one, borrowing from Janis Joplin to stress his point:

Oh lord, won't you buy me a Mercedes Benz?
My friends all drive transits, they drive me round the bends
To become a touring theatre, you have to get down to Lands End,
So oh lord, won't you buy me a Mercedes Benz?
(ACGB, 1974a, 38/35/1)

The subject of vans, and their attendant problems, is a reoccurring one, and unsurprisingly so given the unquestionable demand to travel to a succession of possibly very geographically separated venues in rapid succession (ACGB, 1977d, 34/125/2). The company would tour *Heroes Fit For Homes* and *What's Going On Here?* (two agit-prop shows referred to by Birchall in correspondence as *Pensioners* and *Law* respectively). In March 1974, Birchall reported that they had done 54 gigs to date, and were still absolutely desperate for a van (ACGB, 1974c, 38/35/1). The Drama Director, Nicholas Barter, replied, reminding him that 'You had assistance towards transport in 1973/4' (ACGB, 1974d, 38/35/1). But worse was to come for WLTW.

A Show Report on performances of *Pensioners* and *Law* on 18 and 20 March is almost unreservedly damming: 'The trouble with both these shows was that they were almost totally undramatic, being little more than illustrated lectures on the history of pensions and law enforcement and police methods)' (ACGB, 1974e, 38/35/1). Nearly a year later, Assistant Drama Director Peter Farago summed up his opinion of the company's merit compared to their fellow politically engaged groups with reference to his visit to see *Strike 1926* at the Unity Theatre on June 1.

> Writing didn't seem that good – compare with 7:84. Acting wasn't that good – compare with Belt and Braces. The political message didn't pack much punch – compare with agitprop companies like Red Ladder and even CAST.

His conclusion: 'a well-meaning, earnest, humourless ramble' (ACGB, 1975b, 38/35/1). In 1974, still only being offered money for van hire rather than purchase, Birchall decided on direct action in support of his case, and the WLTW staged a protest demonstration at the July meeting of Council (ACGB, 1974e, 36/3). It was not well-received and the ACGB was growing increasingly less polite in responding to his shotgun tactics of appeals for finance mixed with analyses of, and suggestions for, the improvement of the institution. One such, to the Secretary General of the ACGB, Sir Hugh Willatt, had its over-familiarity commented on by Dick Linklater. 'He addresses you as "Dear Hugh". I don't know whether this is friendship, familiarity or impertinence' (ACGB, 1974g, 38/35/1). In the event, the committee awarded WLTW £12,500 for 1975/76 (ACGB, 1975b, 43/43/13). Birchall, who wanted £20,000 for each of two groups, expressed his dissatisfaction once more (ACGB, 1975c, 38/35/1). In March, the newly formed Touring Committee recommended a one-off grant of £3,600 as support for a second company's activity, but this did little to appease Birchall (ACGB, 1975d, 98/35/9). In April, he launched a direct offensive in a letter to Farago in which he sought to highlight the inadequacies of the ACGB: 'If members of your departments had had some experience at working in the field, experiencing the cash flow problems, the endless applications, tortuous delays etc [...] there might be a basis for such discussion' (ACGB, 1975e, 41/79/2). The Assistant Director's response was immediate and pulled no punches: a line had been crossed:

> I don't think that I want to prolong this specific, somewhat futile, time and paper-wasting correspondence much further.
> If you want my opinion, I give it.
> If you don't like my opinion, disagree with it.
> If you don't want it, don't ask for it.
> It seems ironic, however, that you talk of 'uninformed opinions' when you make statements which themselves would appear to be uninformed.

1   I, and various members of the Department, have 'worked in the field'.
2   " " " " " " " have experienced 'cash flow problems'.
3   " " " " " " " have experienced 'endless applications'
4   " " " " " " " have experienced 'tortuous delays'
5   I personally must admit to finding your letter offensive, but that of course is only my subjective opinion. (ACGB, 1975f, 41/79/2)

By this time, the situation within WLTW was becoming increasingly complicated, with internal disagreements over the kind of subject matters with which the company would be concerned. Birchall had begun to withdraw and had started to plan a move up north where he thought that he might find more politically sympathetic audiences. (ACGB, 1976c, 41/79/2). In 1978, he started Itinerant Theatre in Sheffield, it being 'a solidly Labour area, offering prospects of Labour Movement support, and council finances, which were not available in Kensington and Chelsea' (ACGB, 1978b, 34/125/2).

Three of the WLTW members, Jenny Rees, Diane Lambert and Siobhan Lennon, produced a plan for the period April to June 1976 which they headed 'Policy Statement'. By June, they had become Pirate Jenny (ACGB, 1976d, 34/125/1). The company was granted £18,000, plus £2,000 GAL for 1976/7 (ACGB, 1976e, 36/6). In the spring of 1977, the company produced a document, 'Pirate Jenny: Now Read On', for 'all members of the Arts Council's Drama Panel'. Its opening paragraph described the move that was projected from what its members thought of as old-fashioned agit-prop: 'We wanted to make political theatre that went "below the neck", whose critical weapons amounted to more than facts and rhetoric[…] In content, we wanted a political theatre that responded more deeply to our audiences' lives. In form, we wanted to explore expressionism' (ACGB, 1977b, 34/125/2).

But if its approach signalled a clean break from Birchall's Workshop version of agit-prop, in organizational terms the act of separation was much messier. Birchall continued to press for grant money that Pirate Jenny argued was now rightfully theirs, so there is a certain irony in that, in 1977, he had argued that a reliance on Arts Council money had become a seduction too far: 'the post-1968 breakaway movement became absorbed into the theatrical mainstream by state funding, and what had begun as a piece of political practice ended up as a job' (Birchall, 1977/8).

Undeterred, Pirate Jenny continued to plan for 1977, and to realize the idea that Birchall had had for WLTW, of running two performance companies at once. The first company (run by Jenny Rees) stayed with the kind of agenda that Birchall had supported, with a play about the Jarrow March, *Whistling at Milestones*, by Alex Glasgow: while the second company (run by Diane Lambert) performed *Bouncing Back With Benyon* by Eileen Fairweather, an attack on the William Benyon-sponsored Abortion (Amendment) Bill – intended to restrict the period of legal termination. Pirate Jenny had made the definitive move towards becoming an outright feminist group.

However, the split with WLTW continued to cause problems with funding, as a result of suddenly having to be judged, for potential subsidy, as a completely new company with no track record. The Drama Director, John Faulkner, replied, explaining that the problems have arisen only in part because of the immediate history – 'Most artistic organisations have an organic growth and I am not certain the plant which emerged was the one that could have been predicted from the packet': they were also a result of the inadequate quota of performances (ACGB, 1977f, 34/125/1). The outcome of all this was that the group's situation was referred to Standards and Reassessment (the committee deputed to monitor companies regarded as problematic by the Drama Panel): the disparity between output and finance – 'only 76 performances given on a grant of £20,000' – being first discussed at the 11th Review Committee in March 1977 (ACGB, 1977g, 34/125/2).

In the winter of 1977/78 the Company toured a new play by David Edgar, *Our Own People*, about racial tensions during a strike in a northern town. The tour took in more than two-dozen venues and the performances of *Our Own People* were scrutinized rigorously during the review process, although the many Show Reports varied from the condemnatory to the impressed. For instance, it was variously thought to take 'agit-prop theatre into a new level of sophistication and complexity'; to be 'a rather lack-lustre production'; and have 'proved a very enjoyable evening' (ACGB, 1978a, 34/125/2). The company's Drama Officer Anton Gill concluded, 'What we have to do is look at Pirate Jenny's performance over this year, taking into account their Review difficulties, and then ask "are they worth it?"' (ACGB, 1978a, 34/125/2). However, Jenny Rees was unrepentant: explaining that 'I am about to crack'. In March 1978, she let rip in a letter to Anton Gill in a manner that made Birchall's previous interventions seem positively tame:

> I am sick to the back teeth with it all, I want to know what support as our officer you give us at these drama meetings, does the acgb think were a bunch of useless idiots, because at the moment that's how we feel we are being treated[...] [W]hat the fucks going on. I will stand up to any of the people in drama to tell us straight what they don't like about us. I will also want to know how they decipher the quality of work or whatever they say is the reason for being downgraded yet again. We are not going to take it, they will be articles in all papers, and what ever power we have we will use.

The Drama Director, John Faulkner, replied somewhat brusquely: 'I must make clear to you that if in future you write a letter similar in tone or content to me or to any of my staff you will receive no reply' (ACGB, 1978b, 34/125/2). But Rees continued to support her company energetically. In September 1978, she again wrote to Faulkner: 'Will you please start to recognize that the grant we receive is an insult. There are numerous occasions when I feel a fool to continue working as hard as I do and the rest of the company do, when members of the Arts Council obviously have very little respect for what we are trying to do' (AHRC, 1978c, 34/125/4).

By February 1979, the ACGB's Finance Director, Tony Field, expresses puzzlement at being asked for further financial support: 'My understanding was that your Company is not currently operating'. Officially, Pirate Jenny had ceased operations on 31 October 1978 although, as is apparent, discussions about how and if ACGB revenue should be made continued (ACGB, 1979d, 34/125/4). An internal ACGB memo from October 1979 reveals that a final attempt to refloat the company was made but proved unworkable, and the document concludes with the recommendation that 'no annual revenue be offered for 1980/81' (ACGB, 1979d, 34/125/4). And with that, a long and exceedingly tangled instalment of alternative theatre history pretty well came to an end.

Venues and Touring

One of the most pressing problems for alternative theatre groups in this period was the availability of performance spaces in which to operate. Many of the earliest post-1965 new groups expressed a positive desire to perform outside of the conventional mainstream theatre: but for many others it was a necessary chore imposed upon them by the ACGB in order to obtain or maintain funding – the rationale being the commitment to making theatre available to all parts of the country. From 1970, tours and their financing by the Council were arranged through DALTA, the previously independent Dramatic and Lyric Theatre Association, and, after a series of shuffles, from 1975/6 by an Arts Council Touring Department. Frequently, the venues were theatres and Arts Centres with a regular programme into which touring companies could be slotted. So that, for instance, between February 1968 and May 1972 alone, as well as staging a full in-house programme, the Traverse hosted 16 events by the People Show, as well as productions by a wide range of alternative theatre companies, including: the Pip Simmons Company (premiering *Do It* which subsequently toured to Leicester, Sheffield and beyond); Lindsay Kemp (*Flowers* and *Sideshow*); Freehold; and Portable (Howard Brenton's *Fruit*, the collaborative *Lay By* and Chris Wilkinson's *Plays for Rubber Go-Go Girls*).

However, it was also the period in which the modern Arts Labs movement started to form a chain of venues, welcoming a mixture of alternative cultural events: frequently, there was a blurring of the line of demarcation between Arts Labs – usually interested in the creation and presentation of cutting-edge art and performance – and Arts Centres – where the emphasis was more solidly on serving the interests of an identifiable community. In 1969, there were fifty such establishments; ten years later only six had survived – the Combination (1967), now at the Albany, the Birmingham Arts Lab (1968), the Great

Georges Project in Liverpool (1968) and York (1968), Beaford (1966) and Hull (1969) Arts Centres. Of course, many new ones were founded during the 1970s, including Chapter Arts in Cardiff (1971), which for many years nurtured Geoff Moore's Moving Being, and by the end of the 1970s were more than 140 Arts Centres in Britain (Itzin, 1980, 9). In addition, new (and existing) theatres began to follow the lead of the Sheffield Crucible which, when it opened in 1971, as well as a main stage had a Studio with a flexible four-hundred audience capacity. So, when the 7:84 company included the city in its 1972 tour, *The Ballygombeen Bequest* played in the Crucible Studio and *Serjeant Musgrave Dances On* in the Sheffield University Drama Studio.

To give an example of the multiplicity of venues that could be found in a given area, we could consider the 1971 Bradford Festival, held from 4 to 14 March. It was a mixture of different kinds of events – music and films, as well as alternative theatre – and made use of the Bradford Playhouse, St Georges Hall, the Classic Cinema, the Library Theatre, the Central Library (University Drama Group and the Max Stafford-Clark Theatre Group), the University (Pip Simmons Theatre Group), Queen's Hall and, finally, the Mecca Ice Rink, where Howard Brenton's *Scott of the Antarctic* was staged (on ice) (ACGB, 1971e, 41/46/2).

However, as companies began to consolidate their position, many sought to find their own base, a base that could serve a double purpose. In October 1970, Drama Officer Dennis Andrews reported on a visit to one such possible site:

> I went over to Halifax at Al Beech's invitation to see the warehouse premises in Upper George Yard (the attractive but rundown courtyard of the local pub) These are in the basement and part of the upper floors of a warehouse which is due to be demolished in 5 years as part of a general re-development in the centre of the town [a recurrent theme]. (ACGB, 1970a, 41/48/323)

It is the home of the John Bull Puncture Repair Kit Company, and Beech wants to use it also as a touring base for other companies: and will be putting in a bid 'both for capital and possibly revenue purposes'. Andrews had told Beech that 'Drama would be likely to want to continue its policy of aiding companies, not buildings', but he learnt that guarantees for visiting companies were already being covered up to 50 per cent by the Yorkshire Arts Association; and he thought it 'a lively place and a growing one controlled by a chap who has a clear sense of priorities and it seems a natural caution with regard to expenditure'.

In the event, it was referred to the EPC, and later received backing (ACGB, 1970a, 41/48/323).

The situation in London was rather different. Not only were the vast majority of the companies based there, but there was a demand not just for touring venues outside the metropolis, but also within. There were some less predictable venues: Ronnie Scott's Jazz Club in Frith Street, for example, which in 1969 hosted five Sunday Festivals (along with live music acts), featuring the People Show, Will Spoor Mime Theatre, Frank Castillo Group, Portable Theatre and the Rio Farming Group (ACGB, 1969e, 41/49), but most of the performances took place in purposefully created alternative spaces. Oval House had been offering a home for rehearsal for local companies and also a venue for touring groups until its closure in 1974, and in 1968 the Open Space was born in Tottenham Court Road. In 1967, Jim Haynes opened the London Arts Lab. It was located in what was always going to be a temporary home in Drury Lane and lasted just two years: if it provided a working model for the way in which theatre and performance could take its place among the other creative arts, it was also a harbinger for the ephemeral life of such venues.

> [It was] everything that conventional theatres aimed *not* to be: scruffy, unpredictable, cheap (and cheerful), noisy, disorganised, disturbing, radical – the late 1960s western counter-culture in a nutshell. Theatre historians have often cited it as *the* seedbed for the alternative theatre of the next two decades [...] The range and number of influential groups that performed at the Arts Lab would seem to bear this out: Steven Berkoff's London Theatre Group, David Hare and Howard Brenton's Portable Theatre, the Pip Simmons Theatre Company, the Will Spoor Mime Company from Amsterdam, Geoff Moore's Moving Being, the Brighton Combination, the Sensual Laboratory, Yoko Ono, the People Show. (Kershaw, 2004, 360)

In 1969, the New Arts Lab, also known as the Institute for Research in Art and Technology (IRAT), opened in Camden town. Roland Miller had put forward a proposal to support a relocated IRAT: to 'meet the difficulty of subsidizing theatre groups that are both homeless and outside the normal run of commercial dramatic work'. Six companies had been approached – Delphic Stage Two, Freehold, North End Troupe, People Show, Portable Theatre, Wherehouse Company – and companies such as Pip Simmons, CAST, Agit-Prop and Moving Being were later added to the list of prospective users. The argument for support was thought to be particularly pressing since the premises of the existing IRAT were to be demolished in March 1971. Interestingly, in his application for ACGB support, Roland Miller lists six 'Out of London centres' who had expressed interest in taking touring productions by the groups involved: these were the Beaford Centre, Devon; Birmingham Arts Lab, Brighton Combination; Edinburgh Combination; Northern Open Workshop, Halifax; and York Arts Centre (ACGB, 1969f, 41/47/4).

In addition, from 1966 lunchtime theatre venues – some of which housed the work of individual theatre companies – began to open in London. That year, Quipu Theatre Club started to make use of the Arts Theatre in St Martin's Lane to perform work by David Halliwell's Quipu company, twice daily at 12.15 and 1.15. The company was supported by modest project grants from the ACGB (as GAL) between 1971 and 1973 (ACGB, 1974h, 98/113). It was welcomed by the then Assistant Drama Director Dick Linklater in 'New Developments', a paper written on behalf of the Drama Panel. He saw it as a 'useful addition to theatre life in London, utilizing as it does much young talent in actors, directors and writers and attracting a largely youthful audience'. His stress on the youthfulness of all involved is significant, and is in keeping with the frequently stressed concern of the ACGB with the creation of new audiences: and he concludes that although very little subsidy has been given, 'the Committee considers that this modest support should be continued' (ACGB, 1967, 41/79/1).

In 1968, Junior Teller, the manager of a West Indian Restaurant, the Ambiance, in Bayswater permitted Ed Berman to present lunchtime theatre in his basement. It was a success from the outset – the more so because by now *Time Out* was beginning to publish regular listings of events, thus both opening up the size of potential audiences, but also allowing individuals to make informed choices about the sort of event that they wished to attend. One of the great critical successes was Roland Rees' production of Ed Bullins' *The Electronic Nigger*. However, very soon the restaurant closed down, leaving Ed Berman with the name 'Ambiance' as a serendipitously appropriate title for what he was attempting. The following year, the Ambiance In Exile was established in Frith Street at another West Indian restaurant, the Green Banana. The restaurant was run by Norman Beaton, an actor originally from Guyana, who went on to become a major force in the development of Black Theatre in Britain, including his involvement with the Black Theatre of Brixton: he is now best known for his six-year (from 1988) occupancy of the title role of Channel Four's *Desmond's*. The tiny performance area in the basement of the restaurant offered a varied diet of productions, including Howard Brenton's *Gum and Goo* (1969) and the first performances of Tom Stoppard's *After Magritte*. Also in 1969, Verity Bargate and Frederick Proud opened their Soho Lunchtime Theatre in a Chinese Restaurant, and in 1970 Quipu re-opened in a French restaurant, both of these ventures in Soho. That year, the first of the above-the-pub theatres opened at the Lamb and Flag in Covent Garden. From 1971 until 1973, this became the place where Recreation Ground honed their work: at this time appealing to a largely non-constituency lunchtime audience, before evolving into a fully fledged socialist touring company.

In 1971, Berman opened the Almost Free Theatre in Rupert Street, with a new Stoppard play, *Dogg's Our Pet*, as half of a double-bill. The Ambiance lunchtime theatre there actively promoted lunchtime seasons of new plays and, in particular, produced two seasons that would greatly influence the world of alternative theatre: the 'Women's Festival' of 1973, from which the Women's Theatre Group evolved; and the 'Homosexual Acts' festival of 1975, which played a considerable part in the formation of Gay Sweatshop. In readiness for a discussion at the 1 January 1971 meeting of the Drama Panel, to discuss the 'Need for Small Scale Theatre Venues in London', a list of all currently available spaces was assembled. There were thirty-three, although the list did include the Cottesloe at the National Theatre and the Royal Court Theatre Upstairs: of these, ten were in receipt of funding from the Drama Department and six from Community Arts/ Regional/Art/Music Departments. Obviously, the list did not include other such (larger) premises as the Almost Free, Action Space, the Combination, the Factory, the Half Moon, the New End, Open Space and Soho Poly (which were included on a supplementary report). For the same meeting, one of these venues, the ICA, delivered a list of small-scale and experimental companies who had appeared there in the previous twelve months. Sixty are listed, with 'etcetera' at the bottom (ACGB, 1971f, 38/9/17). Towards the end of 1971, the Drama Department prepared a report on 'The London Fringe', which included a list of all the 'theatres of the London "fringe"': it revealed that far and away the biggest recipient of ACGB funding (more than double any other performance venue) in 1976/7 was the ICA, because, as an internationally renowned arts centre, it received revenue 'from ACGB sources other than the Drama allocation' (ACGB, 1977g, 38/9/19). The ICA was, consequentially, thought by many practitioners to reside at the point where alternative gave way to elite culture: and although companies such as the People Show did perform there, more politically committed ones, 7:84 and Belts and Braces included, were unwilling to, because they thought that the audiences would be too bourgeois for their material and too small to assist in their financing (ACGB, 1979e, 34/2/7). In their turn, a great many of the regional venues expressed their unhappiness at being offered touring companies that were too experimental or too political for their audiences. There was, then, at the heart of the touring policy, a central flaw – the assumption that simply because a community lacked a theatre, what it was crying out for was performance that subverted the expectations of conventional mainstream activity. As many companies discovered to their cost, this was by no means the norm.

Popular Theatre Companies

The term 'popular theatre' is, in its way, as contentious as the labels 'fringe' or 'alternative'. Clearly, in a general sense, it has flourished in its various forms in the whole of the modern era. But in the period under review in this volume, it can be seen to be taking on a more consciously anarchic form than was usually the case in the past. It sought not to pander to the common denominator of popular (of the people) sensi- bilities, but rather to challenge them, to draw from established routines of the circus and a host of other performative playgrounds, expanding and stretching them, if only to see what would happen. In reality, its influence is so pervasive, its tricks and its ploys so seductive, that it could be quietly insinuated in many other sections of this chapter, but perhaps in particular finding a place in agit-prop and in street and community theatre. We offer it a separate home here in order to stress its importance in the overall development of fringe and alternative performance.

In April 1971, the writer and sculptor Hermine Demoriane visited the Tate Gallery in London and accepted the open invitation to attempt the tightrope walk set up by Robert Morris. Fired by this, she took up wire-walking and, over the summer of 1972, she – by her own admission – somewhat inexpertly performed at various festivals and fetes in London, as well as working with COUM at that year's Bradford Festival: 'when COUM re-enact 300 Spartans, E build a replica minefield NOGO area across Art Gallery doors, real corpses, smoke, real mines. And Hermine walks amid the trees. Plus a few more COUM goodies.' (ACGB, 1973f, 98/91). At the beginning of 1972, Demoriane wrote a charming letter to the ACGB in which she outlined her experience to date and her desire to create a walk over the

Serpentine, in London's Hyde Park, with 'the rope set just at water level, to create the illusion of walking on water'. She added the final thought: 'Afterwards anyone could walk it with no risk but a swim.' She attached a modest list of equipment needed for the project, which came to the grand total of £93.70 (ACGB, 1972d, 41/47/2). Dermoriane's request was met – the ACGB having assured itself that she met the criteria, as shown by an internal memo from Nick Barter that 'she does not regard herself as a trained circus performer but as an artist exploring a particular skill for art ends'. He reinforced this by further stressing that Dermoriane had worked with 'street theatre troupes, The Welfare State, The Natural Theatre Company and in festival situations' (ACGB, 1973g, 41/47/2). She had already worked with COUM at the 1972 Bradford Arts Festival and was soon booked for a series of festival events by Mary Turner of Action Space, including the first night of the Manchester Festival on 17 May.

> The entertainments will take place in both a large square and a closed-off street [...] and will include Street Theatre, lots of Music, Fire-drinking, Pub Shows, Stunts of every sort, Dancing Bears, Bishop Pricking, Gross Over-Indulgence, Vulgarity and General Merriment. (ACGB, 1973e, 41/47/2)

Now, obviously this small grant to an ambitious wire-walker does not rank high in an account of the alternative theatre movement, but it gives access to a whole range of activity that tends to go more or less unnoticed in accounts of performance history: a range of activity that is wonderfully conjured up in Turner's listing of vulgar delights on offer. Barter firmly insists that this money will be given not to a circus performer, but rather to an artist: although there were many groups whose working practices had been drawn from a great tradition of skills – juggling and magic, acrobatics and clowning, farce and melodrama, and so on – particularly in the context of festivals and celebrations. One such is the Natural Theatre Company, a street theatre troupe formed in Bath in 1970 and today going stronger than ever, albeit in an admittedly very different and non-alternative form. Similarly, the London Bubble Company, founded in 1972, still exists. Like the Natural Theatre, they were committed to introduce non-theatre-going audiences to a notion of interactive performance that placed the emphasis on play and fun in the very non-formal context of parks and open spaces, community halls and such like. The Bubble Company was brought to wider public attention after *Return to the Forbidden Planet*, their musical take on Shakespeare's *The Tempest* by way of the cult 1956 sci-fi film *The Forbidden Planet*, and originally performed by the company in a tent. The musical successfully translated to London's West End where, in 1989, it won the Laurence Olivier award for 'Best Musical'. Until 1977, the Bubble Company had been wholly subsidized by the Greater London Arts Association (GLAA), as it operated on a seasonal basis, but, in that year, the company planned to operate throughout the year. It made its first application to the ACGB for at least £125,000 per annum and this was significant because it represented the potential collapse of the division between art and entertainment which the Council sought to maintain, a fact all too evident to the then Drama Director, who wrote: 'This is the first instance of such a referral and marks an important point in the relationship between the Council itself, advisory panels and regional arts organisations'. Perhaps not surprisingly, the company was not initially successful in its bid (ACGB, 1977i, 38/9/19).

For many of these popular theatre companies, finance was extremely tight, often to the point of non-existence. The Salakta Balloon Band moved to London from Italy in 1974, when it was run as a co-operative – as were many such groups – under the stewardship of Marie Green and Johnny Melville, who had previously worked with Freehold Theatre. Originally, the company was based at Oval House, but in 1975 it accepted an invitation from Battersea Arts Centre to become its resident group. This account by Melville illustrates the not untypical somewhat casual way in which most of these groups developed:

> Battersea Arts Centre […] gave us a lot of freedom and nice space in which to work for free. We just paid them back by doing performances. The first year saw Marie Green and I learning a lot of new tricks. For example, we'd arrive at a kid's playground and they'd ask us to juggle, and at that point we couldn't juggle. So we'd go away and learn how to juggle for a few weeks. The same happened with acrobatics. So over the months we built up a repertoire of skills […] We also had a couple of jazz musicians who liked to dress up as clowns and would improvise with us. ('Unfinished Histories' webpage, Salakta Balloon Band)

The GLAA subsidized half the individual performance fees asked by the company, but members lived a very much hand-to-mouth existence and it was not until 1976 that the ACGB gave the Salakta Balloon Band a grant of £8,000 (ACGB, 1977k, 34/125/2). However, in that year Melville fell out with David Haley who had joined the company as an administrator – an insisted-upon appointment that emphasized the Arts Council's determination to make companies more answerable financially, and perhaps the very reason for the falling out. Melville had formed Kaboodle with other members of the company and asked the ACGB for a further £15,000. In any event, Salakta was not awarded any further money until the Council reassessed its status. And that really was that.

The importance of Ed Berman during this period, and the sheer variety and volume of events that he was responsible for, means that he literally could pop up at any point in a chapter that seeks to delineate different kinds of alternative performance – just as he would have done at the time. In 1968, Berman founded Inter-Action, a charitable trust that promoted community involvement through interactive perfor- mance and creative play. He also founded and ran the Ambiance Theatre Club and was responsible for introducing the work of dozens of new playwrights to audiences. Similarly, until 1979, when it closed, Berman's Almost Free Theatre was a major venue for alternative theatre and his company, the Dogg's Troupe, produced new work by Tom Stoppard. In addition, he and his team can be credited with the urban farm, which became a nationwide movement. Oh, and he also had a bus – a red London Routemaster Bus – that was unlike any other, as this description shows:

> One side, the street side has not two but five decks: the destination roller at the front is a fruit machine, spinning eyes, teeth and breasts as well as apples, bananas and oranges [...] From the top window in the front of the Bus a crowd stares down at you; a Ralph Steadman cartoon issues instructions to motorists from the rear bottom window; and in the window above this, a clearly visible chunk of sky. If the Bus is at a standstill, it is likely you will find the driver playing an electric piano mounted on the bonnet beside him. A Bus conductor – possibly several conductors, all in special uniform – accompanies him with a guitar and words. (Wintle, 1973, 1973, 7)

As well as functioning as a vehicle to transport passengers (for free) to and from festival activities – and making frequent stops to allow people on and off – the bus itself provided entertainment. There was a cinema downstairs, offering short films and slide shows, and a theatre on the top deck where short plays and sketches are performed – scripts for which can be found in Justin Wintle's 1973 compilation, *The Fun Bus*.

Berman was intent on engaging and entertaining his audiences, not with hectoring them or offering to put the world to rights. For the most part, he was very successful: 'One or two faces would remain determinedly glum […] and just once in a while a prude might be upset, for example, by the transvestite capers in the *Bus Hijack Mystery*. Even so, though they were free to leave they stayed' (Wintle, 1973, 81).

Berman apart, the other most influential figure in the development of a popular alternative theatre tradition in this period was the eccentric and multi-talented Ken Campbell. Already established as actor, director and playwright, in 1970, he formed the Ken Campbell Roadshow. It existed initially on a hand-to-mouth basis and the shows were a bizarre and surreal mixture, 'based on collecting stories, working on them and then re-enacting them in some novelty fashion […] to start off wearing suits, start off in the bar or wherever we were as perfectly ordinary geezers and then launch into a show that got progressively wilder' (ACGB, 1971g, 43/43/2). The Roadshow was a part of the 'Come Together' Festival at the Royal Court Theatre in October 1970. With just £200 from the ACGB at the outset (ACGB, 1970b, 36/2), its original *modus operandi* was simple: first, a non-paid rehearsal period of two-to-three weeks, while also working up a bookings list and scrounging or buying cheap costumes from Oxfam, which was then followed up by performances and a share out of whatever profit there was.

Towards the end of 1971, Campbell began to have more ambitious plans for the company and sought the modest sum of £300 from the ACGB for costumes and props for his next show, *An Evening With Sylveste McCoy*. The title for the show – from which the Roadshow performer and future Doctor Who took his stage name – derived from 'a song that an old lady sang to us in a Pub in Chorley'. Campbell's brief summary of planned proceedings gives a real sense of what he and his company were about:

> So what we do in the show is present the character of Sylveste McCoy (the surname taken from a joke about cork suckers, sock tuckers and I'm the real McCoy). A full legendary fellow. His message is that nothing is impossible. He explodes (really) a bomb on his chest. He's sentenced to death and cheats the rope, finally a length of rope tied in a simple knot, put round his neck and pulled on from either end by sports from the audience. He escapes from handcuffs, chains, locks and Berlin Mail Bag. He makes an attempt (really) on the world record time for having a ferret down your trousers (fifty seconds

– held by the great Dick Daubley while entertaining the troops in the desert in 1942 or 3). (ACGB, 1970b, 36/2)

In the first two years of its existence, the Roadshow received a total of £1215 from the ACGB: by the end of April 1972, Campbell was beginning to realize that his increasingly ambitious plans would need greater assistance and he put in for a further £6,400. His ambitions were less to do with the scale of the work and more to do with the effect it produced on his audiences: 'When I used to act a lot in Rep farces, however much the audience laughed I always had the feeling that there was a lot further you could go, if only the characters could burst out of the walls of the play.' He wanted chuckling to turn to laughter, laughter to turn to a roar and 'once you've heard roars nothing will do but utter hysteria'. He went on to describe a recent performance at the Open Space where, at the end, the audience were shepherded on to a coach and subjected to a 'spoof opera on the top deck', after which they arrived at Hampstead Heath, where the bomb was exploded (ACGB, 1972f, 43/43/3).

Campbell had ended a letter to drama officer Peter Mair thus: 'The Three Stooges. The Crazy Gang. Abbot and Costello. Helzapoppin. These and others are our heroes at the moment' (ACGB, 1971g, 43/43/2). And it is evident from his work that he was looking back to draw inspiration from earlier anarchic stage and film comics, rather than seeking it from contemporary models. In an April letter to Nick Barter, he writes of his desire to devise a stunt show that would:

force a team of would-be comics into a now almost disappeared really wild school. The Working Men's Clubs force great comic talents into becoming mere tellers of jokes. Just about all those sensational clowns of the silent films began by being jugglers or tumblers or acrobats or rope-spinners, and so on. The job to be done today is to capture today something of their spirit. And I think that the Roadshow can now claim to be on its way to be doing it. (ACGB, 1972f, 43/43/3)

Among Campbell's other projects was 'The Smallest Theatre in the World', an off-shoot of the Roadshow, which consisted of a motorbike and a sidecar and could play to a maximum audience of two. When the Roadshow folded in 1973, its originator and owner of the motorbike Marcel Steiner took 'The Smallest Theatre' to America, while Campbell continued working first on his own and then with

Richard Eyre. This was during Eyre's important period in charge of the Nottingham Playhouse (1973–7) and he both directed Campbell and produced his 1974 play *Bendigo* before opening the Cottesloe Theatre in London's new National Theatre in 1976, with his eight-hour sci-fi epic *Illuminatus!* Topping even that, in 1979, Campbell celebrated the end of the 1970s with a 10-play, 22-hour hippy saga, *The Warp*, 'a sort of acid Archers co-written with the poet Neil Oram' (Coveney, 2008). He was truly one of the most original theatrical practitioners of his time. However, Campbell's was not the only way in which a modern popular theatre mode would be formed.

Another very important company, Footsbarn, worked in a very different way. Established in 1971 by John Cook and Oliver Foot (the brother of the campaigning journalist Paul Foot), Footsbarn's name came from a barn in Cornwall owned by the Foot family. Although the company used many of the techniques of popular theatre, comic masks and clowning included, their performances were based – sometimes very loosely based – on settled, indeed, often canonical texts by Shakespeare, Molière and the like: what they brought to these texts was a desire to share with an audience the fun and exuberance of an irreverent retake on the classics. Many of their performances in Cornwall and Somerset took place in a circus tent, although they were not against the occasional visit to a theatre. By 1979, they had become the Footsbarn Travelling Theatre and were playing the Glastonbury Festival. But by 1981, the decision to leave Thatcher's Britain was made and, until recently, the company was based in France and toured mainland Europe. This absence from Britain has resulted in the company being rather written out of performance history in this country. Their importance, however, was re-established with their 2008 production, *Shakespeare's Party*, a wonderful mash-up featuring Juliet walking a tightrope, though not played by Hermine Demoriane. The theatre critic Lyn Gardner summed up the significance of the company in her review:

> Now, Footsbarn's influence can be detected in a subsequent gener-
> ation of companies. Without Footsbarn, we may never have had
> Complicite, Kneehigh and Told by an Idiot: companies which reach
> out across the footlights and embrace the audience, recognising that
> circus and clowning are not dirty words. (Gardner, 2008)

By the end of the 1970s, the notion of popular theatre had been extended considerably, something that the ACGB was increasingly forced to acknowledge in its distribution of subsidies. In the mid-70s, despite all Barter's earlier worries, it even found itself directly funding a company of clowns: Clown Cavalcade, formed by Carol Crowther and Brian Dewhurt. Crowther wrote scripts for the company, including a clownish take on *Alice in Wonderland*, *Harlequinade*, which was taken to the 1976 Edinburgh Festival. However, at the end of the 1970s, Arts Council funding was removed and the company became a conventional commercial production company instead. It was a fate that befell many small companies as post-election spending cuts began to bite. But the influence of the popular theatre revival would continue to be felt – and in some of the apparently most unlikely places.

Agit-Prop Theatre Companies

The term 'agit-prop theatre' derives from the creation of a Department of Agitation and Propaganda after the 1917 Russian Revolution. As is implicit in the title, the activities of the department – which very importantly involved both theatre and performance – were concerned with publicizing the fact of and encouraging the development of the revolution. Its appropriation for a specifically dramatic or performative usage comes via, in particular, the work of Bertolt Brecht in the 1930s. The central tenet of agit-prop theatre is a commitment to a basically Marxist position that political struggle is class-based and that the target audience is the proletariat.

It is important to acknowledge that there is a significant history of radical theatre in Europe and America predating the companies under consideration in this volume. For example, in England, the Workers' Theatre Movement gave birth to Unity Theatre in 1936, which was housed in Camden in north London until the premises were destroyed by fire in 1975. In the period 1965–79, there were a great number of groups actively proselytizing for political reformation, change or revolution, even. However, there is not space here to consider the work of companies such as North West Spanner, founded in the early 1970s in Manchester by Ernest Dolton and Penny Morris, in order to take hard-hitting agit-prop theatre to factories and working men's clubs; or General Will, formed in 1971, out of Chris Parr's work with the Bradford University Theatre Group, and launched with four of David Edgar's earliest plays, starting with *The National Interest*; or, indeed, to consider so many others, including the 7:84 companies (although they are considered in Chapter 8 of this volume).

Agit-Prop Theatre Case Study: Red Ladder and Belts and Braces move towards the 1980s

However, we can date the creation of a modern British agit-prop movement to around 1965. In that year, CAST (or Cartoon Archetypical Slogan Theatre), generally recognized as the first of the new wave of alternative theatre groups, was formed. Although they were solidly committed to playing to working-class audiences whenever possible and offering a socialist analysis, the company was also intent on creating often anarchical fun. Muldoon's political line was not far off that of the graffiti painted on a wall in the Paris of May 1968: 'Je suis Marxiste, tendance Groucho'. If this serves to demonstrate the difficulties encountered in attempting to categorize elements of the emerging alternative theatre scene – difficulties that are mirrored in the struggles of the ACGB's Drama Panel, and its increasing proliferation of subpanels to decide exactly from where potential subsidy should be funnelled – it is still the case that CAST can be seen as a resolutely socialist group.

In the midst of the politically exciting events of 1968, CAST hosted a meeting at the Unity Theatre for people who were 'both political and cultural' (John Hoyland, 1978, quoted in Itzin, 1980, 39). Out of this initial meeting an AgitProp Information Service was set up that operated as 'a comprehensive information and communications service for all those who are working towards a revolutionary transformation of our society' (1968 AgitProp Information Service brochure, quoted in Itzin, 1980, 40). In March 1968, the first of two protest rallies that year gathered in London's Trafalgar Square to march to the American Embassy in Grosvenor Square, in protest against the US involvement in the Vietnam War. It was an appropriate meeting place: it had hosted a major Chartist Rally in 1848 and, in more recent times, had become very much linked with public protests. Indeed, in 1958, it provided the starting point for the very first Aldermaston March organized by CND, and had subsequently become a focal point for such radical opposition.

The AgitProp Information Service was asked to provide some street theatre in support of the then occupied Hornsey and Guildford Colleges of Art. From this small beginning, a group calling itself the AgitProp Street Players evolved, putting together and performing shows for local communities on topical issues such as rent rises (see Itzin, 1980, 39–50 for details). By 1972, the group had found a workable theatrical style that allowed political issues and entertainment to mix freely and the members had become more ambitious, playing directly to trade unions and responding to the crisis years of Edward Heath's government. The group then changed its name to Red Ladder, a reference to the hand-prop that had become a standby for their shows; it received its first small Arts Council grant in 1973. In 1974, the company moved into what was for them largely new territory with *A Woman's Work Is Never Done: Or, Strike While the Iron is Hot* which took on the issue of the empowerment of women within both domestic and workplace contexts. Itzin sees this as a move 'away from classic agitprop and towards a new kind of realism' (Itzin, 1980, 48). Possibly, partly in reaction to this move, Red Ladder lost a number of its members, who formed Broadside Mobile Workers Theatre instead, taking performances directly to the workplace. They were about to be joined by another new AgitProp group, The Belts and Braces Theatre Roadshow Company.

Arguably a part of a second generation of specifically socialist groups, Belts and Braces had its roots solidly in the period immediately prior to its formation in 1973. Its founding members brought to the company a solid set of alternative theatre pedigrees. Gillian Hanna had worked with 7:84, as had Gavin Richards, who had also been with the Ken Campbell Roadshow, along with Eugene Geasley and Jeni Barnett, who had also been a part of the Pip Simmons group. This range of experience facilitated the group's immediate acceptance for funding by the Arts Council's touring wing, DALTA (Dramatic and Lyric Theatre Association), something that was possibly also aided by the fact that not only was the company's second production a theatrical adaptation of Robert Tressell's proletarian classic, *The Ragged Trousered Philanthropists* (*The Reign of Terror and the Great Money Trick*), but it was also a collaborative project with the by then well-established 7:84. And then – following in the footsteps of Brecht – an adaptation of George Farquhar's great eighteenth-century comedy *The Recruiting Officer*, relocated to a contemporary England. The 'smart and lively fringe theatre group' found considerable favour from the off in their regional tours, and Richards particularly impressed a local reviewer of a Manchester production: 'This modern recruiting officer is a real cookie [...] and he is played with easy brilliance by Gavin Richards, who can even hold an audience's attention while he delivers a lecture' (Jones, 1974). A reviewer of *The Recruiting Officer* at the Duke's Theatre, Lancaster, also praised Richards' performance before concluding: 'This was great theatre [...] well thought out and entertaining' (P.A.R., 1974). These remarks express well the desire of Belts and Braces to unite political 'education' with an overall atmosphere of popular entertainment, something that was spelt out in its announcement of a second year of productions: 'The aim of the company is to combine the widest possible range of theatrical, musical and entertainment skills in shows that have a direct bearing on current social and political questions.' To this end, although the group played the regional theatre circuit, their real target audience was to be found in their preferred performance venues – pubs, clubs, prisons, working men's clubs and community centres (ACGB, 1974i, 98/37). Indeed, the company's very next production, *The Front Line*, was commissioned by individual trade unionists.

Belts and Braces was soon encouraged to expand its horizons and, in October 1974, DALTA touring officer Lynne Kirwin sent encouraging letters to potential venues, advising them that the new show was 'specially designed for larger stages and theatres'. The company had expanded to fourteen actors and musicians (it had its own band) and after a short season at London's Jeanetta Cochrane Theatre it would be available for touring from February to April 1975 (ACGB, 1974j, 98/37). The play, *Weight*, was a great success and, by August, responsibility for the financial support of the company was moved from DALTA to the Drama Department, an acknowledgement that it was now playing with the (comparatively) big hitters (ACGB, 1975g, 98/37).

However, there developed a growing feeling that political content was being over-privileged at the expense of the theatrical: the company's 1977 *A Day in the Life of the World* received very negative reviews from Arts Council's representatives. A 21 July Show Report opened, 'I saw half this show last night, and half was enough', a sentiment shared in a handwritten comment; and John Faulkner thought that 'the whole enterprise had the air of having outstripped its essential scale'; while Peter Mair attempted a partial defence, but thought it 'below Belts and Braces' usual standard':

> Firstly, in the manner of content, where the inclusion of just about every establishment/capitalist bogey that B & B perceive caused an overlong and unfocused first act [...] My second objection was that the commitment of the cast [...] was absent in a surprising number of the company [...] Although the presentation in many ways was slick and professional, the unforgivable attitude of "as long as the message is right, the performance standards don't matter" was beginning to appear [...] They are very defensive and did not take kindly to gentle criticism [...] and just retorted that all the material [...] had to take precedence over artistic finesse.

This last piece has been underlined in pencil and a note added in hand, 'Perhaps ACGB is the wrong body to supply funds in that case!' (ACGB, 1977l, 34/2/7). It points neatly to the frequent difference between the public ACGB support for the political groups and the private, real thoughts of many individual members of the ACGB. However, this apparently problematic production was not the only issue for the company at this time.

There was always liable to be tension between what the ACGB wanted of a company and what a company wanted for itself. The demand for a specific number of new productions and a minimum number of tour dates/venues could not, or would not, always be met. In 1976, the process of internal review had already started: although it was accepted that Belts and Braces produced work 'of a high standard', there was not enough of it, the books were not balancing and the proposal to undertake an overseas tour – a good way of boosting income, as many companies discovered – meant that they would not undertake the agreed twenty-two weeks of performance in Britain: and thus the subsidy should be reduced (ACGB, 1976g, 34/2/7). It was a familiar catch-22 situation for touring companies.

Meanwhile, Red Ladder had come to a carefully thought out decision about where they wanted to be. Seeking to redefine both what it was to be a touring company and also to relocate their target audience, they perceived that they wasted time 'grinding up and down motorways', being based in London yet finding 'a greater cultural receptivity to our work in the north'. Furthermore, they noted that the current *Alternative Theatre Handbook*'s list of small-scale touring companies numbered them at 130, of which 70 per cent were based in London. Thus, Red Ladder's 1977 decision to move to Leeds and tour mostly in a local area 'bounded by Leeds, Wakefield, Huddersfield, Halifax and Bradford' was predicated on a number of factors. In Yorkshire 'the traditions of live entertainment [were] still popular, albeit in in a highly commercialized form on the club circuits'; that would allow them to develop a base for their own work and for that of visiting companies; and it would give the company an advantage in being settled where they were already popular, as well as possibly enabling them to attract greater funding from Local Authorities. However, the most important aspect of the decision was one that they felt would change the whole way in which audience constituency would be constructed – and it is one of fundamental significance for all political groups of the period. Red Ladder felt that touring constantly nationwide meant that the company could never form a relationship with any community to which they performed.

By narrowing the geographical base of their activity and by making repeated visits to the same locations, they had no illusions about their continuing status as outsiders; but if 'it cannot be OF the communities it plays for it can be more PART OF them' (ACGB, 1977m, 34/134/6). Their detailed plans worked out well and clearly found favour with the ACGB. In 1976/7, of the total £521,000 subsidy that was allocated to a total of twenty-four clients that had been subsidized for the last five years (making up 61 per cent of the total of £850,000 available), only Welfare State (Galactic Smallholding) and 7:84 (£40,000 each) received more than Red Ladder (£30,000) (ACGB, 1976h, 38/9/13).

The company combined elements of the traditional working men's clubs variety nights – though always with a political twist – with more directly agit-prop material; and were careful to reference the particular community they were playing to, with local references about the transport system, for example. There were downsides to the closer proximity to regular audiences though. Not only did the company's work become better known, but its newly developed premises in the New Blackpool Methodist Church in Leeds did, too. In October 1977, following a series of attacks on the premises – including notices on the door such as, 'Red Scum, you have three weeks to get out: remember Lewisham', a reference to the riots following a National Front march earlier that year – Chris Rawlence wrote to Peter Mair: 'the arson threat was accompanied by more British National Party stickers and it is clear to us that they and other ultra-right-wing groups do not like the idea of a community theatre group working in Leeds'. Links were made with the Eleventh-Hour Brigade who had claimed responsibility for burning down the Socialist Workers' Party premises in London. The Arts Council declared its public support, but an internal memo makes their stance more clear: 'If we do start bombarding chief constables or the Home Secretary with complaints, they will believe us to be a mouthpiece. If we tell the complainants that they are making a mountain out of a molehill, we shall be branded as lackeys of something or another [...] They are a company to whose costs the Council makes a contribution on artistic grounds – that is all.' At the bottom of the memo is the one-word comment, 'excellent' (ACGB, 1977n, 34/134/1).

In London, Belts and Braces were attempting to deal with a very different situation. In April 1977, the company's Paul Hellyer was complaining about 'The struggle to maintain and develop [...] in the face of reactionary economic and political thinking by the Government and ruling class, which results immediately for <u>us</u> in an adequate grant for the year', something he argues that makes getting desirable bookings even harder (ACGB, 1977o, 34/2/7). In 1978, they started to tour their adaptation of Dario Fo's *Accidental Death of an Anarchist*. Although, in one of the strangest Arts Council Show Reports ever, Drama Panellist Gloria Parkinson largely pans what she calls: 'The something anarchist: there were no programmes', this was not an opinion shared by audiences or by ACGB staff. Indeed, at the foot of Parkinson's Show Report, someone else has added in hand, 'I saw the show at the Half Moon, and thought it almost brilliant' (ACGB, 1979f, 34/2/1). Despite this, and other glowing accolades from ACGB representatives, the production created enormous difficulties for the company. In January 1979, Belts and Braces had a deficit approaching £30,000, no money to pay the cast and three court orders for debt: they were also one of the groups listed on the leaked Drama Panel proceedings as about to have their funding withdrawn.

However, by March 1979, Gavin Richards was able to claim triumphantly that the success of *Accidental Death* would allow them to 'break the back of the accumulated deficit in one year' (ACGB, 1979g, 34/2/5). What had caused this turnaround? By 5 March 1980, the play had transferred to London's West End to Wyndham's Theatre, where it ran to packed houses until 24 October 1981: in that period about 1 million customers saw it and it was the greatest financial triumph enjoyed by the alternative theatre movement in this period. The company could not resist crowing, issuing a press release the following January that talks of the company's increasing perfection of its skills even as the West End has 'grown flabby and complacent'. Stopping only to point out the irony that 'only a few months ago Belts & Braces were on a secret list of clients who were for the chop', they hammer home the paradox of the situation:

> For some profit-starved West End managements the prospect of going dark may still be preferable to handing over their theatres to those calling for the overthrow of capitalism. Ian Albery of Wyndhams obviously feels it is necessary to live dangerously. On our side we have enough confidence in our product to risk the minefields of commercialism in exchange for a large comfortable venue to which we can invite the dissidents who number our supporters.

And at the bottom of the Press Release stored in the Arts Council Archives, an internal hand has written, 'A classic! Wonderful! Putting the boot in left right and centre!' (ACGB, 1980, 34/2/7).

British Black and Asian Theatre Companies

In 1976, Jatinder Verma had been one of the founders of Tara Arts, a company that very successfully developed connections between Asian and British culture, in a way that raises questions about the construction of cultural models. Its first production of Rabindranath Tagore's *Sacrifice* opened at the Battersea Arts Centre in 1977. In forming the group, Verma was well aware that he was breaking new ground. Almost thirty years later, in 2004, he talked of a gap in British theatre, a gap that in another sense was not a gap:

> In the 60s and up to the mid-70s, the only Asian Theatre was language theatre: Marathi, Gujarati, Urdu plays, staged occasionally by and on behalf of particular language communities. These were means of recovering lost, or losing, languages among the communities come to settle here. A public expression of the sentiment for what our earlier generations had lost. Equally, such productions were a means of claiming ownership, and thereby giving meaning, to what was undoubtedly a mean life in cold, grey Britain. A means, in sum, of affirming one's identity. (Verma, 2004)

The issue that is raised concerns the creation of an English-speaking Asian and – by my extension – Black theatre in Britain. Michael Pearce talks of the 'significant consequences for black British theatre' of the emergence of the Black Power movement in the United States in the mid-1960s: 'its emphasis on collective opposition, self-determination and self-consciousness, resonated strongly with the younger generation, especially among black activists and artists. For them, identification with the by then mostly independent "third world" former colonies was becoming tenuous. The experience of African Americans as a disenfranchised minority in a white Western country was one with which they could more easily relate' (Pearce, 2015).

The year 1965 had seen a key visit to Britain by civil rights leader Malcolm X. By 1968 – the year of both the 'evenements' in France and of Enoch Powell's infamous 'Rivers of Blood' speech and just one year after US Black Panther associates Stokely Carmichael and Angela Davis had been among an international cast of radical and revolutionary theorists/activists at the International Congress 'Dialectics of Liberation' at London's Roundhouse – a British Black Panther movement was in existence. That same year, the American exile Ed Berman founded the Ambiance Lunchtime Theatre Club and, in 1970, he ran what, as it transpired, would be the historic 'Black and White Power' season, featuring the work of African American writers Leroi Jones and Ed Bullins and kick-starting the career of the West-Indian born playwright Mustapha Matura.

However, the connections that Pearce alludes to relate to the performance of Black American plays rather than to the formation of Black British Theatre Groups. The earliest, The Negro Theatre Workshop, was first set up in 1961 with two principal aims: 'to give Negro actors experience and writers a chance to see their own work performed', as then ACGB Assistant Drama Director Dennis Andrews explained in a 1965 letter to Secretary General Hugh Jenkins. However, his following comment makes it clear that he doesn't see the company as British and that he views the ACGB as a part of the Colonial Project of civilizing the natives: 'It is hoped incidentally, that actors and writers helped in this way will eventually return to their own countries to develop cultural amenities there' (ACGB, 1965b, 38/9/5).

By 1967, this company had been joined by the African Music and Drama Trust (the Ijinli Company), both supported by moderate grants from the ACGB. Assistant Drama Director Dick Linklater, however, recognized that 'these two companies of coloured actors have recently emerged, each with a distinct character and each attempting to achieve fully professional status as British citizens' (ACGB, 1967, 41/79/1). Something of the spirit of the 1960s' civil rights movement had rubbed off, as there is now no question of referring to them as non-British. Nevertheless, there is a clearly perceivable tension between the way in which the newly emerging companies viewed themselves and how they actually were seen by their potential financial supporters, the Arts Council. This can be further demonstrated by reference to the Dark and Light Theatre Company, which was founded in 1969 by Jamaican-born Frank Cousins. On 10 March 1972, the 10th meeting of the Experimental Drama Committee considered at length the situation of the company, following a meeting with Mr McColvin, the Lambeth Amenities Officer. Lambeth had agreed to give Frank Cousins full-time use of Longfield Hall, 'which they had done free of charge including rent, heat and light expenses plus a £100 grant'. Now there were worries 'about Frank's administrative ability, about the choice of plays and about the audience or lack of it'. It seemed likely that Lambeth would no longer offer financial support: the Greater London Arts Association were not prepared to give a revenue grant and applications had been made to the Gulbenkian and to the local community relations board, the latter of which was very interested in the idea of a local tour. There was a long discussion about the best way to proceed and, reading the minutes it is not difficult to see that questions of artistic and administrative competence were being weighed against social issues: 'since the social aspect was a very important factor in the work, Frank ought to try a good many of the Trust Foundations in existence which might be prepared to donate something towards this if not the drama aspect of the work'. The minutes record two further instances of this distinction being made, after recalling that the Dark and Light application for 1972/3 was £9,000 for four productions, which was 'disproportionately large in comparison with any other company. However, because of its wider social implications, as a mixed-race company, it was felt it could not be easily compared with other groups'. Then, after much discussion, it was recommended that the company be awarded £1,500 for a three-month review period, 'subject to a tour being set up within the borough and elsewhere in multi-racial areas [...] and applications being made to various trust funds which might donate in respect of the social importance' (ACGB, 1972g, 43/42/7). The major point for the committee was that, as the group's name suggested, it was a company consisting of both black and white actors, and thus a useful item in community policy terms for promoting racial harmony.

Cousins parted from the company in 1975 and it was taken over by Jamal Ali, Rufus Black and Norman Beaton; the latter had run the Green Banana, when the In Exile lunchtime theatre sessions – including an early play by Matura – had taken place in the basement. The company also changed its name to one that celebrated an entirely different notion of community, one that was in keeping with the changing political consciousness – the Black Theatre of Brixton. Belatedly the company was given the £1,200 left out of the £23,525 contingency fund in the allocation for Drama: and then a further £2,500 was found from the Community Arts budget (ACGB, 1976i, 36/6). Although the company only lasted a further two years, it had been the most significant conduit for the production of new plays by black writers.

> By the time it folded, in 1977 it had produced Jon Henrick's *Evolution of The Blues*; Shiman Wincalbert's *Kataki*; Amiri Baraka's *The Slave*; Richard Crone's *The Tenant*; Robert Lamb's *RAAS*; Manley Young's *Anancy* and *Bre'r Englishman*; T-Bone Wilson's *Jumbie Street* and Jamal Ali's *Twisted Knot*. The Black Theatre of Brixton had produced more black plays in two years than the whole of English theatre had in the previous twenty-five'. (National Theatre Black Plays Archive)

In the spirit of these new sensibilities, the Keskidee Centre was opened in 1971, in Islington, north London, founded by Oscar Winston Abrams, originally from Guyana. In addition to hosting a great variety of Black theatre, music and poetry, it was the first Black community arts centre. In 1974, the Drum Arts Centre opened in Birmingham: among its activities was the promotion of new plays by black writers.

It was becoming ever more apparent that the Arts Council's inability to come to terms with what was becoming an increasingly important part of the cultural townscape could no longer be tolerated: in 1976, it published Naseem Khan's *The Arts That Britain Ignores: The Arts of Ethnic Minorities in Britain*. It was a report that would prove to be particularly influential in the history of theatrical sponsorship in the 1980s, and would change the way in which the AHRC would make decisions on subsidizing Black and Asian companies, but already its mere publication was an indication that things were changing. In London, in 1977, for example, the ACGB supported six '"Ethnic" companies working within their own community': though 'some of the companies listed received funds for one-off projects, others as contributions towards costs' – Black Theatre of Brixton (£18,500); Black Theatre Workshop (£400); Caribbean Cultural International (£500); Drum (£3,000); Keskidee Centre (£7,000) and RAAP (£500) (ACGB, 1977p, 38/9/19).

In 1972, Alton Kumalo (originally from Rhodesia and South Africa), frustrated by the lack of opportunities for black actors, formed the Temba Theatre Company. Given that the Dark and Light Company was still a multiracial one, Temba can lay claim to being the first all-black professional theatre company. Concentrating on new work by black British and African playwrights, the company had originally been formed to tour Kumalo's play, which he had also directed and took the leading role in, also called *Temba* (a Zulu word for 'trust' or 'hope'). The company was offered a modest £670 for the period 1973/4, and in 1974/5 £2,000, and then a further £2,000 supplement for touring new plays by black writers, including a stopover season of three of Athol Fugard's works at the Sheffield Crucible. Later, Kumalo wrote of the first few years of the company's existence as being difficult, until the Arts Council gave them an annual grant (£9,450 in 1975/6, rising to £23,000 in 1976/7 and to £30,000 by 1979/80), and ACGB minutes indicate that they were thought of as good value for the money. In 1975 the company toured Athol Fugard's *The Bloodknot* and then, in the next production, Richard Drain's *Caliban Lives*, the focus was turned firmly on the relationship between Britain and its former colonies. A company member, Julian Bryant, recalls the tour and the play's reception:

The show had already been trialled at the Studio at Sheffield Crucible, but needed simplifying for a community tour. This was to go on a fortnight tour of one night stands, in university theatres [...] and areas where there were significant black populations such as Handsworth, Toxteth, St Pauls in Bristol – all areas where there were serious riots a few years after. In Handsworth we played a building being converted into a community centre, still without windows and full of brick dust. Another venue, too small to contain the show, had a floor covered with beer cans and bottles. The tensions within these communities were apparent at the time; I had doubts that the message of the play was right, urging black people to rise up and take revenge for years of colonial exploitation – Caliban as the image of the oppressed black man. This concern was shared by a member of the audience at the Mumford Theatre in Cambridge, who stood up at the end and accused the production of racism. A post show discussion ensued. (Bryant, website)

However, problems began to emerge of a very different kind and were foreshadowed in an ACGB Show Report: as a production, it was praised for the way in which it offered a warning that unless this country improved 'its treatment of racial nationalities then there is little hope for anything other than riots, hijackings and hostage-taking in their worst forms'. However, the writer also felt that although he gave 'a superb performance' 'the play should have been directed by someone other than Alton Kumalo, since it needed someone to stand back from the play and not be involved in playing the lead'. In many ways, Kumalo was the company and when he was fulfilling engagements abroad, things slipped, not least the company finances. By 1978, Temba was failing to meet its commitment to new productions, and by the end of the following year, it looked as though the end was nigh. The company that had staged the first British production of Fugard's *Sizwe Banzi Is Dead* (1973) was in danger of folding. And this was the last thing that the ACGB wanted:

There is currently no other company doing the same style and type of work as Temba, and which could step into its shoes. There is also a demand for Temba productions and strong support for them from a number of regional arts associations. The possible demise of the Temba Theatre Company would therefore have to be considered in the light of the possible deprivation of sections of the community who wish to see the sort of work that Temba is doing.

Peter Mair's internal memo to Dennis Andrews of February 1978 is effectively a coded call for Temba, as a Black group with a Black constituency, to be treated as a special case, in ways that are importantly different in context but surprisingly similar in substance to the argument previously put forward for support the fledgling Dark and Light Theatre Company. In the event, Temba were given the finances to balance the books and survive, and in 1984 Alby James took over control of the company and attempted to broaden its ethnically based appeal (ACGB, 1979h, 34/159/2).

Towards the end of the 1970s, new companies were formed. In 1979, Charlie Hanson and Mustapha Matura formed the Black Theatre Co-Op to tour the latter's plays, starting with *Welcome Home Jacko*. In 1980, the Carib Theatre Company was founded by Yvonne Brewster and Anton Philips, two actor–directors of Jamaican origin, and would present the first two seasons of Black Theatre at London's Arts Theatre. Interestingly, in her account of Black and Asian theatre activity in Birmingham, Britain's second largest city, Claire Cochrane notes that as 'the first wave of post-war non-white immigration into Birmingham was largely from the Caribbean' so 'in the 1970s and 1980s it was within this community that most of the grass-roots activity was to be found' (Cochrane, 2006, 158). Despite this, although she is able to find evidence of such activity in the 1970s, most frequently associated with specific performance sites – not just the Birmingham Rep but locations such as (from 1978) the Handsworth Cultural Centre, founded by the Probation Service, and the Midland Art Centre (1979) – it is not until the next decade that Black and Asian theatre begins to really develop (Cochrane, 2006, 160–1).

It wasn't until 1982 that the Theatre of Black Women was formed. These two major areas of theatrical development – Black Theatre and Women's Theatre – receive a much fuller treatment in the second volume of this series. Suffice it to say that by the end of the 1970s, not only was there a very different sense of the role that the Arts Council felt it should play in the development of both areas, but there was a solid base of Black, and an emergent one of Asian theatre in Britain. Indeed, by the start of the 1980s, there were already 29 such companies named in Colin Chamber's account of the history of British Black and Asian theatre (Chambers, 2011, 156–7). Starting from almost nothing, that is an impressive development, but one which still had a long way to go.

Feminist and Gay Theatre Companies

This section is intentionally short, as developments are covered in detail in volume II of this series, a great number of the feminist companies dating their foundation from towards the end of the period covered in this volume: for example Beryl and the Perils (1978); Cunning Stunts (1977); Gay Sweatshop's Women's Company (1977); Hormone Imbalance (1979); Spare Tyre (1979); Mrs Worthington's Daughters (1979). So, although the 1970s saw the birth of Feminist, Gay and Lesbian Theatre and much significant activity in these areas, just as the 1980s would come to seem like the decade when Women Playwrights really started to make their presence felt, so too did these and many other companies.

There were a number of reasons why Women's Theatre should have started to develop in the 1970s. It is not that there was anything exactly new about the concept of a politically motivated theatre for women – earlier in the century the Suffragette Movement had been very active in that area, for instance – but it was no co-incidence that its emergence in the modern period coincided with the aftermath of 1968 and the birth of the Women's Liberation movement in 1970. One of the first public manifestations of its arrival on the scene was the disruption of the annual Miss World Contest in London: the WL activists were supported by members of a new company, the Women's Street Theatre Group.

> Their performances cohered around striking visual parodies exemplified in *The Flashing Nipple Show* and an agitprop piece in which [Susan] Todd represented the church, Buzz Goodbody played capitalism and Michele Roberts [...] appeared as a downtrodden woman chained between the two. The WSTG also participated in an 'auction' of women on the London Underground and commandeered the Ladies lavatory in the Miss Selfridges store on Oxford Street. (Megson, 2012, 49)

This mixture of basic theatre and provocation is entirely in keeping with a group that was seeking to intervene rather than to entertain, but as Women's Theatre developed through the 1970s it would result in frequent disputes that pitched politics against professionalism. Nevertheless, the raising of consciousness about inequality and the role of women in society, both at home and in the work place, was inevitably going to spread to the world of the alternative theatre groups which were, after all, supposedly concerned with – among other things – changing the world. For example, when the AgitProp Players changed their name to Red Ladder, the company's next production was *A Woman's Work is Never Done, or Strike While the Iron is Hot*, and it took an emphatically pro-feminist line:

> It had an episodic structure and it took a central character through an enjoyable learning process. The question of equal pay and parity was graphically illustrated by the man's pint of beer and the woman's half-pint [...] What you saw was a working-class woman on the threshold of becoming a revolutionary. (McCreery, 1978 lecture)

This was an example of a company consciously moving to embrace a feminist perspective. Elsewhere, things seemed to go much as before. Gillian Hanna was a member of the previously discussed agit-prop group Belts and Braces. In 1975, she noted two things: firstly, that yet again a new production by the company would offer nothing more than a token – and a small stereotypical token at that – part for a female actor; and secondly, that a large number of highly qualified and dedicated women, many with a very good theatrical track record, had turned up to audition for this one small part. Hanna called a meeting to which all the women who had auditioned were invited and from this a new group, Monstrous Regiment, was formed – although, from the outset, the company also had men in its cast. Given the experience of the group's members, unsurprisingly the ACGB awarded them a reasonable initial grant of £7,000 GAL for the January–March 1977 tour of their first two productions, *Scum* and *Vinegar Tom* (ACGB, 1977q, 36/37). At the end of the year, Drama officer Howard Gibbins reported back on two touring plays by the company: 'Two of the best shows I have seen for a touring company. Monstrous Regiment are in the same class as Joint Stock, Hull Truck and some Foco Novo shows' (ACGB, 1977r, 34/105/1).

From October to December 1973, Women's Street Theatre was responsible for five productions that formed Ambiance Lunch-Hour 'Women's Theatre Festival' at the Almost Free. It was after this success that the problems arising from its evolution – of mixing amateur and professional performers – began to tell. The company split and the Women's Company, consisting of professional actors and directors, was formed; and another company, the Women's Theatre Group (later to be Sphinx), took shape in 1974. The Women's Company wrote collectively to the ACGB seeking financial support in April of that year. The gist of their argument was as follows: 'We cannot accept that serious work which speaks effectively for women can be undertaken by people with neither developed skills nor sufficient commitment to abandon their careers to become full-time practitioners' (ACGB, 1974k, 41/79/4). Despite the appeal, the Women's Company was unable to attract funding and after it had mounted a couple of productions at the Round House and the Almost Free that year, it then folded.

In contrast, by 1977, the Women's Theatre Company described itself 'as a collective of seven women, based in London and touring all over the country, playing to schools, youth clubs, trade union meetings, women's centres and working men's clubs. We are concerned with presenting political issues from a woman's point of view'. The company had successfully toured *My Mother Says I Never Should* and *Work to Role*, and were about to open in London with *Pretty Ugly*, all three plays aimed at twelve to fifteen year olds (ACGB, 1977s, 34/164/1). They were by this time in receipt of a total of £12,500 from the ACGB for 1976/7 (ACGB, 1977t, 36/7). To make a comparison, Monstrous Regiment had received £25,000 for the same period (ACGB, 1977u, 34/105/1).

However, when the company learnt that their annual grant would only rise to £14,000 for 1977/8, they successfully arranged a meeting with drama officer Anton Gill. In an internal memo, he explains that they had expressed the feeling that there 'is an unfair imbalance in levels of subsidy', and expresses his support for increasing the offer considerably: a hand-written comment in the margin reads 'Sexist of course!' (ACGB, 1977v, 34/164/1). But, the anonymous male writer was not in tune with sentiment elsewhere, and the work continued to find favour with audiences and the ACGB reviewers alike. In 1979, the theatre academic Jill Davis reported on their production of *Soap Opera*: 'A smashing show [...] which was packed with an already sympathetic audience who obviously <u>loved</u> the show, although a lot of the audience were standing or in uncomfortable seats' (ACGB, 1979i, 34/164/1). By the end of the decade, though, let down by the Scottish Arts Council and the GLAA, they were in a bad financial state. However, the company was still planning three new shows – *Parlour Music* (an adult show), *Your Health* and *The Wild Bunch* for schools (ACGB, 1979j, 34/164/1). Financially down they might have been, but certainly not out, as the 1980s would show.

Monstrous Regiment also, like many a group in what were finan-cially very difficult times, found itself stretched financially and was at one time put under review: but the company made it through into the Thatcher years. However, by 1979, they and other feminist companies had come under the increasing pressure being mounted by the ACGB to become more professional in the administration of their affairs, to consider applying for charitable status and so on. But both WTG and MR were formed in the spirit of 1960s' and early 1970s' notions of sisterhood, and their declared policy of always making collective decisions was a problematic one for a bureaucratic organization such as the Arts Council. An exasperated staff member described attending a company meeting:

> Frankly, if this was a good example, their meetings are almost impossible to report. The bulk of decision-making seems to take place in the constant day-to-day interaction of the company members. They come together informally but frequently to make sure everyone is fully informed. (ACGB, 1979k, 34/105/1)

The ACGB's insistence on the appointment of an administrator did nothing to counter this democratic impulse. The problem that was endemic in so many of the alternative theatre companies – that they be run as a co-operative, on essentially democratic lines, with everyone's voice being entitled to be heard and, even, equal pay all round – was particularly the case for feminist groups, who saw the issue of a shared sisterhood as central to their mission. Liz Trafford of Red Ladder and of Pirate Jenny, the group that also moved to embrace a feminist stance, stated:

> Groups got together because they wanted to say particular things. It was actually out of that that a collective way of working emerged, rather than people saying they wanted to oppose hierarchical structures. (Mansfield quoted in Goodman, 1993, 1)

However, not only did that make debate about both day-to-day and long-term planning more difficult and more prolix, but it was increasingly seen by the ACGB as evidence of poor administration, one of the cardinal sins in the developing world of public subsidy.

By this time though, there was more crossover between men's and women's groups. In 1977, *Any Woman Can* and *Mr X* became the first bill to feature both the women's and men's Gay Sweatshop companies. The original company had been formed in 1975 after Ed Berman – seeking to follow the success of the Women's Season at the Almost Free the previous year – advertised for gay actors to take part in what was to become the 'Homosexual Acts' season. From this auspicious beginning Gay

Sweatshop was launched: that same year, the new group was invited to stage a piece at the annual conference of the Campaign for Homosexual Equality (CHE) which had local groups established in most towns. They invited Gay Sweatshop to perform at the annual conference in Sheffield. With the help of an ACGB-project grant, the company collectively put together *Mr X*. It was well received and led to demands for a tour to play to gay audiences around the country. In the following year, the company had a lunchtime season at the ICA in London, where, among other pieces, they reprised *Mr X* and premiered Edward Bond's *Stone*.

The ACGB acknowledged the immediate success that the company had enjoyed, and gave them a non-recurrent programme grant of £15,000 for 1977/8. Noël Greig joined the company just as it divided into separate men's and women's groups, the former debuting with a co-written play, *As Time Goes By*, by himself and Drew Griffiths, one of the founding members. Greig had already a long history of involvement with both gay politics and gay theatre. One of the joint founders of the Brighton Combination, he had then worked with Inter-Action before joining the Bradford-based agit-prop company General Will to direct David Edgar's *Dunkirk Spirit* in 1974, a crudely comic history of capitalism, ending up as a member of the cast as well. David Edgar said: 'Some way into the run, Noël mounted a coup d'etat (during a performance) against a company which, he argued, shared no common oppression, claiming the General Will for gay rights' (Edgar, 2009). From thereon, General Will was reformed as a company dominated by gay and lesbian members.

In 1978, both sections of Gay Sweatshop formed a central part of the first *Gay Times* Festival at Action Space's Drill Hall. In 1979, some members of the Sweatshop and of Pirate Jenny, a group by then struggling for its very existence, split to form the lesbian company Hormone Imbalance. Despite a series of hiccups, both groups continued to work separately, and on one occasion – with *Iceberg* in 1979 – together. However, in 1980 the ACGB reduced them to project subsidy status and, having to lose their administrator as a result, they temporarily folded in 1981: though they were to re-emerge two years later.

New Writing and Adaptation Companies

In a rather obvious sense there is arguably no need for this section to exist, as virtually all theatre companies produce new work and it is now a truism to say that every production of a play text is an adaptation.

However, some alternative companies' interest in new writing and/ or adaptation is so central as to constitute the sole reason for their existence. In 1988, David Edgar sought to make a distinction:

> Between the literary, cerebral, intellectually rigorous but visually dry work of the university-educated political playwrights of the 1960s and 1970s, and the visually stunning, but intellectually thin experiments of the performance artists in and from the art schools. (Edgar, 1988, 175)

Of course, Edgar never thought the division was an absolute one, nor did he wish it to be unbreached, talking in the same passage of his desire for a 'synthesis' between the two positions. But certainly, many of the companies – and, indeed, many members of staff and panellists of the ACGB – did perceive it as such and that would become central to what is now a very contemporary debate about text-based and non-text-based performance. So, I want to consider here companies whose prime interest was with the production of new writing and adaptation – and in this context the English Stage Company at the Royal Court, and in particular the Royal Court Upstairs, have to be included, although a somewhat strange set of bed fellows emerge when we make the attempt. Chris Megson considers the relationship between two of the companies most concerned with the promotion of new writing, Portable and Joint Stock, in his chapter on the former in this volume: although it is important to stress here that while the two companies adopted a very different approach to the production of a text, they shared a sense of the primacy of that text.

The problems of taking on examples of companies whose work consists largely or entirely of pre-existent texts can be no better illustrated than by considering The London Theatre Group, formed by Steven Berkoff in 1968 to perform his own works: works that could be described as adaptations, but in a rather particular way – perhaps 'interpretation' would be a more useful word? Highly dependent on movement, the dialogue of the originals is frequently abandoned in favour of alternative channels of communication. This was evident in the version of Kafka's *The Trial* in 1972, and most famously in his acrobatic retelling of the same writer's *Metamorphosis* in 1973. Berkoff attempted to describe his company's aim in a 1973 letter to the ACGB in pursuit of financial support: 'Our most recent work "Miss Julie" is perhaps our most advanced study, in combining and developing a form of "music theatre", which attempts to fuse dance/opera/mime.'

At that time he was planning and rehearsing for the tour of the next production, an 'adaptation' of Edgar Allen Poe's story *House of Usher* (ACGB, 1973h, 43/43/7). Curiously, after this Berkoff went on to create a series of memorable verse dramas, *East* (1975), *Greek* (1980), *Decadence* (1980) and *West* (1983), plays 'so powerful, so visceral' that Aleks Sierz sees them as a precursor to 'In-Yer-Face Theatre' (Sierz, 2001, 25–6).

The company most associated with adaptation as a major tool to emerge in this period is, undoubtedly, Shared Experience. It was started in 1975 by Mike Alfreds, a director with a very extensive history of productions, and, from the outset, he had a very clear idea of what his new company would be about: something that he explains in a very detailed outline of aims and intentions accompanying an initial request for subsidy to the Experimental Drama Committee in November 1975: 'Our aim is to create a POPULAR theatre, appealing to a wide range of people and providing FLEXIBLE and IMMEDIATE performances, specific to each audience and occasion. We want the audience to feel welcome as the focus of a warm, joyfully shared event.' Alfreds was interested, above all, in storytelling and the company's first production was a three-part adaptation of the traditional stories of *An Arabian Night*, which opened at Sheffield's Crucible Studio on 20 November. That it should have been produced in the smaller of the theatre's two performance spaces was appropriate for two reasons: first, this was a new company set on proving its worth; and second, the artistic director, Alfreds, had promised that 'the shape of the show can adapt to any space or type of theatre', preferably 'a space in which the audience is free to move around' (ACGB, 1975h, 34/142/2). On entering the Studio, audiences were invited to sit on the floor, with cushions provided by the Sheffield United football club.

An Arabian Night was an immediate success and, 'as a vote of confidence in Shared Experience's work', the company was awarded £16,000 plus £2,000 GAL on the recommendation of the New Applications and Projects Committee (NAPS): an extremely large figure for a company only newly formed. They toured small venues with the three productions throughout 1976 and 1977, meanwhile applying for an enlarged subsidy for 1977/8. In any event, they were offered £20,000, to which Alfreds responded with a robust letter to then Drama Officer Clive Tempest, telling him it was insufficient to be able to afford an administrator to take the load off of him; salaries will have to remain static and it would be necessary to raise booking fees. The last of these particularly incensed Alfreds as it meant that 'we will rapidly become an "elite" group only playing for wealthy or large-capacity organizations – which defeats one of our aims: to be available to all sorts of audiences and venues'. The ACGB responded to his invitation to appear before them, which he did, on 19 May 1977, but no way of adjusting the figures could be found (ACGB, 1977w, 34/142/2).

In the interim, rehearsals for the second production, a three-part adaptation of Charles Dickens' *Bleak House*, went ahead, with a total of just seven cast members to fill this massive story, and a successful tour was embarked on. A good sense of the company's pared-down performance mode can be gauged from an extract from a Show Report by Jonathan Lamede. He had not much liked *An Arabian Night*, but thought this was 'a tremendous improvement on it […] a beautiful show':

> The Company, dressed in dark-hued, everyday clothes, using a few chairs, no set and no props, bring the book marvellously to life. Simplicity and economy are the hallmarks of this group's approach. Each of the many characters is beautifully defined and presented to us without tricks, and with the minimum of theatrical means. The humour is quiet but effective, the warmth of the work is pervasive and winning[…] Mike Alfred's narrative approach has enormous appeal to audiences, I believe, and accounts for the great popularity of this group. It works perfectly, and the group's approach and team work – from the first moments when they simply mingle with the audience as they come in – could not be faulted. The 'sound effects' consisted of murmurs, clicks and tappings by members of the group and were excellently judged and very effective indeed – the most effective work of this kind that I have ever come across. (ACGB, 1978d, 34/142/2)

The problem that the company faced, as far as finance was concerned, was that Alfreds' desire to be available to even the smallest venue did not square with the perception of them as a popular group being able to command higher fees in larger venues. It was a dilemma that the ACGB could not, or would not, address: the annual grant did increase as the decade drew to a close, but not that significantly – in 1978/9 Shared Experience received £22,500 plus £2,500 GAL, and in 1979/80 £27,000 plus £3,000 GAL. However, the company soldiered on, moving in new and exciting ways to redefine the notion of theatrical adaptation (ACGB, 1978e, 34/142/2).

Theatre-in-Education (TiE)

Theatre-in-Education was one (more organized, more self-defining) of a range of post-war initiatives that linked drama for children and youth. Since the establishment of the Arts Council of Great Britain in 1946, there had been a growing demand from practitioners to properly fund theatre for young audiences. In 1965, the Arts Council published the conclusions of its Young Peoples Theatre Enquiry (ACGB, Annual Report 1966) that strongly recommended support for the field. That year also saw the establishment of a team at the Belgrade Theatre in Coventry that marked a coming together of a repertory theatre supported by Arts Council subsidy, and a team with an education brief to work with schools in the theatre's social and geographical orbit. This model, supported by shared Arts Council and Local Education Authority funding, set the template for the classic model of Theatre-in-Education. The year 1965 was also when Jennie Lee published her *White Paper on the Arts*, as the new Minister for the Arts. Embedded in that text were ideas about a new generation with its own identity and needs: 'Nor can we ignore the growing revolt, especially among the young, against the drabness, uniformity and joylessness of much of the social furniture we have inherited from the industrial revolution' (Lee, 1965). It also saw the government's recommendation that the national education system should adopt the comprehensive model. Implicit in all four developments was a concern that art and education should serve one another, should serve the regional community in which they were based and, above all, should unite to create a more socially just and self-aware society.

One of the driving energies of this period is hybridity – a leeching of influence, embraced by both educationalists and theatre artists, through membranes of discrete academic and journalistic classification. The hybridity principle was nowhere more active than in the creation of the genuinely hybrid artistic form of Theatre-in-Education. The dialogue/dialectic between drama and education was nothing new – the role of drama to instruct and consolidate dominant cultural and social norms (and to challenge and even create new versions of them) is rooted in the history of drama. This was, however, a period initially characterized more by challenge and creativity than conservative consolidation. The defining feature of Theatre-in-Education, in its classic form, was some element of participation and problem-solving by the audience/participants, most frequently in role but not in character.

The model for the TiE movement (as it was to become when similar projects sprung up in cities such as Bolton, Leeds and Peterborough as well as London) was aligned with two state institutions that appeared also to hold out hope as executors of a vision rooted in wartime optimism, the BBC and the National Health Service. Theatre art for young people in schools was seen as analogous to the idea of broadcasting and health as essentials to developing an articulate and socially just generation. What became established as Theatre-in-Education came largely from a post-war generation untouched by direct experience of the world wars, a major factor in forming their worldview. The hair-trigger moment of global apocalypse around the Cuban Missile Crisis was only three years passed, and the rebellious energy it released met the growing tide of a self-confident youth culture in the Western world. Together, they confirmed in place a critical, creative, and often combative, culture. The sources of personnel for the pioneer TiE groups at first tended to be the teacher training colleges and university departments rather than drama schools. This evolved over the period as initially untrained performers acquired performance and acting skills and began to push for more challenging work. One unintended consequence of the arrival of the TiE model was a debate about professional status. To many, the actor–teachers were not good enough teachers because they were unqualified, and the theatre profession in turn looked down its nose at teachers with, they assumed, few performance skills. One important factor in fighting off these negative pressures was the arrival of an Equity TiE contract in 1973 that recognized the professionalism of this new hybrid workforce. The demand for work for young people in education created a nexus of anxieties for the Arts Council. As budgets began to shrink following the economic crises of the early 1970s, choosing what to fund became inseparable from choosing what to cut, and for many Arts Council finance officers anything that smacked of children and youth – all presumed to attend school and/or youth clubs – should be the responsibility of the education sector or social services. One illustrative memo from the Arts Council archive sums up the challenge that the new hybridity was offering. It concerns the work of Inter-Action, doing much of its work with children and young people on the streets and playgrounds of cities. The Arts Council sought to offload Dogg's Troupe, Inter-Action's young people's street theatre, onto the Greater London Arts Association. The devolution of the street theatre company was perceived by Inter-Action's founder Ed Berman as a betrayal of a principle that Dogg's Troupe's work was artistically sound as well as socially useful. An internal, hand-written memo by a drama officer states that:

Berman had been given £80,000 capital grant by the Home Office for his 'urban aid for community' work [...] Ed is anxious for us to know that this doesn't mean he has no need of Arts Council money. In fact he now needs it even more...!! In response, another officer has hand-written: 'This is a help (isn't it) if his "community work" is subsidized by the Home Office, we're absolved from responsibility for it and it clears the picture with regard to other "community" projects. We stick to the "Arts" side of things.' (ACGB, 1971a, 34/39)

This short, informal exchange encapsulates the challenge presented by the new cohort of allied artists and what we might now call social entrepreneurs. The ACGB's relationship to all funding that spoke of education, either overtly in title or covertly in intention, had always been anxious and conflicted. Keynes, in his BBC broadcast of 1945, had signalled his distaste for the chalk dust of the schoolroom when it came to subsidizing the Arts, and successive Arts Council finance officers had resisted the siphoning off of 'art' money into 'education' projects (Keynes, 1945). It was a recurrent theme: as, for example, in B. A. Young's internal memo, in 1974: 'I don't know much about TiE but believe firmly that it should be much more the responsibility of the D.E.S. direct' (ACGB, 1974a, 38/9/14). This was less ideological than a way of trying to protect the shrinking arts budgets from draining into pools that should, in their view, rightfully have been the business of local education authorities. The classic TiE form was one of the greatest challenges to this protectionism because, at its best, it patently satisfied artistic criteria while proudly announcing its educational credibility.

The porosity of the initial TiE movement came about as other influences from the Alternative Theatre movement made themselves felt, and the sense of a political direction from many wings of the political left established itself. The significance of Play, deriving from the theoretical work of education theorist/practitioners, such as Vygotsky, Dewey and Bruner, moved the focus of theory and practice into what became 'child-centred' and 'progressive' modes of teaching. These linked up with the practitioners of Play in Drama both as a rehearsal tool and devising mechanism that would be shared by writers and directors as well as performers. Among many active in these cross-border influences were Berman, Albert Hunt and Clive Barker. All were contributors, directly and indirectly, to Arts Council policy-making for young people and all shared an appreciation of Play as non-authoritarian and critical to human development in the child. Hunt's work was mainly with art college students in Bradford, Berman's work with his company Inter-Action concentrated on work in public places with children of all ages and Barker brought his membership of Joan Littlewood's Theatre Workshop company and Weskers' Centre 42 project to bear as an agent of intelligent theatre for working-class audiences. Littlewood's instinctive method was to play with theatre conventions and Barker took that interest into more formal academic study when he joined the staff of Birmingham University. He also shared close links with Hunt and with Berman's Inter-Action, maintaining a creative dialogue with them and the Arts Council.

While the Inner London Education Authority (ILEA) funded London teams like Cockpit and some core companies such as Belgrade TiE stayed mainly in the classic, school-based formation, many other companies embraced additional forms. In London, Greenwich Young Peoples Theatre included a powerful Youth Theatre wing. In the Pennines, M6 Theatre and Pitprop Theatre, both with roots in the classic TiE model, took on touring community theatre and youth theatre.

Case Study: Key Perspectives and the Demise of Classic TiE

Particularly indicative of the spread of hybridity/porosity of influence around the core of TiE was the work of Key Perspectives/Perspectives Theatre Company based in Peterborough between its founding in 1973 and its uprooting to the East Midlands in 1983. Established by a group of graduating students from the drama course at Bretton College in Wakefield, the company chose Peterborough as its base at the invitation of the Cambridgeshire Education Officer John Boylan and of the first director of the newly built and Arts Council-supported Key Theatre, Terry Palmer. The group had offered itself to other locales, including Redbridge and Glasgow, but it was Boylan's enthusiasm that persuaded them to choose the Key as its base. Their offer was to create theatre for the local communities of Peterborough and the region, with an emphasis on young people and children in schools, but also offering a once-a-year stage show. Typically, the devising company for this worked with young people in schools to co-create these shows, drawing on craft and storytelling work that went on to form the basis for characters and narratives. By 1978, the company was unique in having two staff designers – Annie Smart, later to work with the Royal Court Theatre and Berkeley Repertory Theater, and Bill Mitchell, later to work with Theatre Centre and Kneehigh and to found Wildworks. Both cite the work of Welfare State as early and enduring influences. The significance of this two-designer set-up is that it placed visual art rooted in the community institutions of schools and playgroups at the heart of the creative process, and could thus appear as close to a model of community arts as classic TiE.

The influences on the company's work were largely those permeating many teacher-training colleges of the time, similar to that at Bretton Hall. The 'active learning', Dewey/Bruner-oriented basis of teaching at Bretton Hall ensured that the originating Key Perspectives team were committed to an intellectual rigour about the group's Theatre-in-Education offering, as well as embracing popular theatre forms for touring community theatre. *Mr. Minchip's Utopia* (1979), for instance, used the form and style of a nineteenth-century travelling theatre entertainment arriving in Peterborough to make connections between the city's 1879 incorporation and the creation of a New Town a century on. The case of Perspectives is indicative of another trend in this period – the breaking away from a previously stable base in a regional repertory theatre. As funding for those buildings became squeezed in the early 1970s, some theatre managements saw the ring-fenced money accorded to the TiE team as a well that could be drawn from under the guise of integrating the team (and usually reducing its personnel). Sometimes the impetus to break from the parent company was to reach for artistic and political freedom of expression. Typical of both trends was the move that took Bolton TiE, one of the most creative and active teams, out of its Octagon base to independence as M6 Theatre Company.

By the end of the 1970s, the core TiE form had matured to a point where a canon of programmes (the preferred term for the whole experiential package of scripted performance, role-play participation and curriculum support material) had been established. Among these were the scripts for Belgrade TiE's *Rare Earth* and *The Price of Coal*, Bolton TiE's *No Pasaran* and *Sweetie Pie: A Play about Women in Society*, and Cockpit TiE's *Marches – From Jarrow to Cable Street*. Reaction to the growth of Far Right groupings and the beginnings of a wave of identity politics energized many SCYPT (Standing Conference on Young People's Theatre) companies in work about gender, disability, sexual and racial injustices. In London, Theatre Centre, GYPT and Cockpit offered strong advocacy and leadership for the field.

The election of a Conservative government in 1979 presaged the end of the classic TiE model, although its foundations had been loosened over the preceding decade by the growth of a counter-revolutionary tide that found public expression in Labour Education Minister James

Callaghan's 1973 lecture at Ruskin College. (Callaghan, 1973) The so-called Black Papers of educationalists Cox and Dyson and others, appearing between 1969 and 1977, signalled a retrenchment from within the teaching profession in the face of the 'progressive' model (Cox and Dyson, 1969a, b, 1970; Cox and Boyson, 1970, 1975). The classic TiE model was seldom banned, just starved of funding by the demands of the National Curriculum and local management of schools. These bureaucratic instruments had, of course, been reinforced by ideological ground-preparation. In 1971, speaking at a regional arts association conference in Newcastle, the newly appointed Minister for the Arts, Lord Eccles, inheritor of Jennie Lee's mantle from the previous year's Conservative election win, planted an ideological flag in the funding soil that simultaneously proclaimed the significance of work for young people and hovered over it with, if not an axe, then censorious scissors. The conference was unambiguously called *Arts and Education*, and the Minister's inaugural address lays into what he describes as the decline of the Christian consensus that life has a meaning, and the same meaning for everybody. Most telling of all perhaps, and remembering that Eccles was speaking at a conference on Arts and Education, is his assertion that his campaign against what he characterizes as 'the rational, the frivolous and the angry in the arts' should be most closely targeted on the young: 'the greatest responsibility must fall on the schools and the mass media, for between them they prepare the young to accept or to reject an optimistic view of humanity'.

What awaited the Perspectives company was the collapse of one leg of the tripartite funding arrangement that kept it afloat at the end of the 1970s. Cambridge Education Authority withdrew its revenue funding in the face of its own cuts, and the local authority, itself hit by cuts, was unwilling to step into the gap. The Arts Council was supportive but finally unable to make up the funding difference and, in 1982, the company moved to the East Midlands Arts area with the same name but effectively a new identity. The Arts Council officer involved in these negotiations noted that without support from an educational funding resource, the lack of any TiE performance may have fundamentally damaged the company's identity. The last two decades of the century were to force on similar teams new searches for hybridity, retreat into more conventional forms and, too frequently, closure.

Community Theatre Companies

In 1968, expatriate American Ed Berman created Inter-Action, a tiny organism that grew to have so many different limbs that he would merit mention in almost any section of this chapter. Inter-Action was an organization predicated on Berman's Inter-Action Game Method, 'based on children's games and not on verbal or intellectual ability (Itzin, 1980, 52). As such, it was all about participation, and not at all about spectating – something that is sometimes true, sometimes partially true and sometimes not true at all for community theatre: as we shall see. He quickly realized that his ideas could be used both in the playground and in the theatre: but it is for his work in the community that he is most revered today.

I start with Berman, partly because of his importance in this area, but also by way of pointing out that not only is the concept of community theatre a very wide one, but it is also frequently a hotly contested one. Indeed, the attempt to define what might be meant by the term 'Community Theatre' in many ways constitutes its actual history. Originally conceived of as relating to performance that in some way related to a specific geographical region – a village, a borough in a large town or city, a specific housing estate, an old people's home, for example – it was always liable to be problematically linked with more specific sections of the given communities, special interest groups: the threat of a third Heathrow runway on the life of a village; the problem of kerb-crawling in a particular borough; the problem of vandalism in a specific housing estate; the effects of the possible closure as a result of council spending cuts on an old people's home; and so on. The sheer diversity of work undertaken by these groups was emphasized by Baz Kershaw in 2004. Having noted that thirty-six or more such groups had been formed in the 1970s, he went on to list some of them, stressing the different ways in which the notion of 'community' was located:

> City-based groups such as Interplay (Leeds), Attic (Winchester) and the Natural Theatre Company (Bath) – all 1970 – were usually committed to working-class neighbourhoods and estates. Companies touring shows in rural areas – Orchard Theatre (north Devon, 1968), EMMA (west Midlands, 1972), Medium Fair (east Devon, 1972), Pentabus (east Midlands, 1974) – typically saw themselves as serving deprived communities. The extraordinary proliferation led to imaginative specialization. Interaction toured with its double-decker Fun Art Bus, Bubble Theatre with an inflatable tent and Mikron Theatre

plied the canal system on a forty-foot narrow-boat. 'Special needs' communities welcomed projects from Stirabout (1974) in prisons and remand centres, from Matchbox (1974) for people with physical and mental impairments and from Fair Old Times (part of Medium Fair, 1978), which created the new genre of reminiscence theatre. Rarely didactic [...] but the underlying links with political theatre emerged when, for example, the short-lived Community Theatre (1972) staged *The Motor Show* for striking car workers and Covent Garden Community Theatre (1975) campaigned with local residents against the insensitive redevelopment of the central London market area. (Kershaw, 2002, 363)

Not all of these community theatre groups – and most notably the urban-based ones – would have accepted Kershaw's 'rarely didactic' description, however; and, certainly, the Association of Community Theatre (ACT) described itself, from the moment of its formation as an extension of a London association in 1974, as socialist.

Between 1975 and 1980, Kershaw had himself been involved with Medium Fair, a North Devon-based group formed in 1973, and one of a number of rurally based companies touring local communities. The Dartmoor Resource website describes the group's habitual deployment of Village Visit weeks, which combined performing their own show with supporting the community to produce its own performance for a Saturday night celebratory conclusion – all this with the added bonus of leaving something more permanent, 'a much-needed bus shelter, a refurbished hall', for example (Dartmoor Resource website). Now, clearly, this kind of rural project approaches the notion of an extant community in a very different way from one that is essentially city-based, and part of whose remit may, indeed, be concerned with identifying and bringing together a community that to many eyes – including possibly their own – is effectively invisible. Given that the majority of community theatre companies in this period were urban rather than rural-based, the kinds of potential hurdles arising from attempts to first identify and then interest a potential community audience were paramount (and I use the term 'audience' in the loosest possible way, for frequently a distinction between performing and spectating would be impossible to make). Questions of intentionality are also very much to the forefront. This is well illustrated by reference to two productions, *Made in Islington* and *Toeing It*, by one of the earliest Community Theatre companies, Common Stock, in 1975. For teenagers, they presented *Toeing It*, introduced in the group's publicity thus:

Just over a year ago the Common Stock and groups of adolescents from Islington worked together on the creation of 'Made
in Islington', a production exploring some aspects of the lives of
contemporary working class teenagers in Central London. It was a
great success with the teenage audiences, and caused very healthy
discussions wherever we took it. 'TOEING IT' starts where 'Made in
Islington left off. With groups of teenagers from North Paddington
and Islington the company has developed a play exploring events
that occur when a group of teenagers occupy a deserted building. It
is both very exciting and highly controversial, and provides an ideal
starting point for discussions about the predicament of adolescents
in an urban environment. (ACGB, 1975i, 98/89)

What is perhaps most interesting about this blurb is the clear sense that
it has not been written to attract the interest of its potential audience,
the local teenagers who would, I suspect, have felt very patronized by
its predominant tone: rather, it is intended to attract the attention of
those grown-ups who are responsible for the care of these adolescents,
not even the parents in particular but the teachers, the social workers,
the youth club leaders – all of whom are possible bookers of the show
and all of whom will have possible spaces in which the piece can be
performed. This does not necessarily take away from the effectiveness
of the piece dramatically, but it does emphasize the point that is made
twice, that the performance is above all intended as a prelude to a
discussion that it is assumed will be initiated by the young audience,
but will always have the safety net of the cast and the carers to cushion
any falls.

The production was, it must be added, extremely well reviewed –
The Sunday Times, for example, saying that the narrative 'is handled
with rough and ready delicacy, their alternations of bluster, bullying,
distress, bravado touchingly but never soppily orchestrated' – but
none of the critics' extracts sent to the ACGB make any mention of
a consequent debate. That is not to say that the debates never took
place but that, after the event, the company wished to emphasize the
performance in its theatrical rather than its social context. A different
version of this dichotomy can be seen in an initial application to the
Arts Council by Inroads in 1973.

In the previous twelve months, the part-time company has been
doing street theatre, as well as playing at technical colleges and '25
tenants groups in and around Salford [Lancashire]', which is where

it is based. Like Common Stock, the company produces work for identified communities, but unlike it, Inroads does not work with sections of those communities to assemble the work. It gives a list of six tried and tested productions: ranging from *The Rents Play*, 'specifically for tenants[...] [showing][...] how tenants should fight back', to *Politicians* described as follows: 'An outdoor game-play for children with Mr Million, Mr Teach, Brigadier Killemall and Mr Music in which the cabinet is so crazy that the children hold their own election and discover that they have to get rid of Mr Million altogether if they want to control the country'. (ACGB, 1973j, 41/46/2)

Here, debate is not the logical outcome of the performance: the conclusions are reached for the grown-up and the youthful audience respectively – and in the latter case, given the characters' names, presumably to nobody's real surprise – and it is evident that the notion of a community-based theatre is eliding into an agit-prop mode. Indeed, Inroads, which had started as a community arts group in York before moving to Salford in 1971, had acted as an umbrella organization for North West Spanner, a militant political group intent on playing as close to the shop-floor as possible. Somewhere in the middle of these two models suggested by Common Stock and Inroads is the development of what comes to be known as Constituency Theatre, where community is redefined in ways that may still include a notion of geographical location – though more usually will not – but is principally concerned with an actual or argued for commonality of interests. In the period covered by this volume the most obvious examples of such constituency work are to be found in the areas of gender and race – two of the major areas of political debate.

In 1976/7, Common Stock was one of seven Community Theatre groups in London to be subsidized by the ACGB. The Covent Garden Community Theatre, Mutable Theatre and Theatre Kit received sums ranging from £2,750 to £500; Mayday/Southdown Theatre and Eastend Abbreviated Soapbox Theatre were awarded sums approaching £10,000; but the two most successful groups in terms of funding were Common Ground, with over £20,000, and the Combination at the Albany, with over £40,000 (ACGB, 1977x, 38/9/19).

The Combination had started in 1967 as the Brighton Combination. Founded by Noël Greig, Ruth Marks and Jenny Harris, it created a flexible space that allowed for a multiplicity of events and activities, more of an Arts Lab than a theatre. In 1971, Combination, as it then became known, moved to the old and run down Albany Empire in Deptford in south-east London, where it continued to combine performance with local social and community work, housing:

> a Pre-school playgroup, Housing Scheme using short-life property for single parent families [organized squatting], Intermediate Treatment Programme, Truancy Project (a kind of free-school after school for hardened truants and latch-key children), Claimants Union, Women's Action Group, Squatting Associations, Youth Clubs, coffee bar, Social Workers, Clubs for old people, for ESN children, for people with problems.

There is no mention of performance in this opening to a 1971 handout introducing the Combination's presence to the people of Deptford. However, it later goes on to suggest the way in which the company want to offer a unique fusion of the values of art and community:

> We are DEPTFORDS ENTERTAINERS not missionaries of Art. Everyone seems to want to bring Art into the Community. The assumption being that Art is good for you. More a cultural barrage than anything else. Redefine your art before you bombard anyone else with it. Does it include graffiti? Is jazz a dirty word? And pop? And films? And video? And Market slang? What are we trying to prove anyway? Everyman is an artist!

This would appear to be aimed at their fellow cultural activists and to the ACGB, to whom it was sent, rather than the local community, and points to what appears to be an attempt to address both their potential audiences and their potential sponsors simultaneously. However, the document ends with the company's colours well and truly fastened to the door: 'In an area where there is no cinema, no Theatre, no Dance Hall, no Club, no Amusement Arcade no nothing! Entertainment is needed! And at a party, or over a beer, people do not want INFIRMATION stuffed down their gullets. Never devalue Entertainment. Live Entertainment' (ACGB, 1971h, 98/35).

Greig left and, through a career that included working with Inter-Action, Bradford's General Will and Gay Sweatshop, became one of the single most important figures in the development of alternative theatre in this period. Harris continued to develop the centre, as well as engaging the theatre company in touring activity, including *Watch It All Come Down* (1972), a musical play about the concrete redevelopment of Deptford. Her sterling efforts, backed by a strongly supportive team, developed the Albany as a major local resource and magnet for touring groups. In the latter part of the 1970s, fifteen Rock against Racism events were hosted there and, when on 14 July 1978 the centre was burnt down, it was thought by many that a local neo-fascist group, Column 88, were responsible, a suspicion hardened by the receipt of a note, 'Got You! 88' (On this, see Bunce and Field, 2014, 191).

Case Study: Action Space

A Show Report from Drama Officer Sue Timothy on Action Space, working as LID at the Oval House on 12 December 1971, opens with an attempt to define what might reasonably be expected 'to be classed as Drama': believing that there must be some kind of 'development of plot, character or idea in the form of an event which finally reveals something. By these terms I'm afraid this project could not be called drama'. It is important to note that what Timothy is struggling with was not the show itself – which she describes as 'All most enjoyable' – but the problem of defining different kinds of performance.

> It was a truly enjoyable project and Action Space had invented a highly enjoyable environmental playground. You could paint your own mask, disappear inside an enormous inflatable with blinking lights in it, play draughts with a monster, drink mulled wine, get tangled in a forest of inflatable transparent tubes, watch a girl in a cage filled with dead leaves and mud, or listen to a man testing the properties of metal and concrete for sound [...] Much of the imagery was reminiscent of the People Show, but the People Show do seem to develop their images in a dramatic way.

As a Show Report, it could serve as a model. It not only gives the reader (and the archivist) a strong sense of what kind of performance it was, but asks important questions of her contemporaries on the Drama side of the Arts Council. She writes that it was 'very bold of the Young People's Committee to help this group with a bursary', though 'unfortunately, the only young people involved in the evening I went to see the show were actually working for Action Space'. She concludes 'that this is exactly the sort of work for which an Experimental Projects Committee is needed' (ACGB, 1971i, 41/46/2).

Nick Barter found himself in the middle of just such an attempt at locating the company, in response to applications for financial support to the Drama Panel and/or Experimental Projects (18 January 1971) and then to the New Projects Panel (ACGB, 1971j, 41/46/1). The applications eventually went to none of the three. Barter had intersected the bid as it was passed from panel to panel, concluding with Art. Jack Henderson, the Camden Festival Organizer, has used the group and his council had given them small grants, being 'very impressed and much better than Inter-Action'. Anxious to help if he can, Barter suggests the Experimental Projects Committee, to which a hand-written note, 'Yes please', is added.

This kind of confusion illustrates well the problems that the ACGB had in sorting out the increasing proliferation of new groups into appropriate funding areas. For, to read Timothy's account above, and with the advantage of historical hindsight, it might be thought that Action Space was a Performance Art Group, rather than a community one. And clearly some of the group's projects do seem to support this: though, in practice, practitioners on both sides of this dualism do appear to have a clear sense of which part of the wood they find themselves in. The fact of playing to (and with) an identifiable audience is, however, a key part of a Community Theatre credo, which is not necessarily so in the case of Performance Art. For example, in 1973, Action Space made a grant application for 'Spaces: a Time Sculpture Dream Piece'. The cast is to consist of four characters in two pairs, the objective being to show 'the dramatic content of CHANGE in SPACE'.

> IN THE FIRST sequence Caroline is a wood worm eating away Alan's house. The house is destroyed by Ken and Kathy. Caroline turns into a fly. She, in a later sequence is an insect which in taking a mud bath becomes a girl and is closer in relationship to Alan. Each pair are testing out ways in which they can reach an ever-lasting unity and to some extent both attain this state but in surprisingly different styles. In simple terms the story and structures used are necessary to each other and their unison in movement is seen as the space in which ideas can flow into the main content.

It is characteristic of Action Space's meticulous planning that the application is not only supported by a full schedule up until the last rehearsal, rehearsal photographs and a film proposal; but the performance is not scheduled, at the ICA, for nearly a year ahead, and trial runs have been arranged at festivals in Harrogate and in Rotterdam (ACGB, 1973k, 41/46/2).

The 'performance' at the ICA was a part of the process of moving there as a base, with the construction of a 'Soft Room' for their events to be constructed and staged– with Camden Council's active encouragement. Thus, for a while they combined the performative aspects of their work with a continuation of community-based work. For Action Space is a company with roots both in earlier notions of community theatre and in the cultural reshaping specifically associated with the events of 1968, the year in which they were founded by Ken and Mary Turner, together with Alan Nisbet.

> Linked to Joan Littlewood's ideas for an Adult Fun Palace and the beginnings of the Notting Hill Carnival [started in 1966, but originally on a modest scale], to the development of Arts Labs around the country encouraging participatory events, and the Turners' work in involving Unions in supporting the arts, the idea was to take revolutionary work out of the galleries and into the community. (University of Sheffield Library: Special Collections and Archives: Ref MS 426)

Action Space had built the Plastic Garden for Joan Littlewood's Tower of London Festival, and once the company had acquired its own space in Camden, in 1971, they began to work with people with disabilities, and to embark on a series of community events. Mary Turner recalls one such event in Kilburn Grange Park, 'a tough area usually omitted from the Camden Festival schedule'. The group's attempt to interest the local kids in particle physics, with the aid of an inflated Cyclotron, ended in a confrontation with local teenagers, and a hastily beaten retreat. Back at base, the police returned Mary and Ken's five-year-old son who had been left behind. 'He reported that the bad boys had looked after him and had taken him to the park keeper who phoned the police' (Turner, 2012, 59–60). This was not the normal outcome, and Action Space became a much booked resource, especially during the school summer holidays. In 1973, the group were active with Inter-Action in organizing the original 'First Burst' festival in Kentish Town, the first of 15 neighbourhood festivals held across Camden that year. Notwithstanding the co-operation on this event, Ed Berman of Inter-Action 'felt we were in competition for the limited sums available' (Turner, 2012, 86).

In 1975, the company moved to the Drill Hall in Chenies Street, London, with plans for a large theatre space and a smaller lunchtime studio, a café and all the accompaniments of an all-purpose Arts Centre. From its completed renovation in 1978, it became a venue not only for their own work and 'Extraordinary Evenings', but for other boundary-pushing groups, such as the Phantom Captain, the Secret Garden, Cunning Stunts, the Merchants of Fantasy and Forkbeard Fantasy. Action Space did not abandon its roots in an Arts culture, but began to develop more intensively the specifically community aspects of its work. Sunday sessions in the totally inflated 'Soft Room' 'became more popular with the children travelling from further afield' (Turner, 2012, 131). So, throughout the 1970s, the company continued to present a somewhat hybrid appearance – not to an enthusiastic and faithful public who largely did not worry about such things – but to potential providers of subsidy. The company had stressed this multiplicity of objectives in 1972: 'Its workings are necessarily experimental, devious, ambiguous, and always changing in order to find a new situation [...] to continually question and demonstrate through the actions of all kinds new relationships between artists and public, teachers and taught, drop-outs and society, performers and audiences, and to question current attitudes of the possibility of creativity for everyone' (Action Space Annual Review 1972; Turner, 2012, 65). Its notion of the community was, then, one that saw the arena as a venue for disputing the apparently rigid certainties of class and status, whether it was in respect of the function of education, the apprehension of difference – the Drill Hall hosted both Gay Sweatshop and a Women's Theatre Festival – or, quite simply, the gap between the haves and have-nots.

A series of three-week seasons were organized at the Drill Hall, as the place began to be used to the full. Gay Sweatshop did a season as part of the Gay Pride Festival, and there was a Women's Theatre season led by Hormone Imbalance. By the end of the 1970s, the sheer volume and variety of activity was beginning to become impossible to handle, and the various parts of the operation split. Given that Gay Pride was already being run from the Drill Hall, it was no surprise that from 1981 it 'became known as a Gay and Women's theatre venue under the direction of Julie Parker, though it always continued to embrace a wider remit with workshops and education programmes' (Turner, 2012, 149). By 1982, that part of the company led by Mary Turner moved to Sheffield, where they were faced both with new community venture prospects and with the loss of Arts Council subsidy, victims in part of their own hybridity:

> The Community Arts Officer in Yorkshire Arts did not think we qualified as a community arts company. He had only seen our touring work [...] [and] [...] he remembered a controversy at a meeting in London where Mary Turner walked out on his presentation. He was

envisaging the end of artists as everybody became an artist. The community arts myth again. He now considerered Mary Turner an elitist for supporting the continued existence of artists and because our projects were built on artists' interests in ways of working socially rather than a social theory. (Turner, 2012 165)

Central to all of Action Space's projects had been the design and construction of performances spaces – frequently inflatables – that drew upon specialist knowledge and skills. The company's interest in the community did not exclude the role of the artist as a specialist, but rather sought to democratize access to the art – to place it within a community and not in a carefully patrolled gallery or museum. Action Space is still continuing to do just that.

Performance Art Companies

Performance is, for them, not a means to communication, nor yet communion, but is quite simply the next step in their course of inquiry and experiment. They are, therefore, artists in a simple uncomplicated way. They are performance artists. If they use no theatre techniques it is not because they are 'bad' theatre. It is because they are not theatre at all. (Jeff Nuttall: ACGB, 1973l, 43/42/7)

Performance Art proved to be the most contentious and contested performative medium of the period. Its roots lay firmly in the Art schools and colleges. And, although Nuttall described the People Show as 'a repertory of Happenings, a different one every fortnight, three performances of each', the pre-history of Performance Art was to be found in Europe and in the USA rather than England (ACGB, 1973l, 43/42/7).

In its British mode, it undoubtedly caused the Drama Department of the ACGB more problems than any other limb of the alternative performance body. It spawned a host of companies, including not only the People Show (whose work is considered in detail in chapter four of this volume), but the John Bull Puncture Repair Kit (1969), the Phantom Captain (1970), the Yorkshire Gnomes (1971), the Birmingham Performance Group (1975), Forkbeard Fantasy (1975) and IOU (1976).

Arguably the most important single figure in the development of Performance Art in this period is Roland Miller. He worked with the

People Show, and elsewhere, but is most associated with the projects he undertook with Shirley Cameron, a sculptor he first met while teaching and performing – a normal dualism for Miller – at the 1970 Barry Summer School. Miller and Cameron's first project had been 'Railway Images' that same year. Miller: 'The intention of this project was to place various images alongside a railway line over a period of days so that train passengers could look out and see in the landscape more than was originally apparent' (ACGB, 1970c, 41/46/2). The account of the project is accompanied by photographs, a copy of the handout given to passengers, and so on.

In 1971, they devised a Cyclamen Cyclists event at the momentous – in terms of the development of Performance Art – Bradford Festival. A team of cyclists, dressed in pink, rode bicycles, painted pink, through the city, stopping at random points 'to perform meaningless ritual like pop traffic wardens waving down invisible aircraft' (Nuttall, 1979a). The ACGB was at a loss over what to do about the subsequent bid for financial backing, but a hand-written addition to a letter seems to have settled the issue: 'Do they want money to cycle from Bradford to Swansea? I'll try the Expt. Projects Committee.' Later that year, Nick Barter attended their *Part of a Party Landscape* and provided a detailed description of an event that concluded thus:

> Roland Miller removed his clothes with the exception of his beret, shoes, socks and gloves, and Shirley Cameron solemnly decorated him from head to toe in pink and white icing while he carried on a highly entertaining monologue about his past life, his student days, an encounter with two prostitutes in Exeter etc. All this spoken against a counterpoint soundtrack of a radio tuned at random behind his head and tapes of the famous Hindenberg disaster broadcast, Edward VIII's abdication speech, Edith Piaf and Ella Fitzgerald. (ACGB, 1971k, 41/47/2)

The use of the word 'random' is telling. In Performance Art, an audience is not always able to distinguish between the rehearsed and the spontaneous. As Miller informed the ACGB in 1973, 'the notion of rehearsal time is irrelevant to our work' (ACGB, 1973m, 41/47/3). Miller and Cameron were performing as People/Time/Space: soon they would become Landscapes and Living Spaces, the contrasts of public and private, organized and chaotic playing a big part in their work. Not only did Landscapes begin to receive project funding, but Miller was invited to become a member of the Experimental Drama Committee, where he played an important role in the development of Performance Art, and in 1973 presented to them, by request, an important paper on the history of Performance Art and Artists in Britain (ACGB, 1973a, 43/42/7).

However, having Miller as both a client and a well-liked colleague caused problems. Nick Barter and Roy Kift became so bored with an event at Oval House in December 1973 that mainly featured 'chatter of Shirley and Roland's own Christmas dinner' that they resorted to throwing bread rolls at each other. Barter concludes a Show Report of an Oval House performance that is much less than complimentary: 'I think someone else ought to cover Roland and Shirley's future events at the Oval before I make a couple of enemies for life' (ACGB, 1973n, 41/46/4). Two years earlier, he had acknowledged that Miller, having taken part in the Paris Beinnale and being given 'the whole of the main staircase at the Rijks Museum in Amsterdam to do what he liked with', was 'a prophet not without honour save in his own country' (ACGB, 1971k, 41/47/2).

This was not an unusual situation. Although Miller and Cameron continued to produce events in Britain, a lot of their work – and thus their funding – came from non-British commissions. This was true also of the Phantom Captain: one of the earliest Performance Art Companies, it made frequent foreign trips, to Holland, Spain, Germany, Austria and the US. With its origins in the experimental improvisation group the Switch (1967), Phantom Captain was founded by Neil Hornick in 1970, and, in its own words:

> specialised in situations/environmental events which explore the hinterland between 'theatre' and 'real life'. Our events tend to dissolve the boundaries between 'stage play', 'art Exhibition', 'audience participation event', 'encounter group' and 'teaching situation' [...] And every performance also functions as an experiment, an exercise and an exploration. Last year had received £350 from ACGB, plus £50 Fine Art grant for my exhibition activity. (ACGB, 1973o, 43/43/6)

The company collaborated with Berman on the Fun Art Bus project, and wrote *The Bus Hi-Jack Mystery* that was performed on the top deck; it also worked on a series of community festivals and carnivals. They are evidently to be thought of as nearer the community/performative edge of Performance Art at this point. They were by no means typical.

In 1970, a somewhat bewildered Arts Council show reviewer attempted to describe what happened when the John Bull Puncture Repair Outfit appeared for the first time at London's Oval House. Although it is not a very sympathetic report, reminding the panellist of a 'badly-planned College Rag: untidy and unimaginatively placed', it does give a very good sense of the occasion: 'The proceedings began with two of the play's protagonists dressed scantily in beach attire, being chased around the coffee-bar by a photographer. This couple were not exactly the most aesthetically pleasing creatures under the Dionysian canopy – the man being white and blubbery and the girl scraggy and emaciated.' Next, they went into the auditorium and were 'sat in the formation of a reflected "Z"'. A repeated holiday slide show was playing, and sand and water was directed at the audience. A 'soul-shattering explosion' with things flying through the air was followed by a 'ritualistic candle-procession, and an Oxfam reject selling excretory-coloured ices at sixpence each, and a kiss and a caress of her breasts for an additional 0.25 nupence'. Five minutes of 'inharmonious sounds' in a complete black-out followed, and then 'piles of dung on a table were set on fire, and an amusing, tipsy waiter brought ever-increasing glasses of beetroot-borsch to the fat man who had previously downed a pint of milk in one go. He was, of course, sick – as near as possible to the audience' (ACGB, 1970d, 41/48/3).

By far the most copious correspondent to the Arts Council during this period was Genesis P-Orridge, the leader of the experimental Performance Art Group group COUM, based in Hull. His frequent and weighty additions to the ACGB archives included unsolicited scripts, imaginative hand-drawn schemes for the future and general thoughts about the world and his place in it. In March 1973, Genesis had written a characteristically all-over-the-place letter to 'Dearset Nick' [Barter], telling him of a recent engagement:

> We've just done a thing at Bretton Hall College of Ed. Report to follow. They didn't like it at all, but eventually after discussion agreed basically it was because they didn't understand it. Which we had warned them about. E have just been ill with food poisoning after visiting London. (Cari Saluti [Genesis P-Orridge] to Nick Barter 20 March 1973, ACGB 98/91)

In exasperation, Barter wrote to him:

> Please do not use us an archive for all your various documents. We have got far too much paper floating around the floor as it is

[…] The understanding of you that the Committee really want is to have a firm date on which they can see you at work. (ACGB, 1973p, 41/47/1)

Undeterred, Genesis P-Orridge's reply was addressed to 'Knick Bahter, Infantile Arts Panel'.

There are two scripts (which is really to say, descriptions of sequences of events) of COUM's performed events in the ACGB files. From 1974, there is *Couming of Age*. A small extract from the nine-page outline will give some flavour of what was on offer to visitors to Oval House on 15–17 March 1974:

Thee woman leads thee young girl nude to in front of thee Altar. They stand facing each other, bodies brushing and slowly kiss. Then […] they proceed to rub oil all over each others bodies, twisting, stroking and caressing each other until they glisten with oil. While this happens, thee man eats thee banana slowly and then lies back sleep. He lies, sleeping, like a sacrifice. Or is he dreaming of those girls? For thee oil rubbing sequence there is beautiful flute music playing. When thee girls have covered each other they go to thee swing and flute music finishes.

The other is for *Airborn Spells, Landborn Smells*. This was performed at the Hammersmith Mini-Performance Art Festival (organized in co-operation with Hammersmith Borough Council and the GLAA), held from 28 July to 4 August 1974: and in addition to COUM, it featured many of the most active participants in the scene – Ian Hinchcliffe and Jude 'Doris' Morris performing as Matchbox Purveyor; Keith and Marie as Situations/Real Landscapes; Tony (as Martha) and Jan Costa; Jeff Nuttall and Rose McGuiure as Jack; and Rob Con with GAAAARSP (ACGB, 1974m, 41/19/6).

What so many of these groups have in common is not only that they come, not surprisingly, from art school backgrounds, but they also defiantly did not originate in London and the South. The Hebden Bridge Gathering, and subsequent celebrations there, and the Bradford Festivals of 1971 and 1972 had succeeded in bringing together a mass of enthusiastically talented and experimental individuals all keen to move into the area of what was already beginning to be called Performance Art. It was in no sense a purist coming-together and at its centre was not only art but music, and in particular that of Mike Westbrook and his fellow musicians. John Fox was on the verge of forming Welfare State with Sue Gill; Al Beach and Tony Banks of the John Bull Puncture Repair Outfit (Halifax) John Darling who was then on the cusp of leaving the People Show and, in 1970, wrote to the ACGB with a request for £1,500 for his new company, the Yorkshire Gnomes (Wakefield), to work in 1972/73: 'the People Show found or created new audiences for their work but these invariably remained theatre audiences in theatre situations [...] One of the motives for the establishment of the Yorkshire Gnomes was the theory that if there is to be a radically new form of drama it must seek new audiences' (ACGB, 1970e, 41/50/2). The credo, if such a word can be applied to such a disparate group of activities, was well summed up by Jeff Nuttall:

> Performance art, a phrase tentatively tossed around like a cooling hot potato, means, I suppose, people performing who don't want to be defined as theatre. The old yardsticks of established skills, acting, producing, audience rapport, entertaining, do not apply, they imply, to them. (ACGB, 1973l, 43/42/7)

It is, then, perhaps not too surprising that when, in 1973, the Experimental Projects Committee was terminated, the 'hot potato' that Performance Art had always been for the Drama Department was handed over to Art for it to sort out. It had proved a performance too far for the Drama Panel.

Chapter 3

CAST

Bill McDonnell

Introduction

When Roland Muldoon retired as artistic director of London's Hackney Empire in 2005, it marked the end of one of the most remarkable careers in post-war popular theatre history. Muldoon's profile on the Empire's web page noted that he 'has been an all-round activist in theatre since the early 1960s' (Hackney Empire, 2005). It was a career that began in 1965, with the founding of CAST, the first of the socialist theatres of the alternative theatre movement. Muldoon told the *Leveller* magazine with typical immodesty: 'we invented the political theatre of the time' (Muldoon, 1978, 18). This was the 1960s, a time of revolutionary possibility and libertarian excess, and CAST were the theatre company that most seemed to embody the aesthetic and ideological tensions of the period. In the late 1960s and early 1970s, they would be feted by luminaries of the theatre world and the rock 'n' roll counterculture. Their first major play, *John D. Muggins is Dead,* was performed at the famed UFO club, where they mixed with the likes of Pink Floyd, Christopher Logue and Mike Horowitz, along with Andrew Loog Oldham and the Rolling Stones. Muldoon recounts how Peter Brook came to see CAST perform, and asked them afterwards: '"Did you get that idea from Artaud? Where were you influenced?" And we said: "Karl Marx"'. And he walked away. But he had us in his film *US*' (Muldoon, 1978, 18). The early CAST, then, was a unique company, much feted and much admired, and they represented, along with the Brighton Combination and North West Spanner, a small but significant group of working-class activists within the counterculture. CAST's particular contribution to the development of revolutionary struggle would be to explore through theatre the problematic relationship between the revolutionary intelligentsia and the working class, between theory and practice. CAST has a paradigmatic history. In its development from cultural 'gang' to subsidized professional ensemble to cultural entrepreneurs, the company exemplified the contradictions, crises and transformation of British oppositional theatres in the late twentieth and early twenty-first centuries. Their demise in 1986, along with other left-wing companies such as 7:84 and Foco Novo, signalled the end of a unique cultural project which had articulated a political and epochal aspiration: the achievement, through revolution, of a socialist society.

Given their longevity and impact, the critical bibliography for CAST is narrow. Accounts of the alternative theatre movement agree that they were the first of the political groups to emerge in the 1960s, that they had a seminal influence upon the aesthetics of oppositional theatre in the period and that, in the eponymous Muggins, they created one of the great comic creations of post-war political theatre (Ansorge, 1975; Itzin, 1980; Craig, 1980; Davies, 1987). Yet, in comparison with companies such as 7:84 or Welfare State, there are few detailed studies, and only this writer's general survey covers the whole period of its existence (McDonnell, 2010).

Company History

CAST's history can be divided into four phases. The first, 1965 to 1971, was the highpoint of the company as a feted guerrilla troupe, mixing experimental and agit-prop forms to produce a distinctive, hybrid aesthetic. The second, 1971 to 1974, was a period of splits and reformations in which, for a while, CAST lost their way, distracted by their counterculture celebrity. Rebirth came in 1975–6 in the form of Arts Council subsidy, and lasted until 1979. That year would mark another watershed, presaging the slow phasing out of touring shows and the incremental and historically important rise of New Variety, which, even before grant aid was cut, took the company in a new direction: one that reached its rich apotheosis in their stewardship of the Hackney Empire, 1986–2005. The year 1979 marks, therefore, a bifurcation in the company's artistic focus and also the beginning of the end of the ensemble. CAST's contribution to popular political culture would continue, but in a different form. This account focuses on the period 1965 to 1979 and, in particular, on the first and third phases, viewing them as the most significant in the company's history.

The original group – Roland Muldoon, Claire Burnley, Ray Levine and David Hatton – had left school at fifteen and drifted, in a mixture of instinctive rebelliousness and class politics, towards the libertarian left, bringing to the counterculture the aggressive cohesion of the Mods' and Rockers' subculture which had shaped them. Muldoon, the group's creative inspiration and spokesperson, was raised as a Roman Catholic in a second-generation Irish family on a council estate in Weybridge, Surrey. After leaving school, he worked for a year at the Bristol Old Vic Theatre School as a trainee stage manager. He met Levine and Hatton at Unity Theatre in Camden, London, where he and Burnley spent two years stage-managing in-house productions (Rees, 1992, 70). In an interview, Muldoon spoke of wanting to bring 'political cabaret' into Unity:

> At Unity they ran an old tyme Music Hall, and Claire and I were the stage managers [...] and we actually got to learn and love the old songs, but realised that the nostalgia was crap [...] it was either folk, which was the Communist Party tradition, or it was old tyme Music Hall! And they weren't the things that turned CAST on, who were by nature rock and roll people. (Muldoon, 2000)

Their vision was of Unity as 'a socialist theatre in the middle of Camden town, as a centre of dissension' (Muldoon, 2000). In April 1965, Muldoon organized a coup against the management committee. When he was expelled for, in the words of the AGM minutes, 'conduct injurious to the society in that he secretly conspired with non-members to overthrow the legally elected management committee', he took the rest of the 'gang' with him (Chambers, 1989, 84–5). Explaining the rationale for the attempted coup, Muldoon commented:

> We weren't in the Communist Party but we were coming round to Marxism. We were young and we were part of an enormous resistance to established politics – CND, Ban the Bomb, Anti-Apartheid, that sort of thing. We wanted to bring this into Unity. (Muldoon, 2000)

A few months after the expulsion, David 'Red' Saunders, a charismatic performer and radical activist, joined the 'gang'. He had met Muldoon and Levine through drama classes the two had been running at the London Working Men's College. The new group named themselves the Cartoon Archetypical Slogan Theatre or CAST. Muldoon glossed the name in an interview with Roland Rees:

> It's Archetypical. Archetype is Jungian. 'Cartoon' that was the style. 'Archetypical' was our philosophy. We were influenced by

the archetypicality of Laurel and Hardy, Charlie Chaplin, and the characters in the movie, *Les Enfants du Paradis*. 'Slogan' because we made the language of the plays out of this sort of imagery. CAST because that made us anonymous. (Rees, 1992, 69)

Fast cutting and extremely physical, the early CAST aesthetic was developed through collective improvisation: a style developed for the public meetings and working-class social clubs that were the group's venues. Their first production was *John D. Muggins is Dead*, which dealt with the war in Vietnam. The twenty-minute sketch explored the links between pop culture and imperialism, between the capitalist system and mass murder. It was this system that CAST also dissected in their next play, *Mr Oligarchy's Circus*, written in 1966. Muldoon states:

We said that capitalism was a circus, the ruling class was the circus master and the Labour Party was its bedfellow. It was a very funny play, very popular, playing at colleges to the radical students' movements in 1968. (Itzin, 1980, 15)

Despite the success of *Mr Oligarchy's Circus*, the group felt that a more precise analysis of revolutionary possibilities was required, one which addressed the critical relationship between student intellectuals and the working class. The result was their third play, *The Trials of Horatio Muggins* (1967). For the earlier generation of political theatre activists, like Ewan MacColl, the group provoked a mixture of admiration and despair:

We were told off by Ewan MacColl for being too counter-culture. He got us back after The Trials of Horatio Muggins and he said: 'You know you're great what you do, but it's terrible, because you take the piss out of capitalism, and then in the same play you also take the piss out of Ho Chi Min, Fidel Castro, and Mao Zedong. And Karl Marx. There's no definition for the working classes. And we said 'Yeah, that's us'. So that wasn't agit-prop was it? As far as he was concerned it wasn't. (Muldoon, 2000)

Yet for all MacColl's concerns, CAST provided, through the Muggins character, a consistent, satirical critique of the development of revolutionary praxis in the period:

Muggins is the English archetype of the bloke who does everything and gets no reward. Charlie Chaplin if you like. An Everyman. Except that in every show she or he had a different name – Harold Muggins, Hilda Muggins, Horatio Muggins, Maud Muggins [...] Muggins represents the working class – the people who are mugged by History. (Itzin, 1980, 5)

In the summer of 1967, the group was invited to the international theatre festival at Nancy in France. Here they made contact with both European and American experimental groups; but it was the links with the USA, built on a commonality of language and opposition to the US presence in Vietnam, which were to prove the most significant and durable. At the festival, they encountered Peter Schumann's Bread and Puppet Theatre, Luiz Valdez's Teatro El Campesino and the San Francisco Mime Troupe.

Among CAST's early admirers were the playwrights John Arden and Margaretta D'Arcy, who wrote *Harold Muggins is a Martyr* for the company. The play, exploring state and police corruption, was premiered at Unity Theatre on 14 June 1968 and directed by Muldoon, who also performed in it. While critical reviews were mixed, the production was a popular success and, ironically, given its provenance, provided Unity with its best box-office receipts for the year. In summer 1969, the company was again invited to the Nancy Festival in France, followed by dates in Amsterdam and Berlin. It was during this brief tour that differences within the group began to surface. The Muldoons now had a small child, issues of childcare and financial stability were increasingly important, and they felt unsupported by the rest of the company. Tensions were put aside as the founding group began work on what was to be their last production together, *Aunt Maud Is the Happening Thing,* CAST's offering for the Royal Court's *Come Together* Festival in November 1970. *Come Together* brought together under one roof a representative sample of counterculture theatre companies, including The People Show, Brighton Combination, the Ken Campbell Roadshow, the Pip Simmons Theatre Group, Keith Johnstone's Theatre Machine and Nancy Meckler's Freehold.

Between 1970 and 1975, CAST produced just one new play, *Come In Hilda Muggins,* which premiered in April 1972, and which crudely critiqued the emergent radical feminist movement for the perceived failings of its class politics. Muldoon called it an 'awkward play' that the group 'dragged around the country' (Muldoon, 1977, 41). It was a transitional period, full of frustrations, during which Muldoon felt CAST had lost its way:

> By 1968 everywhere one went and looked there was talk of
> Revolution, with the exception that is of the traditional working
> class. That was CAST's trouble: it was going everywhere but in the
> direction it wanted to go in. (Muldoon, 1977, 41)

The group sat on the sidelines while militant sections within the working
class began mobilizing against the new Conservative government, led
by Edward Heath, which had been elected in June 1970. The period of
this government, 1970–4, witnessed an intensification of rank-and-file
activism within the trade unions, generating an industrial militancy
which polarized society and public opinion. The Upper Clyde Shipyard
'Work In' during February 1971 and the miners' strikes of 1972 and 1973
raised expectations of radical social and political change. Yet during a
period in which many on both left and right of the political spectrum
believed a revolution was imminent, the country's self-proclaimed
political guerrilla theatre was silent, a silence which embraced not only
domestic crises and the proximal neo-colonial conflict in the north of
Ireland, but critical world events, such as the 1973 CIA-sponsored coup
in Chile against Salvador Allende's socialist government. It was not
until 1974, following the re-election of Harold Wilson and a Labour
administration, that a revised incarnation of CAST began work on the
play that secured their future, *Sam the Man* (1975), the success of which
brought them their first Arts Council grant in 1976. With subsidy, the
revolutionary 'gang' became the revolutionary theatre company and
CAST created, as their first funded production, a provocative trio of
short dramas under the collective title *Three for the Road*, focusing on
the conflict in the north of Ireland, the Right to Work campaign and
public spending cuts. The following year, they turned once again to
the relationship between the Labour Party and the unions in *Goodbye
Union Jack*, a polemical satire on Labour's Social Contract with the
trade unions. In October 1977, the company began work on a new play,
Overdose, with the aim, says Muldoon, of analysing 'changes in popular
ideology since the industrial revolution' (CAST, 1979, vi). It was an
ambitious project, absorbing three months of the group's energy before
it was abandoned. Needing a replacement production to satisfy the
conditions of their Arts Council grant, the group turned to a text that
they had been working on before *Three for the Road*, called *Confessions
of a Socialist. Confessions* was given its first performance at a benefit for
the film *The Right to Work*, at the Architect's Association in Bedford
Square, London on 3 February 1978, with Muldoon as the lead. The
play would remain in the repertory for many years, developing in 1979

into the solo act *Full Confessions of a Socialist*, the vehicle for Muldoon's entry into the American radical theatre market. In May 1978, and in response to the rising influence of the racist National Front (NF) party, the company produced *What Happens Next?* Supported by the Anti-Nazi League, and riding on a swell of anti-fascist activism, the play toured widely across Britain throughout 1978 and 1979. Between 1979 and 1985, CAST would create a series of plays in response to the Thatcherite project. Productions such as *From One Strike to Another*, *Hotel Sunshine* and a revived *Sam the Man* would, respectively, explore government attacks on Trade Union rights; the rise of the nuclear threat; and the perceived historical failures of the Labour Party. But for the most part, until the Arts Council cut their funding, Muldoon focused his considerable talents on setting up New Variety: music hall for the post-revolutionary age.

Artistic Policy and Methodology

In their programme notes for the *Come Together* Festival, CAST wrote of themselves: 'CAST produces all its own material. The most important thing about CAST is that it is a group. It is through the group that the plays are evolved and by the group that the plays are presented.' They were an ensemble that had dispensed with the usual structures and relationships of theatre, and had 'no equivalent to the writer–actor– director, no prepared script to begin from' (*Come Together* Programme, Royal Court Theatre, 1970). Instead, the group was defined by an ethos of egalitarian creativity: 'we were an improvisation theatre company, improvising like jazz, on a given form', Muldoon told the *Observer Magazine* (1991, 23), and said they had developed 'a house style, almost a philosophy' (Muldoon, 1977, 40). CAST consistently rejected the idea that they were an agit-prop company, and tagged themselves 'agit-pop' in a bid to focus on their eclectic cultural roots, and distinctive aesthetic. And while Muldoon himself was indubitably the creative linchpin of the company, Claire Muldoon was critical to its aesthetic. A wonderfully gifted actress, a fine comedienne in her own right and a balletic and expressive performer, her contribution to the company's success and longevity has been as decisive as it has been underwritten. Historian David Caute offers an arresting account of the company's early aesthetic:

> Charles Marowitz was fascinated by Roland Muldoon's CAST, a
> guerrilla troupe which sought out working-class audiences to offer

furious indictments of capitalism and the Labour government in a style which was more Brecht than Brecht and more Artaud than Artaud – chalk white make-up, a brash delivery and crude earthy humour. CAST's comic *Mr Oligarchy's Circus* in which the Labour Government sold itself to capitalism was still playing to radical student audiences in 1968. (Caute, 1988, 251–2)

CAST's reference points were eclectic: Chuck Berry and Bertolt Brecht, Jerry Lee Lewis and Karl Marx. CAST may have shared aesthetic features with the classic agit-prop troupes, but their political intent was different, Muldoon argued:

> Agit-prop, as I understand it, is coming from the Russian experience, and you're there saying 'Strike!' You're telling people what to do. You've got to strike. It's not a discussion. You've got to do it because the gain to the Russian Revolution is this. Whereas we were artists, saying, this is our subject, *the battle between theory and practice, as you might have it,* in an artistic form, and that is not agit-prop, as I understand it. (Muldoon, 2000, my italics)

In a fascinating 1978 interview with the *Leveller* magazine, Muldoon was asked what he thought the purpose of political theatre was. His response is revealing, and is worth quoting in full:

> What's its purpose? (*Long pause*). I don't know! (*Laughter*). I never really did. It's the working class that have to make the decisions. I don't think that political theatre is at the forefront of those decisions, because those decisions are really made because of the reality of the political situation. I believe the purpose of political theatre is to raise the analysis. To put meat on the bones of socialism. Political theatres are not the vanguard. I don't believe that's the job of theatre. I still think we have to alert people to the problems of our society and hint and suggest at the socialist process. (Muldoon, 1978, 19)

This goes to the heart of the company's refusal to propose either a model for a new society or to set out a route to it. There are moments when the plays hint at what a socialist society might be like (for example in *Confessions of a Socialist*), but it was a vision moderated by a radical scepticism, a refusal of historical determinism. There is a correspondence between Muldoon's theatre philosophy and Brecht's: their predilection for what Brecht called 'crude thinking' (*das plumpe*

Denken), a term explicated by Walter Benjamin: 'Crude thoughts [...] should be part and parcel of dialectical thinking, because they are nothing but the referral of theory to practice [...] a thought must be crude to come into its own in action' (Benjamin, 1992, 21). CAST's theatre philosophy was grounded in 'crude thinking', in 'thinking against'; it was a rough, dialectical theatre, which confronted theoretical complacency. 'The great turn on for us', Muldoon told the *Leveller*, 'was to make audiences laugh *against* themselves, laugh against their own restrictions and beliefs. They used to laugh, shake their heads at the irony of what we were saying' (Muldoon, 1978, 19). Arts Council Drama Officer Jonathan Lamede agreed, writing in an internal memo that, if the company had difficulty finding audiences, it was evidence of CAST's courage in confronting the shibboleths of left and right, and illuminating their shortcomings 'by the application of a truly subversive mind' (ACGB, 1978b, 34/34/3).

Rare filmed fragments of an early performance of the 1967 play *The Trials of Horatio Muggins* give an invaluable insight into the group's aesthetic. The context was a documentary, *The Year 1967*, made by the Vietnam Solidarity Campaign about a fund-raising event that had brought together luminaries of the counterculture, including writer and polemicist Tariq Ali, poet Adrian Mitchell and folk singers Frankie Armstrong and Ewan MacColl. In the film, we see a group of young people, men and women, applying white face make-up: they are dressed in black and are vaguely androgynous. The film cuts to Adrian Mitchell reading poetry. It cuts back to the opening images of *The Trials*. Downstage right a body lies prone across three chairs. A white faced figure hovers. From the darkness upstage four more figures advance. They are dressed in black; their faces are chalk-white, like those of mime artists. Their movements are balletic. The central figure holds a red flag. They form a tableau, which is briefly held. They move forward again with an admirable precision and unity. They move and pause three times, and then speak in unison. Their voices are hard, impersonal and metronomic: 'We /are / the / Cartoon / Archetypical / Slogan / Theatre / and/ we / demand / revolution / now!' (1967). They dissolve the image and retreat upstage. Then one of them notices the sleeping figure. She moves forward until she is leaning over him. Turning, she gestures to the others to approach. They again move forward as a unit. They deliver their slogan now at the prone figure. They call on him to wake. As he stirs, they begin to shout at him: he must arise and organize the class for revolution! As he sits up and yawns, we notice that he is dressed in ordinary clothes and has no make-up. He ignores them, turns to the audience and speaks: 'What the fuck do you lot want, eh, waking me up like that!' The film audience laughs and cheers. Horatio Muggins gets up slowly and puts on his trilby. The group begins to upbraid him for his failure to act. The proletariat is asleep, they tell him, and must awake and take its preordained role in the coming revolutionary struggle. Muggins shrugs, yawns, smiles at the audience. The film cuts to scenes of demonstrations.

After the original group split in the early 1970s, the history of CAST was shaped by the difficulty of transmitting this foundational aesthetic: 'Starting again was very difficult. We had to teach the new members the style and approach to theatre that we had developed collectively over the years. We sorely missed the talent that had departed' (Muldoon, 1977, 41). Indeed, the story of CAST after 1979 can be seen, in part, as the story of the failure to find a way to communicate the original style, a problem resolved through the development of an artistic methodology in which Muldoon became increasingly the auteur of works he created *through*, rather than with, others. Kate Rutter, who joined the company in 1979, found this shift politically and artistically problematic. Political activist, feminist, member of the Socialist Workers' Party and a talented musician and writer, Rutter was disappointed in CAST's methods, telling me in an interview: 'I expected when I came to CAST that there would be a more collaborative process, and that the creativity would be more evenly spread than it actually turned out to be' (Rutter, 1999). Instead of a socialist collective, what Rutter found was a creative oligarchy, in which the Muldoons 'controlled the money: they controlled the process: there was only creative space within the parameters they had set: there was no way you could break out of those parameters. I felt restricted creatively and also politically' (Rutter, 1999). It is no coincidence that the only successful post-1979 shows were those in which Muldoon acted: *Sedition 81* and *The Return of Sam the Man* were built around him, and utilized to great effect his prodigious performance gifts. Appropriately *The Return of Sam the Man* was also the group's last play, closing a historical arc which had begun with the original production.

Funding and Company Structure

Two narratives define the ACGB archives on CAST: the first narrative is the decisive impact of subsidy on the company's structure and audience demography; the second narrative covers the institution's responses to the political crises occasioned by CAST's commitment to revolutionary socialism and their support for Republican irredentism in Ireland. The files throw new light not only on the company's internal organization and political aims, but, critically, challenge the perception that grant aid operated throughout the period as a brake on political radicalism.

In comparison with other socialist theatre companies, such as Red Ladder and 7:84, CAST came late to the arts subsidy table. In an interview in *Play and Players*, Muldoon noted that by 1973 the company was in danger of being rapidly left behind 'by the wealthy groups in their flash Mercs' (Muldoon, 1977, 41). He continued, in a passage that manages to be self-critical even as it satirizes the wealthier groups:

> We developed an inferiority complex. It was being said in fashionable quarters that didactic theatre was old hat, and the finger seemed to be pointed at us. On the other hand, the 'new political theatre' was coming to be accepted. 7:84 badges could be seen in Oxford Street, even their records could be seen on bed-sitting room shelves. Red Ladder took the legendary road north. Big plays, big audiences, big vans led to nods of approval from the Trade Union leadership. (Muldoon, 1977, 41)

If ever there was a historically propitious moment to be a state-funded revolutionary theatre, then this was it. Arts Council funding to Regional Arts Associations trebled between 1970 and 1979 (Sandbrook, 2013, 20). Subsidy to left-wing groups was also increasing, enabling companies such as Red Ladder, North West Spanner, Banner Theatre and 7:84 to establish successful regional bases and audiences. When CAST eventually applied to the ACGB in 1976, they received a £6,000 project award. Over the next nine years their funding would increase incrementally, reaching a relatively modest £47,000 in 1984–5, before being cut. The organizational impact of subsidy on CAST's *modus vivendi* was considerable, requiring the company to keep proper financial records, and to take a professional approach to the planning and delivery of tour schedules. Funded companies were obligated to complete regular audience returns and company reports, to hold minuted management meetings and to submit audited accounts to back up annual applications for grant aid. They were also required to give Drama Panel members enough notice of performance dates to enable them to attend and assess their work. It would be an understatement of Olympian proportions to say that CAST failed to deliver on these requirements. The 'gang' had always operated with an improvised company structure, with members sharing administrative roles, and this approach persisted post 1976. One constant source of friction was the chaotic organization of tour schedules. In an indicative letter, Drama Officer Clive Tempest wrote to the company warning that, 'The heat seems to have gone out of the assessment of CAST, but that may not be to your advantage. If work continues not to be seen, I foresee problems later on in the year' (ACGB, 1977a, 34/34/1). Part of that heat was doubtless generated six weeks earlier when Dusty Hughes, then at the Bush Theatre, Stratford East's Clare Venables and critic Benedict Nightingale received letters from Tempest urging them to go and see CAST at Oxford. They dutifully turned up, but CAST did not, blaming a van breakdown. CAST's Arts Council files are replete with exasperated memos about these and other organizational failures, particularly from finance officers. An urgent memo from Jonathan Lamede to John Faulkner on 10 October is typical in its tone: 'Celebrate finally! CAST's booking returns are in but the attendance figures are very sketchy' (ACGB, 1978e, 34/34/3). The defining trope of this history is of sympathetic officers seeking to advocate for a company whose artistic creativity was underpinned by an idiosyncratic management system. On 12 May, Lamede wrote an internal review of the company's work which encapsulates the relationship: 'CAST may have its administrative shortcomings [...] but there is not much work of this quality of intelligence, warmth and imagination around. I do feel that RM (Roland Muldoon) is a talent to be cherished' (ACGB, 1978b, 34/34/3).

Funding also affected the company's audience base. In 1969, in a 'Letter from England', American activist Roger Hudson had praised the group's political insight, distinctive aesthetic and 'frenetic La Mam-ish montages', but lamented that their audiences were the 'trendy left' and that 'they've seldom performed for workers' (Hudson, 1969, 192). Although CAST would remain resolutely a London-based company, subsidy expanded its national audience base exponentially, allowing it to build support for its work across Britain, and especially in the old engineering and Communist Party heartlands of the Midlands, Glasgow and West Scotland, and South Wales. In another irony, then, Arts Council subsidy brought CAST, for the first time, into sustained contact with working-class and trade union audiences. What the company lost, however, was the capacity to respond to immediate political events. The need to plan tours and productions months in advance curtailed CAST's interventionary impact. Muldoon again:

> There is pressure on groups to be more productive in terms of quantity than is particularly healthy in terms of quality. This tends to

make groups lose touch. Take the firemen's strike in 1977, a dramatic event when the firemen were challenged by the Social Contract and defeated in just a month. But what could a theatre company do about it between Christmas and January? What happens is they write more and more abstractly, move away from the real concrete issues upon which an exciting relevant theatre should comment. (Itzin, 1980, 20)

It could be argued that what CAST lost in flexibility was more than compensated for in the exponential increase in its audience base, and the financial and organizational stability which made its work possible. In 1979, they appointed Warren Lakin as administrator, a decision which finally brought order and continuity to the group's relationship with the ACGB. An incremental increase in subsidy, from £24,500 in 1979–80 to £35,000 in 1980–1, meant that actors would be employed on proper Equity contracts, and recruited not from political sympathizers, as in the past, but through formal auditions. The gang had become a professional theatre company, and Muldoon was its *de facto* artistic director and auteur.

Resisting Incorporation: Subsidy and Censorship

CAST's first funded production, *Three for the Road,* offered an unambiguous message to anyone who thought that subsidy would dilute their political commitment. The production included a controversial piece on the Prevention of Terrorism Act:

They'd just introduced the Prevention of Terrorism Act. So what we had was an interrogation by two hard blokes to prove that this guy who's got Republican sympathies, a Republican granddad, lives in Liverpool, all the rest of it, would be guilty, and was therefore a reasonable suspect. Then the suspect turned the trial round and he talked to them, he asked them questions about themselves, who they were, how they came to their decisions [...] it was the other way round [...] the terrorists were, if you like, the British Government. (Muldoon, 2000)

It was the first CAST production to be seen by Arts Council Drama Panel reviewers, at a lunchtime performance at the ICA in December 1976. It is hard to imagine a less appropriate venue, or audience demographic. Drama Panel reviewer Betty Richie (ACGB, 1976,

34/34/1) wrote that the production 'had little claim to be described as theatre', and that the other reviewer, Roy Kift, had left halfway through. The production would have passed quietly into history had it not been for comments made by Muldoon in a *Leveller* article the following year:

> We had the State's money and we were going round telling the audience that the State locked people up without trial. We thought: 'Three months and they'll fucking come around and that's it. Somebody will ring up the Arts Council and say: "You know you're funding the IRA". But the great thing was the Arts Council never came to see us at all. (Muldoon, 1977, 18)

As we have seen, it was not for want of trying. CAST's next production, *Goodbye Union Jack*, was well received by Drama Panel reviewers. Sandy Craig, writing from 'a godforsaken pub in godforsaken Reading', wrote that it 'was very interesting [...] more than that, good [...] CAST have been going for years and have pioneered a lot of the styles and techniques associated with political theatre' (ACGB, 1977c, 34/34/3). Another Drama Panel member, Roger Lancaster, who caught the show at Wolverhampton Polytechnic, was equally positive:

> Agit-prop style but with more ingenuity and style than many I've seen. The best section of the show concerned the NF [the National Front] [...] this was excellent theatre and actually frightening in the accuracy with which it simply but directly presented the Front's point of view [...] my spine tingled [...] for this sequence alone they deserve support – on artistic grounds for presenting accurate and disturbing political theatre. (ACGB, 1977b, 34/34/3)

One of CAST's most passionate and effective advocates within the Arts Council was Jonathan Lamede, then chair of the New Applications and Projects Committee. His view was powerfully shaped by his first encounter with the company's work, *Confessions of a Socialist*, and he wrote a glowing review:

> The show was madly funny [...] Roland Muldoon himself was a revelation. I had not seen him perform before, and was really impressed by the casual, confidant, comic skill which he was able to show [...] he really is a superb comedian [...] a superb socialist comedian. I was impressed not merely by [his] comic abilities but by his keen and fertile intelligence. (ACGB, 1978a, 34/34/3)

CAST would have cause to be extremely grateful for Lamede's advocacy in the following years. The responses of Drama Panel members were not always complimentary, of course, a matter of aesthetic differences and of ideological leaning. But the evidence from the archive is that, far from acting as a brake on CAST's radicalism, drama officers became, in effect, ideological shields for the company, defending their revolutionary analysis and provocative attacks on liberal democracy against their right-wing critics. The call for revolution would be financially supported, the Arts Council politely told the company's critics, so long as it was an artistically excellent call. Two events would test this liberal commitment.

The first was the 1978 production *What Happens Next?* The initial sign of trouble emanated from the environment and amenities committee of Mid-Devon District Council, whose minutes, reported in an editorial in the *Exeter Express and Echo* (1978), excoriated the South West Regional Arts Board for sponsoring 'subversive political activity'. They expressed their 'distress' at having an anti-Nazi play, 'produced by a group of Trotsites (*sic*)', and warned the South West Regional Arts Board that they would be withdrawing their annual stipend in protest: all £270 of it. This was the first salvo of what Jonathan Lamede came to view as a concerted attempt by right-wing elements within and without of parliament to remove the group's funding. On 19 October, Lamede circulated an urgent memo to Drama Panel members, writing:

Something seems to be brewing in connection with CAST: why has it blown up only after CAST have put an anti-NF play on the road? It seems to me that people objecting to the staging of plays against Fascism should tread very carefully. (ACGB, 1978f, 34/34/3)

The memo was a response to a series of letters to ACGB complaining about the production and the company. One, written by MP Ray Whitney, began by sympathizing with the Secretary General over the difficulty of avoiding social and political issues when funding, but continued:

I must register my concern at press reports of Arts Council grants to extremist groups such as CAST [...] can we really justify the transfer of public funds to those dedicated to the destruction of the very society which creates such bodies as the Arts Council? (ACGB, 1978c, 34/34/2)

The reply from ACGB was to become a standard one in the developing storm. It emphasized that all decisions were taken on aesthetic merit.

'To do otherwise' wrote Drama Director John Faulkner, 'would imply censorship, moral or political, and it is in my view emphatically not the role of the Arts Council to exercise censorship.' He goes on to say that the group's work is 'generally of a high standard' (ACGB, 1978d, 34/34/2). Lamede agreed, noting in his own review that *What Happens Next?* 'shows this company's characteristic intelligence and refusal to look for easy answers or use simple-minded agit-prop techniques'. He praised the National Front rally scene in particular, thinking it 'exceptional in some ways' (ACGB, 1978i, 34/34/3).

Not all panel members thought so highly of the production, however, with Lois Lambert describing it as a 'very bad play, and for the most part badly acted, with the exception of Roland Muldoon' (ACGB, 1978g, 34/34/3). What was not in doubt was the at times violent public response to the production, underscored in another internal memo from Lamede, which asked Drama Panel members not to reveal details of Muldoons' address because of threats to the couple made by the National Front (ACGB, 1978h, 34/34/3). Local racist gangs forced the relocation of performances of the play at York, Northampton and Wolverhampton, on one occasion threatening to burn down a community hall used by local pensioners. In an interview with the *Cambridge Evening News* Muldoon notes: 'Never before in its 13 year history has it (CAST) met the opposition it is now meeting' (Thompson, 1978). The controversy was stoked in part by CAST's claim that the production was sponsored by the Anti-Nazi League and the Arts Council, an assertion which their right-wing critics used to attack Arts Council policy, and which, in turn, greatly annoyed Drama officers. Notwithstanding, when the 1979–80 grant application round came, Lamede again defended the group in a memo to John Faulkner, which reads: 'Company is led by RM who in my opinion, and in that of members of the NAPS (New Applications and Projects) committee, is a truly original talent and a man of immense vitality and intelligence.' The group's work, he went on, 'stems from a political intelligence often subtler and far more alert that that of many other theatre groups [...] If their work makes people uncomfortable this is all to the good, since in this case this is often a reaction to CAST's flair, imagination and vitality'(ACGB, 1979, 34/34/3). In a symptomatic decision, the company's annual funding was renewed, but was to be released in three tranches, each dependent on panel members seeing shows and audience returns being, well, returned.

Lamede was correct to view the response to *What Happens Next?* as something more than the reactionary fulminations of rural Tories. In retrospect, it can be seen to mark the beginning of a sustained political campaign against the group and its subsidy which persisted until its grant was cut in 1985. Complainants would include Tory MPs and town councillors, retired generals and right-wing students and, critically, the right-wing press. In March 1980, the *Daily Telegraph* ran an article, accusing CAST of being a pro-IRA company, pointing to the 1976 production *The Other Way Round*. The article cited Muldoon's interview in the *Leveller*, quoted above, as evidence. CAST's response was to threaten the *Telegraph* with legal action for libel. The then Chair of the Arts Council, Sir Kenneth Robinson, wrote an elegant response to the paper, pointing out that the man and his work were not necessarily conterminous and that, consequently, Muldoon's 'private views are not necessarily expressed in his artistic output and wouldn't form part of an assessment of his work' (Robinson, 1980). When, on 12 July 1984, Secretary General Luke Ritter wrote to CAST to confirm that they had lost their appeal against the loss of subsidy, he reassured them that it was not based on artistic or political criteria: 'I do want to emphasise that the withdrawal of subsidy was made on strategic grounds. The Council would wish me to make it clear that there is much to commend artistically in the company's work' (ACGB, 1984, 34/34/3). In the margin, rather intriguingly, someone has scrawled in bright red ink: 'Ha!!'

CAST's final ACGB grant, for 1984–5, was £47,000; a sum dwarfed by the £153,000 the company received the same year from the Greater London Council to support their New Variety venture. The company was already moving in a new direction, and while Muldoon joined in the campaign to reverse the ACGB's decision with typical political energy, privately he welcomed it: 'We did everything we possibly could to make sure that, as Trotsky said, you get dragged out of office, kicking – but I was relieved I didn't have to write any more plays' (Muldoon, 2000).

Key Works

When men and women, engaged in quite modest, local forms of political resistance, find themselves brought by the inner momentum of such conflicts into direct confrontation with the power of the state, it is possible that their political consciousness may be definitively, irreversibly altered. (Eagleton, 1991, 223–4)

Here Eagleton restates the challenge that lies at the heart of classic Marxism, of the theory of historical materialism, and CAST returned to it again and again in their plays. Simply expressed it was this:

How were men and women to be brought to an awareness of their condition as alienated labour, and liberated from the ideological indoctrination which led them to reproduce, daily, their own servitude and oppression? Like Eagleton, CAST believed the answer lay in organized political struggle. However, effective struggle demanded the bringing together of intellectuals and workers, theory and practice, the discipline of the vanguard allied to the collective power of the masses. It was the feasibility of this, and therefore of revolution, that CAST's key works explored with intellectual rigor and satirical acuity. Their plays were short, improvised pieces, none more than 35–40 minutes long: there were no complex plots or dramatic conflicts to dwell upon, or written scripts to critique. They were interventionary pieces: responses to specific political crises. The 1968 play *Muggins' Awakening* provides an early example of CAST's interventionary approach. The background to the play was Enoch Powell's incendiary 'Rivers of Blood' speech, given in Birmingham on 20 April of that year, the anniversary of Hitler's birth. Following the assassination of Martin Luther King, Jr, in Memphis, Tennessee on 4 April, the black ghettos of America's great cities had been convulsed by violent race riots. Pointing to these, Powell provocatively predicted racial war in the UK premised upon the demographic colonization of the British Isles by black and Asian immigrants. Conservative Prime Minister Ted Heath responded to the public outcry by sacking Powell from the shadow cabinet. The reaction from a large section of the white-working class, however, was aggressive support for Powell. East End dockers and market stall holders converged on Parliament on 26 April calling for him to be reinstated, while on 7 July there were violent clashes between Smithfield Market traders and students protesting against Powell's speech.

Within the International Socialist movement (later the Socialist Worker's Party), these events gave rise to a critical shift in the analysis of the relationship between class and imperialism. In this new thesis, the working classes of advanced capitalist societies were guilty of the worst kind of narrow nationalism: they were racists at home, and willing collaborators in the imperialist adventures of their masters abroad. As a consequence, the revolutionary torch had passed to the liberation movements of the South, and to the proto-socialist societies of Cuba and China. This analysis achieved two objectives for left-wing intellectuals: it freed them from further failed attempts to make links with the British working classes; and it allowed them the satisfaction of fighting revolutions by proxy. In *Muggins' Awakening*, CAST challenged this analysis in a manner which upset both their growing supporters

in the International Socialists and their new Arts Lab admirers: first
by arguing that the IS analysis was deeply flawed, and ignored the
oppression of workers in the west; second by satirizing Peter Brook's
US by lighting matches and pretending to burn imaginary butterflies
while the audience was invited to clap. The awakening of the title
referred not to revolutionary consciousness, but to Muggins' growing
awareness of his own alienated existence (to be explored more fully in
Confessions of a Socialist, see below), and the failure (a trope of CAST's
work) of the Labour Party, in power since 1964, to deliver a more just
society. Built upon visually arresting images and comic, Socratic-style
dialogues between party and class, ideologue and Muggins, *Muggins'
Awakening* explored the gap between ideal and flawed reality, as did
their next major work, *Aunt Maud Is The Happening Thing* (1970),
CAST's offering for the Royal Court's 1970 *Come Together* Festival.

Like *Muggins' Awakening*, *Aunt Maud* was created as a commentary
upon immediate historical events. In June 1970, Harold Wilson's
Labour Government had been voted out of office, and replaced by a
Conservative administration headed by Edward Heath. The centre of
political gravity was moving rightwards, and *Aunt Maud* addressed
the challenge facing the left by showing capitalism as a dead force
constantly being forced to come back to life for the lack of a credible
political alternative. It was the last piece to be created by the 'gang',
and the reviews, which constitute the most concrete record of the
performance's aesthetic and dramatic impact, were largely fulsome. The
Listener's theatre critic D. A. N. Jones was typical in his praise:

The Cartoon Archetypal Slogan Theatre is a company preferring
factory canteens to playhouses. They present with a dancer's
elegance, sly, truthful and quietly impassioned fables about proles
under capitalism. 'Aunt Maud' looks like a blend of Chamberlain
and MacDonald, but he has beautified his dusty pinstripes with
a flashy cravat and sporty baseball boots, to create a modern TV
image. He rises from his bed, a bed of nails which, turned upside
down, becomes a giant Punch and Judy box, or a TV screen from
which he can bemoan his agonising burden of responsibility, plead
for sacrifice and national unity, explain economics in the match-box
style. He asks the working class how they would like his difficult job.
This class is represented by a dutiful Lancashire lass, sharpening a
sword on a grindstone, for sale to white or black Africans, to Arabs
or Israelis, as her master dictates. This thoughtful, spirited and disciplined company should be looked out for. (Jones, 1970)

In retrospect these earlier plays can be seen as dry runs for the
production which was to become CAST's greatest success of the 1970s,
and the most incisive and precise statement of the group's political and
theatrical philosophy: *Confessions of a Socialist* (1978).

Confessions of a Socialist is the story of Harold Muggins, a universal
gottleib junction maker, who misses the People's Revolution because
he's busy blowing his redundancy money on a package holiday in
Spain. His children despise him and his wife hates him. He works at
a factory producing parts for machines that he has never seen. His
solution is to steal the holiday money and go for a night out with his
mates. A sequence of comical set-pieces take us from pub, to club, to
curry house, to a visceral enactment of Muggins vomiting from the top
floor window of an Indian restaurant after one bhindi bhaji too many.
Sweating, fearing he is dying, Muggins experiences an epiphany. If
God will let him live, he will change his life. He has wanted the world
to change: it is he who must change for the sake of the world. In a
wonderful mimetic sequence Muldoon's alter ego leaps from bed the
next morning and rushes to work:

> **Harry** I was there so early they thought it was the night shift coming
> back. I went into the factory. I wiped Swarfega on my hands. I went
> up to my Universal Gottleib Junction Joint machine, and I said
> to myself: this day I'm going to have a Zen relationship with my
> machine. I'm going to push up the thermometer of productivity. I
> am going to be someone the whole world looks up to. I am going
> to become one with my environment! Oh yes, I said to myself, I'm
> going to produce Universal Gottleib Junction Joints till they run like
> rivers!! (CAST, 1979, 4)

The Beach Boy's song 'Good Vibrations' fades in. Muggins offers a
striking image of alienated humanity: he begins to move, jerkily at first,
then more precisely. He becomes the machine: his limbs become its
parts; he is it and it is him; he is at one with his machine because he *is*
a machine. It is a precise performative articulation of Marx's concept of
alienation as set out in *Grundrisse*:

> The worker's activity, limited to a mere abstraction, is determined
> and regulated on all sides by the movement of the machinery, not
> the other way round. The knowledge that obliges the inanimate parts
> of the machine, through their construction, to work appropriately as
> an automaton, does not exist in the consciousness of the worker, but

acts upon him through the machine as an alien force, as the power of the machine itself. (Marx, 1977, 374)

The image is undercut. Muggins is called by the charge hand. There is a crisis of over-production, and Harry is sacked. Before he leaves he is asked to make one more Universal Gottleib Junction Joint so that they can put it into a machine which will produce them automatically. Muggins was a machine, and now a machine will be Muggins. In a final act of defiance, Muggins takes the redundancy money, but walks out without making the Gottleib joint. Freed into enforced leisure he decides to spend his pay-off on a family holiday in Spain. While he is away there is a successful socialist revolution in Britain. Once home, he is summoned by the Revolutionary Works Council at his old factory, and asked to make one last Universal Gottleib Junction Joint so that it can be reproduced by machines. The play turns on this deliberate echo: under capitalism automation means redundancy; under socialism it heralds a release into an idealized social existence. Muggins is now offered a wide choice of social and communal activities: he can learn dialectics, become a computer expert, an actor, a painter. He asks if he can go fishing by the canal, and his wish is granted. Ecstatic at the possibilities of a life free from wage slavery, Muggins offers his own idiosyncratic but moving take on the new world:

> **Harry** I thought to myself, this is absolutely marvellous. This is paradise on earth, I said. I can go fishing by the canal. I think the whole world can go fishing by the canal. And if there wasn't enough canals, that'll be something we can all do together, to build them. And people who think it's cruel to fish can have plastic fish! I thought, why not? Everything's possible. None of these dreams I had when I was a child about heaven being a place where Tizer came out of the tap! No, I thought, it can all be here on earth. (CAST, 1979, 20)

The speech is Muldoon's comic restating of one of Marx's rare forays into utopian speculation:

> In communist society, where nobody has one exclusive sphere of activity but each can become accomplished in any branch he wishes, society regulates the general production and thus makes it possible for me to do one thing today and another tomorrow, to hunt in the morning, fish in the afternoon, raise cattle in the evening, criticise

after dinner, just as I have a mind, without ever becoming fisherman, herdsman or critic. (Marx, 1973, 54)

Muggins' vision is undercut by the shrill of an alarm clock. It has all been a dream. Yet it could be made true, Muggins/Muldoon offers, out there, in the world, through organized and willed political action. As the lights fade, emblematic slides from a history of struggle, of revolutionary achievement and totalitarian repression appear. These are the historical choices facing humanity, the play argues: socialism or barbarism, production for need or production for profit.

While economic exploitation remained a focal issue for CAST and the revolutionary left, the critical struggle of the mid-1970s was with racism and an aggressive nationalism. Between Powell's Birmingham speech and the then Conservative leader Margaret Thatcher's remark in 1978 about the British people's justifiable fear of 'being swamped' by immigrants, the decade marked a critical rise in support for the fascist National Front. In by-elections in 1976 and 1977 the NF had pushed the Liberals into fourth place, and secured local council seats in London's Tower Hamlets, and in Blackburn and Leicester. As ever, Muldoon's political antennae were acutely sensitive to the shift in the political climate:

Political groups who are interested now in how wages alone are exploited must wonder what they are going to say to their audiences. They should be thinking about alienation and what has led to the rise of the National Front, the seeming collapse of socialist ideology as a challenge to the capitalist state. (Itzin, 1980, 13)

What Happens Next? (1978) was CAST's response to the crisis. Set in 1976, the play traced the rise of the NF through the experiences of Ralph (played by Muldoon), a shop steward and life-long Labour supporter. Attacked by his punk teenage daughter for his failed radicalism, we see him being courted by Reg, a patriotic stallholder, and his NF minder, the urbane Archie. Meanwhile there is a crisis at Reg's factory, where the nightshift (mostly black workers) are threatening to strike over a productivity deal, and are calling for the support of the (mostly white) daytime shift. Ralph takes up the night shift's cause and, in short sharp scenes, we see the strike develop, and the barriers of race replaced by (it is being argued) a more fundamental mutual class interest. Some of the scenes are extremely funny, as Ralph/Muggins throws himself into reggae nights and Asian cultural evenings in an effort to build new bridges with his 'black comrades'. When the strike is undermined by Dave, white convenor, the new found unity dissolves in bitter recriminations. Back at home, with his reputation as a 'black-lover' doing the rounds of local pubs, Ralph is again criticized by his daughter for not doing enough to defeat racism. She storms out leaving him alone. A small package falls through the letterbox. Ralph picks it up. There is a violent explosion and a sudden blackout, which is held. The performers then come forward and sum up the show's analysis, asking their audience: what happens next? Fascism or Socialism? Supported by the Anti-Nazi League and riding on a swell of anti-fascist activism, the play toured widely across Britain throughout 1978 and 1979.

All of CAST's plays were grounded in an activist epistemology, which, returning to Eagleton, we can formulate in this way: the workers do not strike because they are aware, but become aware because they strike. The great Polish Marxist, Rosa Luxembourg, in her analysis of the revolutionary role of the general strike, dismissed the 'theory of the lovers of the "ordered and well disciplined" struggle', noting that the strike is 'not the crafty method discovered by subtle reasoning for the purpose of making the proletarian struggle more effective, but the method of motion of the proletarian mass, the phenomenal form of the proletarian struggle in the revolution', and later, and this concept lies at the heart of the plays, that in times of political crisis it is the 'sections which are today unorganised and backward who will, in the struggle prove themselves the most radical, the most impetuous element' (Luxembourg, 1970, 234). Or, as Muldoon put it: 'the arguments are great, and the theory is great, and the practice is hard and the enemy are at our door. That was the policy of the plays' (Muldoon, 2000).

Critical Reception

Despite their longevity, CAST never received the kind of consistent national attention commanded by companies such as 7:84 or the People Show. There were a number of reasons for this, the most critical of which was political: that is to say, the revolutionary and interventionist nature of their performance work. CAST did not perform at, and were not interested in, the kinds of middle-tier venues that attracted national critics. Their venues were by and large union meetings, community halls and public houses, and their performances were for audiences organized by trade union activists and the revolutionary left. They were also, until 1976, a metropolitan company, who rarely ventured outside London, a fact reflected again in the critical reception of their work.

Before 1968, public mention of the company was confined to campaign leaflets, press releases and listings in underground newspapers such as the *International Times*. However, there were two moments when the company and national critics intersected, and they are worth our attention. The first was the 1968 production of *Harold Muggins* with Arden and D'Arcy, which brought them brief, if generally negative, critical coverage in the national press. Simon Trussler in *Tribune* offered a more considered response: 'If *Muggins* simplifies issues, as good propaganda invariably has to, it never simplifies people, stylise them how it will' (Trussler, 1968). The 1970 *Come Together* Festival brought another spike in national interest, with *Aunt Maud*. *The Times'* Irving Wardle was enthusiastic:

> One of the things which raises the show above the expected agit-prop level is that it demands thought and criticism rather than simple assent. Also its broad musical hall Marxism allows it to cover a lot of social and historical ground. Finally the form is as strong as the message. It abounds in powerful comic images, like Gertie's lathe where she sits sharpening a sword; at once a picture of drudgery, and a promise of what may happen if she remains unsatisfied. (Wardle, 1970)

And while Vincent Guy in *Plays and Players* found the group's performance 'Excruciating!' (Guy, 1970), Helen Dawson in *The Times* thought it a 'genuinely Marxist view of British industrial history, compact, impressively thought out and sustained, a good sharp puncturing of the democratic bubble ... CAST was telling us that it was all up' (Dawson, 1970). For Wardle, the company stood out above all their contemporaries: 'CAST strikes me as the only political theatre group worth the name. Their archetype is Muggins, the eternal working-class sucker, who has turned up variously as John D. Muggins, Horatio and now as Gobbling Gertie Muggins' (Wardle, 1970). In these reviews, and in the earlier responses of Brook and Marowitz and so on, is confirmation that the early CAST was an exceptional company in some ways, offering a unique fusion of agit-prop and experimental practises, of sophisticated political analysis and dramatic inventiveness.

It was these qualities which had attracted Drama Officers like Lamede, and which had underpinned his support for the company. Indeed, the reviews of Drama Panel members at Arts Council England during the period represent another important form of critical reception, offering, as they do, the most consistent response to the company's work in the period. However, elsewhere critical responses to the company were largely confined to socialist journals and left-wing magazines.

A CAST Chronology

All CAST's shows were toured. Up until 1972 the tours were to venues primarily, but not exclusively, in the South of England. From 1976, national tours took them across Britain, usually spending a week in each of the Regional Arts Associations (RAAs), and offering five to six performances, in return for guarantees against loss from the RAA. Below I have divided the productions into two periods and given the names of core members. While others joined for specific shows, those listed constituted the primary personnel in the period.

1965–72

Core Group Members: Roland Muldoon, Claire Muldoon, Red Saunders, Ray Levine, David Hatton.

Productions
1965   *John. D. Muggins Is Dead*
1966   *Mr Oligarchy's Circus*
1967   *The Trials of Horatio Muggins*
1968   *Muggins' Awakening*
1968   *Harold Muggins is a Martyr* (with John Arden and Margaretta D'Arcy)
1970   *Aunt Maud is the Happening Thing*
1972   *Come in Hilda Muggins*

1972–9

Core Group Members: Roland Muldoon, Claire Muldoon, Dave Black, Dave Humphreys, Derek Couturier, Eithnie Hannigan. These were joined mid-1979 by Ray Meredith and Kate Rutter.

Productions
1975   *Sam the Man*
1976   *Three for the Road*

1977   *Goodbye Union Jack*
1978   *Overdose [Abandoned]*
        Confessions of a Socialist
        What Happens Next?
1979   *Waiting for Lefty* (with North West Spanner).
        Full Confessions of a Socialist

Chapter 4

THE PEOPLE SHOW

Grant Peterson

Introduction

Once called Britain's first experimental group of the 1960s, the People Show is the country's longest surviving alternative theatre group. The company's legacy is located both in its impressive longevity and the immense influence it made on Britain's theatre landscape. Sixties' theatre maverick Jim Haynes anticipated the impact of the company early on, writing: 'their work is the work of complex intelligent artists with an equal appreciation of technical, dramatic, and pyscho-sociological possibilities of the medium. I suspect that this is the best (and probably the only) way to a fluid mixed-media theatre' (Haynes, 1967, 58). The People Show fused visual arts with experimental performance tactics, breaking away from conventional theatre practices. The company's approach developed decade by decade and inspired generations of artists and theatre companies, both on the fringes and in the establishment of British theatre.

I was absent during most of the company's history because I was born in 1979 and immigrated to Britain in 2005. The first performance I saw was *People Show 118: The Birthday Tour* in Bristol. The show celebrated the company's fortieth anniversary by showcasing its history, and thus functioned as an apt introduction. Following this, I became interested in the company's early history and the group's relationship to countercultural activities of the 1960s. In addition to discussing the company's artistic methods, funding, key works and critical reception, this chapter unsettles familiar categories of British alternative theatre history by providing a new lens through which to examine the People Show's early years.

Mark Long, co-founder and long-term member of the People Show, once warned that it can be 'quite dangerous talking about' the company because the history of such a diverse group should be represented by many voices, not just one' (Hulton, 1981, 34). In that respect, this chapter puts numerous accounts into play with one another in order to tease out their contradictions and gaps and thus present a larger picture of the company's complex history. The chapter is focused on the company's first fourteen years (1965–80), a fourth of the company's life span and a period that deserves close review. The company's more recent history is briefly examined at the end of the chapter, including the Arts Council's total withdrawal of funding in 2008. The resiliency of the People Show over five decades makes the company's legacy one of the longest and most impressive in alternative theatre history.

A History of the Company's Development

Histories of the People Show usually begin in 1966 when Jeff Nuttall was asked to create a piece for the Notting Hill Gate Festival. Nuttall teamed up with musician Mike Westbrook and invited performers who, as co-founder Mark Long says, 'just happened to be living upstairs and downstairs and next door to him' in the Abbey Art Centre (Hulton, 1981, 2). In addition to Long, the group of 'wayward oddballs', as Nuttall referred to them, included Sid Palmer, John Darling and Laura Gilbert. None were used to Nuttall's eccentric working methods which included the use of nudity and interaction with the audience (Nuttall, 1979, 20). According to Long, Nuttall 'was having quite a lot of difficulty in those days in getting people to do those things' (Hulton, 1981, 2). After a rushed rehearsal, a conflict over planned nudity and 'a bit of grass', the performance piece was presented in Powys Gardens. In what some called a 'happening', the performers unrolled a sheet of polythene over the audience, although Long's account recalls how fish nets were thrown onto the audience (Long, 1971, 48). The event included Nuttall reading a list of random objects, Long and Darling distributing jam-smeared newspapers and a pre-arranged woman in the audience shrieking and fleeing the space (Nuttall, 1979, 22–3).

After the Notting Hill Festival, Nuttall contacted Bob Cobbings, a former collaborator and owner of Better Books, a London alternative bookshop, to organize a performance in the shop's basement. Determined to 'open a theatre that was underground of the Underground' (Nuttall, 1979, 23), Nuttall used the basement literally and figuratively as a way to undermine the buttresses of the literary world and text-based theatre practices. The title of 'People Show' emerged from the first Better

Books performance in October, known as *People Show 1* (some subsequent show titles built on this: *People Show 2, 3*, etc.). Explaining the reasoning behind this choice, Nuttall wrote: 'We presented ourselves as sculptures. We cut holes in the cardboard and through these carefully cut holes we displayed bits of us – my belly, Mark's feet, one of Laura's very pleasant breasts' (Nuttall, 1979, 31). Rather than perform traditional texts with clear storylines, the company presented themselves 'on show' in a series of juxtaposed scenes and activities that visually and dramatically challenged audiences. Nuttall roughly scripted several early performances, but the company spent much of its energy seeking out new methods of improvisation and experimenting with ways sound and light could evoke chosen themes. Shows were assembled from the company's given set of materials: a dingy basement, performers' bodies and cheaply salvaged props and sets. Jack Moore, in the *International Times*, wrote how the company's first show was 'in the conspicuously un-converted basement of Better Books'. Moore continued, 'Jeff and his anti-professional aggressors' created a show that 'has mostly to do with physiological actualities, [and] lasts about fifty minutes' (Moore, 1967, 15).

Moore's emphasis on the show's 'physiological actualities' attends to the company's frequent use of sexually explicit scenes and nudity. The company's preponderance of, particularly, female nudity later drew accusations of sexism and misogyny, but Nuttall claimed the work aimed to progressively liberate sexuality. Gillian Whiteley more recently contends that the company's exploration of obscenity resulted in problematic forms of sexism (Whiteley, 2011, 121). Whiteley cites how People Show performer Shirley Cameron 'was profoundly uncomfortable' and ambivalent about performing scenes involving simulated rape and sexual intercourse (129). However, it is also helpful to consider that the company began two years prior to the abolition of state censorship with the Theatre Act of 1968. The group's voyeuristic objectifications certainly invite criticism, but can also be understood as a critically radical response to previous conservative constraints on the (nude) body in performance. By performing in an unlicensed venue, the People Show pushed boundaries that conventional theatres could not and raised new questions about performer–audience relationships. John Ford summed up these and other key features of the company in a 1970 *Time Out* article.

> The People Show is probably the most accurate name/description a company will ever find. They are not 'actors' in the traditional sense

– they are people who have explored improvisations in an audience environment so thoroughly that they have the confidence to throw out the 'acting' which shelters behind someone else's character. They have the guts to be themselves in front of others, something a lot of us have yet to learn [...] And what they present is not a play, it's a show, a display, an exhibition, an entertainment [...] Perhaps they have learnt from the Absurd, but from the English tradition that inspired the Goon Show rather than the intellectualisation of Continental writers. Their surrealism is that of painting, not theatre. They have no director, no leading figure. (Ford, 1970, 64)

Ford's description outlines what became the group's distinguishing characteristics: a negation of traditional narrative, authorship, character and directing, at the same time as exploring methods of self-reflexive performance, collective devising, improvisation and audience engagement. Ford also identifies how the company's aesthetic of absurd juxtapositions elicited both humour and critical reflection. Importantly, the self-reflexivity embodied in People Show performances resonated with art movements of the time, including happenings (for example, work by Allan Kaprow). These hybrid events similarly tested boundaries of the 'live' moment or, as Nuttall described the first People Show, as being '*in its nature*, right in the middle of creativity' (Nuttall, 1979, 23).

Before proceeding, however, there is a provocative historiographical blip worth exploring, particularly because the genealogy it suggests productively complicates familiar histories of the company and established models of British alternative theatre. Instead of the widely recognized founding year of 1966, some accounts place the People Show's beginnings in 1965. Examples of the 1965 attribution include Marvin Carlson in *Performance* (2004, 116), Sandy Craig in *Dreams and Deconstructions* (1980, 20) and Peter Hulton in *Theatre Papers* (1981, 2). Reasons for the discrepancy are unclear and may reveal simple mistakes, or reflect the obscurity of the People Show's genesis. This deviation might also speak to the flurry of activities in 1965 that are loosely associated with the People Show's beginning.

For instance, some writers discuss the significance of Nuttall's experience in poetry and music festivals, as well as his work with the multimedia experimental Group H (Henri, 1974, 115; Rees, 1992, 30–2; Whiteley, 2011, 117). However, few accounts take note of Nuttall's key role in the Sigma group and the *sTigma* event of 1965 (Henri, 1974, 115; Hulton, 1981, 3; Whiteley, 2011, 112–16), and none evaluate the connections and relevance to the People Show. A genealogy that extends the People Show's development to Sigma and *sTigma*, I argue, opens new ways of understanding the company.

The Sigma group was founded on the basis of an Artaud-inspired manifesto, 'sigma: A Tactical Blueprint' written by Alexander Trocchi, a Scottish novelist and Situationist best known for his novels *Young Adam* and *Cain's Book*. The group called for a political awakening of society through radical art forms cultivated from collectives, and promoted through methods that dissolved boundaries between artists and spectators. In 1964, Nuttall teamed with Trocchi and the Sigma group to produce a collective realization of Sigma, a name tellingly derived from the mathematical symbol $\sum$ meaning 'to designate all, the sum, the whole' (Scott, 1991, 195). Playing on the group's name and ideas of martyrdom, the multimedia installation was titled *sTigma* and ran for three months in 1965. Housed in the basement of Better Books, *sTigma* consisted of an immersive labyrinth with difficult passageways and tunnels that led audiences through experimental soundscapes, environmental sculptures and to a final performance. Spectators had to navigate the 'zig-zag corridor of polythene through which you could glimpse your goal, a group of figures' (Nuttall, 1970, 225–6). Bruce Lacey, a contributor, described *sTigma*'s sensorial assault:

> All the audience comes into this darkened basement. Around the walls we've drilled holes which I'm pouring red liquid down. So there's blood running down the walls […] I am going around in a rubber suit with a helmet on, spraying smoke, like poison gas. (Lacey, 2000)

The *Observer* described *sTigma* as 'The Experience' where attendees found themselves 'negotiating a haunted house, getting covered in feathers, and crawling on your belly through a tunnel of lorry tyres' (Seddon, 1965, 23). BBC's wireless Third Programme broadcast a documentary about the event (Duchene, 1965, 5) and there was a show guestbook signed by celebrities such as Mick Jagger (Watkins, 2011), all of which helped turn the event into a *cause célèbre*.

The People Show's founding is not only near both geographically and temporally to *sTigma*, but the company's early work bears striking resemblances to it as well. Performing in the same basement of Better Books, *People Show 1* staged the disembowelment of a performer hung from a butcher's hook who had meat pulled from a bodysuit (Long, 1971, 48). In comparison, *sTigma*, according to Lacey, featured a pregnant woman who was theatrically disembowelled through a similar grotesque parade of offal (Lacey, 2000). In both cases, vivisections of human bodies can also be read as symbolic deconstructions of theatre as an institutional body. Moreover, the pregnant woman in *sTigma* was an arranged audience plant, not dissimilar to the shrieking woman who fled the People Show's first festival piece. Further comparisons continue: *People Show 1* featured an actor throwing feathers at the heads of audience members – a repurposing of materials from *sTigma* – as he poetically declared: 'This is the nightmare crotch that only opens up to your hand when night comes down on your head like a warm hood' (Nuttall, 1979, 12). Also, both pieces used polythene sheets as visual and physical barriers for the audience to overcome. In many respects, *People Show 1* contained similar bodily metaphors, feathered assaults and performer/audience tactics that *sTigma* explored a year before.

Two months after *sTigma*'s closure, Nuttall wrote in his independent magazine, *My Own Mag*:

> I suggest it would now be a good thing if sTigmas sprang up in church rooms, unused basements, deserted prefabs all over the world. Not, of course, like the London sTigma necessarily, but the name retained could give the lethal people a disconcerting and accurate feeling that, however varied and wild they may be, certain activities and activators a common sane purpose and these activators have been dubbed by Alex Trocchi sigma [...]. To be sigma, as I understand it, is to hold the following simple premise – people must now change or become extinct. (Nuttall, 1965, n.p.)

Here, Nuttall's anxieties can be connected to pervading fears that the post-war generation experienced in the face of possible nuclear annihilation. This is something Nuttall writes more about in *Bomb Culture* three years later, where he attributes much of the subcultural artistic output of the 1960s to a countercultural anxiety that dissipated into disillusionment by 1967. In the 1965 excerpt above, however, it is evident that Nuttall's excitement to tour *sTigma* was rooted in an optimistic sociopolitical purpose of achieving the revolutionary vision of Sigma and Trocchi's manifesto, albeit with some changes. 'Rather than the plethora of nausea we had constructed', he wrote, the new *sTigma* projects would include what was previously lacking: 'the moral seriousness, the wit, and the confrontation with self and nothingness' (Nuttall, 1970, 145).

Despite associations with British theatre traditions, the People Show's history is often connected to visual arts practices more than theatre. Nuttall's background in assemblage art (Whiteley 2012, 114–21), as well as his involvement with jazz, is credited for shaping much of the People Show's artistic direction. The company's founding members generally lacked theatre backgrounds and were more interested in visual, musical and mixed-media experimentation (Nuttall, 1979, 25–6). Long even argued that the company's emphasis on visual composition was so central that new members with strong theatre backgrounds struggled (Hulton, 1981, 21). At one point in the company's early history, audience members expecting traditional theatre were promptly corrected by Gilbert, 'I'm not an actress! We are not a theatre group!' (Long, 1971, 55). The group's 'fine-art tradition of visual as opposed to verbal communication', Robert Hewison wrote, characterized the People Show's style, one that 'encouraged an exploration of process rather than product' (Hewison, 1987, 192).

Because happenings were less prevalent in the UK compared to the US and the continent, the People Show figured prominently as the 'first experimental group in Britain' (Long, 1971, 48). 'When The People Show began in 1966', Long wrote, 'There was no experimental theatre in Britain, not any. There were no groups. The only theatre in London was the West End, and that was it' (Long, 1971, 48). Constructing the history of the company as a singular model of experimental performance, Long (and Nuttall in various accounts) championed the company as an under-acknowledged group that reshaped Britain's theatrical landscape. Sandy Craig added to this narrative in his influential book, *Dreams and Deconstructions*, arguing that the company was 'the earliest and still the most influential performance art group' (Craig, 1980, 24).

Moreover, the People Show's categorization as a 'performance art' group – despite contestations from its members – played a significant part in the theorizing of British alternative theatre. The literary canon is replete with arguments that attempt to distinguish politically driven and stylistically driven performance groups, often constructing an imaginary divide between agit-prop and avant-garde. This is evident in works such as Craig's and Catherine Itzin's respective accounts in 1980. Later writers like David Edgar, John Bull and Baz Kershaw consider alternative theatre categories as a spectrum with opposing poles, commonly placing Cartoon Archetypical Slogan Theatre (CAST) on one end as an 'overtly politically' leftist group and the People Show on the other as an 'overtly a-political' avant-garde counter example (Kershaw, 2004, 360). Such distinctions may offer broad categories but, as Bull has pointed out, 'it would be misleading to suggest that, in practice, the division has been absolute' (Bull, 1984, 25). Techniques of the avant-garde and agit-prop intermingled and the 'relationship has been mutually symbiotic' (Bull, 1984, 25).

The People Show's early connection to *sTigma* offers fertile ground to interrogate symbiotic relationships between the political and artistic, unsettling common binaries of alternative theatre history. Nuttall garnered critical lessons from *sTigma* that, as evidence suggests, directly led to tactics and aesthetics redeployed in the People Show. He insisted that new versions of *sTigma* he wanted to stage would illustrate 'the eloquent and architectural use of space and proportion rather than the angry claustrophobic impositions of the sTigma' (Nuttall, 1970, 145). Nuttall hypothesized that *sTigma* failed because of the unstable 'cross purposes' of the various artists involved: himself and Criton Tomazos as 'moralists with CND backgrounds' and the others as 'antimoralists with no background of social protest' (Nuttall, 1970, 145). Nuttall's observation prefigures the political/artistic dichotomy that dominates later debates. He diagnosed the problem with *sTigma* and his generation of artists more broadly: 'Moral shame, moral absurdity, moral abuse, moral paradox, and moral outrage had frozen us at a point of almost total negativity' (Nuttall, 1970, 129). The remedy, according to Nuttall, was 'the numbing of the moral sense and the use of the sensation, the pain and the anger as propulsion' (Nuttall, 1970, 129). His transition from a political aggressor to a disillusioned but passionate artist can be traced from *sTigma* to the founding of the People Show.

Later iterations of *sTigma* never manifested – at least not in name. Moreover, Nuttall had reversed his opinion by 1968. Rather than restaging *sTigma* everywhere, he wanted to bury it: 'let the daylight in and forgot it as best we could', he wrote. 'We forgot the plans to reconstruct it on a bus and take it round the province. We forgot our plans for shock happenings on London Transport' (Nuttall, 1970, 227). Nuttall's abandonment of the project is revealing, and may reflect the splintering of Sigma, or Nuttall's condemnation of Trocchi's spiralling drug use. But Nuttall's dramatic turn also coincides with the development of the People Show.

The founding of the People Show is therefore a provocative and important departure from *sTigma,* not least because it reanimated many of *sTigma*'s theatrical devices, but also because Nuttall's approach was consciously adapted. The company transformed *sTigma*'s harsh dystopia into dreamy surrealism, its sensorial cacophony into immersive discordance, its sadomasochistic nihilism into poetic despair and its assault on the audience into an idiosyncratic engagement. The People Show, however, struggled to refine these polarities. Long explained how the group experimented with finding the right balance in its methods of audience engagement (Long, 1971, 48). The company eventually excelled at creating interactive performances and surrealistic atmospheres, and explicitly strayed from any sense of political legibility. Craig argued that the mood evoked by the company work 'is a nostalgia for the lost aura and the lost innocence of art, while homologously, the dream-like progression of events pulls the audience psychologically into the lost past of the subconscious' (Craig, 1980, 24–5). Craig once contrasted the People Show's lack of political investment to Welfare State's socio-politically applied theatre. Kershaw built on this comparison by describing The People Show's performance as 'decontextualised carnivalesque', in the sense that the work relies on aesthetics no longer attached to oppositional political intentions (Kershaw, 1992, 71).

In this respect, there is an irony in how Nuttall doubted *sTigma*'s political potency, or at least its salience, but went on to found Britain's most prominent 'a-political' performance company. To divest an aesthetic from previous political roots, however, is not unique to the People Show. For instance, aesthetic tactics inspired by the liberal politics of the Bath Arts Workshop were transformed by the Natural Theatre Company into street performances often stripped of political intent. Describing this phenomenon in relation to the People Show, Kershaw wrote, 'The very iconoclasm that represented a radically unfettered creativity was sometimes dangerously reliant on a formalist aesthetic that consisted of a curious reconstruction of art-for-art's-sake ideology: self-referential, ego-bound, reactionary' (Kershaw, 1992, 71).

Although Kershaw has argued that the People Show's work was removed from 'an oppositional community' (Kershaw, 1992, 71), later writers, such as Gillian Whiteley, suggest the company's aesthetics embodied important potential. In line with Herbert Marcuse's 1969 description of a generation's need for a 'revolution in perception' (Marcuse, 1969, 37), Whiteley analyses 'the ways that the *creative* powers of the imagination – particularly the irrational and affective – could catalyse new political possibilities' (Whiteley, 2011, 111). By radically challenging existing dogma, Whiteley argues that the work of Nuttall and the People Show represented a 'threat' to existing orthodoxies because, as Nuttall wrote, 'the root of political development is creative and irrational' [and a] 'persistent entanglement of the imagination with politics' (Nuttall, 1970, 8). This ethos, Whiteley writes, 'is a central, if problematic, element in his writing and artistic practice' (Whiteley, 2011, 111).

Such observations recognize political undercurrents inherent in much of Nuttall's work. The early development of the People Show suggests a similarly complicated relationship between imagination and politics. Aesthetics once explicitly connected to oppositional (even revolutionary) politics were transformed by, as Nuttall said, a 'numbing of the moral sense' (Nuttall, 1970, 129). A People Show genealogy that includes *sTigma* and extends back to 1965 can productively challenge existing histories by complicating common 'a-political' categorizations attributed to the company. Excavating the relationship between the People Show and earlier histories offers a perspective that uncovers some of the political underpinnings to the People Show's early tactics and aesthetics.

Funding and Company Structure: 1966–80

As with the People Show's founding, a historiography of the company's funding up to the early 1980s reveals a similarly speckled portrait of diverse accounts. Arts Council of Great Britain (ACGB) records tell of the group's first turbulent fourteen years, documented in council meeting minutes, company-authored policy projections, funding requests and personal letters. In contrast to the company's proud claim in 1986 that the 'People Show has always been a good house-keeper' (ACGB, 1986, 34/122/4), records from 1975–80 reveal the company's late or missing reports, its financial deficits, its performers' low wages and its occasionally dysfunctional meetings, including the misbehaviour of company members (Nuttall addresses these alleged incidents in his 1979 memoir). While the Arts Council struggled with the company, these difficulties were sometimes excused as a conse-quence of the company's style, or as Drama Officer Jonathan Lamede reasoned, the group 'function in a way that is beyond the grasp of bureaucracy' (ACGB, 1979a, 34/122/1). Similarly, Drama Director John Faulkner championed the People Show for its outstanding quality in spite of its temperamentality: 'Their cohesion,' he wrote, 'is like that of a spider's silk. Thirty times stronger weight for weight than steel, but it will float away on a breeze' (ACGB, 1980b, 34/122/1).

In some accounts, the People Show's funding is marked as beginning with an annual subsidy in 1974 of £6,000. However, this starting point skips gradual increases of funding starting in 1970 in the form of small bursaries. Both Nuttall and Roland Miller (a company member from 1968–70) cite the 1968 formation of the Arts Council's 'New Activities Committee' as the crucial starting point for the funding of fringe groups like The People Show. Nuttall addressed this shift in his 1979 memoir, while Miller wrote his critique in a 1973 paper specifically prepared for the Council's drama committee. In it, Miller explained how the first initiatives included 'a series of Regional Gatherings [held during 1969–1970], in which not only the experimental theatre groups like The People Show, Portable Theatre, Warehouse La Mama, and others appeared, but also such "art" activities as light shows, inflatables, and avant-garde music which incorporated performance' (ACGB, 1973, 43/42/5). Miller wrote of how the funding supported multidisciplinary performance work beyond existing theatre practices including hybrid forms of music and visual arts. But Miller also wrote how this shift signalled the start of funding streams being disseminated not from the Council's Music and Art Panels, but from its drama allocation. Miller prophetically wrote, 'it marks the beginning of a trend towards classification that has produced the present situation in which performance art is associated closely with drama' (ACGB, 1973, 43/42/5).

The classification Miller identifies helped set what Beth Hoffman has described as 'the habits of differentiation' endemic to performance art genealogies of the UK and distinct from North America and continental Europe (Hoffman, 2009, 103). As Nick Kaye has also argued, in contrast to performance experiments emerging from the fields of music and visual arts, 'British "performance art" of the late 1960s and early 1970s was not only shadowed by the strength of the politically radical and largely text-based alternative British theatre, but shared some of its practices and concerns' (Kaye, 1994, 2). The People Show's growth, therefore, represents an early example of this genealogical distinction. The backgrounds of company members reflected skill sets outside traditional drama and the company's collaborations with musicians and visual artists initially challenged funding streams designed for drama.

The relationship that emerges during the seventies between the Arts Council and the company is an occasionally stormy one, marked with moments of doubt and procedural nudging. Applications by the company reflect their frustration: 'There were no grants at that time for groups, only for writers and building based companies' (ACGB, 1986, 34/122/4). The challenge for the People Show was how its explicit negation of a central playwright and director, along with its unwillingness to secure a permanent theatre space until 1980, distanced it from the characteristics that generally attracted funding. This conflict of categories is also evident in Arts Council records of 1972, with its perception that the company's work 'was becoming increasingly theatrical in content' and 'should be subsidized on a similar scale to Freehold/Portable' (ACGB, 1972, 43/36/2).

As the mid-seventies progressed, the company's modest subsidy was augmented by income earned from tours and the resourcefulness and sacrifices of its members, 'both from their time and from their pockets' (ACGB, 1986, 34/122/4). The company's thrift was well established during its early years in Better Books, then at the London Arts Lab and eventually on what Michael Coveney called the 'campus and cellar circuit' (Coveney, 1980, 36). As the People Show's reputation grew, the group accepted offers to go abroad where its work, as claimed by Long, was artistically and financially more appreciated. 'I mean we couldn't work if we didn't go abroad,' Long told Hulton in 1981, 'that's really what keeps us going, the money we earned abroad' (Hulton, 1981, 5). Touring also helped the company gain a reputation for its adaptability and skills at using cheap materials (Hulton, 1981, 5). 'A show such as No. 84,' an internal council memo reads, 'would cost £1,000 to produce and is suitable for a range of performance spaces' (ACGB, 1980b, 34/122/1). The People Show's affordable and transmutable aesthetic can also be connected to Nuttall's earlier assemblages.

Paradoxically, for a company that defined itself as a collective, People Show funding up to the 1980s was routinely linked to the virtuosity of particular performers. This started as early as 1971 when the Experimental Drama Committee 'felt that since Roland Miller and John Darling had now left, consideration [for funding] should be deferred until their current work with revised personnel had been seen' (ACGB, 1971, 43/36/2). The Drama Panel awarded £2,000 to the company that year but in 1973/4 justified its funding decisions on the strength and worthiness of particular company members. By the financial year of 1974/5, the council was convinced of the company's reliability. Council records state, 'the Committee agreed that their originality and truly experimental nature warranted their being supported at a high level since over the years they had done such startling and original work' (ACGB, 1975, 43/36/1). But even after yearly increases in its revenue grant, anxieties rose about the company's ability to retain its strongest members. For example, Drama Officer Clive Tempest was concerned about the company's low productivity and wrote defensively in an internal memo, 'Subsidy for the People Show at the moment is an investment in the considerable talents of Mike Figgis and Mark Long' (ACGB, 1977, 34/122/1). Yet, Tempest also warned that Long and Figgis expressed a 'tiredness', but that they were committed to staying in the group and were seeking 'new directions'. 'By the end of the year,' Tempest asserted, 'I feel confident that the council will have had its money's worth' (ACGB, 1977, 34/122/1). However, the next year *People*

Show 73 was deemed an 'apparent failure' by Drama Officer Lamede, in part because of the addition of three new members who undermined the quality of the performance (ACGB, 1978, 34/122/1). The Arts Council linked the company's value to the talents of its strongest members and continued to do so into the next decade.

The Council's habit of awarding funding on an implicit valuation based upon individual members contradicts the artistic policy of the People Show as a collective. This paradox may on one hand be a reflection of the company's less acknowledged tendency towards the virtuosity of its key performers. On the other hand, company programmes often included unsigned members' quotes on performance practices that suggested a collective creative process (Wilson, 1979, 19). In this manner, the People Show's structure and ethos tended to pull it in one direction while, perhaps, Arts Council funding schemes pulled in another. Nonetheless, by the end of the 1970s, the company was on course to expand into the mainstream. The Policy and Projections statement of 1979/80 highlighted how success in larger venues and the quadrupling of its income potentially enabled the company to become a commercial repertory company (ACGB, 1979c, 34/122/4). Lamede's meeting minutes corroborate the group's popularity. 'It seems,' he wrote, 'that this year the People Show have more work than they can handle. The Royal Court, Riverside Studios and Hampstead Theatre are all interested in taking shows, and Birmingham Arts Lab wants a one month's residency' (ACGB, 1979a, 34/122/1). The company's popularity, however, did not keep speed with the group's finances. The report emphasized how the company was still committed to bringing its work to smaller venues but would need more assistance from the Arts Council. The report complained, 'Our subsidy is failing increasingly to keep pace with our development; thus the gap between our needs and our resources continues to widen.' According to Lamede, the company needed money to hire a second administrator who would manage the expansion of the company, including the conversion of a studio theatre, and even aid the development of adventure playground projects (ACGB, 1979a, b, 34/122/1).

The company was also frustrated about receiving less funding than similarly sized groups. Interviewing Long in 1980, Coveney wrote, 'The Arts Council annual grant, currently £28,000, is substantially less than that offered to more traditionalist, text obsessed groups like Joint Stock and Foco Novo' (Coveney, 1980, 36). Not only were People Show members anxious about being outside what they saw as prioritized categories of text-based theatre but, according to the company administrator, Bradford Watson, the fourteen-year-old group was feeling 'overtaken by some of the younger groups that have arisen in the past few years' (ACGB, 1980c, 34/122/1). Watson argued that if the company was to maintain and grow its audiences into the following financial year of 1981/2, a revenue grant of £77,000 (nearly four times the funding received four years previously) would be required. Unhappy with the Arts Council's recommended figure of £50,000, Watson responded that it was '£30,000 short of our real needs' and 'We are now, it seems, to be further penalized by being forever held back from decent subsidy in favour of others. We are beginning to find this intolerable' (ACGB, 1980c, 34/122/1).

Realizing the limits of funding and the consequences of expansion, Watson wrote how the shift to larger shows and venues had resulted in members' energies being 'spread too widely, over too many projects'. Instead, the company finally decided to downsize both the scale and number of productions, focusing on small venues and its cabaret shows (ACGB, 1980d, 34/122/1). Members realized that it was 'clear that we were not going to be accepted, in this country, into the mainstream of established theatre' (ACGB, 1986, 34/122/4). In a way, this shift distinguishes the People Show history from groups that attempted to professionalize away from fringe circuits (for example, Portable and the Natural Theatre Company). It also suggests how funding structures influenced the downscaling of the People Show's working methods and possibly influenced its longevity. Had the company continued to expand beyond its means, it may have risked folding. In the end, by doing smaller projects and its cabaret series, the company proved sustainable and continued to receive funding over the next three decades.

Key Work Produced in this Period and its Impact

In 1980, the ACGB's Drama Director John Faulkner received an internal memo from the Deputy Secretary General expressing doubt about the ability 'to identify (let alone assess) artistic quality' of the People Show. Faulkner responded by arguing that the Drama Panel maintained an 'extensive knowledge' of the company based on a continuity of its work over the years, 'since the impact of their work is long term not show by show'. Faulkner wrote that the company contributed significantly to the theatre establishment, 'by showing what is achievable with different, often oblique, forms of communication and these possibilities are exploited by directors and actors and should be respected by writers' (ACBG, 1980b, 34/122/1). Faulkner's defence of the People Show encompasses what was, by then, commonly accepted about the company's influence and importance. However, it took fourteen years and several shifts in company working methods to earn wider acknowledgement. Despite Faulkner's emphasis on the company's 'long-term' impact, the following list of shows marks particular moments of significance in its early history.

- *People Show 9: Mother* (1967–8). The influential theatremaker Joan Littlewood arranged for the company to perform *Mother* at the Theatre Royal in Stratford East, London. This attracted national and international attention and resulted in numerous festival appearances and tours (Behrndt, 2010, 32). The show included Syd Palmer, Laura Gilbert, John Darling, Mark Long, Jeff Nuttall and Muriel England.
- *People Show 11: Something Else* (1968). This show was taken to the Traverse in Edinburgh. It consisted of a sheet draped across the middle of a split audience. On one side of the sheet was a tragedy being performed while a comedy was performed on the other. Reactions of the audience could be heard on both sides and at one point, holes were cut in the sheet for performers and audiences to peer through. This piece marked a creative shift by using the absence of words to heighten an audience's critical faculties of perception and reflection. Snoo Wilson wondered if the show 'was any less true about the political reality or any other kind of reality, than [Peter] Brook's *US*' (Wilson, 1979, 12). Jack Moore, founder of international theatre group, the Human Family, recalled *Something Else* as the most influential show of his life (Moore, 2013). The show included Laura Gilbert, John Darling, Mark Long and Muriel England.
- *People Shows 22–4: Beachball, Tennis,* and *Walter* (1968–9). These productions toured and were part of the Edinburgh Festival. According to Long, they included several nude performers as well as a sexually explicit scene with a clothed female and a dummy. This set of shows was labelled 'obscenity' by the Scottish press and received requests for its cancellation (Long, 1971, 53). Following the lifting of theatre censorship, Long credited this set of shows as acting as a 'catalyst' for a theatre environment previously void of nudity. The shows included Laura Gilbert, Mark Long, Jeff Nuttall, Roland Miller and John Darling.

- *People Show 31: Glass* (1970). Performed in London and Edinburgh, *Glass* was considered 'a major turning point' for the company, marking a shift away from improvisation and towards sophisticated staging and lighting (ACGB, 1986, 34/122/4). *Glass* was structured to run for exactly 29 minutes and 25 seconds; it featured a woman in a black dress and a series of objects including a glass tree, a red rose, a white mirror, red lipstick and additional clothing, all revealed in a tightly constructed light design (Long, 1971, 55). The series of images coincided with a sound recording of a woman's daily activities interrupted midway by a car crash (Long, 1971, 55). The show included Laura Gilbert, Mark Long and John Darling. It was at this point that the company began mastering technical elements and shows became more thematic and deliberately more aesthetically beautiful. Company records state, 'The tools [became] more sophisticated and the deeper creative demands greater. The People Show was now recognised' (ACGB, 1986, 34/122/4).
- *People Show 33: Stretcher/Gunman/Sacks/Phone Box* (1970). This series of three separate shows and an intimate interactive outdoor piece was presented at the Royal Court Theatre, London as part of the highly influential *Come Together* Festival. The shows were different in scale, the smallest being *Phone Box,* which involved a personal invitation to an encounter at an outdoor phone box (Long, 1971, 59). The performers included Terry Day, Alan Barker, José Nava, Laura Gilbert, Mark Long and John Darling.
- The *Come Together* Festival was a key moment in British theatre history as the first major instance when an established and self-styled 'writers theatre' welcomed the work of the fringe. Simon Trussler argues that this event functioned as 'the first vicarious sampling of the fringe' for conventional theatre goers (Trussler, 2000, 340). The English Stage Company's Artistic Director William Gaskill said the festival was intended to place experimental theatre 'in the context of a Writer's Theatre, and partly in the hope that there may be cross-fertilization between the different kinds of work shown and for future work in the theatre generally' (Gaskill, 1970, 15). In other words, The People Show, along with companies like Cartoon Archetypical Slogan Theatre (CAST) and practitioners such as Pip Simmons and Ken Campbell, showcased works that, following the lifting of theatre censorship, were seen as attractive and potentially co-optable forms for the mainstream. Or, as Snoo Wilson said later of the People Show, 'They are, as Blake said of Fuseli, very good to *steal* from' (Wilson, 1979, 10).

- Ronald Bryden described one of the People Show's *Come Together* performances and how it 'very nearly cleared out the audience too, with a combination of smoke bombs, verbal aggro and symbolic equations (a brassier filled with baked beans) of consumer goods with imperialism' (Bryden, 1970, 32). Echoing *sTigma*'s use of smoke and assaults on the audience, performance tactics in *People Show 33* reflected four years of honing a particular People Show style. After this event, the public's awareness and perception of the company notably shifted. Just a year later, Dusty Hughes in *Time Out* said, 'They've been rejected by most people connected with the theatre and yet they must be one of the most important things to have happened over the past five years' (Hughes, 1971, 40).
- *People Show 74: The Billie Holiday Show* to *People Show 79: Hamburg* (1978–80). Company records recognize that this series of shows represented a period when the company made a decisive turn: 'A moment for conscious change had come' (ACGB, 1986, 34/122/4). Shifting from former success in larger venues, the company decided to go 'back to basements' and focus on developing cabaret shows and refining its style of intimacy. In particular, People Shows *75*, *77* and *79*, respectively the *Cabaret Show*, *Billie Holiday Show II* and *Hamburg*, sought to perfect the company's cabaret aesthetic. Not all of these shows received acclaim or large audiences, but *Hamburg*, for instance, was presented at London's Institute of Contemporary Arts and the *Cabaret Show* toured internationally and was considered a significant success. In fact, the cabarets were so successful that the company was accused by performance art 'purists' of abandoning previous principles and selling out (Craig, 1982, 44). Company records reflect on this period of work and its contribution to wider developments of the cabaret genre, claiming that cabaret was non-existent before 1980, but that within 'two years the world seemed to be saturated with cabaret venues and alternative cabaret acts' (ACGB, 1986, 34/122/4).

Artistic Policy and Working Methodology

Outlining an artistic policy of the People Show is a difficult task, not least because of the company's eclectic and divergent working methods. Deirdre Heddon and Jane Milling even suggest that to propose 'the existence of "models" can be "problematic and disingenuous" because it overlooks the company's processes of fluidity and contradiction over time'

(Heddon and Milling, 2005, 78). Depending on the show and its conditions, the People Show has both used text and abandoned it. It has done wildly improvised shows and highly structured-to-the-minute shows; silent shows and cabarets; high-tech shows and low-tech shows; heavily rehearsed shows and shows with no rehearsal at all. Thus, it is important to understand that the company's 'methods' were not set in a traditional sense but open to the different desires and demands of the moment. Long embraced the company's inchoateness, stating, 'There has never been a group idea of a show, there has never been a common denominator, which is one of the reasons the People Show survives, I'm absolutely sure' (Hulton, 1981, 34). The descriptions herein are thus limited in scope and cannot accommodate the full breadth of members' opinions or the numerous methods engaged in by the company. However, it is an attempt to represent what could arguably be considered the company's core methods – no matter how inconsistent or selectively employed.

To begin, company members rarely considered themselves actors in the traditional sense. Many held backgrounds in visual arts, music, vaudeville, mime, circus and acrobatics. The company experimented with unconventional methods of characterization drawn from experiments of the 1960s, happenings and the field of performance art. Contrasting acting styles of the People Show to traditions of Stanislavski and the American Method, David Jay argued that 'With the People Show the role is purely the extension of the actor's personality. Such an approach demands immense subtlety and intelligence, yet the liberation of the actor is much more authentic than in the posturings of the Yippie theatre' (Jay, 1971, 28). Rarely committed to a 'role' or 'character' in the traditional sense, performers often played hybrid versions of themselves. Characters were commonly presented in highly abstracted ways (for example, the woman in *People Show 31: Glass*). By featuring poignantly small fragments of character through image or minimalist staging, Long stated, 'You don't know much about them, you don't know if they are married, you don't know where they were born [...]', but 'in half a minute there one has achieved what a lot of people take hours to get across' (Hulton, 1981, 9–11).

Because character was often composed in relation to theatrical space, the company was frequently concerned with the use of space and lighting. 'We are working around visual structures', Long explained, 'A series of visual images is worked on beforehand and we often embroider these—with our bodies, with our words and with our reactions—to enlarge the images for the audience' (Long, 1971, 57). Key to achieving the desired effect was the People Show's use of lighting, which Long stated resembled American dance companies (Hulton, 1981, 8). 'It's much more atmospheric if you like, much more flexible, much more about lighting, feelings, mood' (Heddon and Milling, 2005, 79). The atmosphere of the People Shows was also achieved by finding the right balance of dynamic sequences. 'Structural decisions, then, are often pragmatic: slow sections are contrasted with chaotic sections; loud with quiet; vertical use of space with horizontal use; the expected with the surprise, or the known with the mystery' (Heddon and Milling, 2005, 79).

The People Show earned much of its early reputation from the way it adapted conventional spaces into absorbing environments. From basements and pubs to phone boxes and fields, the group transformed and incorporated the given space into the show's thematic fabric. Constructing the set is also integral to the company's collective creative process. 'Everyone is involved in the physical labor as well as in making artistic and practical suggestions' (Kirby and Wilson, 1974, 59). For many shows, the company salvaged objects from junk yards, pawn shops and open air markets. Kirby and Wilson observed, 'They are all intrigued with things out of the past: old lace, military medals, Victorian clothes, yellowed account books of a defunct business, broken umbrellas, anything they think would add to the visual texture of a show' (Kirby and Wilson, 1974, 57).

One of the most valued methods of the People Show was its commitment to collective devising. The company eschewed the role of the traditional director and worked towards non-autocratic forms of co-operation that embraced the individuality of each contributor. 'The vital thing in the People Show', Long asserted, is that 'every member of the group exists in his or her own right, totally in their own right; and if that isn't happening it doesn't work' (Hulton, 1981, 22). In this sense, shows were generally 'authored' by the sum contributions of its performers.

The company's openness to chance and unexpected events during rehearsal also extended to the way it employed structured and unstructured improvisations. For example, Kirby and Wilson noted that 'audience reactions are sometimes magnified in importance or allowed to restructure an image or vary a performers' action' (Kirby and Wilson, 1974, 65). A company show usually underwent changes and development during performance weeks. 'They change,' Long said, 'because we find out a lot about a show and about ourselves in it during a performance. There is only so much one can achieve in rehearsal' (Hulton, 1981, 11).

Starting points for a show varied widely. As Long stated, 'It is very difficult to talk about how a show gets put together [...] There is no general principal of how shows get put together because the conditions always vary' (Hulton, 1981, 5). Starting points have included found objects (feathers and polythene), a performance space (The Traverse), a form of theatre (*commedia dell'arte*), talents of particular performers or previously discarded ideas (Heddon and Milling, 2005, 78).

In many senses, the company embraced indeterminacy. Images and activities showcased were intentionally designed to evoke subjective interpretations and encourage self-reflection. 'The result', as David Jay wrote in the *Times Educational Supplement,* was 'to bring the theatre in line with the concerns of artists and sculptors, of conceptual art and the examination of the image [...] For the audience the requirement is not just to see but to discover what is going on, to conceive the idea as well as perceive its execution' (Jay, 1971, 28).

Whether it was by covering audiences with polythene sheets or addressing spectators directly, shows sought to awaken the senses and explore less familiar recesses of thought and imagination. As Michael Kustow explained, 'It attacks you not at the level of reason, but of apprehension, in both senses of the word, perception and a frission of fear, for the emotional colouring of their mosaic of sound, gesture and pictures is as dark as ever, reminding us of the knots of our lives, the surprising tangles and nooks of our consciousness which may lead to heaven or to horror' (Kustow, 1975, 24).

Critical Reception

Criticism of the People Show during its early years ranged from perturbed taxpayers to scholars and fellow theatre practitioners to the company's own members. Discourse on the People Show usually centred on issues about the company's artistic merit, its political value or its wider impact on British theatre practices. A telling example of how the company's artistic value and even its funding status were sometimes challenged is a letter received by the ACGB in 1980. In it, an angry Helen Turnbull complains about *People Show 86.*

> The entire play was an utter and complete insult to adult theatre-goers, although I dare say there will be hundreds of 'trendy' Hampstead-type people who will adopt the 'Emperor's Clothes' attitude and praise the hour-and-a-quarter of drivel, and may I say,

unadulterated crap. This play will not cause even a ripple compared to something like The Romans in Britain, but nevertheless you have financially supported something I consider this to be a wicked waste a [*sic*] dwindling resources. (ACGB, 1980e, 34/122/2)

Concerned about theatre legacies and a perceived lack of quality in the company's work, Turnbull expressed common anxieties of the period. The difficulty of watching a People Show performance was something widely acknowledged, even by company members. Viewing a show for the first time 'is not the most enjoyable experience', Long said, but 'people tend to like it the second or third time or fourth time more. There is that little process of education, getting rid of that looking for a story and plot' (Hulton, 1981, 36).

Beyond the challenge of unpuzzling the structures of People Show work, criticism from scholars and theatre practitioners concentrated on the company's political potency – or lack of it. Long complained that the group's name was sometimes misread as 'The People's Show' and resulted in critiques about the company's lack of Marxist content (Hulton, 1981, 35). Nuttall claimed sociologist Laurie Taylor reviled the group 'for not being a theatre of the people' and failing to entertain or politically enlighten the working classes (Nuttall, 1979, 30). Left-wing theatre practitioners like Albert Hunt were also said to have 'despised the lack of "sociological content"' in People Show performances (Coveney, 1980, 36). Company members, if they responded at all to such critiques, agreed that the company title and its shows were not sociological, but rather presented an exhibition of people. In this way, political readings of shows were not encouraged by company members. Just as Nuttall separated from *sTigma* for its perceived political failures, the People Show evaded political legibility. Political cogency was largely left up to audiences to interpret.

The People Show's characteristically indeterminate style welcomed multiple readings. Writer Snoo Wilson, theatre critic Michael Coveney and later scholars like Gillian Whiteley countered critiques about the company's apolitical vacuity. Coveney, for instance, reasoned that the excessive drunkenness in *People Show 51* was 'a wonderful, distorting stage essay on the social phenomenon of public drinking' (Coveney, 1980, 36). More broadly, Wilson argued that the stylistic choices of the company encouraged a type of self-awareness and political consciousness relevant to the times. 'The structure of the shows', he wrote, is 'something to do with the way things fall apart in the memory, and they benefit from it retrospectively, but what of course the performers are remembering for us is something else' (Wilson, 1979, 12). The contemplative retrospection that Wilson identified embraced People Show work as wrestling with, not excluding, politics. In a similar manner, Whiteley argued that Nuttall and the People Show work to push the way 'imagination – particularly the irrational and affective – could catalyse new political possibilities' (Whitley, 2011, 111).

But perhaps the most persuasive writing on this matter is by Roland Miller after he left the company. Writing about performance art and its potential to inspire critical reflection, Miller wrote,

> Performance art throws the responsibility for actions carried out against the expectations and conventions of society, firmly onto the individual responsible, without the interpretive screen of 'propaganda' or 'symbolism', 'allegory' or 'legend'. Performance art is immediate and personal, and I think vitally relevant in form and content to the present social, political situation. (ACGB, 1973, 43/42/5)

Regardless of whether or not audiences or critics ascribed politics to the People Show, by the 1980s the company's influence was well acknowledged. Craig suggested the company (along with CAST) 'may truly be described as seminal' and 'more influential' than the Living Theatre, Joan Littlewood, La Mama, Open Theatre and Bruce Lacey (Craig, 1980, 20). Max Stafford-Clark, artistic director of the Royal Court from 1979 to 1993, similarly claimed that the group was more influential than Grotowski, Artaud or the Living Theatre (Coveney, 1980, 36). Despite the company's growing reputation, the Arts Council continued to struggle with how to categorize it. 'Where does it fit?', asked its Drama Director, 'It is far more than a stubborn survivor of 60's experiment: so are Welfare State, Triple Action, I.O.U., Shared Experience' (ACGB, 1980b, 34/122/1).

The People Show is credited with supplying mainstream theatre with new forms of expression and for influencing alternative theatre groups. The company's direct and diffuse influence may be due, in part, to its members (particularly in the first ten years) leaving the company and starting up new companies. For instance, early members John Darling and Laura Gilbert went on to found, respectively, John Bull Puncture Repair Kit, The Yorkshire Gnomes and Jail Warehouse. Nuttall claimed a far-reaching influence for the company, including the plays of Howard Brenton, Pip Simmon's Theatre Group and extending even to television's *Monty Python* and *Rowan and Martin's Laugh-In* (Nuttall,

1979, 110). The People Show's numerous tours and outmatched longevity impacted multiple generations of alternative practitioners. For example, Geraldine Pilgrim of Hesitate and Demonstrate, and David Gale of Lumiere & Son, acknowledged the role People Show had on their work (Gale et al., 2013). These, however, are only a few examples of the legacy of the People Shows from 1965–6 to the 1980s.

On the brink of its fiftieth anniversary, the People Show remains active with Long still as a core member. In 2007, the company's Arts Council England (ACE) funding reached £133,104 but was completely cut in 2008 along with that of 150 other companies (Duchin, 2008). Despite losing regular funding status with ACE, an exceptional grant of £72,000 was given to the company in order to complete *People Show 119: Ghost Sonata* (Duchin, 2008, 5, 13). ACE funding grants were awarded to the People Show in 2010, but only at a fraction of previous grants (Duchin, 2012, 2010). In 2013, with a budget nearly halved, the company relocated from Bethnal Green Studios (where it had rented out rehearsal space for nearly thirty years) to the Brady Arts Centre. Most recently, the company adopted twenty-first century technologies including a company blog, a podcast on iTunes and social media accounts on Twitter and Facebook. To once again survive dramatic funding cuts with an active sense of renewal, the People Show demonstrates the resilience and creativity that continue to maintain its legacy as Britain's longest running alternative performance group.

A List of Key Productions

A comprehensive list of People Shows (up to 125 and counting) is available on the company website (http://peopleshow.co.uk/archive/). Earlier iterations of the People Show website from 2002 to the present can be found at the Internet Archive (http://web.archive.org/web/*/http://peopleshow.co.uk). This index allows access to previous versions of the company's website and includes information no longer featured on the current site. For instance, the record from 2008 contains a different history page and includes information such as the general manager, board of directors, rental information, as well as a notice about the cancellation of ACE funding. Archived pages up to 2013 include show descriptions, performers' names and information about images and videos now removed. The site offers a digital – if sorely incomplete – historiographical record of the company's self-presentation and provides a new way of exploring the company's history.

Chapter 5

PORTABLE THEATRE

Chris Megson

'Happily Homeless'

On 5 November 1970, the transit van of the Portable Theatre company was involved in a traffic accident while touring two plays in the Shrewsbury area. At the end of that week, David Hare, who with his friend, Tony Bicât, co-founded Portable in 1968, signed off the usual return form to the company's funding body, the Arts Council of Great Britain (ACGB), which recorded the cumulative ticket sales and box office income for the previous seven days. He added an explanatory note to the bottom of the form: 'Van crashed on Thursday night, and injuries meant cancelling two performances. I am hoping to claim the missing fees from the insurance of the driver of the other car responsible for the crash' (ACGB, 1970a, 43/43/11). Over thirty years later, Bicât recalled the incident:

> David was not with us when, returning from playing *Fruit* in Wales, we had a serious crash: an idiot in a Mini drove out in front of us. The van (with me driving and five actors in the back) turned over and spun round. Miraculously, no one was hurt. We were in a brand new VW van, hired because ours was so broken down. (Bicât, 2007, 24)

The incident, which illustrates some of the practical risks involved in small-scale touring, led Bicât into a protracted tussle with the ACGB. In his own words, he 'accused the long-suffering Arts Council of trying to kill us, pointing out that had we been in our crappy old van we would all be dead' (Bicât, 2007, 24). A few months after the accident, in February 1971, the Council's New Drama Committee discussed Portable's situation and the minutes of this meeting acknowledge the company's 'critical need for a new van, for which they put in an application for a capital grant of £1,000' (ACGB, 1971a, 43/43/1). Bicât even

demanded an interview with Lord Arnold Goodman, then Chairman
of the ACGB, to discuss the matter; at this meeting, one of Goodman's
officials claimed that Portable had already spent its allocated budget
and there was no more money available to fund a replacement vehicle.
According to Bicât, Goodman began to harangue his official at this
point, in front of the Portable delegation, and ended his tirade with the
rather ostentatious declamation, 'Give these people what they want!'
(Bicât, 2007, 24). The Chairman's support for the company, however,
was tempered by his final remarks to Bicât:

> As we left the room, Goodman called me back: 'You should get a
> building; if you get a building, we'll give you lots more money.' Little
> did I know that I was hearing the raison d'être of UK theatre subsidy
> for the next thirty years. We got a new van and continued to be
> happily homeless. (Bicât, 2007, 24)

Introduction

The accident brings into focus Portable Theatre's *modus operandi* as
a touring group, but also its fractious relationship with the ACGB.
The company– named after the then ubiquitous 'portable' radio – was
established as first and foremost a nomadic entity. While touring was
an economic necessity for the alternative theatre movement of the
time, Portable's commitment to touring was central to its desire to
perform new work in non-theatre venues and, in so doing, to distance
itself from the formalities and institutions of building-based theatre:
'As young men,' recalls Hare, 'neither Tony nor I had any wish to have
our work seen as being part of the English theatre' (Hare, 2005, 161).
Given the company's embrace of 'portability' as a means of escaping
the perceived stranglehold of 'English theatre', the iconic van was a
vital resource in enabling the company to realize its vision. Goodman
seems to have recognized this but, at the same time, his urbane parting
shot to Bicât – advocating bricks-and-mortar stability over the risks of
the open road – marks one of the fault-lines that began to trouble the
relationship between Portable and the ACGB.

Theatre scholars to date have discussed Portable's work in a number
of monographs and essays, usually focusing on the uproarious style of
its productions. Richard Boon, for example, describes the company's
approach as 'anti-theatrical, anti-cultural and anti-humanistic [...]
designed to provoke, antagonise and confront its audiences' (Boon,

1991, 139); Maria DiCenzo similarly notes the 'graphic, hostile and provocative' techniques deployed in performance (DiCenzo, 1996, 20). Catherine Itzin identifies the company's 'anti-establishment anger' (Itzin, 1980, 189), while John Bull describes Portable productions as 'a series of assault courses in which the audience was frequently as much the target as the ostensible subject-matter' (Bull, 1984, 16–17). This chapter considers the aims, history and working context of the company, with a particular focus on Portable's attitude towards 'style' – specifically, its attempt to reject style in theatre, a word its directors associated with the decadence of dominant culture and the ghettoization of alternative theatre. As we shall see, debates about style were intrinsic to the countercultural foment of the late 1960s in which Portable was deeply enmeshed.

Aside from the issue of style, the company's relationship with the ACGB forms the second preoccupation of this essay. In addition to the scholarship indicated above and the published recollections of Portable practitioners such as Bicât and Hare, there is a wealth of documentation available in the V&A Museum's Theatre and Performance archive, ranging from the records of individual theatres that hosted Portable on tour, to the voluminous minutes and memoranda, internal reports and personal correspondence, stored in the labyrinthine ACGB files. 'As we comb an archive catalogue [...],' argues theatre historian Joseph Donohue, 'it is useful to remember that time is always moving on even while we contemplate the past and its works, and our links with them' (Donohue, 1989, 194–5). In a similar vein, Jane Milling describes a 'curious paradox' in writing a historiography of the recent past: '[t]he apparently cool objectivity of an idealised scientific, fact-filled history will always run alongside the warm recollection of an emotion-laden experience of personal relationship to social, economic and political structures and events' (Milling, 2012, 30, 31). Archival resources may appear to record a historical past with 'cool objectivity' but in fact they offer an indexical and always partial representation of that past, thereby setting terms for the analytic scrutiny of that representation and the potential 'links' connecting past and present.

Drawing on archival records as a basis for an interpretation of the company's work, it is evident that there was a transformation in Portable's self-image over the years of its existence: the company started out performing pared-down pieces in small, intimate venues but, later, it sought to play larger spaces as its directors tired of what they perceived to be the hermetic fringe network. Over the five or so years of Portable's longevity, the funding structures of the ACGB placed limits on the company's evolving sense of ambition, especially its attempt to keep risk-taking at the centre of its artistic strategy.

History of the Company's Development

One of the first references to Portable Theatre in the ACGB archive is included in an internal memo on 'Fringe and Experimental Theatre Companies', dated December 1968. The document introduces the company and sets out its stated aim

> to take intimate theatre wherever it is wanted. The success of the scheme depends on the company remaining small and mobile – a company that can be picked up and put down in the middle of any group of people whether that group is educational, social or cultural [...] Without being condescending, the aim is to carry the work of the actors into work with the audience after the play. The aim is inspirational rather than didactic. We don't aim to teach drama, but to create it. (ACGB, 1968, 43/36/1)

Here, the company is presented as a kind of prototypical 'pop-up' theatre 'that can be picked up and put down in the middle of any group of people'. The future success of the company is linked to its small size but there is also a concern to inspire audiences through and beyond the performances. The company was one of the first of the new fringe companies to tour beyond the capital and metropolitan areas; it was also, in two respects, a writer's theatre: it commissioned new writing (the play-text was always the premise for stage production), and it produced a number of plays, especially early on, about famous writers. In its early days, Portable's potential to be mobile, intimate, literary and broad in appeal were defining characteristics that won it approval from the ACGB, which regarded the company as crucial to the burgeoning ecology of British new writing.

Portable's first show was *Inside Out*, a one-act adaptation of Franz Kafka's diaries compiled by Bicât and Hare, and staged at Jim Haynes' Arts Lab in Drury Lane in October 1968 (it was remounted the following January). The play was submitted to the ACGB's New Play Scheme, and Portable received a small grant. Funding was increased in the following years, enabling the directors to commission playwrights including Howard Brenton and Snoo Wilson, who both joined the company in 1969. In a continuation of the eclectic literary orientation of Portable's subject matter, Hare wrote *Strindberg*, a monologue adapted from that playwright's diaries, which was produced in 1969 at the Oval House (with the actor Maurice Colbourne in the title role), alongside John Grillo's monologue *Gentleman I*. Hare, who started his career in theatre working as a director, wrote his first original play for Portable – the one-act *How Brophy Made Good*, also in 1969 – which he co-directed with Bicât. *Brophy* departed from the biographical focus of previous plays and honed the uncompromising aesthetic that quickly became associated with the company.

With the arrival of Brenton and Wilson, Portable intensified its engagement with topical, often shocking, subject matter. According to Hare, Brenton planned to write 'a history of evil "from Judas Iscariot to the present day"' (Hare, 2005, 161) although Brenton himself claims that it was, in fact, Hare and Bicât who 'had a grand scheme of making a number of shows called *The History of Evil* – which seemed a really silly idea! None of the plays got written, but *Christie [in Love]* was meant to be one' (Wu, 2000, 20). At this time, Brenton was living in a basement flat in London near to the former home of the serial killer John Christie, and the idea for the play began to take shape: 'What I did was to write comic scenes, comic situations, but stretch them intolerably by using massive pauses or bad jokes, which an actor has to try and tell so badly that an audience doesn't laugh, even at its being bad' (Itzin and Trussler, 1975b, 8). *Christie in Love* is arguably the first Portable show to seek actively to discomfort its audience by reversing or utterly confounding its expectations. For Bicât, '[i]t remains the best play we did' (Bicât, 2007, 21), while Hare contends that, with the production of *Christie*, 'Portable Theatre found itself and was truly born' (Hare, 2005, 161). The play won the John Whiting Award in 1969 and was staged at the Oval House in November and the Royal Court Theatre Upstairs the following March. Brenton's subsequent play, *Fruit*, also directed by Hare, toured in 1970, often doubling with the production of Hare's *What Happened to Blake?*

In its first year, Portable toured over 30,000 km: Augusta ('Gus') Hope, the company's much-admired administrator, secured bookings by sending press releases to schools, universities and even army camps (Bicât, 2007, 19, 22). By 1971, the group had three pieces showing at the Edinburgh Fringe Festival, all of them offering an incendiary response to contemporary culture by drawing on violent and pornographic material: Chris Wilkinson's *Plays for Rubber Go-Go Girls*, the group-written *Lay By* and Wilson's *Blowjob*. The ACGB wanted Portable to remain small in scale and resisted the company's desire to create a reduced number of larger, political shows for medium-sized venues. As Bicât and Hare became preoccupied with other projects from the early 1970s, Malcolm Griffiths took the helm at their invitation, and ran what became the Portable Theatre Workshop Company (POTOWOCA); Hare and Bicât remained 'sleeping directors' (Bicât, 2007, 27). Griffiths, like his Portable colleagues, was a graduate of Cambridge and had worked in the late 1960s as associate director at the Citizens Theatre in Glasgow and artistic director of the Castle Theatre in Farnham. When POTOWOCA was established, the ACGB insisted that the company hire a professional administrator, but this proved to be disastrous and, within eighteen months, the company was bankrupted and Griffiths' Workshop evolved into the Paradise Foundry. By this point, Griffiths – a major figure in the history of British alternative theatre – had co-founded the Independent Theatre Council to represent the interests of emerging companies and was also active in promoting new writing through his service on the Drama Panel of the ACGB.

Funding

Portable Theatre received strong support from the ACGB in its first couple of years: its grant in 1968–9 was £89; by 1970–1, it was £4,500, and in 1971–2 it had increased to around £7,970 (including a capital grant of £1,000 for the replacement van). The tone of the written correspondence between Portable and ACGB staff remained civil but the directors' frustration with both the limited subsidy and the Council's bureaucratic requirements is usually tangible: in November 1970, for example, Hare wrote to Chris Cooper, the ACGB's Drama Officer, assuring him that '[i]n about two weeks we will put our annual statement of aims and achievements, thereby causing the usual ill-feeling and displeasure all round' (ACGB, 1970c, 43/43/11).

The ACGB minutes give a consistent impression of Portable's expansionist aspirations even in times of escalating financial crisis. On 4 February 1971, following an interview with Bicât and Griffiths, the New Drama Committee noted that Portable planned six new productions for the year ahead, anticipated 'average income of £110' per week and 'aimed to widen [the] field of writers a little' (ACGB, 1971a, 43/43/1). The Committee, in turn, acknowledged that 'they were a good group who had found some excellent writers and […] would use their money well'; moreover, it was '[f]avourably impressed with Malcolm Griffiths' (ACGB,

1971a, 43/43/1). The minutes of the Experimental Drama Committee (EDC) of 4 November 1971 report Griffiths' election to Portable's Board and the establishment of a subsidiary Workshop company to be run by Griffiths while Portable focused on developing larger projects (ACGB, 1971b, 43/43/3). In December, the ACGB greeted this proposal circumspectly, fearing it would reduce the company's experimentalism and commitment to new writing (ACGB, 1971c 43/43/3).

The worsening economic climate led to an intensive revaluation of ACGB criteria for funding. At the ACGB's Drama Panel meeting in March 1972, 'Fringe and Experimental Drama' was allocated £85,000 for the forthcoming year: over forty applications had been received for this money and only half would be subsidized (ACGB, 1972a, 43/43/3). There were discussions at this meeting about how to define 'experimental' and 'what degree of technical skill was demanded of these companies': 'had they enough imaginative vigour; was the Council getting the best for its money; should one judge adequacy by length of survival; had the scope of work or the public for it been enlarged in three to five years?' (ACGB, 1972a, 43/43/3). Jenny Harris, a member of the Panel and director of the Brighton Combination, pointed out that 'touring was extremely tough, as provincial audiences were not yet attuned to experimental work as they were at a home base [...] when fringe groups became well-known they became pressurised into "succeeding" with a finished product, and this was detrimental to the origins and intentions of their work' (ACGB, 1972a, 43/43/3). The pressures on the ACGB at this time were best expressed by the writer Roy Kift, a member of the EDC: 'Mr Kift felt that the main problem was that the Committee had a pint of paint with which to paint the Forth Bridge' (ACGB, 1973b, 43/43/7).

In the context of these considerable pressures, Portable pledged to raise its number of working weeks from twenty-seven to thirty-five in 1971–2 and increase the number of productions. The company was also committed to paying the new Equity minimum rates for rehearsal and performance. Portable's financial problems were, however, greatly intensified in 1972 as the burden of operating in continuous debt became intolerable and the company received only £8,000 from an application for a revenue grant of £11,850 for the following year. In an angry letter to the ACGB in December 1972, Portable's directors stated that they 'always received from the Arts Council less than it asked for: and always what we asked for was a temperate working minimum' (ACGB, 1972b, 43/43/5); they also clarified that only one permanent member of staff (Griffiths) was in receipt of a proper salary:

> None of the rest of us has had more than £400 each in all since 1968.
> It is impossible to estimate how much we are owed, both in fees
> (even at the lowest professional level) or in expenses unclaimed [...]
> We bitterly regret ever letting ourselves be subsidised by the Arts
> Council at an unrealistic level. (ACGB, 1972b, 43/43/5)

In fact, Portable was struggling with no less than three kinds of
debt – inherited debt, the debt of the Workshop company and the
debts incurred by that year's large-scale collaborative venture, *England's
Ireland* – and the list of principal items of expenditure makes for
depressing reading: bank overdrafts, personal loans, unpaid bills, owed
wages and accountants' fees. The impact of debt, exacerbated by the
financial failure of *England's Ireland*, led directly to the fragmentation
of the company.

On 16 January 1973, at a meeting of the EDC, Nick Barter (Assistant
Drama Director) reported that 'the bank was threatening to foreclose'
on Portable (ACGB, 1973b, 43/43/7). It was recommended that the
ACGB find £3,000 as a supplementary grant for the remainder of
the 1972–3 financial year, primarily because *England's Ireland* had
produced 'shortfalls [that] were jeopardising the future of the workshop
company'. A new permanent company would aggregate around the
Workshop: '[t]he present board of the company wish to resign but will
not do so until the company is solvent'. It was also advised, somewhat
ominously, 'that the Assistant Director should write to Portable and
suggest that next year's application should include a realistic fee for an
administrator' (ACGB, 1973b, 43/43/7).

On 8 February 1973, Griffiths wrote to Barter about the Workshop
company's budget for 1973–4 (ACGB, 1973c, 43/43/6). During the
previous year, the total number of performances was 124 and the
company reported an audience in the UK of 11,680 but the estimated
deficit at 31 March 1973 was £2,814.36. From this point on, the
Workshop fought to separate itself from the financial mire of its parent
entity, Portable Theatre Ltd:

> It is not possible to give a breakdown of income and expenditure for
> the current year since the Portable Theatre Workshop accounts are
> entangled with the whole of Portable Theatre's accounts. The whole
> question of how much the Workshop has in fact spent this year is
> a matter of some dispute and until the Administrative Director of
> Portable Theatre has produced the relevant information it is not
> possible to give a breakdown. (ACGB, 1973c, 43/43/6)

The priority areas identified for increased efficiency were secretarial and financial administration, planning of touring and scheduling of rehearsals, and contact with writers: 'the company should devote its energies far more to its main reason for existence – the presentation of new plays in the best possible way to as many people as possible' (ACGB, 1973c, 43/43/6). The Workshop applied for a revenue grant of £11,619 with an additional capital grant of £500 (to replace sound equipment) 'as an autonomous group and no longer under the umbrella of Portable Theatre Ltd' (ACGB, 1973c, 43/43/6). The EDC, at its meeting of 13 February, recommended a grant of £10,000 and a £500 capital payment; it also 'agreed' that the separation from Portable 'would be generally to the good' (ACGB, 1973d, 43/43/6). A variety of opinions about Portable's work were expressed at this meeting; the discussion, as was typical of the EDC, was engaged and informed. Some committee members suggested a money-saving reduction in weekly wages from £30 to £25; the playwright John Grillo, a member of the committee who had also written for Portable, defended the company's plans as 'interesting' (ACGB, 1973d, 43/43/6). In the end, however, the financial difficulties of the Workshop persisted and eventually proved to be overwhelming.

Around this time, there was a curious attempt to breathe new life into the vestiges of the old Portable company. The theatre producer David Aukin wrote to Nick Barter on 9 March 1973 explaining his wish to establish a non-profit distributing company on the grounds that 'a number of people and theatre groups [...] have asked whether I would take on the responsibilities of the management and administration of their companies'; these groups included 'the David Hare/Snoo Wilson part of Portable Theatre' (ACGB, 1973f, 43/43/7). He followed up this letter on 19 March with a statement to N. V. Linklater, Drama Director of the ACGB, in which he outlined Portable's plans for 1973–4: '[w]e are still convinced that the major need in the theatre at the moment is for touring companies presenting new work on a large scale, but we have been forced by the financial failure of *England's Ireland* to look again at how the company should be organised' (ACGB, 1973g, 43/43/8). A new Board for Portable was tabled, with Aukin, Hare, Wilson and Max Stafford-Clark as co-directors, and their proposed future projects included *Blood of the Borgias* – a new play by Brenton and Hare – and a musical by Wilson and Nick Bicât (Tony's brother); the amount of funding requested was £13,500. Aukin sent a further letter on 19 April, clarifying that '[f]or the larger shows we would like to tour [to] 500 seat theatres. For a smaller project we would go to the Arts Centres and Studio theatres' (ACGB, 1973h, 43/43/8). At its meeting of 15 May 1973, the EDC expressed concern about the company's ability to fill 500-seat theatres but recognized, nonetheless, 'that if the Fringe was to become middle scale, this would seem to be a good group to initiate such a development' (ACGB, 1973i, 43/43/7).

Aukin's plans, however, were to take a different turn. On 20 August 1973, Stafford-Clark wrote to Barter sharing his plans to produce a verbatim play, *The Speakers* – an adaptation of Heathcote Williams' book of the same name, about Speakers' Corner in Hyde Park – under the auspices of Portable Theatre (ACGB, 1973j, 43/43/8). It was hoped that the project could be funded from an ACGB application (eventually for what was to be the amount of £1,135) to be submitted on behalf of Portable. In the end, this initiative was rejected because, under the terms of the grant, no money could be offered until firm bookings had been made, yet Stafford-Clark was not in a position to accept bookings, at least until the completion of the five-week workshop phase of the project. He attended the EDC meeting of 7 September and reported that eight actors were so far committed to *The Speakers* (with more to follow): 'Mr Stafford-Clark said that a great deal of interest had been shown, although he felt it was important that the work should be subsidized as an end in itself' (ACGB, 1973k, 43/43/8). On 12 October, the EDC learned that a grant of £1,000 had been awarded from Council reserves, reflecting the ACGB's confidence in Stafford-Clark and his collaborator, the veteran director Bill Gaskill (ACGB, 1973l, 43/43/9). *The Speakers* eventually became the first production of the Joint Stock theatre company, co-founded by Stafford-Clark, Aukin and Hare in 1974, and the role of Portable in the genesis of this landmark company should not be overlooked. On a less happy note, at the end of the 7 September meeting, Nick Barter 'reported that the [Portable Theatre] group were now entirely in the hands of their creditors' (ACGB, 1973k, 43/43/8).

The ACGB paper trail on Portable reaches its terminus with a letter, dated 3 March 1975, from Malcolm Griffiths to Peter Farrago, Assistant Drama Director. Farrago had invited Griffiths to sit on the Fringe and Experimental Drama Committee but the letter rejects the offer: 'to accept your invitation to work on it would be to accept the capitalist construct of culture which the Council is determined to shove down our throats'. Griffiths attacked the 'wholly insufficient funds' and the Council's perceived policy of divisiveness in its relegation of groups into numerous sub-categories ((ACGB, 1975, 43/43/13). With its forthright denunciation, this document encapsulates the frustration of many theatre artists with the whole apparatus of ACGB subsidy by the mid-1970s.

Artistic Policy and Key Productions

Portable practitioners sought a theatrical means of communicating the content of plays without too much aesthetic distraction. Implicit in this project was an attempt to foster a new set of dramatic conventions for the direct expression of content in such a way as to attract an audience hitherto unacquainted with theatre-going. In an interview given in 1975, Hare singles out the importance of content in the process of making theatre. Portable, he claims, embarked on a:

> deliberately and apparently shambolic style of presentation, where people simply lurched onto the stage and lurched off again, and it was impossible to make patterns. That is to say, we worked on a theatrical principle of forbidding any aesthetic at all. (Itzin and Trussler, 1975a, 112)

It is difficult to envision any piece of theatre emerging in an aesthetic vacuum (all cultural forms are shaped by aesthetic codes and conventions) but Hare's comments underline Portable's fierce investment in content-led drama. In a much later interview, given in 1990, Hare contextualizes Portable's deliberate stand against 'patterned' theatricality in a commentary that is worth quoting at length:

> We had lost faith in […] institutions, we thought that Britain's assumption of a non-existent world role was ludicrous, and we also thought that its economic vitality was so sapped that it wouldn't last long. So, we wanted to bundle into a van and go round the country performing short, nasty little plays which would alert an otherwise dormant population to this news. And by doing so we hoped to push aside the problem of aesthetics, which we took to be the curse of theatre. People were more interested in comparing the aesthetics of particular performances than they were in listening to the subject matter of plays. And we thought that if you pushed aesthetics out of the way by performing plays as crudely as possible […] you could get a response to what you were actually saying. (Gaston, 1993, 214)

In an interview from 1973, Brenton makes an identical observation that helps explain why the company lost traction as the fringe became more established:

> Portable was very conscious that […] you get a new kind of relationship, which in a way is straight to the content of the piece.

[…] Audiences started asking 'Why don't you act like the Freehold?'
In other words, they became theatrically literate and the discussions
afterwards stopped being about the plays' content and began to be
about their style. (Hammond, 1973, 26, 27)

In both Hare and Brenton's accounts, style is conceived as an obstruction
to the potential dialectic between a play's subject matter and its
audience. Indeed, there is evidence that Portable took every opportunity to assert content as the primary feature of its work. Publicity
flyers such as those for the staging of *Christie in Love* at the Brighton
Combination in December 1969 render, in rather abrupt terms, the
bare content of the play: 'Reginald John Halliday Christie killed at least
six women. First he killed them. Then he fucked them' (THM, 1969,
/273/4/2/7). The brusque language apes the headline-grabbing style of
tabloid newspapers, but also prepares the ground for the deliberately
'crude' theatricality of Portable performances. A more subtle example
of the priority given to content is the programme for the *Come Together*
Festival, a major event in the British counterculture, which was held at
the Royal Court Theatre in late 1970. Each of the visiting companies
and artists at this festival was allocated a one-page entry in the
programme but Portable's, unlike most others, focuses wholly on the
play and the playwright, and reveals nothing at all about the company
itself (THM, 1970c, 273/4/1/78/1). In the Royal Court programme for
What Happened to Blake?, the single piece of information provided
about the company is the almost wilfully vague 'Portable plays on open
floors all over the country' (THM, 1970b, 273/4/2/17).

Given Portable's reification of content, it seems anomalous that
commentators have attended so intently to what the company was
so keen to efface: namely, the issue of aesthetics. An early critic of
Portable, Ronald Hayman, attacked the company in 1970 for privi-
leging style over subject matter, for indulging shock for shock's sake:

In script and *mise-en-scène*, [Hare and Brenton] had to find means
of grabbing the public's attention and then holding it […] producing
deafening effects for their own sake and deceiving themselves about
their motives for wanting to shock. (Hayman, 1970, 93)

John Bull notes that productions offered 'a consistent vision of nihil-
istic disintegration, relying heavily on "uncool" dramatic shock tactics'
(Bull, 1984, 40), and Richard Boon argues that audiences were pushed
towards 'an increasingly sophisticated appreciation of the pieces as

experiments in *style*' (Boon, 1991, 144). To understand the apparent incongruity of Portable's emphatic focus on content and the attentiveness to style in critical reception, it is important to acknowledge that 'shambolic' content was itself systematized as an organizing principle of Portable stage aesthetics. In his illuminating essay on the endeavour to reconstruct past performances, theatre historian Robert K. Sarlós argues that '[s]tyle is comprehended in the bits of apparently disconnected information that filter down to us regarding the spatial arrangements, the color, or the texture of scenic elements' (Sarlós, 1989, 201). As important, he comments that '[o]nly through [...] milieu can style be perceived and identified' (Sarlós, 1989, 201). It is worth looking more closely, then, at Portable's affirmation of shambolic crudity as an antidote to the 'curse' of style in English theatre. Notice, for instance, the terms in which Brenton praises Hare's direction of his play *Fruit*:

> David Hare staged it deliberately against what is regarded as elegant theatre, which is what the piece needed, dirty linen. It had a scrubbed kind of staging which wasn't pleasing to the eye, only pleasing to a sense of the play, and in a way was very beautiful, so functional. (Hammond, 1973, 26)

If we follow Sarlós' injunction to examine what is 'filter[ed] down to us' through the material remains of theatrical performance, it becomes possible to apprehend the 'scrubbed' aesthetics of *Fruit* more fully. In advance of its tour of this play and *What Happened to Blake?*, Portable sent a letter of confirmation to the venues it was due to visit (THM, 1970a, 273/4/2/17). This document includes a section titled 'STAGING FRUIT' that outlines the company's basic requirements in respect of stage properties and furniture (notable among these is 'a completely useless T.V. set that is completely irrepearable [*sic*] & doesn't have to survive the performance') (THM, 1970a, 273/4/2/17). The briefing also sets out the ideal spatial configuration for the show:

> WORKING AREA. We like to stage it in an area roughly 30 or 40 foot wide at most with the audience mostly in front of us, but curling round the sides of the acting area also. All this area should be well lit, and it is an added blessing if the stage left side of the area roughly 15'x 9' can be lit by itself. A microphone is also a help where possible. (THM, 1970a, 273/4/2/17)

What is apparent here is the company's preference for intimate staging, with an audience on three sides, and the almost Brechtian clarity and minimalism of design: in other words, it is a spatial architecture designed to administer the fullest possible exposure to, and illumination of, content.

In accounting further for Portable's attachment to content-driven directness, it is helpful to turn to Sarlós' notion of 'milieu'. An important element within the countercultural activism of the late 1960s was the influence of the Situationists. Brenton visited France in 1969, shortly after the revolutionary events of the previous year, and was particularly inspired by his reading of Guy Debord's *The Society of the Spectacle* (1967) – a key Situationist text that sets out a complex critique of modern life as an alienating 'spectacle' of capitalist consumption. In the Situationist analysis, the citizen–spectator's condition is defined by passivity, disenchantment and lack of engagement with any kind of authentic experience: Debord portrays the spectator as a catatonic victim transfixed by the seductive illusions of commodities. The shambolic, crude, lurching, anti-theatre of Portable needs to be contextualized as precisely antagonistic to this 'milieu': especially under Brenton's influence, the company attempted to take up the gauntlet thrown down by Debord and develop an artistic practice, outside the rarefied enclaves of 'culture', which breaches the spectacle of public life. In this regard, it is notable that Brenton describes *Fruit* as 'a really great outburst of nihilism [...] one of the most beautiful and positive things you can see on a stage' (Boon, 1991, 57), a comment that resonates with Situationist verve.

In Brenton's playwriting, the Situationist desire to rip apart the 'spectacle' manifests in the collision of styles and astonishing bravura of set-piece scenes. In *Fruit*, the protagonist Paul destroys his television set by kicking it to pieces and then stamping on it (hence the company's request for 'a completely useless T.V. set'). What is more, the play concludes with a petrol bomb thrown against the theatre wall: the script ends with a memorable authorial aside bedded into the final stage directions, 'God knows how we're going to get away with that'. Christopher Innes is critical of this final scene, arguing that it reveals the 'confusion of aims' in the play as a whole:

> Brenton's intention is clearly to enable spectators to go home and make their own [petrol bombs] – yet the petrol bomb is thrown through the proscenium arch at the audience. The potential fellow revolutionaries are the ones assaulted. At the same time, the destructive properties of an actual explosion were trivialized as pyrotechnical effects, implying that violent revolution could be painlessly achieved. (Innes, 1992, 191)

The criticism here is rather misdirected: Innes conjures a mythical 'proscenium arch' when, in fact, the play toured to many non-traditional spaces lacking proscenium design. The corrective is more than pedantic since the proscenium implies an architectural separation of the audience from the action onstage, which, as Portable's briefing note makes clear, was not their intention (we might also recall the programme note for *Blake*: Portable 'plays on open floors all over the country'). Moreover, Innes condemns the production for using pyrotechnics that break the spell of illusion, yet the use of asides in the play, the jolting lighting and sound effects, and brittle dialogue create a heightened mode of performance far removed from seamless naturalism. Richard Boon offers a more precise summary of the meaning of *Fruit*'s explosive finale: 'in a very real sense, the play is not just about "disrupting the spectacle", it seeks to disrupt its own spectacle [...] the making and throwing of the bomb seems to smash through the accepted barrier between events on stage and the reality of the world of the audience' (Boon, 1991, 58). The intimacy of the performance space and the action of the play cohere in an attempt to electrify the spectators' engagement with content. This point carries additional force if we consider another aspect of the socio-political 'milieu' at the turn of the decade: the tour of *Fruit* coincided with the emergence of a group of young anarchists – the Angry Brigade – who, in 1970, launched a year-long bombing campaign that targeted banks, embassies and other public buildings. *Fruit* not only draws attention to the political despair driving young people into acts of violence but instantiates a theatrical corollary of Angry Brigade attempts to rupture the spectacle of British public life. Given that the Situationist critique of culture fed into the emergence of punk later in the 1970s, the television-smashing, 'God-knows-how-we're-going-to-get-away-with-that' theatricality of *Fruit* can be regarded, in retrospect, as prototypical punk gestures. Portable's concern from the outset to refute 'style' is, therefore, part of its self-presentation as a writer's theatre of rhetorical directness allied to (literally) explosive new content.

The group-written plays of 1971–2, *Lay By* and *England's Ireland*, mark the strategic shift of the company towards larger projects rooted in highly controversial subject matter; through these collaborations, Portable endeavoured to maximize its escape velocity from the fringe. The company submitted a draft plan to the ACGB outlining its aims for larger projects: 'to try and take new plays to large theatres for one-week runs; to tour with the plays that the resident managements feel at present they cannot risk economically [...] the pilot project, touring the country in July and August, is the *Northern Ireland Show*, which has been written by seven writers working together' (THM, n.d., 273/4/3/30/1). If we recall the information provided about the company in the Royal Court programme for *Blake* in 1970 – 'Portable plays on open floors all over the country' – it is instructive to compare this statement with that provided in the Royal Court programme for *England's Ireland* in 1972: 'The Company presenting *England's Ireland* is Portable Theatre, which presents new work to large audiences in big theatres, rather than confine it to the conventional "experimental" venues' (THM, 1972, 273/4/3/30/1). Portable's ambitious trajectory over two years, from 'open floors' to 'big theatres', is marked in these two comments.

Yet the practice of group writing also carried forward Portable's ambivalence about style. For Brenton, collaborative writing on this scale inhibited authorial indulgence: as he put it, 'personal writing of the worst order, what Snoo Wilson calls "personal farts", goes to the wall' (Hammond, 1973, 29). Hare's comments on the collaborative plays offer a similar perspective that, once again, puts the emphasis on content:

> As a writer, I know that most of the time people will say to you: 'Oh, I see, this is funnier than your last work. Oh, you're developing that point. Oh. It's more serious in tone. Oh, it's in that familiar David Hare way'. Now, to put seven names on a play is to put, in a way, no name on a play. Nobody can work out whose voice it is. And so the idea was that if you did that, then you would be forced to concentrate on the content of the play. (Gaston, 1993, 217)

The first of the group-written projects, *Lay By* (1971), was co-authored by Brenton, Hare, Wilson, Brian Clark, Trevor Griffiths, Stephen Poliakoff and Hugh Stoddart. The trigger for the play was a newspaper story about a court case on the subject of rape. *Lay By* offers a kaleidoscope of perspectives on the plight of Lesley, a struggling drug user and porn model, who accuses a van driver called Jack of raping her, with the complicity of a divorcee called Marge, after Lesley hitches a lift with them on the evening of 27 May 1970. The action retraces the events of this encounter while detailing Lesley's difficult life and background; it also offers a putative critique of the exploitation of women in the sex industry and criminal justice system. The imprint of Portable is evident in the confrontational relationship which the play establishes with its audience – at one point, a Pornographer '*comes forward and gives out hardcore photos of gang-bangs, sodomy, fellatio etc*' (Brenton et al., 1972,

16) – and in the juxtaposition of vaudevillian or cartoon elements with moments of unflinching naturalism. At the start of *Lay By*, two actors, one playing a ventriloquist's dummy, relate the facts of the case against the backdrop of a monochrome *'cut out drawing of a van'* (Brenton et al., 1972, 7); later in the play, Lesley injects herself with heroin in such realistic detail that this single action stretches over the course of a lengthy scene:

> *She gets out syringe, spoon. Melts up some heroin in a spoon over a match, draws it up into the syringe. She ties a rubber tube round her arm above the elbow and injects a vein. She finishes, tucks the tube into her trousers, exits as the speeches end.* (Brenton et al., 1972, 48)

The problematic sexual politics of the piece arises from its attempt to indict processes of female sexual objectification by reproducing, and thus fetishizing, such processes within the play's image structure. Early on, Lesley is subjected to a degrading form of interrogation by a private investigator called Barber: 'Did you consent to fellatio? Were you raped? Can you say anything about the contraceptive cream and how he used it? Who did you tell first?' (Brenton et al., 1972, 26). Barber proceeds to strap a dildo onto Jack and he instructs Lesley to fellate the dildo to show how events on that night unfolded. The casual violence in the play reaches an apotheosis in its final sequence, which takes place in a hospital: Lesley is brought in on a stretcher, apparently the victim of a road accident. Dick and Doug, two hospital orderlies, carry out a horrendously intrusive and violent assault on her body: they pump her legs back and forth, lift her off the stretcher, swing her and drop her on the floor. Lesley wakes up and they return her to the table but, when she tries to resist, they push her back; finally, as the lights begin to fade, Lesley dies. Dick and Doug then wash her body in a bucket of blood and lower her into a large bin; the naked and inexplicably dead bodies of Jack and Marge are then delivered and the two men perform exactly the same procedure on them. As they do so, they engage in idle philosophical speculations that echo the earnest musings in Chekhov's *Three Sisters*: 'I'm going to keep going because that's all I can do. And someday maybe we're all going to know what it's all about. Maybe not in my lifetime – Christ, Doug, I'm getting on – maybe not in my kids' or my kids' kids', but some day some man's goin' to tear the universe apart, say this is what it means' (Brenton et al., 1972, 67). As they talk, two churns of water are poured into the dustbin, fruit pips are shovelled into the mix and the confection is stirred by Doug with a broom handle. He 'dips his hand in the bin and brings it out with a big gob of jam on it' (Brenton et al., 1972, 71), which the two men proceed to eat. The final line of *Lay By* ostensibly refers to the preparation of this macabre human jam but stands as an ironic querying of the uneasy provocation extended by the play itself: 'You could have stirred it up a bit more' (Brenton et al., 1972, 71).

England's Ireland, written by Bicât, Brenton, Hare, Wilson, Clark, David Edgar and Francis Fuchs, is a more explicitly political drama that deals with the Irish Republican Army (IRA), the Orange Order, internment and the deeply contentious role of the British Army in Northern Ireland. The play unfolds as a series of extended sequences on divisive issues such as paramilitary violence woven together with factual data, documentary material and surreal theatrical atmospherics. The opening scene, for example, stages an IRA raid on an English engineering barracks in the mid-1950s, intercutting this with comments on expensive wine made by the five most recent Home Secretaries, from Henry Brooke to Reginald Maudling, who cluster onstage. The politicians' portentous deliberations on wine are counterpointed with a Voice giving background information on the unrest in Ulster from the mid-1960s, specifically the Civil Rights disruption in 1968.

The major sequence of Act One focuses on internment and dramatizes a Catholic man's treatment by the Royal Ulster Constabulary (RUC), an experience that is rendered analogous to the travails of Jesus (the man is called 'O'Christie') from the arrest at Gethsemane to his crucifixion and its aftermath. The scene begins with O'Christie praying for protection but he is interrupted by British soldiers who arraign him: they spit in his face, knock him down, slander his Catholic faith, strangle and feminize him, throw him into a truck and pass him, finally, '[i]nto the loving arms of the Royal Ulster Constabulary'. Following this, the soldiers lean O'Christie against a wall, torture him and put him before a fake firing squad: throughout this episode, the soldiers describe their actions in the present tense in a quick-fire mode of Brechtian distanciation. O'Christie is then 'crucified' on a rope ladder hanging from a helicopter, which is heard flying overhead: as the helicopter ascends, O'Christie screams ('A HUGE, INHUMAN, GODLIKE CRY'): 'My God My God why has thou forsaken me.' The conclusion of the scene is implacable in showing that the actions of the British army have galvanized recruits for Republican paramilitary organizations. An Angel appears and addresses the audience:

Angel Be not affrighted. Ye seek Jesus of Nazareth which was
crucified: he is risen. He's gone through the wire.
(*enter* O'Christie, *above, beret and dark glasses with a machine gun*)
O'CHRISTIE: Oh ye of little faith. I have come into my kingdom.
(*High above, he fires his machine gun into the audience.*)
Tape THE HYMN 'Christ the Lord is risen today Hallelujeh'.
(*blackout*).

In Act Two, the ghost of James Connolly invokes the spirit of the Easter
Rising of 1916 as inspiration for the present struggle; a man explains
how to make a 'gelignite stick with a thermal fuse' (recalling the finale
of *Fruit*) and claims that a bomb is about to detonate (it does so at the
end of the scene); another man carries his own guts in a bag as evidence
of a mistimed bomb attack: 'We would rather drown our children
in their mothers' blood, rape our grandmothers on Sundays and eat
them afterwards, tear down every monument and institution with
our bare hands so that nothing will remain of the hated British rule.'
The second half of the play also includes a scatological pastiche of the
Orange Order: seven men enter the stage dressed identically in bowler
hats with each carrying a golden bowl. The group stand in a line and
'Draw the water of the English Ascendancy' – in other words, they each
urinate into their bowl and, with backs turned to the audience, drink it.
One man picks up a trowel and runs into the ring of Orangemen which
conceals him. He defecates, hidden from view, and his excrement is
shovelled onto the floor with each man stamping on it in a scabrous
parody of Orange territoriality.

In total, eleven actors perform over sixty roles in *England's Ireland*
with music composed by Nick Bicât. In the closing moments of the
play, the company steps forward to address the audience with 'Stories
to tell our children'. Each of these 'stories' gives a snapshot emblem of
'the Troubles': Protestants marching up William Street to burn down
the cathedral; a British military lorry skidding and killing a six-year-
old boy. The actors then fire questions at the audience about current
political developments:

All The Whitelaw initiative argues that the sooner things return to
normal the better. But what is normal?
Is unemployment at 43% in Anderstown and Ballymurphy normal?
Is the Special Powers Act normal?
And is £11 per week a normal wage?

It is difficult to imagine a more arresting or provocative drama on the subject of Northern Ireland, which, in the course of its bitter critique of British complicity in violence, stages the machine gunning and then bombing of its audience. As noted earlier, *England's Ireland* had a deleterious impact on Portable's finances largely due to its contentious subject matter: as Brenton put it, '[w]e couldn't get into big spaces; they wouldn't have us. [...] 50-odd theatres refused to take it' (Hammond, 1973, 27).

Critical Reception

James Warrior, one of the actors who appeared in the tour of *Fruit* and *What Happened to Blake?*, recounts a memorable performance in a church hall in Aberdeen:

> The audience turned out to be entirely composed of non-conformist Presbyterian ministers and their wives. There were about 50 of them in all. They had come to see what they expected to be a reverential presentation of the great religious, visionary poet and painter, William Blake. David Hare, of course, was more interested in the fact that Blake used to shag his own sister [...] Worse was to come. (Bicât, 2007, 23)

At this point of the tour, rehearsals for *Blake* had not yet fully commenced and so Hare announced to his Aberdeen audience that *Fruit* would be performed instead. As Warrior recollects, '[the audience] watched the first half of the play in complete silence [...] when the interval came, not one single person came back' (Bicât, 2007, 23). Hare no doubt refers to this episode in his 1989 lecture on Raymond Williams, when he acknowledges ruefully that Portable '[performed for] bewildered audiences in church halls up and down the country' (Hare, 2005, 160).

The tour of *Fruit* and *Blake* is fairly well documented in the ACGB archives, and the papers give an interesting insight into audience attendance. The company had performed the previous week – that is, the first week of September 1970 – at the Traverse Theatre in Edinburgh. On the return form sent to the ACGB covering the period of their Edinburgh visit, Hare notes: '[f]ull every night w. inevitable pre-arranged comps' – the seating capacity at the venue was only ninety per night but 407 tickets were sold for the Edinburgh shows. According to the return form for the following week's excursion to Aberdeen (week ending 14 September), Portable performed *Fruit* once – this is the incident recounted in Warrior's commentary – though Hare's handwritten note claims there were '[a]pprox 150 in the audience', which is a significantly higher figure than Warrior's recollection of fifty; the rest of the week was committed to 'rehearsals', presumably of *Blake*. The weekly reports indicate that Portable performed to 'full houses' at Bretton, Sunderland, Bingley – where 270 tickets were sold for two showings of *Fruit* – and at the Royal Court in London; in addition, 150 tickets were sold at Stockwell College of Education, 160 at Rolle College in Exmouth, 175 at Leeds University and 200 at Eastbourne College. Hare notes, however, that there were '[b]ad houses at Skelton [and] Workington' (35 and 100 tickets, respectively) and audience turn-out at the Gulbenkian in Canterbury was a '[c]omplete disaster' – the company played five nights in Canterbury, with audience numbers ranging from twenty-nine to fifty-two per show in a venue that seated 300 (ACGB, 1970a, 43/43/11). It is unwise to extrapolate general conclusions from evidence pertaining to only one tour but – at least as far as *Fruit* and *Blake* is concerned – Portable sold the most tickets when it played at the colleges, universities and arts centres comprising the well-trodden fringe circuit.

Aberdeen's audience of thin-lipped Presbyterians may have been untypical but its negative reaction was not: reflecting back on the early stages of his career, Hare recalls that 'the days and the nights were alive with hatred directed at you' (Homden, 1995, 13). Theatre critics at the time chided the company for indulging, or at least offering cultural reinforcement to, the pervasive doomsaying that characterized British politics (and indeed other branches of culture including literary fiction) in the early 1970s: J. W. Lambert questioned the company's 'strong leaning towards the zestful projection of schizophrenia and sadism' (Lambert, 1974, 45), while Peter Ansorge regretted that the company was 'half in love with easeful crisis' (Ansorge, 1975, 20). Underlying these comments is an anxiety that Portable playwrights transgress the protocols of English realism by forsaking a coherent dramatic thesis in favour of paranoia and nihilism.

It is worth examining the reception of *Fruit* to gain a more nuanced understanding of critical reaction to Portable's work. Following on the heels of the 1970 General Election, which resulted in the surprise victory of the Conservative Prime Minister Edward Heath, the production of *Fruit* was often viewed as a comment on the contemporary political scene. Some spectators were particularly intrigued by the possible veracity of the play's content, specifically the link between the homosexual prime minister in the play and Heath. Brenton, however, felt that the frisson of homosexuality distracted audiences from the wider politics of his play: 'In the discussions after the play, they were often very angry indeed [...] It was just after the General Election, so all the questions were about "Is that true?"' (Hammond, 1973, 26). Michael Billington's review of *Fruit* for *Plays and Players*, which is at once curiously circumspect and insistent in its corre-lation of the play with current affairs, exemplifies Brenton's point: 'the Establishment figures who are [Brenton's] victims include a secretly homosexual prime minister and a drunken Socialist leader, neither of whom is hard to identify' (Billington, 1970, 49).

If British audiences tended to fall back on literalist interpretations, another strand of criticism shows that Portable's concern about 'style' was, at least in part, justified. When the company toured *Fruit* to the Netherlands, Brenton disapproved of the respectful response of some Dutch audiences to the play. Rather than treating his writing as 'dirty linen', they tended instead to valorize it as 'art': Brenton describes a performance in Amsterdam when an English businessman barracked the play as a travesty of politics; this outcry solicited the following response from Dutch spectators, a response that appears to have caused Brenton apoplexy: 'No, this rewrite of *Richard III* is a rich piece of English avant-garde' (Hammond, 1973, 27). The comment exemplifies the difficulties faced by Portable writers trying to resist processes of cultural and continental appropriation.

Conclusion

In spite of Portable's relatively brief existence, its legacy is enduring and significant. The company opened up new opportunities for writers and proved there was an audience for new work and touring. Portable's big collaborative shows *Lay By* and *England's Ireland* laid the foundations for Hare and Brenton's later co-written *Brassneck* (1973), arguably the first 'state of the nation' play of the 1970s, and *Pravda* (1985) (Bicât, 2007, 28). Indeed, Brenton's recent work at the Globe Theatre (*In Extremis* (2007) and *Anne Boleyn* (2010)) bears more than a trace of Portable inventiveness:

> The sense always came from the idea that, just as you could make a circle with a group of half-drunk students in the middle of a rock concert and set up a theatre for fifteen minutes, so in a theatre of

any size you can do anything [...] you can do it, you can *drum it up*. That sense has never left me, of what you could do. Of course, at the Globe, this is essential [...]. (Megson, 2012, 220)

As described earlier, Max Stafford-Clark sought to produce *The Speakers* with the Portable company: there is an oblique correspondence between Joint Stock's endeavour to engage audiences directly with documentary subject matter and Portable's aspiration to convey content to an audience unrestrained by ossified theatrical convention. Joint Stock's relationship with Portable personnel was cemented later in the 1970s when Hare wrote *Fanshen* (1975) for the company and then directed Bicât's first play, *Devil's Island*, for Joint Stock at the Royal Court in 1977. Many of Hare's subsequent plays have pursued a documentary or quasi-documentary format – including *The Permanent Way*, directed by Stafford-Clark in 2003 for Joint Stock's successor company, Out of Joint.

Portable's distinguished alumni of actors include Maurice Colbourne, Brian Croucher, Paul Freeman, William Hoyland, Sue Johnston and Colin McCormack. The company also had an influence on another major group that rose to prominence in the decade: two Portable actors, Colbourne and Neil Johnston, went on to work with Freehold. And, beyond the 1970s, the influence of Portable writers is felt in the work of the so-called 'In-Yer-Face' playwrights of the 1990s: as Graham Saunders observes, '[i]f one were to trace similarities in [Sarah] Kane's drama to a particular group of dramatists, it would not be found in her immediate contemporaries, but rather a group of playwrights who emerged in the late 1960s and early 1970s [...] Edward Bond, Peter Barnes, Howard Brenton and Howard Barker' (Saunders, 2002, 19).

In its endeavour to subordinate style to visceral 'throat-grabbing' provocation, Portable Theatre resurrected an almost Artaudian strain of modernist experimental performance shaped, crucially, by the 'milieu' of the 1960s counterculture and the literary predilections of the English theatre. As such, it remains one of the most important and pugnacious new writing companies in modern British theatre history.

List of Productions (All Productions Toured)

1968   *Inside Out* by Tony Bicât and David Hare. Directed by David Hare. Arts Lab, London.

1969   *Strindberg*, by David Hare (monologue performed by Maurice

Colbourne) in double bill with *Gentleman I*, by John Grillo
(monologue performed by Grillo). Arts Lab, London.

How Brophy Made Good by David Hare. Directed by Tony
Bicât and David Hare. Oval House.

Amerika by Franz Kafka. Adapted by Tony Bicât.

Purity by David Mowat. Directed by David Hare.

Christie in Love by Howard Brenton. Directed by David Hare.
Oval House.

1970   *Pericles, the Mean Knight* by Snoo Wilson (1970). Directed by
Snoo Wilson.

Device of Angels by Snoo Wilson.

The Creditors by August Strindberg. Directed by Snoo Wilson.

Fruit by Howard Brenton. Directed by David Hare.

What Happened to Blake? by David Hare. Directed by Snoo
Wilson.

1971   *The Maids* by Jean Genet. Directed by Tony Bicât.

Pignight by Snoo Wilson. Directed by Snoo Wilson.

Food and *Zonk* by John Grillo.

Plays for Rubber Go-Go Girls by Chris Wilkinson. Directed by
Malcolm Griffiths. The Other Pool, Edinburgh.

Blowjob by Snoo Wilson. Directed by David Hare. The Other
Pool, Edinburgh.

Lay By by Howard Brenton, Brian Clark, Trevor Griffiths,
David Hare, Stephen Poliakoff, Hugh Stoddart and Snoo
Wilson. Directed by Snoo Wilson.

1972   *When We Dead Awaken* by Henrik Ibsen.

England's Ireland by Tony Bicât, Howard Brenton, Brian Clark,
David Edgar, Francis Fuchs, David Hare and Snoo Wilson.
Directed by David Hare and Snoo Wilson.

Chapter 6

PIP SIMMONS THEATRE GROUP

Kate Dorney

Art to me is not about reaffirming people's values, but about
questioning the derivation of those values – Pip Simmons (in
Coveney, 1978b, 16)

The Pip Simmons Theatre Group (PSTG) is one of the many alternative theatre companies which burst on to the scene in the late
1960s, were acclaimed as fringe royalty and then faded away in a
blaze of indifference from funders and commentators alike. As well as
providing a history of the group, this chapter will attempt to understand how and why this happened. The initial enthusiasm with which
the company's work was greeted by alternative theatre critics has
been echoed more recently in Mike Pearson's 'imperfect archaeology'
of the Mickery Theatre in Amsterdam, where both Simmons and
Pearson received support and encouragement from Artistic Director
Ritsaert ten Cate (Pearson, 2011). Beyond Ansorge's report from the
frontline in *Disrupting the Spectacle* (1975), Theodore Shank's account
of *An Die Musik* (1975), Coveney's spirited celebration of the group
in *Plays and Players* (1978) and Pearson's vivid accounts in *Mickery:
An Imperfect Archaeology* (2011), there is a dearth of commentary
on the company and their work. Simmons and various incarnations
of the PSTG continued to make work into the late 1980s, but merit
only occasional references in most accounts of UK alternative theatre,
devised performance and the origins of site-specific and immersive
practice written during the past three decades. Curiously, many of
these use production stills from PSTG shows (particularly *Do It!*, *The
George Jackson Black and White Minstrel Show* and *An Die Musik*) to
illustrate their accounts, even when the group is only mentioned in
passing. Drawing on contemporary reviews and interviews, Pearson's
recollections, and material in the archives of the Arts Council of Great

Britain (ACGB) and English Stage Company, this chapter will give a flavour of the company's work, their methodological approach and offer some thoughts on why the company has disappeared from British theatre history's consciousness.

PSTG specialized in highly stylized and confrontational shows which demanded intense, disruptive and destabilizing elements of audience participation. Shouting 'come on you can't always be pigs' at audiences as an incitement to chase each other through the auditorium (Ansorge 1975, 33) was one shock tactic; assaulting audiences with fake tear gas and guns was another. Making them wear masks for a site-specific version of *The Masque of the Red Death* (1977) predates Punchdrunk's comparable use by more than thirty years, but doesn't warrant so much as a footnote in contemporary scholarship on participatory or immersive theatre or on Punchdrunk's work. Jospehine Machon's *(Syn)aesthetics: Redefining visceral performance* (2009) and *Immersive Theatres: Intimacy and Immediacy in Contemporary Performance* (2013) have nothing to say on PSTG. Nor does Gareth White's illuminating *Audience Participation in the Theatre* (2013), but it does point to one possible reason for PSTG's invisibility in that, as with most other work in the field, the historical background cited for participatory work is North American:

> Famous examples of audience participation are often notable events in the progress of experimental performance. The Living Theatre's *Paradise Now*; the Performance Group's *Dionysus in '69*; Yoko Ono's *Cut Piece*. (White, 2013, 7)

Neither White nor anyone else mentions the company that tried to sell you slaves, put a gun to your head or encouraged you to beat them up. Living Theatre's commitment to forging a new kind of relationship with the audience was pioneering but at the UK production of *Paradise Now*, the worst that could happen to a member of the audience was that they were confronted by nearly nude actors imploring them to relax (Lambert, 1969), had slogans shouted at them or felt compelled to join the 'love pile' of actors in g-strings 'lying in a heap and stroking each other gently' (Lewis 1969, n.p.). It might have been embarrassing or liberating but it was not the same as finding yourself: 'handcuffed at the interval to a blacked-up actor who followed me to the bar like a bowing and scraping human rebuke, answering "Yes, Massah" to everything I said' (Kustow, 2000, n.p.).

Dutch theatre critic Jac Heijer described the premiere of PSTG's

Black and White Minstrel Show (1972) as 'a slap on the head for every well-intentioned white person who is sympathetic to the plight of discriminated against black people' (Pearson, 2011, 196). *An Die Musik*, the group's meditation on the Holocaust and the Anne Frank industry, left audiences in stunned silence in 1975 and 2000 – a fitting response to a production that sought to remind an audience becoming used to the sanitization of the Holocaust by Hollywood of the horror of the camps and the Fascism that powered them. But silence does not seem a fitting critical legacy for a group that helped redefine the audience/performer dynamic, a contribution unacknowledged even in Holland, where the company's work enjoyed greater appreciation than in Britain:

> Simmons's influence – in his attitude to space and to audience – has, he [Max Arian] thinks, been lasting, though largely unacknowledged and often by hearsay or historical osmosis, as young contemporary practitioners in the Netherlands once again favour extreme styles of expression and the relocation of audience. (Pearson, 2011, 67)

There are a number of ways in which we can account for the silence around the PSTG. Firstly, Simmons' disillusionment with British theatre and the theatre press means that press coverage of the group and its work is modest, and published interviews with Simmons and co-founder Chris Jordan rare. Secondly, unlike, for example, Welfare State, no one from the group has gone on to have an academic career, nor do the group seem to have been taken up as a topic for academic study, so there is no book about PSTG or anything like *The Welfare State Handbook* to provide a way for the work to live beyond the memory of its production. Thirdly, unlike Foco Novo and CAST, there is no history of PSTG written by their founder. The result is that, with the exception of Pearson's recent work, analysis of PSTG work effectively stops in 1978 on their tenth anniversary. Catherine Itzin's influential *Stages in the Revolution* (1980) confines most of its commentary to work produced before 1973, and simply notes that *Woyzeck* happened but has nothing to say about the site-specific nature of the work. She concludes that the PSTG 'became less overtly political in their subject matter, further developing their own distinctive, very visual and surrealistic performance style' (Itzin, 1980, 75), a style that was going out of fashion in the 1980s when spectacle largely came to be associated with mega-musicals and was thus seen to be suspect.

Working Methods and Funding Structure

The PSTG received its first ACGB grant of £1100 in 1970, when they were classified as an experimental touring group. The following year the grant was increased to £7311 (Portable's was £8000), and the year after £8678. Along with many other ACGB-funded companies, from early on the PSTG struggled to work within the Council's funding and regulatory framework, and that struggle continued well beyond the chronological scope of this volume. The tension between the company and the Council reinforced Simmons' perception of the latter as uninterested and unsupportive, while the Council regarded him as a maverick whose work, though consistently imaginative, did not always reach their quality threshold.

Despite coming under the experimental rubric, PSTG's work was always considered to be drama rather than performance art by the ACGB. Assistant Drama Director Nick Barter saw it that way in 1971, as did Roland Miller in 1972 and in 1973. Jeff Nuttall described the PSTG as 'among the best of' the 'theatre people' (ex-theatre school, ex-university, literate, predominantly *literary* insofar as they are fixated on the delivery of words and the communication of either message or story' (Nuttall, 1973, 175). Thus, the company was at an advantage in that the Council understood their work and, by and large, thought it excellent: but at a disadvantage in that the classification of them as experimental touring placed as much emphasis on the touring as it did on the experimental, and therefore required the development of work that could tour intensively for between twenty-four and twenty-eight weeks each year. Having contributed to the establishment and support of a network of smaller venues across England including Arts Labs, studio and university theatres, the Council felt obliged to keep them provided with shows. As PSTG's composition changed and evolved new ways of working, the requirement to tour intensively became increasingly untenable. As early as the published script for *Superman* (1970), it was clear that the group prized a long development period, with Simmons noting in the Preface: 'It was not our intention to provide a working script but to suggest possibilities to a group with five months spare time' (Simmons, 1970, 89). Once in receipt of regular funding, spare time was a thing of the past. The company oscillated between adaptations of literary texts – for example, *Alice in Wonderland* (1971) and *Dracula* (1974) – and projects created by responding to the politics of the time, such as *Do It!* and *Towards a Nuclear Future* (1979). In the beginning, scripts were created and directed by Simmons, with music performed and written by Chris Jordan. As the group coalesced, they began to experiment with improvisation. Reflecting on *Alice*, Simmons noted that the show had been important because 'we started improvising freely. It was a kind of fantasy, a dramatic anarchy contained in the performance' (Anon, 1976, n.p.). By the end of the 1970s, the group had moved to the creation of environmental work and perfected what Clive Barker calls:

> a provocative dialectic between stage and auditorium and a marked lack of concern for dialectic between characters on the stage, which Simmons sees as characteristic of a dead literary theatre. In many cases the values of the audience are challenged directly by making it a protagonist in the play. (Barker, 1979, 18)

In interviews, Simmons and other members of the company proudly mention their lack of formal training and the diversity of their professional experience, all of which arguably helped in achieving a direct rapport with the audience, whereby the performers made no attempt to distance themselves or hide behind characterization. Simmons was fond of making analogies between their shows and the energy created at football matches and rock concerts and, like the performers at those events, the group derived its energy from directly acknowledging and interacting with its audience: whether the audience liked it or not. The chief tactic of the company's work, particularly in the early 1970s, was to force the audience to take sides. From the mid-1970s onwards there was a shift towards a more immersive aesthetic, in which the audience were cast as performers, or at least incorporated into the *mise en scène*, becoming guests at the masque in *Masque of the Red Death* (1977) for example.

History of the Company's Development

Phase one 1968–1972

> transglobal vibrations that accompanied the dreams and spontaneous naiveté of the drug culture. (Coveney, 1978b, 15)

Led by Simmons, a Jewish working-class East Ender who had dropped into the Hampstead Theatre School and dropped out again with a group of actors who 'had either left the school prematurely or been rejected by the conventional theatre' (Coveney, 1978a, n.p.), the group began work in 1968, emerging from and performing at Drury Lane Arts Lab. There is confusion over the ordering of the group's first shows. Barker cites *The Masque Routine* adapted from George Kaiser's *The Philanthropist* (Barker, 1979, 19); *Time Out* has it as *The Meaning Behind the Word*, based on the word-game texts of Jean Tardieu (*Time Out* 1971, 63). According to its 1971 'Guide to Underground Theatre', the company 'still distrust words but have evolved their own style of music and movement to put across strong simple stories with the maximum directness and impact' (*Time Out*, 1971, 63). Their early aesthetic had something in common with the Yippie movement later examined in their show *Do It!* (1971). They engaged in apparently ludicrous and aggressive acts, but for a serious purpose. The directness wasn't just limited to their performance style: legend has it that when they were invited by Eugenio Barba to attend a seminar on English Fringe Groups at the Odin Teatret in Denmark in 1971 they were surprised to be asked to 'discuss their work' and instead fired water pistols at each other, shouting 'discuss this' (Dudeck, 2013, 84). Simmons described their warm-up 'as playing football for hours' (Ansorge, 1972, 22), but this apparently flippant approach co-existed alongside a fierce critique of society:

> A typical evening in the company of the Pip Simmons group combined the energy of a football match or pop concert with a decisive attack on mainstream liberal values. The shows were steeped in cynicism, excitement, despair and good music. (Ansorge, 1975, 30)

The 'good music' was composed and performed by Chris Jordan, co-founder and long-term PSTG member whose commitment to whipping up a frenzy was equal to, and indeed, outlasted Simmons'. In 1978, he was reported to be 'openly dubious about the recent tendency to suppress group hysteria in favour of more direct methods of addressing the audience' (Coveney, 1978b, 18). This remark, made the year before the company's *Towards a Nuclear Future*, which did indeed directly address the audience in a debate about nuclear energy, nevertheless reinforces the idea that for ten years the PSTG aimed to create group hysteria among the audience – an exhausting experience for faithful audiences and longstanding performers.

After the closure of the Arts Lab in 1969, the company toured their work around the UK's newly created fringe circuit including the Edinburgh Traverse, Birmingham Arts Lab, Chapter Arts, Cardiff and the London venues Oval House, Royal Court Upstairs and the Open Space Theatre. But if the Drury Lane Arts Lab was the PSTG's cradle, then the Mickery in Amsterdam was their nursery, a place where they learned, experimented and retreated to when the exigencies of the British arts funding system proved too much (for too little). It was their portal to the European arts and performance circuit that provided stimulation and opportunities for creative collaborations, as well as better wages and facilities. It also set an example that UK venues could not follow.

Superman, first performed at the Mickery on 11 May 1970, combined covers of early rock 'n' roll hits (including 'Teenager in Love' and 'Money (that's What I Want)') alongside original music composed by Jordan and performed by a live band under his direction. According to a PSTG policy document, the Mickery performances,

> were massacred by the press and at the same time marked a turning point for the group. Their disastrous reception in Holland only served to accentuate their conviction about their work and led to the victory of *Superman* in England, the first real hit of their repertoire. (ACGB, 1978i, 34/123/1)

Written and directed by Simmons, the play's scenario is drawn from 'Rock 'n' Roll Superman', an episode in DC Comics' *Superman's Pal; Jimmy Olsen* (1958), in which Jimmy reluctantly agrees to impersonate his superstar cousin Jerry 'Rock 'N' R'Olsen' at gigs, after the star contracts chicken pox. Jimmy learns the moves and mimes to a pre-recorded vocal which has a profound effect on Superman who can't stop dancing when Jimmy performs, because his watch (normally used to transmit messages to Superman in secret) broadcasts the music to him at high intensity. Superman becomes a laughing stock when his uncontrollable dancing stops him from preventing a crime perpetrated right in front of him. Simmons used the comic strip as a basis for an examination of the excitement that rock 'n' roll originally generated and the way it, and other forms of popular entertainment, became a means of zombiefying the masses and manufacturing consensus. The two-dimensional cartoon characters are joined by a cast of vacuous television critics, fans, groupies and a chorus who both narrate the action and play the various mobs.

Unusually, there is a published script for the show bearing a dedication to President Nixon and musician Screamin' Jay Hawkins, 'whose efforts to recapture the early 50s do not pass unnoticed', it was published in Methuen's *New Short Plays 3* alongside works by Howard Barker, Donald Howarth and Robert Grillo (Simmons, 1970, 89). Reviews and witness accounts testify to the visceral nature of the piece, but the script provides an opportunity to examine the detail of the work. Simmons' introductory note acknowledges the source text and a range of addition material 'plagiarised and borrowed unscrupulously' (notably from Nietzsche), but also instructs the reader/performer that 'the style of playing implied by comic strip should be applied at all points so the final product has as its basis a carefully explained sequence of events involving a collection of colourful, but in every case, two dimensional characters' (Simmons, 1970, 90) – like the breathless appreciation of Olsen's fans who greet every statement with 'wow'. The script also suggests something of the mad physicality and frequent nudity of the signature PSTG style. Superman does keep-fit exercises; actors impersonate a car, and in one scene, a groupie trying to seduce Superman strips while the Chorus perform unspecified 'masturbatory rituals' which though,

> related in their vocal rhythms to the GROUPIE's stripping, should appear to ignore her and should be directed outward at the audience [...] it is both a meditation between the GROUPIE and the audience and also a comment on the audience as they watch the 'exciting' dance before them: it should deride the audience's experience by physically mirroring their 'mental processes. (Simmons, 1970, 100)

It is conceivable that this scene is also a satire on *Paradise Now*'s 'love pile' and the opportunities it offered the audience for voyeurism. Pearson recalls the show's impact in Edinburgh:

> Jimmy Olsen's 'Rock and Roll Son' picking up messages from the superhero with a large papier-mâché head through his electric guitar. Cartoon style acting, rock music, theatrical irreverence – we were amazed, won over! (Pearson, 2011, 72)

The next show, *Do It! Scenarios from the Revolution*, was adapted by Simmons from Yippie activist and founder Jerry Rubin's book of the same name. 'Yippie' was the term coined in the late 1960s to describe members of the Youth International Party, a loose association of US anarchists with a background in street theatre who both engaged in direct action and staged interventions and events aimed at disrupting political processes and also encouraged a questioning of the way in which the US was governed. Their activities included an attempt to levitate the Pentagon and an intervention that brought the New York Stock Exchange to a halt when activists started tossing money in the air. But their most famous intervention came during the Democratic

Party Convention of 1968, when they staged a series of events and a 'Festival of Life' in Chicago which 'burlesqued the whole process of electoral politics' including proposing their own Presidential candidate, a 145lb pig called Pigasus the Immortal, as an alternative to Richard Nixon (Hoffman, quoted in Bottoms, 2006, 303). Their activities at the conference ended in widely televised violent confrontations with riot police. Commissioned by the Traverse Theatre and 'based on an idea by Mike Rudman' (English Stage Company, 1971d), *Do It!* first explored the storming of the Democratic Convention, and then the trials that followed. Like *Superman*, the acting style was two-dimensional: the characters wore large papier-mâché heads and were accompanied by a rock score composed by Jordan. Unlike *Superman*, the music was heavier, the story was based on real events and some of the characters were based on real people. Given their predilection for confrontation, one might have expected the PSTG to sympathize with the aims and methods of the Yippies, but their desire to question kneejerk liberal attitudes remained intact. Simmons told critic Ronald Hayman that the group wanted to explore how an audience would react:

> [I]f they were provoked in the way the kids threw shit at the pigs (=police). So our actors ran through the audience in a very obscene way. We were asking 'If you'd been a guard at the Pentagon, what would you have done?' (Hayman, 1973, 214)

Critic John Peter had a visceral reaction to the show:

> The show was about the Vietnam War and was written and created by the actors. I was not there to review it. In the first act, something which was not actually tear gas, but smelt and looked like it, was released. It rather upset me because I had been on the receiving end of a tear gas attack in Budapest in 1956.[1] I still think it's infantile to do this to a theatre audience. This was in the Young Vic and I was sitting in a gangway seat. In the second half, at one point, actors came down the gangways with toy revolvers in their hands. The actor who came down my gangway put a pistol against my head. I asked him repeatedly to remove it. He said 'Why, what's the matter? What's your problem?' I said, 'My problem is that I don't like this'. He insisted, so I finally got up and threw him down the gangway.
>
> I don't think this is a funny story but it gives you a good picture of what used to be the naïve side of British political theatre. It's done by grown-up adolescents who probably never suffered serious hardship

and almost certainly were never at the receiving end of political violence. (Peter, quoted in Stefanova, 2013, 135)

Peter's reaction may have surprised the actor in question, but it was at least a genuine reaction to the situation he found himself in. Michael Rudman's recollection of the energy and excitement generated by the show, or at least one member of it who 'burned an American flag because Pip Simmons suggested it. I'm sorry Mr Consul, sir. Of course we'll buy you a new one. I had no idea they burn so easily' (Rudman, 1973, 128), feels more contrived at this distance, but both accounts give a flavour of the intense level of commitment demanded of the audience at a PSTG show. Contemporary immersive theatre or experiential theatre is rarely so confrontational or political – audiences are encouraged to become part of the show but are rarely physically abused without their consent.[2]

Do It! opened at the Edinburgh Traverse in February and appeared at the Theatre Upstairs at the Royal Court at the invitation of director Roger Croucher who went to some lengths to get the show programmed and the press in. The PSTG had a long list of press they didn't want invited, including *The Stage, Daily Mirror, Daily Express, Financial Times, Daily Mail, Daily Sketch, Sun* and *Daily Telegraph*. They were keen for the 'underground press we like' to be invited and Croucher chased the Court's press office to make sure they turned up. In a memo to the Royal Court press office he wrote:

> I'm very worried that only two press tickets have gone to the Underground press for the first night of PIP SIMMONS. Since this is an electrifying and sensational show, I feel it is wrong for it not to widely seen. I do not understand why, as agreed, the Underground Press isn't there in force for the first night. (English Stage Company Archive, 1971b)

The word must have got out, for a few days later Croucher notes that 'we are admitting new members at a rate of about 30 a night for this show' (English Stage Company Archive, 1971c), while a letter to PS's administrator confirms that 'DO IT was seen by a total of 1,460 people, 105 on comps' (English Stage Company Archive, 1971a). These numbers would become increasingly important in the Arts Council's assessments of whether touring groups were fulfilling the terms of their funding.

The show received mixed reviews, with Irving Wardle describing it as: 'an exercise in crude power, aiming to slug the audience into a state where they no longer recognise the basic dishonesty of the stage–spectator relationship' (Wardle, 1971). Nicholas de Jongh provided a more balanced account in the *Guardian*, noting the cumulative effect of music, lights and actors to create a 'prolonged climax of confusion which compels the ears, confuses the eyes and gives a total impression of being in the midst of a revolution' but also commenting on 'stretches of relaxation and sprawling inconsequence which should be replaced by sharper material' (de Jongh, 1971). The next show certainly delivered in that regard.

The George Jackson Black and White Minstrel Show (1972) had its premiere at the Mickery. This time the two-dimensional quality of the cartoon-style playing matched the two-dimensionality of the minstrel stereotype then familiar to British viewers from BBC's television's *Black and White Minstrel Show*.[3] There had also been a highly successful stage version and it is typical of Simmons' confrontational attitude to mass entertainment that he should expose the questionable racial politics of the light entertainment version by hi-jacking its supposedly inoffensive mask for an investigation of the struggle for equality. George Jackson was a black American who had learned revolutionary politics in prison and joined the Black Panthers. Initially jailed for a year, his sentence had been extended indefinitely and he had recently been killed trying to escape from prison (having taken hostage and killed several guards and white prisoners). The programme note for the Royal Court run gives a sober history of the minstrel tradition up to the television version. It ends:

> Our version of the Black and White Minstrel Show is an attempt to replace the show in a modern context. How far it remains pertinent remains only a question of whether the jokes are funny. (English Stage Company Archive, 1972a)

A veteran of PSTG shows would know the jokes were never just funny. *George Jackson* began with a white slave owner's white supremacist monologue, a speech so offensive that Jac Heijer declared that 'the awful racialist jokes and repartee' were so excruciating 'I was somewhat relieved I couldn't follow the English text' (English Stage Company, 1972b), although he also noted that 'the show was equally unkind to Black Panthers' (Pearson, 2011, 197). The racist jokes were not the only offensive element; they were compounded by the white supremacist addressing the audience as if they too were racists and slave owners. He then held a slave auction and it was at this point that actors ran into the

audience begging to be bought. In the interval, members who participated in the auction then had to decide how to treat their new chattel:
would they use them or liberate them? Were they pigs or Yippies? In
the second half, 'Jackson' appeared in boxing gloves and fought a white
gorilla before being handcuffed, tied up in a sack and suspended above
the floor for his great escape. The audience watched the sack sway
and throb as the hero fought his way out of his handcuffs and shot
a fist through the sack giving the Black Panther salute. 'Immediately
shots were fired and inside, the body stretched in its death spasm. The
show was over' (Ansorge, 1975, 34) and the audience were once again
complicit in an atrocity they had failed to halt. Those who had come
seeking comfort about their own liberal position were disabused, and
indeed abused.

Phase Two 1973–6: Residency at Toneelraad

In 1973, exhausted by years of continuous touring in an attempt to
clock-up the weeks required to fulfil the conditions of their Arts Council
grant, Simmons disbanded the company following the Council's refusal
to grant his request for a minimal grant to support them during a
period of reflection and reassessment. It was a request that simultaneously demonstrated how their exposure to the Mickery – and European
– funding structures had provided them with a new perspective on
how state subsidy could work, while also showing their lack of understanding, or inability to accept, the workings of the British system. Even
the Council's Experimental Projects Committee (1969–73), which had
just been dissolved, could not have agreed to such a radical propo-
sition: the Drama department only funded work, not the headspace
for creating it. To put his frustration into perspective, Simmons was
by no means the only person to be frustrated by ACGB's parameters:
Peter Brook had recently decamped to Paris after failing to persuade
the Arts Council and other funders to provide him with the resources
to experiment without the guarantee of a show. His International
Centre for Theatre Research was funded by the French government,
the Gulbenkian and Ford Foundations and charitable foundations.
Simmons' more modest respite was offered by a residency funded by
Toneelraad Rotterdam, the city's arts board that provided him with time,
space and resources to reflect and reassess his direction. Simmons was
required to produce two shows on the theme of horror, and the result
was *Dracula* (1974) and *An Die Musik* (1975): one typifying the group's
interest in adapting literary texts; the other working from the image

of Jewish orchestras in concentration camps to produce a meditation on the horrors of the Holocaust. Simmons created a new company, Children of the Night, for the residency, working again with Ben Bazell, Sheila Burnett and Chris Jordan and welcoming Peter Oliver, formerly the director of Oval House and husband of the PSTG's administrator Joan, into the group along with Rod Beddall and Emil Wolk – both of whom would become long-term PSTG members. In an interview during the restaging of *An Die Musik* in 2000, Simmons described the show's impetus as stemming from their feeling that, having made *Dracula*, they needed to produce something 'a bit more profound' (Simmons, 2000). Discussions with the Dutch about the Second World War led to the decision to make a show about the Holocaust, offering an alternative view to the nascent Anne Frank industry, building on the aftermath of the Broadway musical and recently released film, and the corresponding growth in tourism around her house (Simmons, 2000). The group, consisting of Bazell, Beddall, Burnett, Peter Jonfield, Jordan, Roderic Lee, Oliver, Woulk and Rowan Wylie, worked with Dutch dramaturg Ruud Engelander to devise the show. In 2000 Simmons, described the process in typically vague terms:

> I worked with a group of actors, some of whom I'd worked with before. Chris Jordan, the composer of the music who I'd worked with since 1968, by that time five or six years, some of them were actually rock and roll musicians, painters, photographers. Two or three of them were actors, one was a mime [artist] who worked with Etienne Decroux and we sat down and talked about how to make the show. It was very much a, how do you call it, an evolved piece, a piece that was made with the actors through two basic images. The first half was an operetta set against music and the second half a concentration camp concert. So, as I say, over eight weeks, ten weeks that we worked on the show it became what it was and a lot of that time was just spent developing a performance as professionally as we could. (Simmons, 2000)

Simmons was always keen to stress the eclectic nature of the performers' backgrounds and his role in simply facilitating them to do whatever they thought appropriate. In 1979, he suggested that the variety of backgrounds made for a tighter bond between them and allowed them to think beyond received ideas of theatre and performance: 'our area of professional expertise is on the whole only what's existed between us. There is a different kind of imagination' (Barker, 1979, 20). The collective imagination that produced the two shows saw a decisive shift in the group's style from cartoon-style terror (the last vestiges of which appeared in *Dracula*, whether intentionally or not) to a more sombre mode.

Theodore Shank described all the elements of the show in detail in *The Drama Review* in 1975, so a brief description will suffice here. It begins with an SS Officer, played by Oliver, introducing the operetta 'The Dream of Anne Frank'. Appropriately enough, the dream is more like a nightmare. An exhausted band, reminiscent of the Jewish orchestras forced to play in concentration camps, provides a mournful accompaniment to the scene of a Jewish family performing a bleak parody of the Sabbath meal. The SS officer 'serves' them in an increasingly menacing way, presenting them with bones, human hair and a live dove and, finally, bread, but only after demanding, and receiving, their jewellery and other valuable possessions. The father is shot and the daughter reads aloud from Anne Frank's diary as they change into concentration camp uniform. In the second half, the son and SS officer have exchanged places and the son now presides over the torture and humiliation of the Jews accompanied by Schubert's 'An Die Musik' and Liszt. The prisoners are forced to ridicule their race: telling racist jokes; exposing a circumcised penis and laughing at it; they are humiliated and beaten and finally stripped naked and gassed while playing Beethoven's 'Ode to Joy'. The show forced audiences to confront the horrors of the Holocaust and to reflect on their capacity for collaboration and complicity in similar situations, regardless of race. At the Mickery the audience were engulfed in smoke along with the actors and then filed out in silence, aware, according to Simmons, that they had witnessed 'a very solemn and necessary ritual', a reclaiming of Anne Frank, and the Nazi atrocities it stood for, from sentimentality (Ford, 1975, 27) and an attempt to come to terms with the Jews' apparently passive acceptance of their fate. Twenty-five years after he first saw the performance, Michael Kustow remembered the piece as,

> furious and confrontational. Its first part was an operetta, the Dream of Anne Frank: the mythifying of Anne Frank into the heroine of a Broadway tear-jerker, was another target of Simmons's ruthless stripping of emotional alibis. (Kustow, 2000, n.p.)

Ford's review quotes Simmons, suggesting the show should only be performed in an occupied country. However, not every occupied country received it with the stunned silence of the Mickery audience: on at least one occasion in Paris, the company encountered audience participation of a very different kind when the stage was stormed by what director Ian Brown,

> presumed was an anti-Fascist group who thought the play was a glorification of fascism. There were about 15 of them and they had some quite violent arguments onstage with the management before the audience was ushered out.' (Brown, 2011, n.p.)

The actors, according to Brown, were as shocked and frightened as the audience. Coveney mentions a Maoist stage invasion in Paris which may be the same event – in his report, the protest was sparked by the fact that the show failed to take account of their point of view. British reviews report walk-outs, by no means unusual for PSTG shows, but critics praised the show for its fury and power, with several speculating on Simmons' own controlled fury at easy attempts to console liberal conscience.

Reflecting on the show in 2000 while touring a new version with the Jewish State Theatre of Bucharest, Simmons told Kustow:

> We were outside the theatre, and against society. I was a lunatic at the time, angry about everything. *An Die Musik* was a shout against hippie glibness, the self-congratulatory, complacent mood of the times. (Kustow, 2000, n.p.)

Anger against 'hippie glibness' had been the recurring theme of the group's early shows beyond the Arts Lab: *Superman, Do It* and *The George Jackson Black and White Minstrel Show* all pour scorn on kneejerk liberal sympathy and go to extreme lengths to discourage the audience from sympathizing with the characters on stage (regardless of what happens to them) and to destabilize the audience's complacency.

An Die Musik and *Dracula* toured the UK and Europe, along with an adaptation of Dostoevsky's *The Dream of a Ridiculous Man* (1976), which they created with ACGB funding. *Dream*, described as 'an extremely slick musical account of a man saved on the brink of suicide by a vision of Paradise, represented as an island of naked, guitar-strumming freaks' (Coveney, 1978b, 15) was well-received in Europe and Britain while *An Die Musik*, which had its British premiere at the ICA, was respectfully reviewed. *Dracula* appeared on the main stage at the Royal Court, prompting an angry letter of protest to the Arts Council from 'a theatregoer of 50 years' experience' (ACGB, 1976a, 34/123/1) and indifferent reviews from the critics. It was misplaced at the Royal Court but popular at the Glasgow Citizens Theatre, playing to 3,590 people in a week, while *Dream* was seen by 2,721 the following week (ACGB, 1976b, 34/123/1). In total, *Dream* and *An Die Musik* clocked up more than 500 performances across Europe (Grant, 1978); increasingly, and from the Arts Council's point of view problematically, PSTG were a major force on the European scene.

Phase Three 1977–9: Experiential Environments

Although *An Die Musik* and *Dream* answered the PSTG's desire to develop new ways of working, the pressure of touring continued to take its toll on the company's creative energy, and three long-standing members left at the end of the tour. The work 'had no base, no theatrical possibilities beyond what it could contain in the back of a van' (ACGB, 1978i, 34/123/2), and the one-night stand mentality of touring made it hard for the company to develop relationships with local audiences. The 'hit-and-run' nature of the touring model was equally unsatisfactory for many of the Arts Centres and other venues hosting companies like PSTG and the project model developed by them in association with partner venues the Mickery, Chapter Arts in Cardiff, Birmingham Arts Lab and University Theatre Newcastle was as much a solution to their creative frustrations as to the PSTG's. Mik Flood, artistic director of Chapter, who worked with the group on *Woyzeck* (1977) and *We* (1978), stressed this when he wrote to the Welsh Arts Council to request extra funds for the project. He begins the letter outlining Chapter's ambition to nurture work that can make use of its spaces and the opportunities they offer, but acknowledges that he must also host 'already prepared "product"' from ACGB's touring grid, and that the grid is satisfactory for such product:

> It is far however from satisfactory for the sort of theatre where the work process and environment for presentation is integral to the final product. For these specialised areas of theatre a few days in one place is simply not enough for the company to draw from the specific nature of the environment, nor does it give enough time to develop the audience necessary to make the work relevant. (ACGB, 1977b, 34/123/1)

The project phase saw the PSTG effectively abandon touring in favour of residencies where they developed '"environments" within which a play can be created which relates not only to the audience and to the actors but to the space available and the immediate "society" which populates the space' (Grant, 1978, n.p.). The first of these was *The Masque of the Red Death* created in and with the Mickery. The show was conceived as 'a party of death held by a group of masked white-shifted aristocrats': the story was divided into seven sections spread over the building in which the audience confronted and were 'confronted by the experience on offer' (Grant, 1978, n.p.). The group used Edgar Allan Poe's text as a way of exploring contemporary fascination with Poe and the Gothic imagination, referencing several of his works and their recurring themes of death, decay and premature burial. Ten Cate had the idea of using all of the Mickery's public spaces for the masque, so the show began in the foyer with Poe lying on a hospital bed attended by the Shadow and ended with him being buried alive in the garden, before reappearing in the Bovenzaal (upper auditorium) as a speaking corpse, and then disappearing, leaving the audience staring at a glass cage filled with rats gnawing a decomposing corpse.

The critics were divided: some were enchanted by the promenade style; others thought it lacked clarity. Heijer received the play as Simmons' extended meditation on theatre and theatre artists: a mix of provocation, pastiche and spectacle:

> When during his Last Supper following an exalted speech about art, Poe magically pulls the skinned rabbit out of his hat, Simmons is really talking about himself and the sort of avant-garde theatre he has been making for ten years. (ACGB, 1977a, 34/123/1)

Did Simmons feel he was being buried alive under the weight of the alternative theatre scene's expectations? Did he identify with Poe, constantly obliged to produce another piece of dark and disturbing work to keep the pennies coming in? Perhaps, but the period during which the piece was worked up was also creatively nourishing, establishing the idea of environmental performance and moving his own brand of spectacle to another level. Even by the standards of the Mickery, a theatre that had pneumatically powered hover-seating units to aid flexibility, *Masque* moved things to a different level of design, production and audience engagement. Designers Frans de la Haye and Dick Johnson echoed Poe's motif of glass panes, conceiving of a rectangle of transparent screens that moved up and down, sometimes confining the audience within the rectangle, at other times leaving them watching the action from the outside. They were cast as 'privileged guests' dressed in white capes, caps and masks, a move which Mike Pearson credits as an inspiration for dressing the audience in ponchos in *The Persians* (Pearson, 2011, 189).

Woyzeck (1977), co-produced with Chapter Arts, developed the idea of site-specificity further still, a former school providing the 'set-starved' Simmons with a giant canvas on which to plot the action. Each of the play's locations was staged in a different part of the building: with the help of Chapter's thirty or so staff, twenty postgraduate students from the Sherman theatre and performers from the resident companies, the audience was moved from the barbershop to a tavern, then to a fairground, a lab, a barracks room and finally to a lake built out in the courtyard which was set alight at the climax of the play. It was an all-encompassing immersive performance. The audience could buy drinks in the tavern, hot chestnuts during the execution and dirty postcards from Chapter's publicity officer (Barker, 1979, 18).

Woyzeck was well reviewed, even if some critics struggled with the idea of site-specific performance: In the *Daily Telegraph* Eric Shorter noted that the 'focus seems to be a fundamental problem as we follow the players about. At whom or what should we look? […] but the evening remains an unforgettable experiment along the lines already furnished some years ago in Paris by such people as Ariane Mnouchkine and Bob Wilson' (ACGB, 1977f, 34/123/1). In the ACGB's Pip Simmons file is a photocopy of a programme essay called 'Watching Out for Woyzeck', also by Shorter, in which he evinces slightly more enthusiasm for the project. He describes the company as 'the only British avant-garde company that matters', but grumbles at 'trudging around a building as if it were a museum or an art gallery, waiting for the next stage (literally) in an exercise to prove that an audience kept on its feet won't be able to fall asleep', but ends curiously upbeat:

> Messing about with dead authors in such a self-indulgent way may have its tiresome aspects. Standing in the rain is one of them. Plodding round a former school in search of the next scene is another. But when it is all over you are made to wonder if theatre of this order (or disorder) isn't more to the point in its sense of adventure than nine shows out of every conventional ten – the point being that the evening experiments not just with Buchner but with our theatrical responses. (ACGB, 1978a, 34/123/1)

In *Plays and Players*, Chris Stuart stressed the extent to which all the elements had come together:

> This *Woyzeck* lays down its own terms of reference, houses them in scenes of breathtaking verisimilitude and invites its packed, gaping audience to partake of the ensuing melee and to profit from the enveloping vitality. (Stuart, 1977, 29)

This major critical success was soured by a huge row with the Arts Council caused by the change in the PSTG's working methods and their failure to keep their funders informed of it. Classified as a touring company, the group was required to take its shows around the touring grid in England and Scotland, not create static work in Holland and Wales. From files in the ACGB archive, it seems that Drama Officer Peter Mair only realized they hadn't performed in England in October, after a probably accidental tip-off from David Gothard, programmer at Riverside Studios, who wrote a rave review of *Masque* to Drama Director John Faulkner, as a ringing endorsement of the PSTG's new direction, urging that someone from ACGB go and see it. The show only had a week to run and no one from the Council made it. Instead, Mair wrote to the company noting they had not yet,

> played in this country at all [...] A grant of £32,000 and a guarantee against loss of £4000 was offered on the company's submission of mounting four productions this year and playing them for between 24 and 28 weeks. I am concerned that there are now only 22 weeks left in this financial year and that you clearly cannot therefore fulfil the amount of weeks that you originally said would be possible. (ACGB, 1977c, 34/123/1)

There was also a letter from Finance Director Anthony Field reminding them that,

> one of the Council's Conditions of Financial Assistance is that no overseas touring or touring in Scotland Wales [sic] may take place without the prior agreement of the Council, and on the strict understanding that no part of the Council's subsidy shall be used abroad. (ACGB, 1977d, 34/123/1)

Thus began a new wave of grievance.

In a long letter and *de facto* policy statement, the company apologized for not having kept the Council informed and provided accounts reassuring it that no subsidy has been spent on foreign work. The letter lays out with extraordinary clarity the company's desire to continue experimenting in how and what they develop rather than churning out 'product'. As the dispute continues, the group's patience begins to wear thin (as does the Arts Council's), and although they continue to apologize for not having informed the Arts Council in advance of their Mickery residence, they also point out with some asperity that *An Die Musik* and *Dracula* toured the UK, having cost the Council nothing in development or rehearsal costs. Supporters weighed in to attest to the quality of *Woyzeck*, including Drama Officer Ruth Marks who found it 'enormously impressive' (ACGB,1977g, 34/123/1), and John Cuming, who declared that: '*Woyzeck* struck me as one of the most enjoyable and moving pieces of theatre I've seen from a British company for some years', adding that, as someone 'working in an arts centre where various touring companies arrived, performed their show, and disappeared along the M4' he was sympathetic to the PSTG and Chapter's desire to develop a new model (ACGB, 1977e, 34/123/1).

After much debate, exchanging of letters and outlining of plans up to March 1979, the Council immediately reduced PSTG's grant from £36,000 with a guarantee against loss of £4,000, to £23,000 with the same amount guaranteed against loss. They also advanced them some of next year's grant so that *Woyzeck*, which, in the end, played to 810 people out of a possible 840, could go ahead. The consequence of this was a cashflow crisis for the company and a threat to the Arts Council that they would disband. A temporary truce was called; the company outlined plans for a collaboration with Sheffield Crucible, Warwick Arts Centre, Glasgow Citz, Gardner Arts Centre and Birmingham New Arts Lab (which never happened and was replaced with *We*), and a collaborative endeavour with Riverside Studios that was initially pitched as a version of Brecht's *Rise and Fall of the City of Mahagonny*, but ended up being a production of *The Tempest*. In February, in view of the company having only completed fifteen weeks of touring, the Arts Council reduced their grant to £18,500 and informed them that all monies paid above that would be regarded as an advance on their grant for 1978/9. The letter came a few weeks after their long suffering administrator Joan Oliver (wife of Peter) had written to Mair reporting that the Citz and Crucible had pulled out of the proposed collaboration, adding:

It is a bit disheartening to be in our present financial position as the creative side of the work is proving to be very exciting and of great value, not only to ourselves either. I find it personally depressing to have to come in every day dreading that another unthought of bill might arrive or that one of the group has reached the stage of needing props or a costume. Even the thought of a set of guitar strings sets me screaming. (ACGB, 1978b, 34/123/1)

To offset the loss of funds, the PSTG developed a touring version of *Woyzeck* that went to the Traverse in Edinburgh in 1978 and won an admiring show report from Drama Officer Jonathan Lamede, who was shortly to become their contact at the Arts Council. The ironic contrast between the Council staff's appreciation of the company's work and corporate attitude to their operation is just one of the contradictions of the way in which Drama funding worked. In their 1978 submission to the Council, the PSTG planned to research and rehearse three new shows for twenty-one weeks before touring them for twenty-eight – fourteen round the UK, eight in London and six abroad. On that basis they were allocated £42,000 of subsidy. In May, they projected ninety-five performances of the show that became *We* up to 31 December, which Lamede estimated as seventeen weeks' work in England and five in Scotland and Wales.

The Tempest, billed as their tenth anniversary show, was originally planned as a grand collaboration between the company and Riverside Studios, where Simmons would be able to use the space to serve the production as he had with *Masque* and *Woyzeck*, but ultimately he ended up with an end-on stage that severely curtailed his ambitions. In Barker's opinion this, along with the Royal Court's presentation of *Dracula*, were 'major disasters for the company. [...] anyone who saw either of these two productions only at these venues will have very little idea of their power when performed in a sympathetic environment' (Barker, 1979, 20). Unfortunately, the fact that it was in London also meant it was a show reasonably well attended by Arts Council personnel, including Finance Director Anthony Field. An internal memo from Field to Drama Director John Faulkner reads:

I was surprised to note that *The Tempest* was playing to '80–90% of capacity'.* I took a number of Professors from the University of British Columbia with me (having dissuaded them from seeing the National or the RSC!) and they sat in a house no more than one-fifth full (and hated it).

The asterisk refers down to a hand-written scribble 'they were exaggerating a little – it actually fell to 60% over the run' (ACGB, 1978e, 34/123/1). Anton Gill enjoyed it: 'I liked it, despite its lack of depth. It was adventurous and it was stimulating and it didn't last too long. What else can one ask?' (ACGB, 1978f, 34/123/2). An anonymous hand has written in red pen to the effect that it had very good and very bad bits but they had no real idea what it was for. According to their submission to the Arts Council entitled 'Our Proposals for Next Season 1978', its aim was:

> to seek to explain our own standpoint through Shakespeare's dark island, attempting to avoid the fairy-like misinterpretation of previous productions, and considering the play in terms of what it actually discusses – political corruption, rape, murder, crude colonialism – a science fiction projection of the renaissance where all the absurdities of the world are contained within one image of shifting landscapes and loyalties. (ACGB, 1978i, 34/123/2)

A show report from Lamede confirms 'a packed though not overly enthusiastic audience' and identifies its strengths as: 'evident in the ability to jettison the received notions of conventional theatre and inject one or two lively new insights into a well-known text'. However, he criticizes 'the company's conforming to their own well-tried formulas' and 'their evident lack of full commitment (in terms of energy and creative percipience) to this particular show' (ACGB, 1978e, 34/123/2). Field has added a note underneath agreeing with Lamede that it was ultimately disappointing, but adding 'I still think Pip and his company have a lot to offer and contribute to British theatre'. It is difficult to see how the company could have reconciled this praise with the systematic cutting of their grant, but it seems unlikely that knowing about it could have made relations any worse. Reporting back on a PSTG board meeting, Lamede noted that the company were upset that so few people from the Council had seen the show: 'they see this as symptomatic of a continuing mystery about "the mechanics of assessment" [..] and that the Arts Council, or the Drama Department, should be continually on hand or on the sidelines patting them on the back and saying "great, great" to all the good ideas that come up' (ACGB, 1978d, 34/123/2). The Council were just as touchy: the company had used every press opportunity to explain their new policy and the Council's decision to reduce their grant as a result. When Michael Coveney's article celebrating ten years of the company was published in *Plays and Players*, someone from the Arts Council went through and underlined every criticism of them. They also exercised their right to reply and wrote back to the magazine rebutting his claims, noting acidly: 'Far from not understanding what Pip is trying to do, we fully appreciate it – now that we know' (ACGB, 1978g, 34/123/2).

If *The Tempest* had been a disappointment, *We* was a success in artistic and critical terms. A four-way collaboration with Chapter Arts in Cardiff, Wales, the Mickery, Birmingham Arts Lab and Newcastle University Theatre, the show was an adaptation of Yevgeny Zamyatin's 1921 dystopian novel, the inspiration for George Orwell's *1984*. The project evolved from the company's attempts to find a creative way to continue their project-based work while fulfilling their touring obligations. Several of the co-producers were interested in exploring a science fiction project, and the group embarked on a period of research, reading works of science fiction. Simmons found *We*, liked its use of direct address (the novel is written as a diary) and it became the basis for the show. *We* is set 2000 years in the future when war has reduced Earth's population to ten million people living within the Green Wall – a hermetically sealed environment. The population (One State) live according to mathematical principles governing every aspect of behaviour, from how often they have sex to how often to chew their food. The narrator is seduced by a woman working for a resistance movement who ultimately betrays the revolutionary cause, leading to her execution. The narrator undergoes surgery to 'achieve perfection and happiness' and the final image of the performance is 'a unity of chanting metronomes swaying from side to side, wreathed in beatific smiles, as the lights fade' (Barker, 1979, 24). It was the company's most technically ambitious show to date, featuring banks of televisions massed at various points relaying messages to the audience, laser beams and kaleidoscopes, while the white one-piece costumes combined to create the antiseptic and regulated environment of One State. It did good business at all the partner venues and received enthusiastic Show Reports from Arts Council assessors. Ironically, Lamede thought it was the slickest show they had done in terms of accomplished performance. Echoing One World's obsession with mathematical perfection, the group were copying Meyerhold's theory of Biomechanics which they had seen illustrated in *The Drama Review* and which Simmons described as 'moronically unbelievable' (Barker, 1979, 25). This is a good example of the tension between the Arts Council standards and the PSTG's desire to examine dramatic cliché. Their decision to adopt Biomechanics as a demonstration of cliché was taken literally as an improvement in their performance standards. Unlike the group and the co-producers, however, Lamede did not discern a new way of working, adding at the end of his show report that,

> I think that once again Pip has fallen prey to his own conditioned reflexes, nowadays, whatever the subject, it seems to evoke the same responses for the group. The results are fairly predictable. Granted that Pip knows this and wants to break out of it, is the answer simply more money and time? No amount of laboratory work and additional resources can break such a situation; the impetus must surely come from something else. Naturally, Pip chooses the material that suits his outlook and uses it in his way. Perhaps he has to make a radical break into new kinds of material. But which, and how, and where? (ACGB, 1978h, 34/123/1)

The question was never resolved. Despite the critical and financial success of *We*, the company was still dogged by cash-flow issues, and once again Ritsaert ten Cate came to the rescue, first lending the company 10,000 guilders and then inviting them to the Mickery for a month-long residency that would provide the company with much needed funds. As soon as the PSTG fulfilled their touring obliga-tions for the Arts Council, they left for a European tour. The tour was followed by the Mickery residency which produced *Towards a Nuclear Future (1979)*, a departure for the company in that its aim was to put the case for and against nuclear energy to encourage the Dutch to make an informed decision about it. Instead of being confrontational, the arguments were rehearsed by two characters, one pro-nuclear, one anti, with Sheila Burnett mingling with the audience as someone 'undecided', and switching sides. In a fitting metaphor for the company's cyclical and troubled relationship with Britain and its funding structures,

> the performance ends as it began, people are sitting in the dark 'in the dark ages', coldly in their blankets, asking themselves how to find a way out, but 'no one will turn on the light'. (Tan and Schoenmakers, 1984, 485)

The light never fully came on in the UK for the company and by the end of the 1980s Simmons, who described himself as feeling 'very much a passé avant-gardist [...] decided to go and live in the woods in Sweden' because 'what I could get together here, was not worth staying for' (Simmons, 2000). Simmons' politics, working methods and personality were less palatable to the instrumentalist approach the Arts Council was required to adopt in the 1980s and 1990s than they had been in the 1970s and the files evidence his struggle to get work funded at the level requested even when collaborating with the likes of LIFT (London International Festival of Theatre) and Arts Admin on a project in the dilapidated London docks (*Crossing the Water*, 1987). He, and the company, were by no means alone in being frustrated by Arts Council policy, neither were they the only company to disband – the Arts Council's history is depressingly full of them.

Conclusion

In 1975 Simmons argued: 'the English are very good at absorbing everything. I mean, they've absorbed us' (Ansorge, 1975, 75). His observation suggests perhaps the most compelling factor in the group's disappearance from the record: their work, which started out as formally and politically radical, was absorbed into the general noise surrounding the beginning of the alternative theatre scene, lumped in with Living Theatre and everything that came after during the 'freak out' of the late 1960s and early 1970s described with typical overstatement by alternative theatre guru Charles Marowitz:

> The freak out was the order of the day, and anyone not advocating its extravagance and excess was in danger of being considered the sort of person who snuck into matinees of Noël Coward revivals or the more galumphing works of Brian Rix.[4] (Marowitz, 1973, 158)

It is hard to imagine Simmons sneaking into a Coward or Rix production, unless it was to arrange a stage invasion. The humiliations inflicted on Rix's characters in plays such as *Reluctant Heroes* and *Dry Rot* had nothing on the lengths the PSTG would go to prick the pomposity of bourgeois conventions and progressive principles treasured by the liberal audiences who supported them but, rather like Rix, to date their legacy has been to be remembered as caricature – reduced to a dim recollection of nudity and smoke.

The Shows

This chronology is drawn from a variety of sources, the most comprehensive of which appears in *Theatre Quarterly* 35, alongside Clive Barker's 'Pip Simmons in Residence'.

1968
The Masque Routine, adapted from *The Protagonist* by Georg Kaiser
Sand by Murray Mednik
Conversation Sinfonietta by Jean Tardieu
The Hangman's Sacrifice by Obaldia
The Enquiry Office by Jean Tardieu
The Meaning Behind the Word, based on the works of Jean Tardieu
Underground Lover by Jean Tardieu

1969
The Pardoner's Tale

1970
Superman
The Hunting of the Snark, adapted from Lewis Caroll
Do It!

1971
Alice in Wonderland, adapted from Lewis Carroll

1972
The George Jackson Black and White Minstrel Show

1974
Dracula, adapted from Bram Stoker (a co-production with Rotterdam Toneelraad)

1975
An Die Musik (a co-production with Rotterdam Toneelraad)

1976
Dream of a Ridiculous Man, adapted from Dostoevsky

1977
Masque of the Red Death, adapted from Edgar Allan Poe (a co-production with the Mickery Theatre Amsterdam)
Woyzeck, adapted from Georg Büchner

1978
The Tempest, adapted from Shakespeare
We (a co-production with Birmingham Arts Lab, Chapter, the Mickery and Newcastle University Theatre)

1979
Towards a Nuclear Future (co-production with the Mickery)

Notes

1   Peter was born in Hungary and came to Britain as a refugee in 1956.
2   I am thinking here of work like Blast Theory's *Kidnap* (1998) in which people volunteered to experience being kidnapped and two of them were snatched and held in an undisclosed location for forty-eight hours and their incarceration was live streamed (http://www.blasttheory.co.uk/projects/kidnap/), or Punchdrunk's immersive theatre shows in which audiences choose their level of interaction with the actors and the action.
3   This long-running light entertainment show featured a group of minstrels – white men in black face – singing a combination of minstrel songs and music hall numbers interspersed by comic sketches and dancing.
4   Noël Coward (1899–1973), author, director and actor of a string of highly successful light comedies from the 1920s to 1940s. Brian Rix (1924), author, director and producer who produced and acted in a string of farces at the Whitehall and Garrick Theatres during the 1950s and 1960s.

Chapter 7

WELFARE STATE INTERNATIONAL

Gillian Whiteley

Introduction

The Welfare State exists to create images in the most unexpected places: in streets, on housing estates, on recreation grounds. A labyrinth made out of junk is sprayed white by the fire brigade with white foam and turns into a frozen winter palace. A burning coracle is thrown into a grey canal. In the drabbest of circumstances, the Welfare State plays out the role of permanent Lords of Misrule. (Albert Hunt quoted in Craig, 1980, 25)

Given its longevity alone, it would be difficult to overstate Welfare State International's significance in relation to the histories of performance art: alternative, experimental and applied theatre and participative forms of practice. Between 1968 and 2006, this collective of artists, writers, musicians, performers and engineers pioneered site-specific multimedia theatre and processional street performance, and developed new models of community art. Rooted in the radical countercultural contexts of the 1960s, their ambitious events combined large-scale spectacle and popular theatre, attracting international acclaim and directly spawning a wide range of other experimental theatre companies and performance groups. As Baz Kershaw remarked, in relation to events such as the iconic *Parliament in Flames* (1976), first staged in Burnley with an audience of over 10,000 people, 'no-one else was producing carnivalesque agit prop on this scale' (Kershaw, 1992, 212).

By the 1980s, consolidated in the publication of Tony Coult and Baz Kershaw's co-authored book *Engineers of the Imagination, The Welfare State Handbook* (Coult and Kershaw, 1983), a DIY guide to basic techniques aimed at sharing their ethos, skills and practices with others, they had developed new forms and prototypes of vernacular arts and theatre. Celebratory theatre, secular rites of passage, such as 'naming ceremonies', and lantern festivals were all signature Welfare State practices that were widely adopted by other companies and arts organizations through the 1990s and beyond. After encountering the Lantern Sea Ceremony in Northern Japan in 1982, Welfare State devised the first Lantern Festival at their base in Ulverston in 1983 and this became an annual community-based event (Fox, 2002, 75–6) spawning many other similar festivals across the UK. Since 2006, John Fox and Sue Gill have continued to develop alternative rites and rituals through, for example, the expansion of a series of practical handbooks, the *Dead Good Guides*. Welfare State's valedictory show, *Longline, the Carnival Opera* (2006), was performed in a circus tent at Low Mill Business Park, Ulverston. The multimedia performance synthesized a range of recurrent themes, narratives and images from forty years' work, while investigating the contemporary political economies and ecological issues around Morecambe Bay. Recurrent Welfare State themes were interwoven with current reflections on the plight of migrant workers, the environmental consequences of nuclear power, the role of local arms and pharmaceutical industries, the impact of local tourism and the effects of global warming. Combining the key elements of *spectacle* and *participation*, *Longline* involved over five hundred performers and included many familiar Welfare State components – community choirs, acrobats, puppetry, live music and a processional lantern finale with fireworks – inviting reflection on its own history back to its origins as a radical itinerant company in 1968.

The rapid expansion of all forms of alternative theatre in the 1970s has been well documented. However, it is worth emphasizing that, besides this being one of their most creative and productive periods, Welfare State was particularly astute at capitalizing on the 'subsidy revolution' in the 1970s. Under Thatcherite policies, the 'market-orientated' 1980s witnessed the demise of many political theatre groups and, as Bim Mason indicated in 1992, the 'virtual disappearance of such activities outdoors' (Mason, 1992, 3). However, while many other companies folded, Welfare State demonstrated a remarkable capacity to adapt; as Mason noted, through that difficult period, the company continued to flourish but it also managed to maintain artistic integrity at the same time as retaining their 'political edge' (Mason, 1992, 24).

Spectacle and Participation: Rethinking Critical Contexts

Mason's association of their work with 'the political' raises the question of how Welfare State has been positioned critically and historically. Since the 1970s, there has been an intense critical debate around definitions and discourses related to 'alternative', 'popular', 'fringe', 'political', 'avant-garde', 'experimental' and 'community' theatre. The longevity of the company, its ever-changing personnel and the interdisciplinary and eclectic range of its activities have presented critics and commentators with multiple problems. Previous cultural, performance and theatre histories have situated Welfare State in various categories – often depending on the orientation of the writer. For example, in an important early survey of performance art and happenings published in 1974, the artist Adrian Henri described Welfare State, first, as an 'art-orientated pop group' and, latterly, as 'anarchic street theatre'(Henri, 1974, 118–19); whereas, writing in the context of 'experimental' and 'fringe' theatre in 1975, theatre critic Peter Ansorge referred to them as one of the most highly regarded groups in 'the underground', providing the 'most spectacular instance' of what he termed 'environmental theatre' (Ansorge, 1975, 41–2). Reviewing the company's twenty-year history in 1988, Michael White made other associations.

> Welfare State International's own twenty-year history as an outdoor travelling theatre may be read, in part, as a reclamation of public space as the rightful milieu and meaningful heritage of popular culture. Moreover, it is space in which to learn and create collectively an indigenous social poetry of a high order within a precise, functional context. It need in no way be parochial and purist, rather it is an eclectic receptive theatre, minimally verbal yet able to assimilate and articulate divergent cultural viewpoints through startling patterns of rich, evocative imagery. (White, 1988, 195)

White could not have foreseen that Welfare State would continue for yet another twenty years, but his comments provide a useful starting point for this re-examination. He also noted that, as 'indigenous animateurs', they 'consistently explored the territory *between* theatrical product and applied anthropology' (White, 1988, 196). Kershaw later commented that by the early 1980s, Welfare State's work was predicated on an 'iconoclastic radical ideology', shaped by a deep opposition to the overproduction and consumerism of the developed world (Kershaw, 1992, 209). Calling them 'primitive socialists', he wrote of their visionary, anarchic approach and 'their claims for the healing power of creativity and the place of "poetry" in a healthy culture' (Kershaw, 1992, 212). Pertinently, in the same text, Kershaw declared 'Welfare State was (and is) unique, impossible to pin down in any of the existing categories' (Kershaw, 1992, 212).

In particular then, the 'hybrid' and 'in between' nature of Welfare State's creative output has perpetually posed difficulties for scholars attempting to position their practice. In this current re-evaluation, I want to dismiss the pressure to place Welfare State in one camp or another and to problematize some of the established critical binaries, as the familiar categories of alternative, oppositional, political, avant-garde, and so on, are not mutually exclusive. In her recent book on 'applied theatre', Nicola Shaughnessy argues this very point, declaring that this creative tension is a fallacy, a false dichotomy, and that such work is, rather, an interplay of formal experiment, *affect* and social-political effect (Shaughnessy, 2012, 14). Her approach provides the most fruitful framework for a re-assessment of Welfare State. Her analysis of applied theatre draws on the vogue for what has been described within contemporary art practice as collaborative, interactive, immersive and participatory practice (Shaughnessy, 2012, 28, 188). Including them as key historical pioneers of 'applied theatre', Shaughnessy places the company in the '*hinterland between* populist community carnival and exclusive experimental theatre' (Shaughnessy, 2012, 22–3; my emphasis). Furthermore, it is significant that Shaughnessy gives primacy to the discourse of *participation* for her analysis of their work.

The history of participatory art practices has been dogged by binaries, tensions and conflicts: equality versus quality, participation versus spectacle and art versus real life. As Claire Bishop, key theorist of the contemporary resurgence of participative art forms, has commented,

> the dominant narrative of the history of socially engaged, partici-
> patory art across the twentieth century is one in which the activation
> of the audience is positioned *against* its mythic counterpart, passive
> spectatorial consumption. (Bishop, 2012, 36)

Welfare State crossed all those boundaries and dichotomies, generating what Norman Denzin has termed '*active* spectatorship' (Denzin in Shaughnessy, 2012, 12). Bishop (2012) charts the historical shifts in re-imagining 'participative identity', from conceptualizing it as 'the crowd' through to current notions of audience as 'co-producers'. Welfare State pioneered co-production, as it was one of their key strategies. Particularly pertinent for this study, Shaughnessy's book addresses 'situated spaces between making and performance' and the contemporary shift from artist to spectator/participant. While any assumption of 'togetherness' must, of course, be problematized, drawing on Denzin's model and Shaughnessy's concept of 'socially engaged art praxis' (Shaughnessy, 2012, 7), I will argue that, through spectacle, collaboration and participation, Welfare State transformed communities into subjects not objects and that their practices demonstrated the possibility of 'emancipating the spectator' for action and even, potentially, for activism. Furthermore, in the new millennium, with the widespread coming together of carnival, festivity, activism and protest in the public sphere (Patrick, 2011) there has never been a better moment to reconsider Welfare State's significance, influence and legacies.

History of the Company's Development

Origins and Formation

> [I]n many ways, Welfare State are the most daring of the Alternative Theatre companies because they are in the business of yoking together the aesthetic and visceral nature of theatre with a developing political analysis and at the same time of making that powerful conjunction available to people who have no interest in theatres or plays. (Coult, 1976, 20)

Welfare State was formed at the end of 1968, that momentous year of 'revolutionary' uprisings which has since acquired mythic status in popular memory. There is no doubt that the collective of artists, performers, musicians and assorted associates was a product of the radical political contexts and countercultural activities of the late 1960s. More specifically though, it emerged from the vibrant alternative cultural scene within and around Yorkshire, primarily under the creative impetus of one particular individual: Welfare State's future long-term artistic director, John Fox, then working at Bradford College of Art. Significantly, Fox did not have a background in theatre. A few weeks before Fox was due to take up a post as Liberal Studies tutor at Bradford, the *Yorkshire Post* carried a special feature on him in their series 'The Young Creators'. Fox was interviewed by Judith Hann at the remote farm in Coneysthorpe, near York, where he lived with his young family; Hann emphasized his versatility in the article. After studying Philosophy, Politics and Economics at Oxford and doing a teaching diploma, he spent four years studying Fine Art under Richard Hamilton and Victor Pasmore at Newcastle University, but promptly abandoned what looked to have been a promising career as a painter.

For Fox, the 'fine art scene' was dominated by elitism, pretentiousness and commodification and, having been involved in local happenings and festivals, he was motivated instead to create 'a more popular art that communicated with ordinary people' (Fox in Hann, undated).

At Bradford and around Yorkshire, there were plenty of like-minded people with experimental cultural practices and approaches. In 1980, Robin Thornber, looking back at that time, argued that the great deal of creative energy being released in and around West Yorkshire was 'based on a nexus between Albert Hunt, Jeff Nuttall and John and Sue Fox's Welfare State' (Craig, 1980, 173–4). Indeed, the Northern, provincial, often non-metropolitan character of this scene was frequently highlighted in various contemporary accounts: for example, Adrian Henri noted that 'the most exciting mixed-media work in England is today being produced by young artists in Yorkshire' (Henri, 1974, 118–19). The circle around the Ardens – John Arden and Margaretta D'Arcy – had been involved in a range of radical performances and alternative community-based activities since the early 1960s, such as the 'Festival of Anarchy', which they had staged at Kirbymoorside, in 1963. Furthermore, the art colleges at Bradford and Leeds provided key contexts for the founding and future expansion of Welfare State. Jeff Nuttall, artist, performer and founder of the People Show, also worked at Bradford. Fox and Nuttall then both taught art at Leeds Polytechnic alongside a plethora of visiting performance artists and poets such as Stuart Brisley, Bruce Lacey and Adrian Henri (see Whiteley, 2011–12).

Initially, Bradford provided the opportunity for Fox to work with Albert Hunt, the radical educationalist and pioneer of experimental and participatory forms of theatre. Greatly influenced by the radical educator A. S. Neill, in May 1965 Hunt joined the staff at Bradford, where he had free rein and the full support of the Principal to set up an experimental anti-authoritarian project-based 'liberal studies' programme. Before moving to the post at Bradford, Hunt had initiated an experimental youth theatre while lecturing at Shrewsbury. In 1967, with the Ardens as tutors, Fox helped Hunt stage *St Petersburg 1917/Bradford 1967: An October Carnival*, a happening-style re-enactment of the Russian Revolution on the streets of Bradford and involving over 300 students from all over Yorkshire (Hunt, 1976; Hunt interview, *Unfinished Histories* project). By the time Fox initiated Welfare State, he was also working in different configurations with various other artists and musicians, such as Cosmic Circus, formed with Mike Westbrook who later also worked extensively with that company. Cosmic Circus events included *Earthrise*, a multimedia exploration of outer space that later formed the basis of a large-scale Welfare State event to herald the first day of spring in March 1970. In the mid-1970s, artist and singer Kate Barnard (who was later to become Westbrook's wife) painted the designs on the travelling trucks and caravans at the Heasandford base at Burnley.

Above all, in the early days, Welfare State was not an isolated group by any means. In the 1970s, it expanded the range of experimental UK-based performance practices, but, more pertinently, it emerged from a rich seam of Northern activity, much of it based around the 'Yorkshire Vortex' (see Nuttall, 1979, 68–9), which included groups such as the Yorkshire Gnomes, Al Beach's John Bull Puncture Repair Kit and Jeff Nuttall's People Show. Many of these individuals and groups collaborated or shared platforms at the end of the 1960s and early 1970s. For example, in November 1970, the John Bull Puncture Repair Kit and The Welfare State presented 'SCAB, a dazzling entertainment in memoriam of Sandie Shaw' at the AUE Union Club in Halifax. A leaflet publicizing the event, promoted by Amnesty International, noted 'a joint production for "Prisoner of Conscience" week which this year highlights the fate of Trade Unionists imprisoned for their views' (WSTC, 1970, 14/2).

Throughout the key decade of the 1970s, the activities of Welfare State can be viewed in distinct phases: the first few years were spent developing forms of nomadic and processional-style street theatre and spontaneous happenings; from 1973 to 1979 they worked from a settled encampment at Burnley; the turn of the decade and 1980s marked a move northwards and the development of participative work and deep immersion within the community in and around the industrial town of Barrow, culminating later in the building of Lanternhouse at nearby Ulverston in the 1990s.

Nomadic Street Theatre and Impromptu Performance, 1968–72

The Welfare State is in many ways the most remarkable mind-blowing group of all. It contains many elements, art school, rock culture, music, pagan ritual – all fusing into a poetic Dionysiac vision of man liberated by revolution. (Hammond, 1973; WSTC 12/1)

The dozen or so artists, teachers and others working around Bradford brought together by John Fox in December 1968 shared a radical outlook and a common commitment to take art into the streets

– early members included Roger Coleman, Roy Dodds, Jane Durrant, Alison Fell, Sue Gill, Steve Gumbley, Nigel Leach, Lizzie Lockhart, Ken McBurney, Rick Parker, Jamie Proud, Rosemary Timms, Chris Timms and Geoff Walker. Beyond that, the initial artistic strategies and aesthetic vision of Welfare State had a range of roots, amalgamating popular folk cultures and esoteric avant-garde art forms. Early happening-style events bore the inspiration of Fluxus, Joseph Beuys and John Cage. Equally, the radical political ethos of international groups such as el Teatro Campesino, San Francisco Mime Troupe and the US-based Bread and Puppet Theatre were important influences.

Aside from these international references, a key characteristic was the way in which Welfare State drew on British (or more particularly English) folk traditions and contemporary popular culture. Looking back, John Fox perceptively described them as operating 'somewhere between populist performance art and applied anthropology' (Fox, 2006). Mummery, for example, was particularly important. Referring to it as the 'last vestiges of English folk culture', Bim Mason outlines the basic scenarios of mummery as challenge, conflict, death and life renewal, all of which were key elements in various Welfare State performances (Mason, 1992, 118). Often improvising and expanding on a basis of rehearsed material, their performances, happenings, events and assembled environments incorporated staple elements from circus, pantomime, puppetry, music hall, festival and carnival, as well as earlier historical cultural forms like court masque and pageantry.

Aptly, Welfare State's first major event, *Heaven and Hell* (December 1968), commissioned by Lancaster University, was a day-long tribute to William Blake at the Ashton Memorial, involving over a hundred performers, a dancing bear and puppets. Street events and performances followed, often involving acrobats, wrestlers, musicians, fire-eaters and dancers. A number of spontaneous events and impromptu processions, such as those through Leeds, were largely unrecorded, captured in the occasional photograph, but mainly in the memories of local participants and art students.

Many early events were akin to happenings transposed into medieval times. In a three-week project, in 1970, at the Beaford Centre in Devon – billed as ' medieval happenings, circus acts, etc' with cabaret and sounds by Mike Westbrook – rubbish was scrounged from tips and local firms to create a Horror Maze and a Geodesic Dome (WSTC, series 14/2) Another typical event in March 1970, heralding the first day of Spring, included music provided by the Westbrook band, a team of racing cyclists and fencers, climbers, weightlifters, army radio operators, a model aircraft display, scaffolds of towers, giant projected images, thirty drum majorettes and a fancy dress pageant. With a pre-punk penchant for horror, in May of the same year, a Welfare State event entitled *Heptonstall* was described in the company's publicity as 'gothic entertainment',

> a simple family circus is invaded by the dead from the Doomsday village of Heptonstall [...] strongmen, dancers, unicyclist and harlequin of life do battle with the King of the Dead, primitive ghouls, and Wild Electronic noise, films, slides and giant puppets. (WSTC, 1970, 14/2)

From early on, music made an enormous contribution, whether it was the rough acoustic strains of the ramshackle twenty-or-so strong Blood-stained Colonial Band or haunting melodies composed for specific performances. Sometimes music would be spontaneously produced, lasting just one show, but often compositions would be layered into later pieces, producing an ever-growing patchwork, a 'source-pool' of sound. 'Mad Song', for example, composed by Westbrook with Fox lyrics in the early 1970s, was used over and over again, metamorphosing into the 'Falcon tune' and song in 'Bellevue' in the *Doomsday Colouring Book* tour of 1982 (Welfare State archive). Welfare State's musical repertoire was extensive and it is impossible to do justice to the role and range of it here (see 'Street and Outdoor Performance and Music' section with musical scores and Appendices listing LP albums (including *John Peel's Top Gear Selection*, BBC Enterprises 1969, and *Welfare State/Lol Coxhill*, Virgin 1975, in Coult and Kershaw, 1990, 31–57, 262–4, 269–70).

From 1968, a string of exceptional individual musicians, such as Lol Coxhill, Phil Minton and Mike Westbrook, played key roles in the company, each making a distinctive contribution to a peculiarly cumulative eclectic house style which combined fey English folk, Dixieland jazz and Albert Ayler-esque improvisation, Eastern and Western classical traditions and a smorgasbord of ethnic music. Rather than a backdrop to performance, music was used to heighten the intensity of the total theatrical experience. Players were often required to perform in punishing prolonged 'vigils': for example, the extensive performance by Lol Coxhill, Lou Glandfield and Colin Wood at the *Memorial for the First Astronaut*, a static sculptured space in the Lancashire countryside (recorded by Mike Kustow in his film, *Stoneyholme*, for London

Weekend Television's *Aquarius* series, 1975). Frequently, Welfare State soundscapes took on a shamanistic role while, at heart, the ethos was always about facilitating a connection between professional and amateur models and creating a common musical language.

> We aim not to lower our standards but to broaden them by creating the theatrical equivalent of the Decathlon. We seek a diversity which is itself professional, but which allows each separate activity to be amateur, in the best sense. Ultimately, we are looking for a new Primitivism, where the shaman gets his ticket by vision, rather than by simply professional expertise. Welfare State's music is central to the establishment of that vision. (Coult and Kershaw, 1990, 57)

The rapid development of impromptu, processional and nomadic street theatre reached a climax in 1972 with a series of events and occurrences: a mammoth series of thirty outdoor theatre performances in three weeks around Yorkshire, a month-long 'South West tour' and the invention of the complex multi-layered character, Lancelot Icarus Handyman Barrabas Quail. The appearance of Jamie Proud's alter-ego Lancelot Quail, at Surrey Hall in Brixton, was significant. Later billed in a leaflet that accompanied Welfare State's 1973 *Beauty and the Beast*, as 'Britain's new folk hero (a working-class hermaphrodite strong-man)', Quail, a New Age everyman, became a recurring reference point for the company and featured right through to the final performance in 2006. In September 1972, Welfare State spent a month conducting the *Travels of Lancelot Quail*, a processional theatrical event which roved from Glastonbury through Somerset, Devon and Cornwall, culminating afloat on a submarine off Land's End.

> We placed standing stones on remote tors, built turf circles on dark moors. Erected a maypole at night on a granite outcrop (for the autumnal equinox), lit giant beacons on inaccessible hills, walked twelve miles across Dartmoor at night, created a symphony in the Cheesering quarry with the Mike Westbrook Band, falling rocks and fire bombs. We have performed to all the cars on the A38 between Glastonbury and Burrow Mump in one afternoon. We have created a naming ceremony for a child in the Hurlers Stone Circle on Bodmin Moor, tried Judge Jeffreys in an ornamental fountain in Taunton, and more or less discovered the sunset in Her Majesty's Submarine, *Andrew*. (Henri, 1974, 119)

Fox's description of the south-west tour, recorded in Henri's book in 1974, captures the postmodern nature of the nomadic troupe's bricolage of bizarre activities. Contemporaneous critics were impressed by Welfare State's makeshift approach, the poignancy of their stories and the wondrous spectacle of the images they created.

> Dirt, a hand to mouth existence and makeshift props are the raw materials of a show concerned only with being alive [...] it was wild and weird, gentle and tempestuous, a lifting and ebbing sea of stories. It is undecided and ambivalent, the bold stories touching off many levels of experience. Its unpredictability and spectacle complete wonder. (WSTC, 1972, 12/1)

Finally, 1972 was also significant for the production of the first Welfare State 'manifesto', a political form of rhetoric in itself. Although many events had obvious revolutionary themes (for example, *Parliament in Flames*) their statements usually denied any direct political engagement.

Why are you called Welfare State and are you political?

> We started with the name seven years ago and it is now well known. In fact, we offer assistance to the national imagination rather than agit-prop. People have a need for ceremony in their lives. Our vision is to make theatrical celebration a reality and available to all (Welfare State, 1978b, n.p.).

In interviews in the 1970s, John Fox acknowledged that 'the right says we are anarchists and the left says we should be reaching the workers'. Denying any interest in agit-prop, he argued that their activities were designed to have poetry, that they were engaged in 'missionary work in the discovery of alternative spiritual values' (Fox interviewed by Theodore Shank in *The Drama Review*, March 1977 in Itzin, 1980, 72). Never didactic, the political ethos of Welfare State was embedded in the organization itself and its creative strategies. Primarily, their collectively written manifestoes professed this 'alternative aesthetic': a unique hybrid approach which combined archetypal myth-making, a Blakeian vision typically reflected in 1960s' counterculture and a New Age rhetoric of magic and ritual.

> The Welfare State make images, invent rituals, devise ceremonies, objectify the unpredictable, establish and enhance atmospheres for particular places, times, situations and people [...] We will

continue to analyse the relationship between performance and living, acting and identity, theatre and reality, entertainment and product, archetype and need.[...] We will react to new stimulus and situations spontaneously and dramatically and continue to make unbelievable art as a necessary way of offering cultural and organic death. (Welfare State, 1972, n.p.)

From Civic Magicians to Engineers of the Imagination, Burnley 1972-1979

Through the classic period of the 'proliferation' of alternative theatre in the mid-1970s (Kershaw, 1992, 87), Welfare State worked out of a settled base in Burnley, a working-class industrial town with a growing Asian population, captured on camera by Daniel Meadows, who documented many of the company's events in that decade. By 1972, the company was already established in Burnley but the collapse of plans to stage an exhibition event in London at the Serpentine Gallery (primarily because they were refused permission to erect their circus tents in Kensington Gardens in Hyde Park) convinced them to stage the event in Burnley instead. Annoyed with the intransigence of the authorities, Fox sent a telegram to the Serpentine, explaining why he had cancelled the planned event; he also despatched a set of photographs of work for them to paste on the gallery floor and, provocatively, a mynah bird, trained to say 'Fuck off bureaucrats!' – apparently, it didn't survive the journey (Fox in Whiteley, 2014).

The company set up their touring caravans and lorries on a reclaimed rubbish tip at Heasandford quarry in Lancashire, and ended up staying five years as part of the Mid-Pennine Association for the Arts' innovative community programme of artists' residencies. Until 1978, with Boris Howarth and Lol Coxhill playing key artistic roles, the company built a self-sustaining community of growing families and associated artists, musicians and performers. For the company, this was an exceptionally productive period in which, besides conducting an experiment in alternative forms of living and social interaction, they created some of their most important and influential performances and developed new artistic strategies and prototypes for vernacular art forms.

The company focused on working in dialogue not only with the local landscape but also with the town's working-class communities. On 1 January 1973, in nearby Barrowford, Welfare State had created an event to celebrate the New Year, leading 'a cavalcade to display the coracle of the dying hermit', burying a canister of 'relics' and planting trees. This led to an invitation from the Council to return to create a midsummer event and the coining of themselves as 'civic magicians', a tag quickly adopted by others. Following a visit to Heasandford, Ian Nairn, a London-based critic, recognized Welfare State's aim to create a 'sense of wonder', quipping that there had been two 'wonders' for Burnley that year: the 'Civic Magicians' and their 'happenings in a disused rubbish tip' and promotion to First Division football. (WSTC, 1973a, 12/1). Clearly, the local population was variously bewildered and confused by the company's activities, but they were also sometimes beguiled into participating.

> Most of the audience-participants at Burnley were children and I'd be prepared to bet that ten years ahead, in bank or factory, someone will think back to that crazy evening when Icarus wed the Queen of the May and wonder what the hell happened to wonder. (WSTC, 1973a, 12/1)

A series of key performances and iconic events followed. One of the first projects, *Beauty and The Beast*, featured the mythic figure Lancelot Quail. Described by Robin Thornber as 'like being in one of those nightmare landscapes by Hieronymous Bosch' (WSTC, 1973b, 12/1), the company spent three months building a makeshift labyrinthine environment from junk for the final performance.

> Much of the audience was street kids. Mostly they just jeered and jibed, their defence against anything unfamiliar […] we may not accept that anything that happens on a rubbish tip could be a major cultural event. But in their lives at least that's just what it was. (WSTC, 1973b, 12/1)

In November 1973, they created the first large-scale bonfire event, directed by Boris Howarth, which later developed into *Parliament in Flames* in Burnley (1976) garnering an audience of 10,000; it was then recreated in Milton Keynes (1978), Ackworth (1979), Tamworth (1980) and, finally, Catford (1981) with 15,000 spectators. Subsequently, there was a suggestion that they create a similar event in Milton Keynes Bowl for an audience of 50,000 but, significantly, the company rejected the idea of working on a spectacle of that scale (Fox in Whiteley, 2014). In 1974, they made their first permanent earthwork at Gawthorpe Hall in Burnley and their first giant ice work at Wath-upon-Dearne. In the following year, they created *Harbinger*, a large-scale sculpture from scrapyard junk, for the International Performance Festival in Birmingham city centre. Besides outdoor site-specific projects, they also worked in galleries – for example, with Bob Frith of Horse and Bamboo Theatre, they constructed a fully operative *Ghost Train* at the Mid-Pennine gallery in Burnley in January 1977. The Burnley period culminated in *Barrabas*, a six-week project, described as a 'total theatrical environment' in which daily performances included film, sideshows, processions and the 'ritual, disembowelling of The Dead Man (and his culture)' (Coult and Kershaw, 1990, 245).

Beyond the Burnley site, Welfare State's ambitious and audacious approach to creativity was mirrored by their efforts at social engagement in some of the most deprived communities in Britain at the time. Typically, in August 1976, the company spent a weekend setting up their tents and equipment on a squalid site at Denistone, a poverty-stricken area in Glasgow, in readiness for a procession through the working-class streets, and a finale performance of *Island of the Lost World*. A commentary, made at the time by Fox, noted the problems of working in a locality where violent gangs and knife crime were rife: lots of equipment went missing overnight and local children fought over tickets. With little if any cultural provision, live theatre was virtually unknown, and the company faced insatiable demands for their performances. Fox's efforts to highlight the social and economic deprivation of the area, and his call for funds to set up a community theatre at the request of the local community, aggrieved the Lord Provost of Glasgow so much that Fox was asked for an apology, and the Arts Council was asked to investigate the company's subsidy. With the Arts Council's support, the controversy dissipated, but the incident is indicative of some of the ethical and political issues surrounding the field of social theatre in the 1970s (ACGB, 1976a, 34/163/1).

Besides creating events in and around Burnley, and carrying out various commissions and tours in the UK, Welfare State also worked in Europe through the 1970s. Their first overseas project in January 1973, *Fanfare for Europe*, involved a travelling performance that started in Hull Market with a 'paranoid clown' and his wife selling tripe and onions. It continued on the North Sea ferry and culminated in a procession in Rotterdam. In summer 1973, they performed another version of *Beauty and the Beast* at the Shaffy Theatre in Amsterdam and De Lanteren in Rotterdam. In 1975, midway through the residency at Burnley, notes made by Fox reflected on their various performances in Holland and on the expanded concept of Quail. Significantly, one of Fox's commentaries, written at the time, reveals some of the aesthetic shifts that had taken place in the work of the company, signalling a new set of preoccupations.

> Now, parody has gone. Now Quail seeks to extend and confirm his identity in relation to purer elemental forces of ice, fire, water and earth. WS now spends much time constructing large landscape sculptures – sometimes without performance of any kind but more usually with climactic musical and processional animation. Illusion has gone. Tangible form has increased. Work exists in landscape. Rarely in theatres. Now, WS is seeking through Ritual Patterns Archetypal symbols Simple concrete images and necessary ceremonies to make a holy but secular theatre accessible to the common man. By travelling in a tribe…usually with a mobile village of lorries and caravans […] the implied relationship between alternative life style and metaphysical poetry is demonstrated. Imagination and play shown in action and objectified in artefacts present a real counter to the tedious illusion of materialist death culture. Now Quail is doing it. Not commenting upon it. A mythical tribe grows round him. Quail becomes maybe the harbinger of the future. (WSTC, 1975a, 12/1)

An earlier note by company member Peter Kiddle expressed the view that Welfare State was not being as effective as it could be in communicating and engaging with the community at large, or with local youth, many of whom were articulate and keen to talk about what was going on – 'no A stream kids these, but stuck somewhere down the alphabet and stuck in school by ROSLA': at the time, the Raising of the School-Leaver Age adversely affected a generation of young people, many of whom had no interest in staying on at school (WSTC, 1937c, 12/1). Kiddle suggested setting up discussion groups and print and filmmaking workshops as a way forward. Others had different views. By 1976, a series of aesthetic and directional differences had developed within the group and a number of individuals, including Steve Grumbley and Lizzie Lockart, split off to form the theatre company IOU (Independent Outlaw University). In 1978, the Burnley base was dismantled and the nomadic on-site Welfare State 'school', which had intermittently taken in local children, folded with it. With Welfare State members registered as 'home teachers', the company's own school had operated since

April 1975. Catherine Kiddle's book recounts the ethos, benefits and problems they faced in running the school.

> So what should we teach these children for whom we now had total responsibility? Knowledge, facts, experience yawned before us, the great blackness of space, infinite and impossible to comprehend. Our own knowledge, our skills, our own moments of excitement and illumination in learning shone out like stars [...] We wanted to give them the stars. (Kiddle, 1981, 32)

The Fox family went to Australia on a 'sabbatical' residency and the company base moved to Liverpool where Boris Howarth worked with Adrian Mitchell to produce *Uppendown Mooney*. On return, in 1979, the Foxes settled in Ulverston with a core group of five full-time employees and over fifty freelance contributors and this initiated a new phase of work starting, for example, with the first Summer School, in 1980.

Early 1980s Onwards

The work of Welfare State from the 1980s to 2006 is outside the scope of this volume. While Kershaw and others have documented the company's prolific output through to the late 1990s, a comprehensive survey and further research needs to be done. However, as has already been indicated at the outset of this chapter, various key developments occurred in the early 1980s and a brief reference, at the very least, is necessary here. Paradoxically, it was in this period that Welfare State combined participation and epic spectacle in a creative symbiosis which, eventually, became unsustainable. The shift to Cumbria represented a desire to establish a permanent base and deep community roots from which to develop new forms of socially-engaged participative practice, but it also coincided with an ever more ambitious programme of large-scale spectacular events (see Kershaw, 2007, 135–6), such as the final *Parliament in Flames* at Catford (1981), *Raising the Titanic*, Canal Dock Basin, Limehouse (1983) or, overseas, *Tempest on Snake Island*, Toronto Theatre Festival (1981) and *The Wasteland and the Wagtail*, performed on a mountain side in Togamura, Japan (1982). Later large-scale projects included *False Creek: A Visual Symphony*, a six-week residency in partnership with Canadian artists and musicians at World Expo '86 in Vancouver, *Glasgow All Lit Up* (1989–90), *Shipyard Tales* (1990) and *Lord Dynamite* (1991). Two documents by John Fox, *A Plea for Poetry* (a paper to the National Arts and Media Strategy Unit) and *Flight From*

Spectacle, both in 1991, signalled a shift in the direction and ethos of the company. As Mason has noted, these events and performances were not only 'site-specific', they were also 'audience-specific'; going beyond the performance, they were about creating a particular audience, often having worked together for weeks on a creative project in technical and craft-based workshops (Mason, 1992, 134).

Welfare State worked extensively with local participants around Ulverston, initiating the annual lantern festival and extending their locale to include Barrow-in-Furness, a town with an economy based on shipbuilding and the manufacture of nuclear submarines and with long traditions of working-class organization and culture. Between January and April 1982, they collaborated with Sheffield City Polytechnic on a full-length 'community feature film', *King Real and the Hoodlums*, based on a script (derived from Shakespeare's *King Lear*) by Adrian Mitchell with music by Peter Moser, mainly filmed on location at Barrow with unemployed local youth. The anti-nuclear narrative had an overtly subversive impact in Barrow, a town whose economic survival depended on making weapons of mass destruction (Kershaw, 1992, 215). Local reception was mixed as *King Real* played with the contradictions of the town's industrial and economic situation.

Audaciously, the company continued their risky strategy of creating ironic 'ideologically double-edged' events (Kershaw, 1992, 220). In 1987, at the invitation of Barrow Borough Council, Welfare State spent six months creating a 'sculptural enhancement' of the Town Hall, which turned out to be 'probably the biggest artwork in Europe' (Thornber, 1987). This was spectacle on a grand scale, with a market, an oratorio composed and collaged from traditional songs by Peter Moser sung by a mass choir, an exploding birthday cake, pyrotechnic displays and acrobatic performances on the building itself. As Kershaw notes, *Town Hall Tattoo* was extraordinary for its 'rich ideological dialectic' (Kershaw, 1992, 220) and for the way it integrated civic celebration, anarchic imagery,

> and a subtle radicalism which poked gentle and good humoured fun at the very values the event appeared to valorise. This was ironic agit-prop on the grand scale, heavily disguised as a straightforward carnivalesque party. (Kershaw, 1992, 220)

Garnering an audience of 15,000, the event was hailed as a critical success and Barrow Council went on to fund Welfare State to work with the town's community for a further three years, culminating in the *Feast of Furness* in July 1990 – a 'total festival' which included story-telling, poetry readings, cabarets, street events and 'Rock the Boat', an anarchic nightclub. The centrepiece of the festival was *Shipyard Tales*, a cycle of plays, devised by local young people and adults, which explored the complex moral issues and paradoxes of a community whose economic survival was bound up with warfare (Fox, 2002, 119). In particular, *The Golden Submarine* provided a typically spectacular finale, a multi-layered work that was simultaneously humorous, celebratory and subversive. Welfare State's efficacy in utilizing the rhetorics of theatre, intertextual narrative and participatory practices enabled them to create performances and events that revealed socio-political contra-dictions and complexities through the kind of 'active spectatorship' referred to earlier. As Kershaw notes in a detailed analysis of this and other participative spectacles created by Welfare State at that time, despite the danger of creating a 'tokenist nod to towards self-determi-nation and empowerment':

> Far from being a crude escapist event, the Golden Submarine was a grand carnivalesque agit prop, participatory celebratory protest, perhaps at its most powerfully subversive. (Kershaw, 1992, 237–40)

Funding and Company Structure

Reflecting the flourishing of British 'alternative theatre' in the 1970s, by the early 1980s Welfare State had grown rapidly from a small 'underground' nomadic troupe to an established company with all the trappings of a business outfit. As Craig put it crudely in 1980, the continual challenge for them, as for others, was 'to set a course between the Scylla and Charybdis of incorporation into the mainstream and cultural ghettoization' (Craig, 1980, 10). There is no doubt, though, that Welfare State was more astute than others in managing to maintain artistic integrity, while accruing funds and subsidies from various organizations.

A number of factors assisted the development of alternative and political theatre in the 1970s – for example, the development of a university-based circuit and the expansion of community-based, non-theatre venues. The gradual increase in public subsidy from the Arts Council, and its recognition of new and alternative categories of drama and theatre-related activity, were key factors for Welfare State. The minutes of the Arts Council's Drama Panel at the end of the 1960s document the emergence of 'Fringe and Experimental' theatre with, in 1968, a specific reference to an 'upsurge' of activity, initiating the setting up of a 'New Activities Committee' (ACGB, 1968, 43/3/1). In common with various other multimedia groups operating at the time, Welfare State was able to capitalize on the fact that the Arts Council's bureaucracy was not quite ready to cope with the interdisciplinary nature of their work. Earlier, apart from the 'New Activities Committee', Welfare State had applied to the Jazz Subcommittee but, as Nick Barter commented in 1973, although they were likely to be funded by the Drama Panel, their work could also attract funds from the Experimental Projects Committee, and Visual Arts, noting rather emphatically that the Arts Council needed 'to avoid triple subsidy' (ACGB, 1973, 41/78/3).

Welfare State's earliest approaches to the Arts Council for funding were via the New Activities Committee, with their first request for a capital grant to pay for the purchase of a piano amplifier and speakers: an amount of £375 was awarded in September 1971 (ACGB, 1971, 41/78/2). The company's correspondence with the Arts Council through the early 1970s documents a litany of appeals for further funds, usually in response to urgent requests to fund vehicle repairs, as was the case following their South West tour in 1972, after which Fox noted they had serious financial problems (ACGB, 1972, 41/78/2).

In 1973, the company registered as Galactic Smallholdings Ltd, an educational charity to act as an umbrella organization for the company to 'initiate research projects into the aesthetics of the alternative' (WSTC, 1978a, 12/1). By 1973–4, at their council-supported base at Burnley, with almost 150 performances and events supported by an Arts Council grant of £14,300, the assets – and liabilities – of the company had become extensive. Supporting documents for funding applications to the Arts Council in the mid-1970s are illuminating. A document, dated 1975, gives a breakdown of grants, expenditure, debts and staff costs, noting that no one received more than half the Equity minimum and the Director, John Fox, was unpaid (WSTC, 1975a, 12/1). It summarizes the company's previous funding: 1968–9 nil grant/41 performances, 1969–70 nil grant/38 performances, 1970–1 £133/87 performances, 1971–2 £2,697/109 performances, 1972–3 £8,570/146 performances, 1973–4 £14,300/143 performances. With two lorries, one Landrover, one Bedford van, a generator and trailer, and with the north-facing Heasandford site in dire need of hard standing and a WC unit, proposed capital expenditure of £35k and expected running costs totalling £7,742 for 1973–4 (WSTC, 1973d, 12/1), even though the company had secured one of the largest public grants in the sector, the continual shortfall of funds to sustain basic living conditions was clearly a major issue. Another document, 'The Welfare State: A Report on the Future', dated July 1974, gave the total estimated grants for 1974–5 as £43,200 – this included money from 'Housing the Arts' and the Gulbenkian Foundation (WSTC, 1974, 12/1).

In 1974, outlining plans to replace the earlier concept of the 'mobile village' with a 'residential nucleus', their pitch to the Arts Council for almost £50,000 hinged on extending both international and partici-pative elements of their work, indicating a potentially fruitful symbiosis of Welfare State's ideological aspirations and public funding policy (WSTC, 1976, 12/1). Even with generous subsidies, the company continued to have cash-flow problems through the decade and the Arts Council generally responded with additional guarantees against losses. On occasion, the company's administrator had to make additional requests for an advance out of the guarantee, to ensure that performers could be paid (ACGB, 1978, 34/163/4). Nevertheless, the company managed to thrive and, with astute financial management, continued to attract public subsidies. By the end of the 1970s, Welfare State was running a large-scale operation with permanent and freelance employees, company directors and an administrator.

The Fox family's 'sabbatical' year in Australia offered a breathing space for the company and, reconfigured and refreshed, Welfare State moved to Barrow-in-Furness in the early 1980s. Policy statements and accompanying documents submitted to the Arts Council in 1979 underlined a shift of emphasis from 'box office returns' to 'grassroots work', with Welfare State planning to focus more on educational and community-based work – a change of direction which, Fox indicated, would require appropriate subsidy,

> Our argument is simply that we have essential work to do for which we are uniquely qualified [...] unfortunately even after 11 years of positive creation our original art is still peculiarly vulnerable to the vagaries of unbalanced not to say unhinged free market forces [...] if we can presume to be valued as a national asset, then may we please be funded accordingly? (ACGB, 1979, 34/163/4)

Consistent work in the community in the area through the next decade subsequently led, in 1999, to the Lottery-funded building of a permanent base for performance, educational and community projects, Lanternhouse at Ulverston. While this represented the culminating achievement of over forty years' work, in many ways it signalled the beginning of the end, as a combination of restrictive legislation, endemic managerialism, the recuperation of 'alternativity' by capital and the corporatization of culture constrained both the aesthetics and, eventually, the ethos of the company. From April Fool's Day 2006, John Fox and Sue Gill archived the company, handing it over with full funding to another organization under the name of Lanternhouse International. Subsequently, Lanternhouse continued to operate as an independent company and, occasionally, a community resource. A poignant coda to this study: it closed in April 2012 and, as I write, the building has been put up for sale.

Artistic Policy and Working Method

Most alternative and political theatre groups emerging from the countercultural scene of the late 1960s were purposefully challenging the dominant methods of cultural production and management. As a collective of artists, musicians, engineers, writers, teachers and poets, Welfare State, with its collective and collaborative approach, was no exception to that. While there were designated 'directors', and particular individuals were given specific roles, the company maintained an anti-hierarchical and egalitarian approach to all aspects of its work. Although specific skills and experience were acknowledged, everyone was encouraged to perform, make music and assist with artistic and technical production.

Collectivity extended to the working methods used to create performances. A substantial Welfare State document entitled 'The Welfare State Internal and External Environment' (WSTC, 1975b, 12/1) outlined 'the decision making process' at great length and in some detail, and suggests that, in theory at least, they aspired to democratic aims. It noted that the company was a collective of individuals sharing a common aim, although it also aimed to provide aesthetic freedom for other work. Aesthetic and ideological tensions were already evident at this time though, and issues came to a head in 1976. In particular, archive documents show that, apart from ongoing financial problems reaching a critical point, a key issue related to some individuals wanting to carry out creative work outside Welfare State, and this led to a group of company members proposing recommendations to instigate a small committee to control the artistic directions of the company (ACGB, 1976b, 34/163/1). An internal Arts Council memo dated March 1976 warned, alarmingly, that Welfare State was 'about to implode' (ACGB, 1976d, 34/163/1): clearly, there were divisions created in respect of how the company should be run. By August 1976, a number of changes had been made to company personnel, and a Belgian, Luc Mishalle, took over from Peter Kiddle as full-time administrator. Mishalle, a musician who had originally trained as an arts administrator, joined Welfare State while doing his 'national service'. As he was a conscientious objector, social work for an arts organization was allowed instead of military engagement. By 1976, as far as Kiddle was concerned though, the personnel management issues previously highlighted for concern by the Arts Council had been dealt with amicably and efficiently. Pointedly, in a letter to Clive Tempest at the Arts Council, Kiddle noted that it had had 'considerable problems' but that Welfare State actually presented a 'model of good management' in the way they had resolved 'industrial problems and changed administration' (ACGB, 1976c, 34/163/1).

That said, in May 1976, Steve Gumbley, Liz Lockhart, Di Davies and Lou Glandfield left to co-found IOU with others. Initially, IOU worked under the umbrella of Galactic Holdings, finally becoming a wholly independent company on 1 April 1977. With a main administrator and no regular policy meetings, the main area for Welfare State's collective activity was concerned with the process of aesthetic decision-making. A typical scenario would be as follows:

> Once gig is in advanced state of negotiation, John Fox visits site with a couple of others. Reports impressions back to company – then we arrive on site. Each person is allotted task. John oversees. (WSTC, 1975b, 12/1)

At that time, 'scripts' were largely a written indication of how Fox, as artistic director, visualized the performance, Rather than detailed directions, they were usually treated as guidance notes, with little formal rehearsal. Writing in the *San Francisco Theatre Archive* in 1978, about the working methods of various experimental theatre companies, Theodore Shank focused on Welfare State's emphasis on the construction of site-specific scenarios, rather than prepared scripts (WSTC, 1978b, 12/1). However, despite the total theatrical experience created, rather than action, the creation of single iconic imagery was of paramount importance for Fox. As he noted, 'we create ambiguous hermetic images which you can hang meaning on, but which don't have any meaning themselves' (Fox in Mason, 1992, 81). Visual aesthetics took precedence over language and, in many of Welfare State productions and performances, this was a major characteristic, as intimated in this vivid description by John Fox of a scene from the *Vigil of Icarus*:

> [O]n a great ziggurat of ice blocks in a sunken marble courtyard a wounded airman weeps at night. Candles are lit in the ice. A nun plays a flute, four cellists lay a lament for twelve hours. Meanwhile circling above the city a frail aircraft trails a painted illuminated backdrop of the wings of Icarus. (WSTC, 1973d, 12/1)

Selected Key Works

As indicated already, apart from archetypal figures such as Quail, Welfare State constantly recycled narratives and motifs. Striking images and talismanic objects commonly recurred in the company's productions. Apart from attracting critical acclaim and large audiences, *Beauty and the Beast* (1973) and *Parliament in Flames* (1976) were key works that functioned in this way and, in doing so, acquired a mythic significance of their own within the company's repertoire. The Mid-Pennine Association for the Arts issued a press release (written by John Fox) for the performance,

> On a plateau above a polluted river skirting green houses, allotments, new factories and NCB sludge, the Welfare State settlement – a cross between a Bolivian tinmine, TS Eliot's 'wasteland' and an Inca stilt village – is growing and extended through scarecrows, subterranean tunnels and living vans decorated with mythical paintings of *Beauty and the Beast*.

Beauty and the Beast was the first major project in Burnley. It involved company members and locals spending three months creating a junk environment that, along with making bonfires, was a staple Welfare State practice. Later, the audience was led by Quail past the caravans painted by Kate Barnard (see above) with mythical figures and creatures, through a labyrinth that resembled a grotesque haunted house of horrors, to witness the staging of a cycle of promenade performances. In summer 1973, they performed another version of *Beauty and the Beast* at the Shaffy Theatre in Amsterdam and De Lanteren in Rotterdam. In late 1977, the company created *The Loves, Lives and Murders of Lancelot Barrabas Quail* on Fulledge Recreation Ground in Burnley as a kind of synthesis of all the previous years' experiences of Quail, the 'everyman' character. In 1983, Tony Coult captured the experience and conveyed a sense of the imagery in such detail that it is worth quoting at length.

> [I]n a complex of tents around what looked like a medieval jousting space, the audience wandered amongst sideshows and giant puppets before entering a 'cinema' to see a film about Quail and his bizarre early life. After the film, there was an opportunity to wander again, to buy tea and hot potatoes, to investigate the strange tableaux repre-senting Quail's inner mind, to listen to the band's music or just to keep warm by the glowing brazier. Finally, the audience sat on either side of the space for the 'play' of 'Barrabas'. Giant puppet figures, and acting performances to match called to the performance space an array of marvellous images to terrorise and torment Quail. As the performance drew to a close, two gross cooks distributed spicy, steaming-hot lardy bread to the audience. (Coult and Kershaw, 1990, 10–11)

Coult argued that 'Barrabas' was a summation of many Welfare State elements. With its universal themes of birth, death and resurrection, he notes that the imagery created was spectacular and beautiful, not because of its polish or perfection, but precisely because it was 'rich, quirky and obviously handmade' (Coult and Kershaw, 1990, 10).

In November 1973, Welfare State created their first large-scale bonfire event that later developed into *Parliament in Flames* in Burnley (November 1976) with an audience of 10,000 people. It was an exhila-rating spectacle with a revolutionary theme that combined affect and effect, particularly given its later restaging at the same time as mass street protests, marches and riots in the early years of the Thatcher government. Over a few days, the company and participants from the local community built a sixty feet high replica of the Houses of Parliament, and a thirty feet high 'guy' which was then subjected to ritual burning, accompanied by feasting. *Parliament in Flames*, directed by Boris Howarth with designer Maggy Howarth and created by Ali Wood, Andy Plant, Tim Hunkin and Tony Lewery with pyrotechnics by David Clough, was then re-created in Milton Keynes (1978), Ackworth (1979), Tamworth (1980) and, finally, Catford (1981), with 15,000 spectators. Although the event acquired the status of one of their 'vernacular prototypes', it retained an immediacy and volatility which, as Bim Mason notes, is only possible outdoors where the environment is impossible to control (Mason, 1992, 85).

One of the company's most remarkable productions, *King Real and the Hoodlums*, was a community film made on a budget of £25,000 with a script by Adrian Mitchell. It was created on location in Barrow between January and April 1982, with the assistance of Sheffield Polytechnic and over one hundred and fifty local participants, many of them shipyard workers and unemployed youth with no acting experience. Made the year after the patriotic fervour of the Falklands War, in a town whose economy was constructed on the arms industry, the storyline took Shakespeare's *King Lear* and turned it into an overtly anti-nuclear fable.

> The film combines the razzmatazz of Punch and Judy with the sad blue-greys of Goya. In its punk-operatic ex-cesses, icebergs of welded-together fridges float by under the shipyard cranes and Lear/Real's daughters totter up thrones of junk to preside over the last rites of consumerdom in a spirit of holo-caustic humour. (White, 1988, 195)

In what Kershaw describes as 'a kind of punk-medieval rabble in a wasted industrial junkyard' (Kershaw, 1992, 215), the three daughters conduct a quest to find what they describe in the film as the 'keys of destruction'. The scene in which Tom and Claudella wander in the 'wilderness' – a post-nuclear desert with a backdrop of factories, inter-jected with montaged images of derelict burning cities and industrial wasteland – is bleak but poignant, as they sing a simple haunting folk melody. Later, in the 'royal bunker', there is a scene of gluttony and feasting, as the power-hungry fat sisters (literally) squeeze out the King and fire him into space like a torpedo. Finally, the bunker blows up, Claudella throws away the 'keys of power' forever and the entire company makes a ramshackle musical procession back into town for a bonfire. Culturally tied to a post-punk 'Rocky-Horror' aesthetic, *King Real and the Hoodlums* is comical but, given its setting, context and audience, it is also boldly and radically subversive: another gloriously triumphant example of Welfare State's capacity to create 'ideologically double-edged events' (Kershaw, 1992, 220). The premier showing of the film at the local cinema was equally 'ideologically double-edged' and, by all accounts, a spectacular experience. After descending from a limousine, all the 'stars' made their entrance via a rather small 'red carpet'. Consequently, Fox recalls that it took a long time to get everyone installed in the cinema and, with an ironic awards ceremony in which the whole cast each received a golden statuette, the evening was 'long, very joyful and exceedingly raucous' (Fox in Whiteley, 2014).

Looking Ahead

Certainly, through the 1970s and into the early 1980s, Welfare State's activities were underpinned by a commitment to collaborative working, breaking down the barriers between lay and professional models and fostering a deep and lasting engagement with participants from local communities. Through the 1980s, when many other companies were closing down, their affective events and performances developed new audiences and fostered 'active spectatorship'. Maintaining a sense of radical dissent, Welfare State revealed the ambiguities and contradictions of late capitalism, wedded to profit, consumerism, arms manufacture and the destruction of the environment. As was emphasized at the outset, the legacy of Welfare State is complex and conglomerate, as it spawned many other experimental theatre and performance groups. More interesting, perhaps, is the new 'performative paradigm' of the second millenium. Kershaw has noted that, 'the new global forms of political, economic, media-based and techno-logical change engendered the performative society: societies that are crucially constituted through performance' (Kershaw, 2007: 11–12). In the last ten years or so, in a performative and choreographic turn, anti-globalization and direct action groups, such as the Clown Army, or the Black Bloc with its spectacular exploding Trojan Horse on the anti-cuts demonstration in March 2011, have adopted Welfare State-style strat-egies. Carnival, mass participation and spectacle have been used as a means of protest, resonating with some of those distantly remembered events that disrupted the status quo in the 1970s, when ice melted and fire burned.

Endnote on Sources

The research for this case-study utilizes the author's personal collection plus private papers and archives of John Fox/Sue Gill (author's personal access); the extensive Welfare State archive (including extensive collections of photographs) held as part of the University of Bristol Theatre Collection (referenced in this chapter as WSTC); and the Arts Council of Great Britain (ACGB) archive held at the Victoria and Albert Museum. In addition, the author drew on interviews with Welfare State company members and associates, some of which were conducted for a retrospective exhibition, *Radical Mayhem: Welfare State International and its Followers,* which she curated for

Mid Pennine Gallery, Burnley, 26 April–7 June 2008. The author's published conference papers include Whiteley, Gillian, 'New Age Radicalism and the Social Imagination: Welfare State International in the Seventies', in Laurel Forster and Sue Harper (eds), *British Culture and Society in the 1970s: the Lost Decade,* Newcastle upon Tyne: Cambridge Scholars Press, 2010, 35–50. Coult and Kershaw (1990) have a chronology of performances and events from 1968 to 1990; chronologies (some annotated by John Fox) up to 2006 are held within the Welfare State archive (WSTC).

Chapter 8

7:84 THEATRE COMPANIES

David Pattie

Founded by John McGrath in 1971, 7:84 was one of the most important and influential political companies to emerge from the alternative theatre movement of the late 1960s and early 1970s. McGrath's commitment to Marxism, and to creating a style of performance that was accessible to working-class audiences in particular, led him and the company to develop a distinctive performance style that incorporated elements from contemporary popular culture, popular traditions of performance, agit-prop, documentary theatre and Epic performance, and to take these shows directly to working-class audiences in Scotland and England.

Wind Will Not Cease, Even If the Trees Wish to Rest: 7:84 in Context

In May 1968, John McGrath travelled to Paris, a city which, for a moment, seemed to many on the left to be on the verge of a full-scale revolution, led by an alliance of radical students and striking workers. He experienced first-hand what he was later to call one of the most important theatrical experiences of his life. The *evenements* (as the protests in Paris and, to a lesser extent, the rest of France became known) were sparked by a number of causes: widespread dissatisfaction with France's ruling elite, and in particular with the presidency of Charles De Gaulle, and a more general animus against capitalism itself (a view held both by radicalized students and by France's sizeable Communist party). Starting in May, a series of sit-down protests and wildcat strikes came very close to toppling the French state. McGrath was caught up in the (in hindsight, rather exaggerated) radical fervour of the time; a Marxist state seemed to be possible – and those who were involved in culture were at the forefront of the change:

I spent most of my time there with Jean-Jacques Lebel who is the great Happenings man. Jean-Jacques literally created barricades and scenes of confrontation, and it was- though it sounds derogatory to say it- a form of theatre. The nightly confrontations with the CRS [Compagnies Republicaines de Securite, the riot police] made one suddenly realise the tremendous dramatic impact of this. That is not to say it wasn't serious; it was immensely serious. But in Paris the street battles were theatre in the sense that they were more than themselves [...] Revolution cannot be reduced to theatre; but at times like this theatre can aspire to express revolution. (McGrath, 2002, 29)

It is not that the Paris events converted a previously sceptical or disinterested theatre worker to the cause of Marxist theatre: McGrath was already a committed member of the British left. Rather, Paris helped to crystallize McGrath's ideas about the power of theatricality in what at that time appeared to many to be a pre-revolutionary period. Theatre could both gesture toward revolution and test the revolutionary process itself; and it could do so by moving out of the theatre, into the spaces occupied by those caught up in that process.

McGrath's time in Paris served as confirmation of an approach to theatre and performance that had been developing through the 1960s. However, any idea that his nascent Marxism was sparked into life by the events of 1968 would be simply untrue. Rather, for McGrath and for other theatre workers of his generation, the political events of the late 1960s served to confirm rather than to create a sense that capitalism was profoundly harmful, and that it was the duty of those on the radical Left to oppose it. For McGrath, this opposition could not be expressed through the theatre channels then available. At this time he was a well-connected member of the London theatrical and cultural community – a community that contained a wide range of left-wing and progressive opinions. He had written for the theatre, for television and for film, his name being associated with not only successful plays (*Events While Guarding the Bofors Gun* (1966)), but also the development of BBC TV's *Z Cars* (1962–78), a ground-breaking series that (at least in its early days) strove to give a scrupulously realistic portrait of both the police, and the social conditions within the communities in which they operated. However, as McGrath put it later, he had become disillusioned with the scope and impact of the work produced on the London stage. 'Prices are far too high' McGrath informed the ACGB, and he had abandoned any idea of establishing a London base, as he wanted to 'extend the range of audiences we play to further and feel we can do this most effectively outside London' (ACGB, 1972a, 34/168/1). How could theatre act as a rehearsal for and analysis of change if the theatrical environment produced and promoted stasis?

Reflecting on this in a series of lectures delivered at Cambridge in 1979, McGrath gave an example of this process in his analysis of the archetypal Royal Court play of the 1950s and 1960s: produced by a theatre which was broadly on the political left, but which attracted an audience drawn largely from the ranks of the London theatre establishment. Any impact the play might have would necessarily be blunted, both by the fact that it was performed to those with an interest in maintaining an unequal *status quo*, and also because the constraints of production dictated that writers place themselves in a tradition which elevated aesthetic success over effective political intervention. Even when writers espoused broadly left-wing, or even explicitly Marxist, causes and ideas, the impact of those ideas was necessarily stifled by the medium in which they worked (McGrath, 1981, 15). Granted, McGrath expressed these views in 1979, when he had nearly a decade's worth of experience in a different type of theatre; one might naturally expect his attitude to the kind of stages he'd left behind to have hardened over the intervening period. But there is more than enough truth in the portrait to make it uncomfortable reading for the playwrights he mentions. The conservative, commercial structures of the theatre industry would smother any radical message, converting it during the play's production and reception into something aesthetically acceptable and culturally safe.

The logical answer to this problem was twofold. Firstly, theatre should be taken out of this cultural straitjacket, and should be targeted specifically at those audiences who were at the sharp end of political and cultural struggle; and secondly, the form that theatre took should be radically readdressed. It is not simply that certain types of art are thought of as intrinsically more valuable than others; it is that the division of culture into that which is aesthetically worthwhile and that which is worthless fosters what might be called an ingrained structure of feeling in the audiences that encounter it. Put simply, if you are told that your preferred cultural tastes are inferior, you are also, by extension, inferior; conversely, some cultural products are treated as more aesthetically valuable than others – in liking them, you affirm your cultural superiority. These cultural judgements do not take place in a social and political vacuum; they are bound up with, and help to naturalize, inequality. Only those who have risen naturally to the top of the social pile (the argument runs) can truly appreciate culture; and the cultures of those further down the social scale are either intrinsically worthless or are only made valuable by appropriation – as the attention of those who think of themselves as culturally superior is brought to bear on material previously thought worthless.

McGrath's developing interest in a radical theatre which challenged both the structures and aesthetic assumptions of a dominant Capitalist culture was, of course, shared by a number of other theatre workers at the time. The emerging alternative theatre scene was also intimately bound up in the counterculture of the late 1960s. For commentators such as Baz Kershaw, the oppositional theatre movement that began to develop in the late 1960s, although it demonstrated a bewildering diversity of approaches and styles, was united in one aim: to engage in celebratory protest – that is, it did not simply aim to present an objective analysis of the state of the capitalist world, but to provide a mechanism through which new versions of a truly just society could be rehearsed and incarnated.

> As such, it played [...] a key role in promoting and popularising oppositional ideologies. And [...] its chief tactic was allied to the emergence of the anti-nuclear, anti-war and civil rights demon-strations in Britain and the USA. This is best described as a carnivalesque resistance to the oppressions of affluence, as promoted by the capitalist, technocratic and meritocratic status quo. (Kershaw, 1992, 40)

However, there was no clear agreement in the alternative theatre sector about the nature of that just society; and this ideological uncertainty was itself a source of cultural and artistic strength. When McGrath formed 7:84 in 1971, the fringe, as it was described at the time, was still in a relatively embryonic stage; by the middle of the decade, it had grown and diversified – and that growth was, in part, fostered by the work and example of 7:84 – both in Scotland and in England. 7:84, then, was an integral part of the emerging alternative theatre movement in England; in Scotland their role was rather different and their impact greater: a point to which I will return later in this chapter.

This is not to say, though, that McGrath's company existed smoothly side by side with other political companies and theatre workers. Its early years were marked by a number of productions in which their performance style was honed and developed, yet it was also shaped by arguments over the approach that political theatre companies should take to their audiences, and to the culture those audiences consumed as part of their everyday lives. McGrath, for example, had infamously attacked Arnold Wesker, who helped set up Centre 42, an organization committed to bringing high culture to working-class audiences. McGrath (probably correctly) identified a strain of cultural patronage in its implicit assumption that those cultures favoured by those in power were regarded as intrinsically more valuable than the cultures of the poor.

This argument also prefigured another later clash of opposing ideas in the 1970s, between McGrath and the playwright David Edgar, about the type of performance style that political theatre groups should adopt. Edgar argued that the use of popular performance forms (and the assumption that those forms spoke directly to an allegedly alienated working class) was something that should be handled warily; in a capitalist culture, it was simply impossible to isolate and employ any performance style that spoke authentically to and for the working classes (see Edgar 1988, 233). For McGrath, such a dismissal was patronizing at best, and betrayed an unacceptable level of cultural pessimism about the transformative potential locked up in working-class culture. It is not that he was blind to the regressive elements Edgar identified (the sexism, the racism, the reactionary nostalgia, and so on); rather, for McGrath, Edgar and those who agreed with him missed the fact that popular forms like the working-men's club demanded a different type of response from its audience, one which didn't isolate the event itself from the lives the audience led outside of the theatre. The alternative, for McGrath, could be found in the famous description in *A Good Night Out* of a typical working-man's club night in Chorlton-Cum-Hardy (McGrath, 1981, 22–5). The performers in such a venue would work to keep the audience interested and involved; all elements of the various performances would have the ultimate goal of 'capturing' their audiences. To keep the audience from drifting, the night would be varied, and would alternate styles and modes of performance: performers would include the audience (within boundaries that the performance could sustain); performers would address the audience directly; and they would tailor their material to the audience – making local references, referring to elements of shared experience, and so on. Where Edgar saw content irreversibly tainted by the operations of capitalism, McGrath saw a form that had the potential to shatter performance categories, and to address the audience on its own territory.

By the time he came to deliver the lectures published in *A Good Night Out*, McGrath had synthesized a list of performance styles and categories that a truly engaged political theatre could take from working-class entertainment forms. In order, these were *directness* (the ability to speak to the audience, without ambiguity, about the realities of their lives); the use of *comedy* and *music* to break up and vary the tone of the performance, and to hold the audience's attention; the conscious appeal to *emotion*; the use of *variety*, so that the evening mixed performance modes, rather than settling comfortably into one set style; *effect* and *immediacy* – or, in other words, a theatre that aimed to be as engaging as possible, and to root itself as closely as possible in the lives of its audience; and finally, *localism* and a *sense of identity*, which meant both that the company should reflect local experience, and that the company should identify with the needs and experiences of their audiences. As McGrath noted, such an approach was not without its dangers: localism could shade over into complete identification; a sense of identity could become nothing more than simple, uncritical celebration; and directness (if pitched wrongly) ran the risk of patronizing or preaching at the audience. However, against these dangers, McGrath argued that a political theatre that followed these principles would lodge itself in the communities who experienced the forces of capitalism at their most unbridled and destructive.

McGrath was not alone in prioritizing and pursuing popular performance techniques: many companies – CAST, Welfare State, Red Ladder and, rather later in the decade, Belt and Braces in England and Wildcat in Scotland (both in their various ways offshoots of 7:84) – used a variety of such styles. Indeed, as various commentators on the fringe – Kershaw (1992), DiCenzo (1996), Catherine Itzin (1981), Sandy Craig (1981), Steve Gooch (1984), Chris Megson (2012), among others – have pointed out, part of its dynamism at this time came from a willingness to attempt a variety of performance forms, and in so doing to widen the performative vocabulary of the British theatre. 7:84's contribution to this – aside from the fact that the company played a crucial role in opening up the debate – was not that it inaugurated new performance styles, but that it showed that effective work could be done by a company who were less concerned with the formal consistency of the work it produced, and more concerned with the bond between the performer and the audience. Ideally, McGrath wished to replace the static, self-absorbed style of performance he associated with British theatre of the 1950s and 1960s with the idea of performance as an open-ended, engaged conversation, with an audience whose lives provided the raw material for the work of the company. In these conditions, theatre could (at least potentially) be more than itself (as McGrath said about the street protests in Paris in 1968); rather than an enclosed, ineffectual rehearsal of political positions, played in front of an audience not directly affected by the debate, theatre could be part of the dialogue through which those most at risk under capitalism came to realize the exact nature of their situation – and how to change it for the better.

The Formation of 7:84 (1971–3)

McGrath and Elizabeth MacLennan had been talking about forming a theatre company along the lines of 7:84 long before 1971, when the new company mounted its first production. In an interview with Clive Barker, McGrath pointed out that one of the reasons why the company came together at the time it did was because, for the first time, a network of sympathetic touring venues and like-minded theatre companies had begun to form in the British theatre. As McGrath later noted, the Arts Council played a crucial role in creating this network; it funded companies like 7:84, enabling them to tour plays for long enough to cover costs (McGrath, 2002, 48). However, McGrath's initial request for subsidy, in a letter to Nicholas Barter dated 20 September 1971, came after the company's first productions of *Trees in the Wind* and the Trevor Griffiths double-bill, *Apricots* and *Thermidor*: and a fairly modest bid it was, too. McGrath asked for just £1,320, the money towards rehearsal costs, saying that he knew it might be too big an ask, and that he could support himself 'on fees for plays and any directing I may do, helped by some writing for films and T.V.' (ACGB, 1971, 43/43/2). Under a Labour government (1964–70), support for the arts had been growing: the Arts Council's budget increased, and its role as a key funding source for new initiatives in the arts was cemented into place. Later in the decade, a politicized alternative theatre sector would argue with itself about the paradox of taking state funding to criticize the state – but, in the early years of the alternative theatre movement, public funding was very welcome. McGrath was an early recipient of this new largesse, not least because he was an already established name and was a member of the Drama Panel; and he had already moved toward the kind of work that the new company would produce, during a fertile period with Allan Dossor's company at the Liverpool Everyman. Dossor, like McGrath, admired the work of Joan Littlewood at Theatre Workshop in East London and the community theatre projects of Peter Cheeseman at Stoke; both directors had crafted pieces of engaged, popular political theatre which came from (and attempted to connect with) particular working-class communities. McGrath's work at the Everyman (the group of short plays *Unruly Elements* (1971), and the plays *Soft or a Girl* (1971) and *Fish in the Sea* (1972)), can be thought of as his first venture into the kind of performance style that 7:84 adopted. *Soft or a Girl* (1971), for example, was a 7:84 show in embryo. It had a simple central narrative (the interweaving stories of two Liverpool families – one working class, one middle class), and it used rock music extensively – punctuating the action with songs that commented on the action; a mixture of different performance styles; and with its roots firmly set in Liverpool. It was also notable because it was a marked success, playing to capacity houses. It showed not only that such a show could be assembled, out of the history of the location and the popular culture of the time, but that there was an audience for this type of work.

However, it would take time to transfer this type of approach to the new theatre company: Dossor's Everyman company was already established, and its links to a local Liverpool audience were already strong. Working with the Everyman did give McGrath access to performers who were interested in the kind of performance style that he wanted his new company to employ. When it formed, 7:84 drew heavily not only on the style established at the Everyman, but also on the personnel with whom McGrath had worked: for example, Victor Henry (Joe, in *Trees in the Wind*, 1971) came from the Everyman (McGrath, 1975, 49). *Trees in the Wind*, the company's first show, was in some ways a rather conventional piece of late 1960s/early 1970s radical drama. Three women – each in their own way incarnating various strands of broad-left feminist thinking in the late 1960s/early 1970s – are confronted by a male character, Joe, who argues that the only way to change the capitalist system is to manipulate it from within. The play argues that Joe is wrong, and that only a complete transition to a new social and political structure will work. *Trees in the Wind* is one of a number of plays of the period which debated the options open to the broad, progressive Left – others included Trevor Griffiths' *The Party* (1973), David Hare's *The Great Exhibition* (1972), Howard Brenton's *Magnificence* (1973) and Pam Gems' *Dusa, Fish, Stas and Vi* (1976). It would fit neatly on to the stage of the Royal Court, or any of the more radical repertory theatres of the period (the Nottingham Playhouse, for example, which provided a home for Howard Brenton and David Hare's

Brassneck (1973) and Brenton's *The Churchill Play* (1974)). The plays that followed drew more directly on the work McGrath had produced in Liverpool; he revived and restaged *Unruly Elements* under the banner title *Plugged into History*, which toured in 1972. Secondly, it meant formulating a company credo which first appeared on the programme for *Serjeant Musgrave Marches On* (1972), a reworked version of John Arden's 1959 play. In it, McGrath noted that the company would have a strong nucleus of theatre workers, organized collectively around a central political and theatrical philosophy:

> They are united by their attitude to society, and to the role of theatre in society, an attitude informed by a socialist awareness. They have no desire to be demagogic, or simplistically 'agitational'. They see their role as trying to raise consciousness [...] They also want to present work which is good theatre, and which gives people a few laughs. (McGrath, 2005, 24)

In line with this credo, the young company produced work by other engaged writers: they toured Trevor Griffiths' *Occupations* (1972), and staged John Arden and Margaretta D'Arcy's *The Ballygombeen Bequest* (1972), alongside *Serjeant Musgrave Dances On*. This commitment to the work of other playwrights (and to work which came through the company itself) was to stand 7:84 in good stead as the decade progressed; McGrath was capable of working at a furious rate, but even he would not have been able to provide material for two geographically disparate theatre groups. This early statement of intent, however, also indicated (without intending to) one of the problems that both 7:84 companies in England and Scotland were to encounter later in the 1970s. Put simply, the work was tiring, both physically and creatively; all the work on tour was done by the company – setting up, performing, striking the set and moving to the next venue. Added to this, the statement set up an implicit tension between McGrath's role as artistic director and the work of the collective: in the future, arguments about the relative distribution of power between McGrath and both of the companies would be a source of unwelcome internal tension – especially when the political atmosphere turned against the kind of work that 7:84 did.

In the beginning, though, the troubles the company encountered came from the outside. In the febrile, politically heated atmosphere of the early 1970s, work which was in any way controversial (and which was funded in part by the state) would come under attack: and both *Serjeant Musgrave Dances On* and *The Ballygombeen Bequest* dealt with the Troubles in Northern Ireland at a time when the sectarian tensions of the 1960s had spilled over into armed confrontation. They did so, moreover, in a way which directly appealed to and implicated the audience; it was not possible to watch either show and to remain at a distance from the events staged. Arden and D'Arcy's play mixed black comedy, melodrama and shock effects (including the torture of an IRA suspect by British soldiers at a roadblock). *Musgrave* (directed by Richard Eyre) employed techniques that would become familiar parts of 7:84's work – direct address to the audience, the incorporation of elements taken directly from the events of the time, and the deliberate restructuring of the performance space, so that the audience and performers could encounter each other directly. *Musgrave's* third act, for example, took place in a theatre space that had been transformed, auditorium and all, into the play's town hall. As John Bull points out, the audience were included in the action, their involvement made explicit in the reworked setting and in the fact that the house lights remained up throughout the act (Bull, 2005, 50).

McGrath's adaptation of Arden's play was an important staging post in the development of the company's mature style, but at the time both plays were risky for a young company who only received project funding from the Arts Council: and not only risky in financial terms. In a Show Report of a performance of *Ballygombeen* at the Bush Theatre, London on 13 September 1972, Nick Barter says that there was a packed audience, but one that was 'searched as one went in' (ACGB, 1972b, 34/168/2). *The Ballygombeen Bequest* was taken out of production because of a threatened injunction by an Irish absentee landlord (who felt that he'd been slandered by the play); and letters of complaint were sent to the Arts Council, one coming from General Tuzo, the British Commander in Chief in Northern Ireland (ACGB, 1972c, 98/112). It is perhaps a sign of the agitational effectiveness of both plays that they attracted criticism from the very people they targeted. In the short term, though, the furore over *The Ballygombeen Bequest* meant that hints that the company had received that the Arts Council would provide long-term, sustained funding did not come to anything. McGrath's and the company's response to this uncertainty were to be decisive. The company did lose some members (Gavin Richards, for example, left to form the socialist theatre company Belt and Braces), but the most important decision taken at the time was to split the company in two. Some of the members of the company would continue in England, and others would go to Scotland (McGrath and especially Elizabeth MacLennan had strong family links to the country) to start a new group. McGrath would act as artistic director for both companies.

Funding for the Companies

Like all new companies, 7:84 had to prove their suitability for Arts Council funding – though it did not hurt that McGrath already had a track record when the group was formed. However, they were initially only given a DALTA GAL (Guarantee Against Loss) of £670 for the tour of *Unruly Elements* (ACGB, 1972d, 36/1). This was slightly added to for the year 1971/2 by the provision of a capital grant of £400, plus a further £400 GAL, from DALTA; with a further £250 from the New Drama Group – under the list, 'New Play Company with Ad Hoc Actors' – and then a supplementary grant of £750 by the Experimental Drama Committee. Given that all these items appeared as matters of report on the agenda of the May 1972 Experimental Drama Committee meeting, it is perhaps not too surprising that questions were raised about why the company was being funded by DALTA as well (ACGB, 1972e, 43/43/4). In fact, the situation was further complicated by the fact that £1,000 GAL had also already been granted by the Drama Panel in respect of 7:84's production of Trevor Griffiths' *Occupations.* (ACGB, 1972f, 36/1); and later that year, the Small-Scale-Touring Committee recommended a further £950 GAL for McGrath's own musical play, *Underneath* (ACGB, 1972g, 36/1). These acquisitions of funding, however small, were a result of the fact that McGrath's work could be seen as straightforward drama, as experimental and as new; and 7:84 met the requirements of both touring and small-scale-touring companies. As so often in Arts Council history, the areas were dealt with by completely different committees. This was one of the side effects of confining companies to project funding initially, as each project had a potential grant life of its own. What it does mean is that all is not quite as it first seems in funding terms. McGrath was clearly cognisant with all this and put in a £1,800 bid for 1972/3 (ACGB, 1972g, 36/1).

Establishing a reputation for themselves as a talented and enter-taining company, 7:84 had a supply of good scripts from McGrath and from other socialist playwrights. A more ambitious double-headed tour from August to December 1972 was planned, of John Arden and Margaretta D'Arcy's *The Ballygombeen Bequest* and McGrath's reworking of Arden's *Musgrave, Serjeant Musgrave Dances On.* The Touring Drama Committee recommended £2,500 GAL for the tour and this was accepted by the September 1972 Council meeting (ACGB, 1972h, 36/1). Both plays addressed contemporary political issues head-on and, in particular, *The Ballygombeen Bequest*'s presumption of taking on the Northern Ireland issue was seen as little less than treason by large sections of the establishment. One month later, the October Council meeting discussed the political worries expressed by the tabled correspondence (ACGB, 1972i, 36/1), and the seemingly confident move towards more substantial funding was rather put on hold: Council's subsequent provision of an additional £520 to the already agreed £2,500 (ACGB, 1973a, 36/1) was little more than an acceptance that a financial commitment had been made.

For a couple of years, as the shape of now two companies was forming, the ACGB offered 7:84 England what was really very minimal support, with money from Small-Scale Touring and New Drama (ACGB, 1973b, 36/1). In 1974, Council rejected a bid for money for two new vans with which to tour, a fundamental requirement placed upon the company (ACGB, 1974, 36/1).

However, shortly after this the tide began to turn. Under Small-Scale Touring, at the beginning of 1975 £7,000 was promised towards any deficit on the *Fish in the Sea* tour; and a Capital grant was given towards the cost of one van. By the year 1975/6 7:84 England received a subsidy of £24,000, plus £2,000 GAL (ACGB, 1975, 36/1), and they were among a swathe of groups receiving supplementary awards in January 1976. They were now apparently firmly back in the fold, and were awarded £36,000 for 1976/7, plus £4,000 GAL (ACGB, 1976, 36/1). However, by August 1978, Drama Officer Anton Gill had concluded that 7:84 (and some other groups) needed close observation and possible investigation by the Review Committee (ACGB, 1978, 38/9/19). The company was already notorious in the Drama Department for its somewhat relaxed presentation of income and audience figures, and the pressure of providing material and maintaining responsibility for two geographically separated companies was beginning to take its toll on McGrath. But, although doubts about the company's suitability for continued sponsorship were beginning to arise, it received funding of £83,000 for 1982/3: but time was running out.

Funding for 7:84 Scotland was provided through the Scottish Arts Council. It started with £2,000 GAL for the *Cheviot* tour, and from a figure of £8,800 for 1973/4, by 1976/7 it was in receipt of nearly £45,000. After a temporary blip in 1979/80, when only £11,000 was granted, by 1980/1 it was raised again to £50,000 and, just after its sister company had ceased to be, in 1987/8 the Scottish Arts Council awarded it over £134,000 (DiCenzo, 2002, 114).

Splitting the Company: 7:84 in England and Scotland

7:84 England (1973–86)

Understandably, it took a while for the two new companies to find their feet, but whereas in Scotland the new 7:84 had McGrath to lead them, the English company lost momentum; after a tour of Adrian Mitchell's *Man Friday* and an adaptation of Robert Tressell's *The Ragged Trousered Philanthropists* (both in 1973), the company produced no work until 1975. By this time the Scottish company was established (and had very quickly become a key part of the Scottish theatre scene – see below) and McGrath was able to give some time to the English company; the Arts Council had also given 7:84 England revenue funding – meaning that, for the first time in its career, the company could plan ahead securely. The first show the revived company staged was a slightly reworked version of McGrath's Everyman Theatre play, *Fish in the Sea* (directed by Pam Brighton); this marked the start of a productive burst of activity, which carried the company through the next two years. It seemed as though, after a hesitant start, 7:84 England could run in parallel with its more consistently successful Scottish sister company. Sandy Craig, associated with the company in its early days, came back as 7:84 England's administrator, and McGrath produced what are arguably two of his most successful, timely shows – *Lay Off* and *Yobbo Nowt* (both 1975) (a reworking of Brecht's/Gorky's *The Mother*, in which a disregarded working-class woman comes to recognize and fight back against the sources of her oppression).

The momentum built up by both of these shows faltered in the next few years: however, arguably what sustained the company during the times when its shows ran into difficulties was the policy that McGrath and Craig put in place when the English company revived. They actively sought out Trades Union and Labour organizations, and fostered strong links with them; in their turn these organizations provided the company with venues, an audience, publicity and, when the company needed it, financial and other means of support. Adverts for the shows would appear in community papers and in the left-wing press (in the Communist party's newspaper, *The Morning Star*, for example). The company also found other ways of publicizing their work; one show, *Bitter Apples* (1979), was advertised in a football programme (for Nottingham Forest versus Liverpool). The company also tried unsuccessfully to persuade Brian Clough, the Nottingham manager, to appear in the advertising campaign (Holdsworth, 1997,

31). There is strong evidence that this policy proved successful; the audiences for 7:84 shows were demographically different to those found in the mainstream theatre. A 1978 Mass Observation report (that also covered Monstrous Regiment and Triple Action Theatre Company) found that 7:84 was able to reach audiences who would not normally think of themselves as theatre-goers (certainly when compared to some other fringe/political groups):

> At Clay Cross 67 per cent of the audience was drawn from a manual worker background (C2, D, E) and 70 per cent finished their formal education at eighteen or earlier, and at Workington the C2, D, E proportion was 37 per cent [with] 40 per cent [having] completed full-time education before they were nineteen. (Holdsworth, 1997, 34)

This process was mirrored in Scotland (it forms the backdrop to McGrath's famous description, in *A Good Night Out*, of the first night of *The Game's a Bogey* (1974) in a Miners' club in Glenrothes). The difference was that, in Scotland, the company was swimming with the cultural tide, for reasons dealt with below; in England, closer ties with labour organizations were forged at a time when those organizations were in long-term retreat, as patterns of work and income distribution changed. This process had not yet taken on the momentum it did during the 1980s, when the incoming Conservative government conducted an ideologically driven war against the organized working classes; but it was already there – and it meant that 7:84 England's marketing and audience-building strategies were based on foundations that were weaker than they first appeared.

After this period of relative stability, the English company's fortunes dipped: McGrath, it is fair to say, gave most of his energy to the company in Scotland, and work in England suffered. The texts – Shane Connaughton's *Relegated*, McGrath's own *The Rat Trap* and Steve Gooch's *Our Land, Our Lives* (all 1976) – were not as strong, and the company began to suffer from the accumulated fatigue of a rigorous touring schedule. In McGrath's absence, arguments broke out over the structure and future direction of the company. It attempted to organize itself democratically, but McGrath's continued role as artistic director meant that any collective decisions had to be reconciled with his image of the company: something which, in practice, proved understandably difficult. In a 1976 letter, Sandy Craig reported on the director David Bradford's decision to pull out of the production of *Our Land, Our Lives*:

He feels that any group through touring tends to develop a strong individual identity and style of work. Thus they present an entity he can approach and work with. However, given that 1) the company [is] going through a number of personnel changes; and 2) the company's relationship to John McGrath who gives identity to the company- it is very difficult for an outside director to assume responsibility for a show [...] Is 7:84 there to perform John's work, or is it something else as well or something including that? Where does the real power in 7:84 lie? (McGrath, 2005, 42)

As we will see below, the Scottish company experienced something like the same tensions, but the difference was that in Scotland McGrath was more of a presence and could deal with these issues directly. This, though, left the English company in limbo (even though McGrath continued to write for them and to have a hand in the organization) and despite some good shows during the period (David Edgar's *Wreckers* (1977), one of the most astute analyses of the politics of the later 1970s, being a notable example) the company went into a sharp decline.

Ironically, the election of the Conservatives in 1979, under a Prime Minister whose plans for the country were in their way as radical as any since the end of the Second World War, sparked the company back to life. It helped that the quality of the scripts they worked with markedly improved; in this period they staged Barrie Keefe's *Sus*, John Burrows' *One Big Blow* (both 1980), Claire Luckhurst's *Trafford Tanzi* and McGrath's *Rejoice* (both 1982). However, the new government's impact on the arts was quickly felt: in 1980 for example, the Arts Council began a review of funding for theatre companies. Forty-one groups were examined, and three were cut. This was a sign of things to come: 7:84 England, who were swimming against the ideological tide (and who had an organizational structure which in some ways militated against consistent work), found itself very vulnerable, in a new, different cultural and political climate.

7:84 Scotland (1973–9)

When McGrath and MacLennan came to Scotland to set up 7:84 Scotland, they were aware that they were moving into different political and cultural territory:

We had become increasingly aware of the cultural and political differences between the situation in the south-east and the north of

England and Wales, and between their preoccupations and those of
people in Scotland. (MacLennan, 1990, 43)

If the company was to take the idea of raising the consciousness of
their audiences seriously (intervening in the debates that were of
most interest to that audience, and in doing so providing them with
both a Marxist analysis and a theatrically effective piece of work),
then they had to take account of the shifting nature of that audience;
and one of the strongest underlying forces in British life in the 1970s
was the resurgence of a particular form of nationalism in Scotland,
fuelled both by the discovery of North Sea oil (which was discovered
in 1969) and longer-term trends (declining heavy industry, the ebbing
influence of Protestant Unionism, which had guaranteed a vote for the
Conservatives in previous elections) conspired to re-enforce the sense
that Scotland was different; at the same time, Scotland already had the
structures of an independent country firmly in place. Scotland in the
1970s seemed very fertile territory for the kind of theatre they wanted
to produce. For instance, Scotland had its own educational, legal and
religious systems – hangovers from the Act of Union in 1707; it had
a long tradition of Labour organization, and left-wing activity more
generally; and the general tone of public life seemed rather more egalitarian than public life south of the border.

The most visible sign of Scotland's growing political distance from
the rest of the country was the electoral success of the Scottish National
Party [SNP] in by-elections and, to a lesser extent, in Westminster
votes, from 1967 onward; however, the SNP could not position itself
as a right-wing nationalist party (labour organizations, and the Labour
party, were far too well-entrenched in Scottish life), and so, beginning
in the 1970s, the SNP began to tack leftwards, and the Conservative
vote went into a long-term decline which gathered pace after Margaret
Thatcher became Prime Minister in 1979. It was not simply that
Scotland moved left at a time when the rest of the country moved
right; it is that, beginning in the 1960s (and, arguably, continuing
through to the present) Scotland engaged in a debate with itself over
the nature of Scottish identity – and whether that identity could find its
fullest expression inside or outside of the wider UK state. Against this
background, 7:84 Scotland's first show (*The Cheviot, the Stag and the
Black, Black Oil*, which toured Scotland in 1973) could not have been
more apt. The idea for a show about the impact of waves of enforced
economic change on the apparently timeless landscape of the Scottish
Highlands had been growing in McGrath's mind for the previous fifteen

years. However, the recent changes in the Scottish economy brought about by the discovery of oil gave the material both a contemporary relevance and a wider cultural impact; the Highland clearances had pitted Highlander against Lowlander, but what to do with the oil was Scotland's problem.

The company McGrath assembled to tour the show was a mixture of members of the previous incarnation of 7:84 (McGrath and MacLennan, her brother David, and Feri Lean, the company's administrator) and a number of Scottish actors and musicians (Alex Norton, Bill Paterson, John Bett, Dolina MacLennan and Allan Ross) with, between them, a great deal of experience of Scottish popular theatre. The three actors – Norton, Paterson and Bett – had worked together in *The Great Northern Welly Boot Show* the previous year; the show, written by Billy Connolly, was an almost perfect version of 7:84 Scotland in embryo: direct, funny and topical, it retold in thinly veiled form the story of the successful workers' occupation of Upper Clyde Shipbuilders. McGrath was aware of the show; and the actors, in turn, were aware of him. Alex Norton told the *Glasgow Herald* in 2011:

I was in *The Great Northern Welly Boot Show* (by Billy Connolly) in Edinburgh, and I saw a poster up for a play by the 7:84 company (the English company), *The Trees In The Wind*. Something in my head told me I just had to see this show and, for me, it was like the road to Damascus. I just knew it was the sort of theatre I wanted to become involved with. In fact, I vowed to myself that if I didn't get to do it, I'd chuck the business. (Norton, 2011)

Luckily for Norton (and for Patterson and Bett), McGrath had already seen the show, and had decided that he wanted to form the Scottish branch of 7:84 with them. These actors could provide him with the same skills that the Everyman performers had in 1971. They had experience of working directly with audiences in Scotland, and they were part of a broad, popular performance tradition – used to engaging their audiences directly, and switching between performance styles and registers as the show demanded.

The importance of *The Cheviot* in Scottish theatre is hard to overestimate. For Liz Lochhead, writing in 1987,

7:84 did rediscover, revitalise and quite blatantly harness to their own purposes something which, if it had any right to be called a 'tradition', had been first bastardised and then allowed to atrophy.

Impossible to remember just how fresh, how very cheeky indeed, seemed Bill Paterson's McChuckemup or Liz MacLennan's Harriet Beecher Stowe monologue or John Byrne's pop-up-book Heilan' set. Hard to recall the unfamiliarity of hearing Dolina MacLennan's Gaelic songs and Allan Ross' fiddle music swell to fill the Citizens' Theatre caused a shiver up the spine and a prickle at the back of the neck. (Anderson and MacLennan, 1987, 1)

As Lochhead points out, the show worked along lines established by popular performance forms that were still within living memory: the music halls and the variety circuit (forms which by the early 1970s had almost disappeared in Scotland, but which were still reanimated each year as Scots comedians and performers came to the larger urban theatres during the pantomime season). Even the idea of the ceilidh (the traditional, informal Highland gathering whose form *The Cheviot* sets out to follow) was not confined to the Highlands. For example, *The White Heather Club* (a sanitized and rather painfully twee version of a ceilidh, which had been a staple of BBC Scotland's programming from 1958 to 1968) had come to the end of its run only five years before. Arguably, what made *The Cheviot* work – and what ensured that 7:84 Scotland came to play an important role in the cultural life of the country in the 1970s – was that the show both used and satirized particularly Scottish tropes and images. David Edgar, in the argument discussed earlier, might have thought of the ceilidh form as part of the fading Celtic twilight, but this is to miss the point – images drawn from that Celtic twilight were themselves both a prominent feature of Scottish popular culture and also a ripe target for satire.

As noted above, Scotland, in the 1970s, had begun a process of redefinition: a show which took as its starting point the clichéd representation of the country's history would have had a direct, contemporary relevance – even if its subject matter had not dealt with the economic transformations of the 1970s. 7:84's first show was an example of the type of political theatre advocated by McGrath in *A Good Night Out*, but it was also an exercise in subversion. It opened with the glutinously sentimental faux-folk song 'For These Are My Mountains' (the kind of song that was a staple of *The White Heather Club*), used as an exercise in communal singing, but every time the song recurred, it was used by the more unscrupulous or powerful characters as an assertion of ownership, rather than as a celebration of kinship. The same dynamic works through the performance as a whole: all of those who assert their dominance over the people and the landscape are the ones who are most keen to dress themselves in the trappings of Scottishness – to prove themselves, in the words of Lord Crask and Lady Phosphate, 'more Scottish than the Scotch' (McGrath, 1996, 172).

The Cheviot inaugurated a series of shows that investigated the nature of contemporary Scottishness: *The Game's a Bogey* (1974) mixed a Marxist analysis of working-class structures in the West of Scotland (refracted through the speeches of the Scot John Maclean, a socialist intellectual from the early years of the twentieth century) with some sharp sideswipes at the commercialization of popular culture – and at the indigenous sectarianism which marked Glaswegian life; *Little Red Hen* (1975) contrasted the radical Scotland of Maclean with the nationalist resurgence of the 1970s; *Out of Our Heads* (1976) looked at alcohol in Scottish culture – a social anaesthetic, which both masked political failure and legitimized macho violence. Each one of these shows juxtaposed stereotypical images of Scottishness (Old Firm rivalry, the 1970s nationalist wrapped in tartan, the here's-tae-us-wha's-like-us bonhomie of the Scottish pub) with sharp portraits of the realities those images obscured. They used one of the basic techniques of agit-prop (simple, clear images and characterization, in the service of social analysis) but rather than employing images that clarified the argument, they employed images that subverted it. This in itself was enough to make sure that the company was an important voice in Scotland's cultural scene; it placed them on the same side as influential theorists such as Tom Nairn, who argued that Scotland suffered, more than most subordinate cultures, from a false view of itself, bound up in stereotyped images of Scottish identity (Nairn, 1977). The image of Scotland needed interrogating, and in the theatre 7:84 was the company that led that interrogation.

The impact of the company, however, went beyond simply presenting shows that interrogated Scottish politics and culture, and their place in the wider international environment. Their very presence was a catalyst: after 7:84 toured the Highlands and the Central Belt (the most populated part of Scotland, running from Glasgow across to Edinburgh) playing non-theatrical venues, the circuits they opened up were populated by a new generation of touring theatre groups, including Wildcat (who were offshoots of the original 7:84 company), Communicado, Clyde Unity and Borderline theatre. This in turn contributed to the development of an expanded Scottish theatrical infrastructure (crucial, given the rather hesitant nature of theatrical development in the country for much of the twentieth century). Ironically, though, at the same time that the company's example had started to be followed, the original team began to break up: the sheer pressure of touring took its toll, and debates over the relationship of the company to the Scottish National movement led to the exit of Dolina MacLennan. McGrath's position in the company was also a point of tension: his work-rate had been impressive, but even this could not compensate for the sheer difficulty of driving two companies forward at once. Stresses within the company were matched by outside pressures: the company was in financial difficulties by the end of the 1970s, because at a time of high inflation the grants 7:84 received were shrinking in value – and company policy was to keep ticket prices affordable for its audiences.

These pressures led to a change in the structure of the company. When it first started, 7:84 Scotland, like the original company, had organized itself as a loose collective (albeit one in which McGrath had more power than the other members, given his pivotal role in writing and directing the shows). As the 1970s gave way to the 1980s, a shifting membership, and the need to get costs under control, meant that 7:84 could no longer sustain a permanent company, and they were forced to move toward a different structure – one in which actors were hired for each show, and where tasks like stage management were no longer handled communally. For McGrath, this structural change was evidence of a wider political change, which was reshaping the UK as a whole:

> All in all, 7:84 was becoming more of a management, the company more of a work-force ranged against their 'bosses'. Because the company was not permanent – we could not afford it on existing finances – there were many 'hired hands' with short-term contracts. They were not involved in making decisions for the future work of the company, and they inherited the decisions of others about all the crucial areas of work. (McGrath, 1990, 94–5)

For McGrath, the new structure of the company wasn't simply a matter of financial expediency; it was part of a wider set of changes, coming from central government, which aimed to replace alternative forms of organization with the kind of top-down, hierarchical power structure that capitalism favoured. This was a more insidious way of altering the political make-up of a group like 7:84 than simply removing its funding: if it was structured like a capitalist company, it would come to behave like a capitalist company. From McGrath's perspective, this was exactly what happened; under the new structure, company members 'wanted us [McGrath and the management team] to be bosses, and them to be fee-earning professionals' (McGrath, 1990, 95).

Partly, this analysis is correct: as noted elsewhere, pressure was undoubtedly placed on funding organizations and theatre groups to abandon the communal structures of the 1970s and to adopt the government's preferred capitalist management structures. Scotland, even though it had its own arts funding structures, was not immune from this pressure. Partly, though, 7:84 came under pressure because their work had in some ways acted as a catalyst for Scottish theatre; and as the new decade dawned, other theatres and touring companies began to crowd in to the territory that 7:84 had to itself in the early 1970s. In particular, Wildcat (the company led by ex-7:84 members David MacLennan and David Anderson) was to Scottish theatre in the early 1980s what 7:84 Scotland had been in the 1970s: they produced the same kind of fast-moving, sharply funny shows – and they did so at a time when 7:84's work was starting to change from the kind of segmented, club night format of the 1970s into something more linear. *Swings and Roundabouts* (1980) relocated Noel Coward's *Private Lives* to a hotel in the Central Belt, and used the parent play's tight structure to evaluate shifting class allegiances in the early 1980s: *Blood Red Roses* (1980) told the story of a militant shop steward, from her childhood in the Highlands, through successful campaigns against multi-national capitalism, to eventual defeat and partial retrenchment. These were good shows (*Blood Red Roses*, like *The Cheviot*, was successfully adapted for TV) but they were no longer unique. In comparison to the early 1970s, Scottish theatre in the 1980s was beginning to thrive – and the kind of work that McGrath and the company produced was not that different to Wildcat, Borderline Theatre or Communicado, or to the plays produced at the Traverse theatre (under Chris Parr's artistic directorship) or at the Tron in Glasgow.

Conclusion

In a *Theatre Quarterly* interview in 1975, McGrath was asked how he would respond if Peter Hall, then director of the National Theatre, wanted to commission a play from him. He said:

I would run about twenty-five miles. The point really is that the National Theatre and the Aldwych [where the Royal Shakespeare Company were based] have got the facilities for really exciting work

[...] But it's everything else that would make me run. Well, really, I don't know that much about National Theatre audiences – except that they don't mean that much to me. I'd rather have a bad night in Bootle. You get more from it if someone's going to come up at the end and say, do you know what's happening in Bootle? (McGrath, 1975, 54)

Ten years later, however, the political and social atmosphere had changed radically. In an interview with *New Theatre Quarterly* (*Theatre Quarterly*'s successor), McGrath noted ruefully:

In fact, it's the Conservative Government and its policy of a long march through the institutions of Britain, replacing all the progressive and liberal people in those institutions with their own – 'one of ours', as Margaret Thatcher keeps saying – that has politicized the whole of Britain's institutional and social life. The Tories have politicized every aspect – the BBC, the IBA, the Arts Council, all the nationalized industries. They have become sites of extreme political struggle, because they've been cleared out. (McGrath, 1985, 396)

As he pointed out, there was something ironic in the fact that techniques of political insurgency associated with the Left were now being used by the Right, and that a revolution of sorts was reshaping the country – albeit from the top down, rather than from the bottom up. McGrath's work in the theatre, the continued life of the company that he had set up in the early 1970s and indeed the whole idea of an oppositional sector of British theatre were under direct threat as a result of this revolution.

A simple reading of the history of the period might suggest that 7:84 as a company waxed and waned as the political tides shifted around them. The kind of collective, socialist work they created in the 1970s, at a time when a thriving new left subculture was able to make common cause with a wider political culture (supported by the Labour Party and the Trades Unions), was no longer possible in the 1980s, both because of the determined assaults of a resurgent right-wing and because long-term patterns of employment and social organization were changing (and the traditional sites of union organization were crumbling). Work that was relevant – and which seemed to be on the side of history – in the 1970s was out of place in the 1980s; a country which in some ways seemed ripe for Marxism had come to embrace the peculiarly paradoxical version of Conservatism that Thatcher embodied – a Conservatism made up, in equal measure, of free-market liberalism and a return to Victorian social pieties. There was, of course, more to the rise and fall of the company than that. 7:84 helped to pioneer a particular way of creating theatre: collaborative (at least to an extent), responsive to events and imbued with a clear political and cultural rationale. They also helped to forge new touring circuits, both in England and (more particularly) in Scotland. And, arguably, in Scotland their legacy is yet to fade: *The Cheviot, the Stag and the Black, Black Oil* was, as has been frequently noted, a key production in the history of modern Scottish theatre, and later work (in particular the Clydebuilt season (1982), which revived texts from the country's hidden theatrical past) helped to bolster and develop a particularly Scottish form of engaged theatre. However, having said that, the company's internal politics were perhaps as crucial in determining its development and its ultimate fate as was the external political situation. The history of 7:84 England and Scotland is at least partly the history of a company and its creator who stretched themselves beyond what was artistically and organizationally feasible – even if they did so with the best of intentions.

Productions

7:84 Productions
1971   *Trees in the Wind* by John McGrath
      Thermidor and *Apricots* by Trevor Griffiths
1972   *Plugged into History* by John McGrath
      Underneath by John McGrath
      Occupations by Trevor Griffiths
1972   *Serjeant Musgrave Dances On* by John McGrath (based on John Arden's *Serjeant Musgrave's Dance*)
      The Ballygombeen Bequest by John Arden and Margaretta D'Arcy

7:84 Scotland
1973   *The Cheviot, the Stag and the Black, Black Oil* by John McGrath
1974   *The Game's a Bogey* by John McGrath
      Boom by John McGrath
1975   *My Pal and Me* by John McGrath
      Capital Follies by David MacLennan and John Bett
      Little Red Hen by John McGrath
1976   *Honour Your Partners* by John McGrath
      Out of Our Heads by John McGrath

1977 *Thought for Today* by David MacLennan
      The Trembling Giant by John McGrath
1979 *Joe's Drum* by John McGrath
1980 *Swings and Roundabouts* by John McGrath
      Blood Red Roses by John McGrath

7:84 England

1973 *Man Friday* by Adrian Mitchell
      The Reign of Terror and *The Great Money Trick*
1974 *Fish in the Sea* by John McGrath
1975 *Lay Off* by John McGrath
      Yobbo Nowt by John McGrath
1976 *Relegated* by Shane Connaughton
      Rat Trap by John McGrath
      Our Land, Our Lives by Steve Gooch
1977 *Wreckers* by David Edgar
      Trembling Giant (a pantomime for children of all ages, with songs) by John McGrath
      Joe of England by John McGrath
1978 *Underneath* by John McGrath
      Vandalour's Folly by John Arden and Margaretta D'Arcy
1979 *Bitter Apples* by John McGrath
      Trees in the Wind by John McGrath
      Big Square Fields by John McGrath

BIBLIOGRAPHY

Chapters 1 and 2

Ansorge, Peter (1975), *Disrupting the Spectacle: Five Years of Experimental and Fringe Theatre in Britain* (London: Pitman).

A Policy for the Arts (1965), Government White Paper.

Arts Council of Great Britain Archive, Victoria and Albert Museum, London (1965a), Nigel Abercrombie, letter to Carol Johnson MP, 12 November, ACGB 38/18/2.

Arts Council of Great Britain Archive, Victoria and Albert Museum, London (1965b), Dennis Andrews, letter to Hugh Jenkins, 15 September, ACGB 38/9/5.

Arts Council of Great Britain Archive, Victoria and Albert Museum, London (1966a), Arts Council 21st Annual Report 1965–1966 'Key Year'.

Arts Council of Great Britain Archive, Victoria and Albert Museum, London (1966b), M. J. McR, 'Memo Box 39 – Royal Opera House', 24 October, ACGB 38/19/2.

Arts Council of Great Britain Archive, Victoria and Albert Museum, London (1967), Dick Linklater, 'New Developments', 12 December, ACGB 41/79/1.

Arts Council of Great Britain Archive, Victoria and Albert Museum, London (1968a), Minutes of 154th (24 April) and 155th (29 May) Council meetings, ACGB 36/1.

Arts Council of Great Britain Archive, Victoria and Albert Museum, London (1968b), Minutes of 1st meeting of New Activities Committee, in minutes of 160th Council meeting, 28 November, 36/1.

Arts Council of Great Britain Archive, Victoria and Albert Museum, London (1969a), Bruce Birchall letter to Ian Bruce, ACGB 41/46/2.

Arts Council of Great Britain Archive, Victoria and Albert Museum, London (1969b), Dennis Andrews letter to Bruce Birchall, ACGB 41/46/2.

Arts Council of Great Britain Archive, Victoria and Albert Museum, London (1969c), Minutes of 162nd meeting of Council, ACGB 36/1.

Arts Council of Great Britain Archive, Victoria and Albert Museum, London (1969d), 'New Arts Laboratory', 28 September, ACGB 41/47/4.

Arts Council of Great Britain Archive, Victoria and Albert Museum, London (1969e), Ronnie Scott's Sunday Festivals programme, 7 March, ACGB 41/49.

Arts Council of Great Britain Archive, Victoria and Albert Museum, London (1969f), Roland Miller, Proposal for Premises in London, August 5, ACGB 41/47/4.

Arts Council of Great Britain Archive, Victoria and Albert Museum, London (1970a), Dennis Andrews report, and hand-written internal note, October, ACGB 41/48/323.

Arts Council of Great Britain Archive, Victoria and Albert Museum, London (1970b), Minutes of 180th meeting of Council, 29 July, ACGB 36/2.

Arts Council of Great Britain Archive, Victoria and Albert Museum, London (1970c), Roland Miller and Shirley Cameron letter to Michael Dawson, Yorkshire Arts Association, 14 November, ACGB 41/46/2.

Arts Council of Great Britain Archive, Victoria and Albert Museum, London (1970d), Unknown reviewer Show Report on John Bull Puncture Repair Kit performance, ACGB 41/48/3.

Arts Council of Great Britain Archive, Victoria and Albert Museum, London (1970e), John Darling request for financial support for Yorkshire Gnomes, ACGB 41/50/2.

Arts Council of Great Britain Archive, Victoria and Albert Museum, London (1971a), Internal Memo, undated, ACGB 34/39.

Arts Council of Great Britain Archive, Victoria and Albert Museum, London (1971b), Minutes of 1st meeting of Experimental Projects Committee, ACGB 43/42/6.

Arts Council of Great Britain Archive, Victoria and Albert Museum, London (1971e), 1971 Bradford Festival programme, 8 January, ACGB 41/46/2.

Arts Council of Great Britain Archive, Victoria and Albert Museum, London (1971f), Small Scale Theatre listings 1971, 1 January, ACGB 38/9/17.

Arts Council of Great Britain Archive, Victoria and Albert Museum, London (1971g), Ken Campbell letter to Peter Mair, 21 September, ACGB 43/43/2.

Arts Council of Great Britain Archive, Victoria and Albert Museum, London (1971h), Combination Theatre Pamphlet, December, ACGB 98/35.

Arts Council of Great Britain Archive, Victoria and Albert Museum, London (1971i), Sue Timothy Show Report on Action Space, 16 November, ACGB 41/46/2.

Arts Council of Great Britain Archive, Victoria and Albert Museum, London (1971j), Ken and Mary Turner applications for funding for Action Space, ACGB 41/46/1.

Arts Council of Great Britain Archive, Victoria and Albert Museum, London (1971k), Nick Barter Show Report on *Part of a Party Landscape*, 27 November, ACGB 41/47/2.

Arts Council of Great Britain Archive, Victoria and Albert Museum, London (1972a), Dick Linklater internal memo, 16 May 1972, ACGB 38/9/11.

Arts Council of Great Britain Archive, Victoria and Albert Museum, London (1972b), Minutes of 8th meeting of Experimental Drama Committee, 8 February, ACGB 43/43/7.

Arts Council of Great Britain Archive, Victoria and Albert Museum, London (1972c), Howard Brenton letter to Nick Barter, 17 January, ACGB 43/43/1.

Arts Council of Great Britain Archive, Victoria and Albert Museum, London

(1972d), Hermine Demoriane Request for Financial Support, January, ACGB 41/47/2.

Arts Council of Great Britain Archive, Victoria and Albert Museum, London (1972e), Letter from Mary Turner, 22 and 23 February, ACGB 41/47/2.

Arts Council of Great Britain Archive, Victoria and Albert Museum, London (1972f), Ken Campbell letter to Nick Barter, 30 April, ACGB 43/43/3.

Arts Council of Great Britain Archive, Victoria and Albert Museum, London (1972g), Minutes of the 10th meeting of the Experimental Drama Committee, 10 March, ACGB 43/42/7.

Arts Council of Great Britain Archive, Victoria and Albert Museum, London (1973a), Roland Miller, 'Paper on Performance Art and Performance Artists', prepared for the Experimental Drama Committee, 28 September, ACGB 43/42/7.

Arts Council of Great Britain Archive, Victoria and Albert Museum, London (1973c), Bruce Birchall letter to Drama Panel, October, ACGB 38/35/1.

Arts Council of Great Britain Archive, Victoria and Albert Museum, London (1973d), Bruce Birchall letter to Drama Panel, 5 September: ACGB 38/35/1.

Arts Council of Great Britain Archive, Victoria and Albert Museum, London (1973e), Bruce Birchall letter to Drama Panel, 5 November, ACGB 38/35/1.

Arts Council of Great Britain Archive, Victoria and Albert Museum, London (1973f), Cari Saluti (AKA Genesis P-Orridge) letter to Susan Timothy, no date, ACGB 98/91.

Arts Council of Great Britain Archive, Victoria and Albert Museum, London (1973g), 1973 Internal Memo from Nick Barter, 12 February, ACGB 41/47/2.

Arts Council of Great Britain Archive, Victoria and Albert Museum, London (1973i), Steven Berkoff letter to Nick Barter, early 1973, ACGB 43/43/7.

Arts Council of Great Britain Archive, Victoria and Albert Museum, London (1973j), Sharon Nassauer to Nick Barter, Experimental Drama Committee, 28 September, ACGB 41/46/2.

Arts Council of Great Britain Archive, Victoria and Albert Museum, London (1973k), Action Space Application for Grant Aid, 22 February, ACGB 41/46/2.

Arts Council of Great Britain Archive, Victoria and Albert Museum, London (1973l), Jeff Nuttall 'The Situation Regarding Performance Art', prepared for the Experimental Drama Committee, August, ACGB 43/42/7.

Arts Council of Great Britain Archive, Victoria and Albert Museum, London (1973m), Landscapes and Living Space Itinerary January–March 1973, ACGB 41/47/3.

Arts Council of Great Britain Archive, Victoria and Albert Museum, London (1973n), Nick Barter Show Report on Landscapes and Living Spaces, 29 December, ACGB 41/46/4.

Arts Council of Great Britain Archive, Victoria and Albert Museum, London
  (1973o), Phantom Captain, letter of application and Company History to
  Nick Barter, 29 January, ACGB 43/43/6.
Arts Council of Great Britain Archive, Victoria and Albert Museum, London
  (1973p), Nicholas Barter letter to Genesis P-Orridge, 6 June, and reply,
  ACGB 41/47/1.
Arts Council of Great Britain Archive, Victoria and Albert Museum, London
  (1974a), B. A. Young, internal memo, 'Drama Policy in 1976/7', 18 July,
  ACGB 38/9/14.
Arts Council of Great Britain Archive, Victoria and Albert Museum, London
  (1974b), Bruce Birchall letter to Drama Panel, 21 February, ACGB 38/35/1.
Arts Council of Great Britain Archive, Victoria and Albert Museum, London
  (1974c), Bruce Birchall letter to Drama Panel, 21 March, and Nick Barter
  letter to Birchall, 5 April, ACGB 38/35/1.
Arts Council of Great Britain Archive, Victoria and Albert Museum, London
  (1974d), RW Show Reports on *Pensioners* and *Law*, 22 April, ACGB
  38/35/1.
Arts Council of Great Britain Archive, Victoria and Albert Museum, London
  (1974e), Minutes of 225th meeting of Council, 25 September, ACGB 36/3.
Arts Council of Great Britain Archive, Victoria and Albert Museum, London
  (1974f), Minutes of 39th Meeting of Fringe and Experimental Drama
  Committee, 3 September, ACGB 43/43.
Arts Council of Great Britain Archive, Victoria and Albert Museum, London
  (1974g), Dick Lindlater letter to Sir Hugh Willatt, 3 October; Bruce
  Birchall letter to Hugh Willatt, 23 September; Willatt letter to Birchall, 16
  October, ACGB 38/35/1.
Arts Council of Great Britain Archive, Victoria and Albert Museum, London
  (1974h), Quipu Production Ltd File, ACGB 98/113.
Arts Council of Great Britain Archive, Victoria and Albert Museum, London
  (1974i), 1974 Belts and Braces Roadshow handout, ACGB 98/37.
Arts Council of Great Britain Archive, Victoria and Albert Museum, London
  (1974j), Lynne Kirwin letter, 1 October, ACGB 98/37.
Arts Council of Great Britain Archive, Victoria and Albert Museum, London
  (1974k), Women's Theatre Group letter to ACGB, 5 April, ACGB 41/79/4.
Arts Council of Great Britain Archive, Victoria and Albert Museum, London
  (1974m), Hammersmith Mini-Performance Art Festival Programme,
  ACGB 41/19/6.
Arts Council of Great Britain Archive, Victoria and Albert Museum, London
  (1975a), Peter Farago Show Report on *Strike* 1926, 2 June, ACGB 38/35/1.
Arts Council of Great Britain Archive, Victoria and Albert Museum, London
  (1975b), Groups subsidized by Experimental Drama Committee in 1975/6,
  ACGB 43/43/13.
Arts Council of Great Britain Archive, Victoria and Albert Museum, London
  (1975c), Bruce Birchall letter to ACGB, 27 February, ACGB 38/35/1.

Arts Council of Great Britain Archive, Victoria and Albert Museum, London (1975d), Minutes of 1st Meeting of New Touring Committee, 25 March, ACGB 98/35/9.

Arts Council of Great Britain Archive, Victoria and Albert Museum, London (1975e), Bruce Birchall letter to Peter Farago, 9 April; Farago letter to Birchall, 11 April, ACGB 41/79/2.

Arts Council of Great Britain Archive, Victoria and Albert Museum, London (1975g), Gillian Hanna letter to Lynne Kirwin and hand-written internal ACGB note, no date, ACGB 98/37.

Arts Council of Great Britain Archive, Victoria and Albert Museum, London (1975h), Mike Alfreds' application to Drama Director, 10 November, ACGB 34/142/2.

Arts Council of Great Britain Archive, Victoria and Albert Museum, London (1975i), Common Stock presents a brand new season, ACGB 98/89.

Arts Council of Great Britain Archive, Victoria and Albert Museum, London (1976a), Dick Linklater memo, 18 March, ACGB 38/9/13.

Arts Council of Great Britain Archive, Victoria and Albert Museum, London (1976b) Peter Farago internal memo to Chairman and Drama Director, 18 March, ACGB 38/9/13.

Arts Council of Great Britain Archive, Victoria and Albert Museum, London (1976c), Bruce Birchall to Drama Panel, January, ACGB 41/79/2.

Arts Council of Great Britain Archive, Victoria and Albert Museum, London (1976d), Jenny Rees et al., undated, and 6 June, ACGB 34/125/1.

Arts Council of Great Britain Archive, Victoria and Albert Museum, London (1976e), Minutes of 244th Meeting of Arts Council, 26 May, ACGB 36/6.

Arts Council of Great Britain Archive, Victoria and Albert Museum, London (1976g), 5th (17 June) and 6th (30 September) Review Committee, ACGB 34/2/7.

Arts Council of Great Britain Archive, Victoria and Albert Museum, London (1976h), Drama 'Fringe' Allocation 1976/7, ACGB 38/9/13.

Arts Council of Great Britain Archive, Victoria and Albert Museum, London (1976i), Minutes of 234th meeting of Arts Council 25 June, and of 246th meeting 28 July, ACGB 36/6.

Arts Council of Great Britain Archive, Victoria and Albert Museum, London (1976j), Letter from Rosemary Heesom, North West Arts to Dick Linklater (19 July), and reply (21 July), together with 'The Fight for the Fringe Campaign' leaflet, ACGB 34/134/1.

Arts Council of Great Britain Archive, Victoria and Albert Museum, London (1977a), 'The London Fringe' Internal Drama Department memo, 30 November, ACGB 38/9/19.

Arts Council of Great Britain Archive, Victoria and Albert Museum, London (1977b), 'Pirate Jenny', April, ACGB 34/125/2.

Arts Council of Great Britain Archive, Victoria and Albert Museum, London (1977c), Drama Department internal memo, 30 November, ACGB 38/9/19.

Arts Council of Great Britain Archive, Victoria and Albert Museum, London (1977d), Pirate Jenny Touring Schedule for *Our People*, ACGB 34/125/2.

Arts Council of Great Britain Archive, Victoria and Albert Museum, London (1977f), Vincent Burke letter to Drama Panel, 15 March; and Drama Director, John Faulkner letter to Burke, 6 April, ACGB 34/125/1.

Arts Council of Great Britain Archive, Victoria and Albert Museum, London (1977g), Review Committee Meeting Minutes 1977/8; and Clive Tempest Memo, 5 September, ACGB 34/125/2.

Arts Council of Great Britain Archive, Victoria and Albert Museum, London (1977i), Drama Department memo to Secretary General, 30 November, ACGB 38/9/19.

Arts Council of Great Britain Archive, Victoria and Albert Museum, London (1977j), John Faulkner, Drama Director, letter to Richard Hoggart, ACGB 38/9/19.

Arts Council of Great Britain Archive, Victoria and Albert Museum, London (1977k), Standards and Reassessment Meeting, 10 March, ACGB 34/125/2.

Arts Council of Great Britain Archive, Victoria and Albert Museum, London (1977l), Show Reports on *A Day in the Life of the World*, from RS (21 July), John Faulkner (27 July) and Peter Mair (8 July), ACGB 34/2/7.

Arts Council of Great Britain Archive, Victoria and Albert Museum, London (1977m), Red Ladder Theatre Company, Programme for Year 1977/8, ACGB 34/134/6.

Arts Council of Great Britain Archive, Victoria and Albert Museum, London (1977n), Chris Rawlence letter to Peter Mair, 5 October; ACGB Press Notice, 7 October; Theatre Writers Union letter to Drama Department, October; internal memo, 6 October, ACGB 34/134/1.

Arts Council of Great Britain Archive, Victoria and Albert Museum, London (1977o), Paul Hellyer letter to Peter Mair, 26 April, ACGB 34/2/7.

Arts Council of Great Britain Archive, Victoria and Albert Museum, London (1977p), 'London Fringe Drama Department internal memo to Secretary General, 30 November, ACGB 38/9/19.

Arts Council of Great Britain Archive, Victoria and Albert Museum, London (1977q), Minutes of 250th meeting of Drama Panel, 26 January, ACGB 36/37.

Arts Council of Great Britain Archive, Victoria and Albert Museum, London (1977r), Howard Gibbins Show Report on *Floor Show* and *Kiss and Kill*, 23/24 November, ACGB 34/105/1.

Arts Council of Great Britain Archive, Victoria and Albert Museum, London (1977s), Women's Theatre Group Introduction for Standing Conference of Young People's Theatre 1977 conference, ACGB 34/164/1.

Arts Council of Great Britain Archive, Victoria and Albert Museum, London (1977t), Minutes of 252nd meeting of Drama Panel, 23 March, ACGB 36/7.

Arts Council of Great Britain Archive, Victoria and Albert Museum, London

(1977u), ACGB letter to Sue Beardon of Monstrous Regiment, 27 April, ACGB 34/105/1.

Arts Council of Great Britain Archive, Victoria and Albert Museum, London (1977v), Anton Gill internal memo after meeting with Women's Theatre Group, 26 May, ACGB 34/164/1.

Arts Council of Great Britain Archive, Victoria and Albert Museum, London (1977w), Mike Alfreds' letter to Clive Tempest, 25 April, ACGB 34/142/2.

Arts Council of Great Britain Archive, Victoria and Albert Museum, London (1977x), Drama Department to Secretary General, 'The London Fringe', 30 November, ACGB 38/9/19.

Arts Council of Great Britain Archive, Victoria and Albert Museum, London (1978a), Show Reports on *Our Own People* from Anthony Everitt, March; Jonathan Lamede, 6 December; Philip Hedley,11 January; and Anton Gill, 13 January, ACGB 34/125/2.

Arts Council of Great Britain Archive, Victoria and Albert Museum, London (1978b), Jenny Rees letter to Anton Gill, 10 March; John Faulkner letter to Rees, 15 March, ACGB 34/125/2.

Arts Council of Great Britain Archive, Victoria and Albert Museum, London (1978c), Jenny Rees letter to John Faulkner, 14 September, ACGB 34/125/4.

Arts Council of Great Britain Archive, Victoria and Albert Museum, London (1978d), Jonathan Lamede Show Report on *Bleak House*, 1 February, ACGB 34/142/2.

Arts Council of Great Britain Archive, Victoria and Albert Museum, London (1978e), ACGB Subsidy figures, ACGB 34/142/2.

Arts Council of Great Britain Archive, Victoria and Albert Museum, London (1979a), Confidential: 'Review of Exploitation of Subsidised Theatres' Product', 20 March, ACGB 98/38.

Arts Council of Great Britain Archive, Victoria and Albert Museum, London (1979b), Shirley Barrie letter to Roy Shaw, 29 March, ACGB 38/9/24.

Arts Council of Great Britain Archive, Victoria and Albert Museum, London (1979c), Minutes of Council, 10 September, ACGB 38/9/21.

Arts Council of Great Britain Archive, Victoria and Albert Museum, London (1979d), Tony Field letter to Jenny Rees, together with filed hand-written note from Howard Gibbins, 20 February; Howard Gibbins internal memo, 17 April; internal memo, October, ACGB 34/125/4.

Arts Council of Great Britain Archive, Victoria and Albert Museum, London (1979e), Hand-written addenda to John Faulkner note to Chris Cooper, 26 March, ACGB 34/2/7.

Arts Council of Great Britain Archive, Victoria and Albert Museum, London (1979f), Gloria Parkinson, Show Report on *Accidental Death of an Anarchist,* no date, ACGB 34/2/1.

Arts Council of Great Britain Archive, Victoria and Albert Museum, London (1979g), Gavin Richards letter to John Faulkner, 14 March, ACGB 34/2/5.

Arts Council of Great Britain Archive, Victoria and Albert Museum, London (1979h), Temba Theatre Files: Financial Details; letter from Temba Theatre Company to ACGB, December 1977; Peter Mair Show Report of *Caliban Lives*, undated; internal memo from Peter Mair to John Faulkner, 14 February 1979, ACGB 34/159/2.

Arts Council of Great Britain Archive, Victoria and Albert Museum, London (1979i), Jill Davis Show Report on *Soap Opera*, 16 March, ACGB 34/164/1.

Arts Council of Great Britain Archive, Victoria and Albert Museum, London (1979j), Minutes of Board Meeting of Women's Theatre Group, 29 August, ACGB 34/164/1.

Arts Council of Great Britain Archive, Victoria and Albert Museum, London (1979k), CD report back from Monstrous Regiment meeting, 15 May, ACGB 34/105/1.

Arts Council of Great Britain Archive, Victoria and Albert Museum, London (1980), Belts and Braces Press Release, 17 January, ACGB 34/2/7.

Bainbridge, Luke (2007), 'The Ten Right-Wing Rockers', *The Guardian*, 14 October.

Barberis, Peter, John McHugh and Mike Tyldesley (2005), *Encyclopedia of British and Irish Political Organizations* (London: Continuum International Publishing).

BBC News (2001), '*Epoch-making poster was clever fake*', 16 March, http://news.bbc.co.uk/1/hi/uk/1222326.stm (accessed 13 September 2015).

Beckett, Andy (2010), *When the Lights Went Out: What Really Happened to Britain in the Seventies* (London: Faber).

Beetham, Sir Michael (2015), Obituary, *The Times*, 28 October.

Bew, Paul and Gordon Gillespie (1999), *Northern Ireland: A Chronology of the Troubles 1968–1999* (Lanham, MD: Scarecrow Press).

Birchall, Bruce (1977/8), 'Grant Aid and Political Theatre 1968–77', *Wedge* 1/2.

Bleich, Erik (2003), *Race: Politics in Britain and France: Ideas and Policymaking Since the 1960s* (Cambridge: Cambridge University Press).

Bosanquet, Nick and Peter Townsend (1972), *Labour and Inequality: Sixteen Fabian Essays* (London: Fabian Society).

Bosanquet, Nick and Peter Townsend (1980), *Labour and Equality: A Fabian Study of Labour in Power, 1974–79* (London: Heinemann).

Boyd-Carpenter, John (1967), 'Why the Pound is Weaker', *The Times*, 13 November.

Brenton, Howard (1973), *Magnificence* (London: Faber).

Brenton, Howard (1975), 'Petrol Bombs Through the Proscenium Arch', *Theatre Quarterly* 5 (17): 20.

Brenton, Howard (1976a), *Weapons of Happiness* (London: Faber).

Brenton, Howard (1976b), 'The Man Behind the Lyttelton's First New Play', *The Times*, 10 July.

Brenton, Howard, and Tony Howard (1979), *A Short Sharp Shock for the Government* (London: Faber).

Bright, Martin (2002), *The Observer*, 3 February.

Bryant, Julian, 'Temba – the early years', http://creatingtheatre.com/about/
early-work/ (accessed 23 January 2016).

Bull, John (1984), *New British Political Dramatists* (Basingstoke: Macmillan).

Bunce, Robin and Paul Field (2014), *Darcus Howe: A Political Biography*
(London: Bloomsbury).

Café, Rebecca (2011), BBC Radio 4 News, 4 December.

Callaghan, James (1973) Lecture at Ruskin College, Oxford, http://www.
educationengland.org.uk/documents/speeches/1976ruskin.html (accessed
8 Novemeber 2015).

Carter, April (1986), 'Campaign for Nuclear Disarmament', in Linus Pauling,
Ervin Laszlo and Jong Youl (eds), *The World Encyclopedia of Peace*
(Oxford: Pergamon): 109–13.

Castle, Barbara (1984), *The Castle Diaries: 1964–1970* (London: Weidenfeld
and Nicolson).

Chambers, Colin (1980), *Other Spaces: New Theatre and the RSC* (London:
Eyre Methuen).

Chambers, Colin (2011), *Black and Asian Theatre in Britain: A History*
(London: Bloomsbury).

Cohen, Stanley (2002), *Folk Devils and Moral Panics: The Creation of the Mods
and Rockers* (London: Routledge).

Cortright, David (2008), *Peace: A History of Movements and Ideas*
(Cambridge: Cambridge University Press).

Coveney, Michael (2008), Ken Campbell Obituary, *The Guardian*, 1 September.

Cox, C. B. and Rhodes Boyson (eds) (1975), *Black Paper 1975: The Fight for
Education* (London: Dent).

Cox, C. B. and Rhodes Boyson (eds) (1977), *Black Paper 1977* (London:
Maurice Temple Smith).

Cox, C. B. and A. E. Dyson (eds) (1969a), *Fight for Education: A Black
Paper* (London: Critical Quarterly Society).

Cox, C. B. and A. E. Dyson (eds) (1969b), *Black Paper Two: The Crisis in
Education* (London: Critical Quarterly Society).

Cox, C. B. and A. E. Dyson (eds) (1970), *Black Paper Three: Goodbye Mr Short*
(London: Critical Quarterly Society).

Craig, Sandy (ed.) (1980), *Dreams and Deconstructions: Alternative Theatre in
Britain* (London: Amber Lane).

Croft, Susan and Unfinished Histories (2013), *Re-Staging Revolutions:
Alternative Theatre in Lambeth and Camden 1968–1988* (London:
Unfinished Histories).

Crosby, John (1965), *The Daily Telegraph*, 16 April.

Daily Telegraph (2007), Enoch Powell's 'Rivers of Blood' Speech, 6 November.

Daily Telegraph (2010), Harold Macmillan's 'Never So Good' Speech in full, 19
November.

Dalton, Ernest (1980), *The Spanner Experiment* (London: Justpress).

Dartmoor Resource (2016), 'Medium Fair', http://www.dartmoorresource.org. uk/performance/theatre-on-dartmoor/theatre-history-of/115-medium-fair-company-the-start-of-community-theatre-on-dartmoor (accessed 15 September 2015).

Davies, Andrew (1987), *Other Theatres: The Development of Alternative and Experimental Theatre in Britain* (Basingstoke: Macmillan).

Denning, Lord (1963), *Lord Denning's Report. Presented to Parliament by the Prime Minister by Command of Her Majesty*, September (London: Her Majesty's Stationery Office).

Dewhurst, Keith (1974), 'One Rarely Sees', *The Guardian*, 24 January.

DiCenzo, Maria (1996), *The Politics of Alternative Theatre in Britain 1968–1990: The Case of 7:84 (Scotland)* (Cambridge: Cambridge University Press).

Eccles, Lord David (1971), Paymaster General with Responsibility for the Arts, Address to Regional Arts Conference, *Arts and Education*, Northern Arts Association, Newcastle.

Edgar, David (1977), *Destiny* (London: Eyre Methuen).

Edgar, David (1988), *The Second Time as Farce: Reflections on the Drama of Mean Times* (London: Lawrence and Wishart).

Edgar, David (2005), 'My Fight with the Front', *The Guardian*, 14 September.

Edgar, David (2009) 'Noël Greig: Obituary', *The Guardian*, 23 September, http://www.theguardian.com/stage/2009/sep/23/noel-greig-obituary

Friedan, Betty (1963), *The Feminine Mystique* (London: Victor Gollanz).

Friel, Brian (2013), *The Freedom of the City* in *Plays One* (London: Bloomsbury).

Gardner, Lyn (2008), Review of *Shakespeare's Party*, *The Guardian*, 21 May.

Gilbert, David (2006), 'The Youngest Legend in History: Cultures of Consumption and the Mythologies of Swinging London', *The London Journal* 31 (1): 1–14.

Goodman, Liz (1993), *Contemporary Feminist Theatres: To Each Their Own* (London: Routledge).

Greer, Germaine (1970), *The Female Eunuch* (London: McGibbon and Kee).

Griffiths, Trevor (1973), *The Party* (London: Faber).

Griffiths, Trevor (1976), 'Transforming the Husk of Capitalism', *Theatre Quarterly* vi (22).

Griffiths, Trevor (1977), *All Good Men and Absolute Beginners: Two Plays for Television* (London: Faber).

Hall, Stuart, E. P. Thompson and Raymond Williams (1968), *The May Day Manifesto* (London: Penguin).

Hanna, Gillian (ed.) (1991), *Monstrous Regiment: Four Plays and a Collective Celebration* (London: Nick Hern).

Hansard (1963), 21 March.

Hawthorne, George (1968), 'Portugal's shirts on Britain's backs', *The Guardian*, 12 January.

Haynes, Jim (1984), *Thanks for Coming!* (London: Faber).

Hebdige, Dick (1979), *Subculture: The Meaning of Style* (London: Methuen).

Hebdige, Dick (1993), 'The Meaning of Mod', in Stuart Hall and Tony Jefferson (eds), *Resistance Through Rituals: Youth Subcultures in Post-War Britain* (London: Routledge).

Heffer, Simon (1999), *Like the Roman: The Life of Enoch Powell* (London: Orion Books).

Hewison, Robert (1995), *Culture and Consensus: England, Art and Politics Since 1940* (London: Methuen).

Hingorani, Dominic (2010), *British Asian Theatre: Dramaturgy, Process and Performance* (Basingstoke: Palgrave Macmillan).

Hoch, Paul and Vic Schoenbach (1969), *LSE: The Natives are Restless: A Report on Student Power in Action* (London: Sheed and Ward).

Hodgson, Geoff (1981), *Labour at the Crossroads* (Oxford: Martin Robinson).

Holmes, Martin (1985), *The Labour Government, 1974–79: Political Aims and Economic Reality* (Basingstoke: Macmillan).

Hutchinson, Robert (1982), *The Politics of the Arts Council* (London: Sinclair Brown).

Itzin, Catherine (1980), *Stages in the Revolution: Political Theatre in Britain Since 1968* (London: Eyre Methuen).

Jackson, Anthony and Chris Vine (eds) (2013), *Learning Through Theatre: The Changing Face of Theatre in Education* (Abingdon: Routledge).

Jones, Beryl (1974), Review of *The Recruiting Officer*, *Manchester Evening News*, 22 May.

Keeffe, Barrie (1977), *Barbarians* (London: Faber).

Kershaw, Baz (1992), *The Politics of Performance: Radical Theatre as Cultural Intervention* (London: Routledge).

Kershaw, Baz (2002), 'Alternative Theatres, 1946–2000', in Baz Kershaw (ed.), *The Cambridge History of British Theatre. Volume 3, Since 1895* (Cambridge: Cambridge University Press): 349–76.

Keynes, John Maynard (1945), 'The Arts Council, Its Policy and Hopes', *The Listener*, 12 July.

Khan, Naseem (1976), *The Arts that Britain Ignores: The Arts of Ethnic Minorities in Britain* (London: Arts Council of Great Britain, Gulbenkian Foundation and the Community Relations Commission).

King, Anthony (2009), '1979 Election: Mapping the Road to Thatcherism', *The Parliament*, 23 April.

Laing, Stuart (1992), 'The Politics of Culture: Institutional Change', in Bart Moore-Gilbert and John Seed (eds), *Cultural Revolution? The Challenge of the Arts in the 1960s* (London: Routledge):

Lamb, Richard (1995), *The Macmillan Years: 1957–1963: The Emerging Truth* (London: John Murray).

Lane, John (1978), *Arts Centres: Every Town Should Have One.* (London: Elek).

Lavery, Bryony (1984), 'But Will Me Like It?', in Susan Todd (ed.), *Women and Theatre: Calling the Shots* (London: Faber): 26–7.

Lee, Jennie (1965), *A Policy for the Arts* (London, Government White Paper).

Levin, Bernard (1970), *The Pendulum Years* (London: Jonathan Cape).

Lewis, Paul (2010), 'Blair Peach: After 31 Years Met Police Say "sorry" for their Role in his Killing', *The Guardian*, 27 April.

Macintyre, Donald (2013), 'It's Time to Revive the Memory of Hugh Gaitskell, the Best Labour PM Britain Never Had', *The Independent*, 4 January.

Mackie, Lindsay (1977), 'The Real Losers in Saturday's Battle of Lewisham', *The Guardian*, 15 August.

MacLennan, Elizabeth (1990), *The Moon Belongs to Everyone: Making Theatre with 7:84* (London: Methuen).

Mansfield, Liz (1982), 'New Perspectives on Theatre Today: Theatre Collectives: Alive and Kicking', *Platform* 4: quoted in Goodman (1993): 54.

Marr, Andrew (2009), *The Making of Modern Britain* (London: Pan).

Martin, Chris (2015), 'From 2 Tone to Grime', *The Observer*, 17 May.

Mason, Paul (2015), 'The Dirty Tricks of the Shrewsbury Trials Expose the Dark Heart of the Radical 1970s', *The Guardian*, 7 December.

McCreery, Kathleen (1978), Unpublished lecture at Kings College, Cambridge, Conference on Political Theatre, April: quoted in Itzin (1980): 47.

McGrath, John (1973), *The Cheviot, the Stag and the Black, Black Oil* (West Highland Press).

McGrath, John (1975),'Better a Bad Night in Bootle', *Theatre Quarterly* 19.

McKitrick, David and David McVea (2001), *Making Sense of the Troubles* (London: Penguin).

Megson, Chris (ed.) (2012), *Modern British Playwriting: The 1970s* (London: Methuen).

Millett, Kate (1970), *Sexual Politics* (New York: Doubleday).

Mitchell, Juliet (1971), *Women's Estate* (Harmondsworth: Penguin).

Muldoon, Roland (2013), *Taking on the Empire: How We Saved the Hackney Empire for Popular Theatre* (London: Just Press).

Murphy, Eileen Murphy (ed.) (1975), *Sweetie Pie: A Play about Women in Society* (London: Methuen Young Drama).

National Theatre Black Plays Archive, http://www.blackplaysarchive.org.uk/explore/companies/black-theatre-brixton (accessed 10 September 2015).

Newton, Scott (2010), 'The Sterling Devaluation of 1967, the International Economy and Post-War Social Democracy', in *English Historical Review* 125 (515) (Oxford: Oxford University Press): 912–45.

Nuttall, Jeff (1968), *Bomb Culture* (London: Harper Collins).

Nuttall, Jeff (1979), *Performance Art I: Memoirs* (London: John Calder).

Osment, Philip (ed.) (1989), *Gay Sweatshop: Four Plays and a Company* (London: Methuen).

P.A.R. (1974), Review of *The Recruiting Officer*, *Lancaster Evening Telegraph*, 23 May.

Pearce, Michael (2015), 'Tracing Black America in Black British Theatre from the 1970s', in National Theatre Black Plays Archive.

Prentki, Tim and Sheila Preston (eds) (2009), *The Applied Theatre Reader* (Abingdon: Routledge).

Rees, Roland (1992), *Fringe First: The Pioneers of Fringe Theatre on Record* (London: Oberon).

Robertson, Geoffrey (2010), 'The *Lady Chatterley* Trial', *The Guardian*, 22 October.

Rowbottom, Sheila (1973), *Woman's Consciousness, Man's World* (London: Pelican).

Russell, Bertrand (1961), 'Civil Disobedience', *New Statesman*, 17 February.

Sandbrook, Dominic (2006), *Never Had It So Good: A History of Britain from Suez to the Beatles* (London: Abacus).

Sandbrook, Dominic (2007), *White Heat: A History of Britain in the Swinging Sixties* (London: Abacus).

Sandbrook, Dominic (2011), *State of Emergency: The Way We Were: Britain 1970–74* (London: Penguin).

Sandbrook, Dominic (2013), *Seasons in the Sun: The Battle for Britain 1974–1979* (London: Penguin).

Schweitzer, Pam (ed.) (1973a), *Four Junior Programmes* (including *The Price of Coal*) (London: Methuen Young Drama).

Schweitzer, Pam (ed.) (1973b), *Four Secondary Programmes* (including *No Pasaran*) (London: Methuen Young Drama).

Seal, Patrick and Maureen McConville (1968), *French Revolution 1968* (London: Penguin).

Shepherd, Simon (1978), 'Pirate Jenny: An Interview with Jenny Rees', *Renaissance and Modern Studies* XXII: 111–31.

Sierz, Aleks (2001), *In-Yer-Face Theatre: British Drama Today* (London: Faber): 25–6.

Sinclair, Andrew (1995), *Arts and Cultures: The History of the 50 Years of the Arts Council of Great Britain* (London: Sinclair-Stevenson).

Snyder, W. P (1964), *The Politics of British Defense Policy, 1945–1962* (Athens, OH: Ohio University Press).

Taylor, Richard and Colin Pritchard (1980), *Protest Makers: British Nuclear Disarmament Movement of 1958–1965, Twenty Years on* (Oxford: Pergamon).

Thomas, Graham P. (1998), *Prime Minister and Cabinet Today* (Manchester: Manchester University Press).

Tonge, Jonathan (2002), *Northern Ireland: Conflict and Change* (London: Longman).

Trussler, Simon (ed.) (1981), *New Theatre Voices of the Seventies* (London: Eyre Methuen).

Turner, Mary (2012), *Action Space Extended* (London: Action Space Mobile).

Unfinished Histories, http://www.unfinishedhistories.com/history/companies/salakta-balloon-band/

University of Sheffield Library: Special Collections and Archives:
Ref MS 426 Action Space Extended, https://www.sheffield.ac.uk/
polopoly_fs/1.5

Verma, Jatinda (2004), 'Historical Developments and Contemporary
Identity', paper given at Asian Theatre Conference, University of
Birmingham.

Walsh, Dermot P. J. (2000), *Bloody Sunday and the Rule of Law in Northern
Ireland* (Basingstoke: Macmillan).

Wesker, Arnold (1963), *Chips With Everything* (London: Penguin).

Wesker, Arnold (1970), *Fears of Fragmentation* (London: Jonathan Cape).

Whitemore, Hugh (1997), *A Letter of Resignation* (London: Samuel French).

Wilson, Harold (1963), 'Labour's Plan for Science': Reprint of speech by the
Rt. Hon. Harold Wilson, MP, Leader of the Labour Party, at the Annual
Conference, Scarborough, Tuesday 1 October.

Wilson, Harold (1971), *The Labour Government 1964–1970: A Personal
Record* (London: Weidenfeld and Nicolson).

Wilson, Harold (1979), *Final Term: The Labour Government 1974–6* (London:
Weidenfeld and Nicholson).

Winchester, Simon (1974), *In Holy Terror: Reporting the Ulster Troubles*
(London: Faber and Faber).

Wintle, Justin (compiler) (1973), *The Fun Art Bus: An Inter-Action Project by
Ed Berman* (London: Methuen).

Witts, Richard (1998), *Artist Unknown: An Alternative History of the Arts
Council* (London: Little Brown).

Wooster, Roger (2007), *Contemporary Theatre in Education* (Bristol:
Intellect).

Wyatt, Stephen and Maggie Steed (1973), *Rare Earth: A Programme about
Pollution*, devised by Belgrade Coventry TiE (Methuen Young Drama).

Chapter 3

Ansorge, Peter (1975), *Disrupting the Spectacle* (London: Pitman).

Arts Council of Great Britain Archive, Victoria and Albert Museum, London
(1976), Betty Richie, Show Report for *Three for the Road*, 16 December,
ACGB 34/34/1.

Arts Council of Great Britain Archive, Victoria and Albert Museum, London
(1977a), Clive Tempest, Letter to CAST Theatre, 7 July, ACGB 34/34/1.

Arts Council of Great Britain Archive, Victoria and Albert Museum, London
(1977b), Roger Lancaster, Drama Panel Show Report, 10 October, ACGB
34/34/3.

Arts Council of Great Britain Archive, Victoria and Albert Museum, London
(1977c), Sandy Craig, Show Report for *Goodbye Union Jack*, 12 October,
ACGB 34/34/3.

Arts Council of Great Britain Archive, Victoria and Albert Museum, London (1978a), Jonathan Lamede, Show Report for *Confessions of a Socialist*, 10 May, ACGB 34/34/3.

Arts Council of Great Britain Archive, Victoria and Albert Museum, London (1978b), Jonathan Lamede, CAST Company Review, 12 May, ACGB 34/34/3.

Arts Council of Great Britain Archive, Victoria and Albert Museum, London (1978c), Ray Whitney, Letter to ACGB, 8 October, ACGB 34/34/2.

Arts Council of Great Britain Archive, Victoria and Albert Museum, London (1978d), John Faulkner, Letter to Ray Whitney, 10 October, ACGB 34/34/2.

Arts Council of Great Britain Archive, Victoria and Albert Museum, London (1978e), Jonathan Lamede, Internal Memo to John Faulkner marked 'Urgent', 10 October, ACGB 34/34/3.

Arts Council of Great Britain Archive, Victoria and Albert Museum, London (1978f), Jonathan Lamede, Internal Memo to Drama Panel, 19 October, ACGB 34/34/3.

Arts Council of Great Britain Archive, Victoria and Albert Museum, London (1978g), Lois Lambert, Show Report for *What Happens Next?*, 25 October, ACGB 34/34/3.

Arts Council of Great Britain Archive, Victoria and Albert Museum, London (1978h), Jonathan Lamede, Internal Memo to Drama Panel marked 'Urgent', 25 October, ACGB 34/34/3.

Arts Council of Great Britain Archive, Victoria and Albert Museum, London (1978i), Jonathan Lamede, Show Report for *What Happens Next?*, 20 November, ACGB 34/34/3.

Arts Council of Great Britain Archive, Victoria and Albert Museum, London (1979), Jonathan Lamede, Internal Memo to John Faulkner, 24 January, ACGB 34/34/3.

Arts Council of Great Britain Archive, Victoria and Albert Museum, London (1984), Luke Ritter, Letter to CAST Theatre, 12 July, ACGB 34/34/3.

Benjamin, Walter (1992), *Illuminations* (London: Fontana Press).

CAST (1979), *Confessions of a Socialist* (London: Pluto Press).

Caute, David (1988), *1968 – The Year of the Barricades* (London: Hamish Hamilton).

Chambers, Colin (1989), *The Story of Unity Theatre* (London: Lawrence and Wishart).

'Come Together at the Royal Court' (1970), Festival Programme, November.

Craig, Sandy (1980), *Dreams and Deconstructions: Alternative Theatre in Britain* (London: Amber Lane).

Davies, Andrew (1987), *Other Theatres: The Development of Alternative and Experimental Theatres in Britain* (Basingstoke: Macmillan).

Dawson, Helen (1970), 'Come Together, a Report', *Gambit* 7: 178–81.

Eagleton, Terry (1991), *Ideology* (London: Verso).

Editorial (1978), *Exeter Express and Echo*, 23 November.

Guy, Vincent (1970), 'Come Together', *Plays and Players* (November): 30–2.

Hackney Empire, *Where Theatre Lies / About / History.htm* (accessed 20 July 2005; last accessed December 2005).

Hammond, Jonathan (1973), 'A Potted History of the Fringe', *Theatre Quarterly* 3 (12): 40–2.

Hudson, Roger (1969), 'Letter from England', *Drama Review* 13 (4): 192–4.

Hunt, Albert (1974), *John Arden, a Study of his Plays* (London Eyre: Methuen).

Itzin, Catherine (1980), *Stages in the Revolution* (London: Methuen).

Jones, D. A. N. (1970), 'Capital Fun', *The Listener,* 5 November.

Kershaw, Baz (1992), *The Politics of Performance – Radical Theatre as Cultural Intervention* (London: Routledge).

Luxembourg, Rosa (1970), 'The Mass Strike, the Political Party and the Trade Unions', in Mary-Alice Waters (ed.) *Rosa Luxembourg Speaks* (New York: Pathfinder Press).

Marx, Karl (1973), *Grundrisse* (Harmondsworth: Penguin).

Marx, Karl (1977), *Selected Writings*, edited by David McLellan (Oxford: Oxford University Press).

McDonnell, Bill (2010), 'Jesters to the Revolution: A History of Cartoon Archetypical Theatre (CAST), 1965–85', *Theatre Notebook* 64 (2): 96–111.

Muldoon, Roland (1977), 'CAST Revived', *Plays and Players*, January: 40–1.

Muldoon, Roland (1978), 'Strife is a Cabaret My Friend', *The Leveller,* 27 April: 18–19.

Muldoon, Roland (1991), 'A Room of My Own', *Sunday Observer Magazine,* 3 February.

Muldoon, Roland (2000), Interview with Bill McDonnell, London, 22 July.

Rees, Roland (1992), *Fringe First: Pioneers of Fringe Theatre on Record* (London: Oberon).

Robinson, Kenneth (1980), Letter to the *Sunday Telegraph*, 17 March.

Rutter, Kate (1999), Interview with Bill McDonnell, Sheffield, 13 October.

Sandbrook, Dominic (2013), *Seasons in the Sun: The Battle for Britain: 1974–1979* (London: Penguin).

Thompson, David (1978), 'Political Play at Cambridge', *Cambridge Evening News*, 22 September.

Vietnam Solidarity Campaign (1967), *The Year 1967*, VHS Recording.

Wardle, Irving (1970), 'Come Together', *The Times,* 24 October.

Chapter 4

Arts Council of Great Britain Archive, Victoria and Albert Museum, London (1971), Experimental Drama Committee (EDC) Notes, 4, 9 February, ACGB 43/36/2.

Arts Council of Great Britain Archive, Victoria and Albert Museum, London (1972), Minutes of EDC meeting, 8 February, ACGB 43/36/2.

Arts Council of Great Britain Archive, Victoria and Albert Museum, London (1973), Roland Miller, 'Paper on Performance Art and Performance Artists, Prepared for the Experimental Drama Committee', 28 September, ACGB 43/42/5.

Arts Council of Great Britain Archive, Victoria and Albert Museum, London (1975), Minutes of ECD meeting, 8 January, ACGB 43/36/1.

Arts Council of Great Britain Archive, Victoria and Albert Museum, London (1977), Clive Tempest, Internal Memo to People Show File, 6 October, ACGB 34/122.

Arts Council of Great Britain Archive, Victoria and Albert Museum, London (1978), Jonathan Lamede, Internal Memo, 20 February, ACGB 34/122/1.

Arts Council of Great Britain Archive, Victoria and Albert Museum, London (1979a), Jonathan Lamede, Internal Memo, 10 July, ACGB 34/122/1.

Arts Council of Great Britain Archive, Victoria and Albert Museum, London (1979b), Jonathan Lamede, 'People Show Review Meeting', 10 October, ACGB 34/122/1.

Arts Council of Great Britain Archive, Victoria and Albert Museum, London (1979c), Report on the People Show: 'Policy and Projections 1979 Onwards', ACGB 34/122/4.

Arts Council of Great Britain Archive, Victoria and Albert Museum, London (1980a), Letter to Deputy Secretary General Richard Pulford from John Faulkner, 11 February, ACGB 34/122/1.

Arts Council of Great Britain Archive, Victoria and Albert Museum, London (1980b), Letter from John Faulkner to the Deputy Secretary-General Richard Pulford, 15 February, ACGB 34/122/1

Arts Council of Great Britain Archive, Victoria and Albert Museum, London (1980c), Bradford Watson, Letter to John Faulkner, 29 September, ACGB 34/122/1.

Arts Council of Great Britain Archive, Victoria and Albert Museum, London (1980d), Bradford Watson, Letter to John Faulkner, 11 November, ACGB 34/122/1.

Arts Council of Great Britain Archive, Victoria and Albert Museum, London (1980e), Letter from Helen Turnbull to John Faulkner, 3 December, ACGB 34/122/2.

Arts Council of Great Britain Archive, Victoria and Albert Museum, London (1986), People Show. Grant Application 1986–7: History Appendix A, ACGB 34/122/4.

Behrndt, Synne K. (2010), 'People Show in Rehearsal: People Show #118 The Birthday Tour', in D. A. Mermikides and D. J. Smart (eds), *Devising in Process* (Basingstoke: Palgrave): 30–49.

Bryden, Ronald (1970), 'Marx in the Drawing-room', *The Observer*, October 25: 32.

Bull, John (1984), *New British Political Dramatists: Howard Brenton, David Hare, Trevor Griffiths and David Edgar* (Basingstoke: Macmillan).

Carlson, Marvin (2004), *Performance: A Critical Introduction* (London: Routledge).

Coveney, Michael (1980), 'From Luton to Caracas', *The Observer*, 36.

Craig, Sandy (1980), *Dreams and Deconstructions: Alternative Theatre in Britain* (London: Amber Lane).

Craig, Sandy (1982), 'Lords of Misrule', *City Limits* 40 (9–15 July): 44–5.

Duchene, Anne (1965), 'Radio', *The Guardian*, 13 March: 5.

Duchin, David (2008), *Report and Financial Statements*, London: charitycommission.gov.uk

Duchin, David (2010), *Report and Financial Statements*, London: charitycommission.gov.uk

Duchin, David (2012), *Report and Financial Statements*, London: charitycommission.gov.uk

Ford, John (1970), 'The People Show', *Time Out* 49 (17–31 October): 64.

Gale, David, Performance and Live Art. Online Discussion. The Argument Room. http://www.livestream.com (aired and accessed 31 January 2013).

Gaskill, William (1970), '*Come Together*: Royal Court's Festival of Experimental Theatre', *The Times*, 15.

Haynes, Jim (1967), 'In My View', *Plays and Players* 14 (10): 58.

Heddon, Deirdre and Jane Milling (2005), *Devising Performance: A Critical History* (Basingstoke: Palgrave).

Henri, Adrian (1974), *Environments and Happenings* (London: Thames & Hudson).

Hewison, Robert (1987), *Too Much: Art and Society in the Sixties, 1960–75* (Oxford: Oxford University Press).

Hoffmann, Beth (2009), 'Radicalism and the Theatre in Genealogies of Live Art', *Performance Research* 14 (1): 95–105.

Hughes, Dusty (1971), 'Howard Brenton Interviewed: ("The phoney ideas you get about art when you write alone for years are honed away by working with people")', *Time Out*, 21–27 May, no. 66: 40.

Hulton, Peter (1981), 'Mark Long, Founder Member of The People Show, in Interview with Peter Hulton', *Theatre Papers, The Fourth Series* 2: 1–36.

Jay, David (1971), 'Fringe, The People Show', *Times Educational Supplement*, 17 September: 28.

Kaye, Nick (1994), 'Live Art: Definition and Documentation', *Contemporary Theatre Review* 2 (2): 1–7.

Kershaw, Baz (1992), *Politics of Performance: Radical Theatre as Cultural Intervention* (London: Routledge).

Kershaw, Baz (2004), 'British Theatre, 1940–2002: An Introduction', in Baz Kershaw (ed.), *Cambridge History of British Theatre, Volume 3* (Cambridge: Cambridge University Press): 291–325.

Kirby, Victoria Nes and Derek Wilson (1974), 'The Creation and Development of People Show #52' *The Drama Review* 18 (2): 48–66.

Kustow, Michael (1975), 'Summer Festival', *Plays and Players* 22 (262): 24–5.

Lacey, Bruce (2000), Interview by Gillian Whiteley, National Life Story Collection: Artists' Lives, 15 and 18 May 2000. British Library Archival Sound Recordings, http://sounds.bl.uk/View.aspx?item=021M-C0466X0099XX-0700V0.xml (accessed 7 June 2011).

Long, Mark (1971), 'About the People Show', *The Drama Review* 15 (4): 47–57.

Marcuse, Herbert (1969), *An Essay on Liberation* (Boston: Beacon Press).

Moore, Jack (1967), ERTAEHT, *International Times*, 30 January: 15.

Moore, Jack (2013), Interview with Jack Moore by author, 30 May.

Nuttall, Jeff (1965), Untitled. *My Own Mag*, no. 12: 4.

Nuttall, Jeff (1970), *Bomb Culture* (London: MacGibbon and Kee).

Nuttall, Jeff (1979), *Performance Art; Volume 1, Memoirs* (London: John Calder).

Nuttall, Jeff (2011), *The People Show*, YouTube, http://www.youtube.com/watch?v=66N7X9bGKLc (accessed June 9, 2011).

Rees, Ronald (1992), *Fringe First: Pioneers of Fringe Theatre on Record* (London: Oberon).

Scott, Andrew Murray (ed.) (1991), *Invisible Insurrection of a Million Minds: A Trocchi Reader* (Edinburgh: Polygon).

Seddon, George (1965), Briefing / Who & Why, *The Observer*: 23.

Trussler, Simon (2000), *The Cambridge Illustrated History of British Theatre* (Cambridge: Cambridge University Press).

Watkins, Islwyn (2011), Interview with Islwyn Watkins by author, 8 March.

Whiteley, Gillian (2011), 'Sewing the "Subversive Thread of Imagination": Jeff Nuttall, Bomb Culture and the Radical Potential of Affect', *The Sixties* 4 (2): 109–133.

Wilson, Snoo (1979), 'The Sense of the Sublime: Snoo Wilson on the influence of The People Show', *Plays and Players* 27 (2): 10–12.

Chapter 5

Ansorge, Peter (1975), *Disrupting the Spectacle: Five Years of Experimental and Fringe Theatre in Britain* (London: Pitman).

Arts Council of Great Britain Archive, Victoria and Albert Museum, London (1968), Anonymous, 'Fringe and Experimental Theatre Companies 1969/70', December, ACGB 43/36/1.

Arts Council of Great Britain Archive, Victoria and Albert Museum, London (1970a), David Hare, 'Arts Council of Great Britain Weekly Return Form', Portable Theatre, week ending 6 September, ACGB 43/43/11.

Arts Council of Great Britain Archive, Victoria and Albert Museum, London

(1970b), David Hare, 'Arts Council of Great Britain Weekly Return Form', Portable Theatre, week ending 8 November, ACGB 43/43/11.

Arts Council of Great Britain Archive, Victoria and Albert Museum, London (1970c), David Hare, Letter to Chris Cooper, 13 November, ACGB 43/43/11.

Arts Council of Great Britain Archive, Victoria and Albert Museum, London (1971a), Minutes of New Drama Committee, 4 February, ACGB 43/43/1.

Arts Council of Great Britain Archive, Victoria and Albert Museum, London (1971b), Minutes of Experimental Drama Committee (EDC), 4 November, ACGB 43/43/3.

Arts Council of Great Britain Archive, Victoria and Albert Museum, London (1971c), Minutes of EDC, 16 December, ACGB 43/43/3.

Arts Council of Great Britain Archive, Victoria and Albert Museum, London (1972a), Minutes of Drama Panel meeting, March, ACGB 43/43/3.

Arts Council of Great Britain Archive, Victoria and Albert Museum, London (1972b), Tony Bicât, Peter Evans, Malcolm Griffiths, David Hare, Snoo Wilson, Letter to ACGB, 6 December, ACGB 43/43/5.

Arts Council of Great Britain Archive, Victoria and Albert Museum, London (1973a), Minutes of Drama Panel, October 1967–14 March, 2 March, ACGB 43/3/6.

Arts Council of Great Britain Archive, Victoria and Albert Museum, London (1973b), Minutes of EDC, 16 January, ACGB 43/43/7.

Arts Council of Great Britain Archive, Victoria and Albert Museum, London (1973c), Malcolm Griffiths, Letter to Nick Barter, 8 February, ACGB 43/43/6.

Arts Council of Great Britain Archive, Victoria and Albert Museum, London (1973d), Minutes of EDC, 13 February, ACGB 43/43/6.

Arts Council of Great Britain Archive, Victoria and Albert Museum, London (1973e), Minutes of EDC, 14 February, ACGB 43/43/7.

Arts Council of Great Britain Archive, Victoria and Albert Museum, London (1973f), David Aukin, Letter to Nick Barter, 9 March, ACGB 43/43/7.

Arts Council of Great Britain Archive, Victoria and Albert Museum, London (1973g), David Aukin, Letter to N.V. Linklater, 19 March, ACGB 43/43/8.

Arts Council of Great Britain Archive, Victoria and Albert Museum, London (1973h), David Aukin, Letter to N.V. Linklater, 19 April, ACGB 43/43/8.

Arts Council of Great Britain Archive, Victoria and Albert Museum, London (1973i), Minutes of EDC, 15 May, ACGB 43/43/7.

Arts Council of Great Britain Archive, Victoria and Albert Museum, London (1973j), Max Stafford-Clark, Letter to Nick Barter, 20 August, ACGB 43/43/8.

Arts Council of Great Britain Archive, Victoria and Albert Museum, London (1973k), Minutes of EDC, 7 September, ACGB 43/43/8.

Arts Council of Great Britain Archive, Victoria and Albert Museum, London (1973l), Minutes of EDC, 12 October, ACGB 43/43/9.

Arts Council of Great Britain Archive, Victoria and Albert Museum, London (1975), Malcolm Griffiths, Letter to Peter Farrago, 3 March, ACGB 43/43/13.

Bicât, Tony (2007), 'Portable Theatre: "Fine Detail, Rough Theatre". A personal Memoir', in Richard Boon (ed.), *The Cambridge Companion to David Hare* (Cambridge: Cambridge University Press): 15–30.

Billington, Michael (1970), 'Portable Theatre, Royal Court Theatre Upstairs', *Plays and Players* (November): 49.

Boon, Richard (1991), *Brenton the Playwright* (London: Methuen).

Boon, Richard (ed.) (2007), *The Cambridge Companion to David Hare* (Cambridge: Cambridge University Press).

Brenton, Howard (1986), *Plays: One* (London: Methuen).

Brenton, Howard, Brian Clark, Trevor Griffiths, David Hare, Stephen Poliakoff, Hugh Stoddart and Snoo Wilson (1972), *Lay By* (London: Calder and Boyars).

Bull, John (1984), *New British Political Dramatists* (London: Macmillan).

DiCenzo, Maria (1996), *The Politics of Alternative Theatre in Britain, 1968–1990: The Case of 7:84 (Scotland)* (Cambridge: Cambridge University Press).

Donohue, Joseph (1989), 'Evidence and Documentation', in Thomas Postlewait and Bruce A. McConachie (eds), *Interpreting the Theatrical Past: Essays in the Historiography of Performance* (Iowa: University of Iowa Press).

Gaston, Georg (1993), 'Interview: David Hare', *Theatre Journal* 45 (2) (May): 213–25.

Hammond, Jonathan (1973), 'Messages First: An Interview with Howard Brenton', *Gambit* 6 (23): 24–32.

Hare, David (2005), *Obedience, Struggle & Revolt: Lectures on Theatre* (London: Faber).

Hayman, Ronald (1970), *British Theatre Since 1955 – A Reassessment* (Oxford: Oxford University Press).

Homden, Carol (1995), *The Plays of David Hare* (Cambridge: Cambridge University Press).

Innes, Christopher (1992), *Modern British Drama 1890–1990* (Cambridge: Cambridge University Press).

Itzin, Catherine and Simon Trussler (1975a), 'David Hare: From Portable Theatre to Joint Stock … via Shaftesbury Avenue', *New Theatre Quarterly* 5 (20): 108–15.

Itzin, Catherine and Simon Trussler (1975b), 'Petrol Bombs through the Proscenium Arch', *Theatre Quarterly* 5 (17): 4–20.

Itzin, Catherine (1980), *Stages in the Revolution: Political Theatre in Britain Since 1968* (London: Eyre Methuen).

Lambert, J. W. (1974), *Drama in Britain: 1964–1973* (Essex: Longman).

Megson, Chris (2012), *Decades of Modern British Playwriting: The 1970s – Voices, Documents, New Interpretations* (London: Methuen).

Milling, Jane (2012), *Decades of Modern British Playwriting: The 1980s – Voices, Documents, New Interpretations* (London: Methuen).

Postlewait, Thomas and Bruce A. McConachie (ed.) (1989), *Interpreting the Theatrical Past: Essays in the Historiography of Performance* (Iowa City: University of Iowa Press).

Theatre Management (THM) files in Victoria and Albert Museum Theatre Archive (1969), Royal Court Theatre Production File, Publicity flyer for *Christie in Love* at the Brighton Combination, THM 273/4/2/7.

Theatre Management (THM) files in Victoria and Albert Museum Theatre Archive (1970a), Portable Theatre, Unsigned letter confirming tour of *Fruit* and *What Happened to Blake?*, THM 273/4/2/17.

Theatre Management (THM) files in Victoria and Albert Museum Theatre Archive (1970b), Programme for *What Happened to Blake?* at the Royal Court Theatre, THM 273/4/2/17.

Theatre Management (THM) files in Victoria and Albert Museum Theatre Archive (1970c), Programme for *Come Together* Festival at the Royal Court Theatre, THM 273/4/1/78/1.

Theatre Management (THM) files in Victoria and Albert Museum Theatre Archive (1972), Programme for *England's Ireland* at the Royal Court Theatre, THM 273/4/3/30/1.

Theatre Management (THM) files in Victoria and Albert Museum Theatre Archive (n.d.), Portable Theatre, Draft plan for *England's Ireland*, THM 273/4/3/30/1.

Sarlós, Robert. K. (1989), 'Performance Reconstruction: The Vital Link between Past and Future', in Thomas Postlewait and Bruce A. McConachie (eds), *Interpreting the Theatrical Past: Essays in the Historiography of Performance* (Iowa City: University of Iowa Press): 198–229.

Saunders, Graham (2002), *'Love Me or Kill Me': Sarah Kane and the Theatre of Extremes* (Manchester: Manchester University Press).

Wilson, Snoo (1999), *Plays: One* (London: Methuen).

Wu, Duncan (2000), *Making Plays: Interviews with Contemporary British Dramatists and Their Directors* (Basingstoke: Macmillan).

Chapter 6

Anon. (1976), 'The Newfound Respectability of Pip Simmons', 22 December.

Ansorge, Peter (1975), *Disrupting the Spectacle: Five Years of Experimental and Fringe Theatre in Britain* (London: Pitman).

Arts Council of Great Britain Archive in Victoria and Albert Museum,

London (1976a), J. H. Wheeler, Letter to the Arts Council, 17 December, ACGB 34/123/1.

Arts Council of Great Britain Archive in Victoria and Albert Museum, London (1976b), Glasgow Citizens Theatre Box Office Return for *Dracula*, ACGB 34/123/1.

Arts Council of Great Britain Archive in Victoria and Albert Museum, London (1977a), Jac Heijer, Review of *The Masque of the Red Death*, NRC Handelsblad ACGB 34/123/1.

Arts Council of Great Britain Archive in Victoria and Albert Museum, London (1977b), Mik Flood, Letter to Gilly Adams, 22 September, ACGB 34/123/1.

Arts Council of Great Britain Archive in Victoria and Albert Museum, London (1977c), Peter Mair, Letter to Joan Oliver, 20 October, ACGB 34/123/1.

Arts Council of Great Britain Archive in Victoria and Albert Museum, London (1977d), Anthony Field, Letter to Joan Oliver, 26 October, ACGB 34/123/1.

Arts Council of Great Britain Archive in Victoria and Albert Museum, London (1977e), John Cuming, John Show Report on *Woyzeck*, 10 December, ACGB 34/123/1.

Arts Council of Great Britain Archive in Victoria and Albert Museum, London (1977f), Eric Shorter, Pip Simmons Theatre Co. Chapter Arts centre, *Daily Telegraph*, 12 December, ACGB 34/123/1.

Arts Council of Great Britain Archive in Victoria and Albert Museum, London (1977g), Ruth Marks, Memo to Peter Mair, 12 December, ACGB 34/123/1.

Arts Council of Great Britain Archive in Victoria and Albert Museum, London (1978a), Eric Shorter, 'Watching out for Woyzeck', January, ACGB 34/123/1.

Arts Council of Great Britain Archive in Victoria and Albert Museum, London (1978b), Joan Oliver, Letter to Peter Mair, 1 February, ACGB 34/123/1.

Arts Council of Great Britain Archive in Victoria and Albert Museum, London (1978c), Anton Gill, Show Report on *The Tempest*, May 19, ACGB 34/123/1.

Arts Council of Great Britain Archive in Victoria and Albert Museum, London (1978d), Jonathan Lamede, Internal Memo re Pip Simmons Board Meeting, ACGB 34/123/2.

Arts Council of Great Britain Archive in Victoria and Albert Museum, London (1978e), Jonathan Lamede, Show Report on *The Tempest*, 15 June, ACGB 34/123/2.

Arts Council of Great Britain Archive in Victoria and Albert Museum, London (1978f), Anthony Field, Memo to John Faulkner, 20 June, ACGB 34/123/2.

298 *Bibliography*

Arts Council of Great Britain Archive in Victoria and Albert Museum, London (1978g), John Faulkner, Letter to the Editor of *Plays and Players*, 4 August, ACGB 34/123/2.

Arts Council of Great Britain Archive in Victoria and Albert Museum, London (1978h), Jonathan Lamede, Show Report on '*We*', 6 December, ACGB 34/123/1.

Arts Council of Great Britain Archive in Victoria and Albert Museum, London (1978i), Pip Simmons Theatre Group, 'Our Proposals for Next Season', undated, ACGB 34/123/2.

Barker, Clive (1979), 'Pip Simmons in Residence', *Theatre Quarterly* 35: 17–29.

Bottoms, Stephen J. (2006), *Playing Underground: A Critical History of the 1960s Off-Off-Broadway Movement* (Ann Arbo: University of Michigan Press).

Brown, Ian (2011), 'My Most Memorable Night at the Theatre', *Daily Telegraph*, 14 March, http://www.telegraph.co.uk/culture/theatre/theatre-features/8369405/My-most-memorable-night-at-the-theatre.html (accessed 10/10/15).

Coveney, Michael (1978a), 'Rocking at the Riverside', *Observer*, 7 May.

Coveney, Michael (1978b), 'Rough Magic: On the Tenth Anniversary of the Pip Simmons Theatre Group', *Plays and Players* (May).

de Jongh, Nicholas (1971), Review of *Do It!*, *Guardian*, 20 August.

Dudeck, Theresa Robbins (2013), *Keith Johnstone. A Critical Biography* (London: Bloomsbury).

English Stage Company Archive, Victoria and Albert Theatre Archives (1971a), Jane Lamb, Letter to Carolyn Hutchinson, 8 September, THM 273/4/2/31.

English Stage Company Archive, Victoria and Albert Theatre Archives (1971b), Roger Croucher, Memo to Gloria Taylor, 16 August, THM 273/4/2/31.

English Stage Company Archive, Victoria and Albert Theatre Archives (1971c), Roger Croucher, Memo to John Catty, THM 273/4/2/31.

English Stage Company Archive, Victoria and Albert Theatre Archives (1971d), Simmons, Pip & Company, *Do It!* Press Release, THM 273/4/2/31.

English Stage Company Archive, Victoria and Albert Theatre Archives (1972a), Pip Simmons Theatre Group, *The George Jackson Black and White Minstrel Show* Press Release, THM 273/4/2/54.

English Stage Company Archive, Victoria and Albert Theatre Archives (1972b), Jac Heijer, Review of *The George Jackson Black and White Minstrel Show*', THM 273/4/2/54.

Ford, John (1975), 'An Die Musik', *Players and Players*, August.

Grant, Steve (1978), 'Beyond the Fringe', *Time Out*, 4 May.

Hayman, Ronald (1973), *The Set-Up: An Anatomy of British Theatre Today* (London: Methuen).

Itzin, Catherine (1980), *Stages in the Revolution* (London: Methuen).

Kustow, Michael (2000), Review of *An Die Musik*, *Evening Standard*, 7 September.

Lambert, J. W. (1969), 'The Dying Theatre', *Sunday Times* 14 June, n.p., Production File for *Paradise Now*, Roundhouse 1969, V&A.

Lewis, Peter, 'Police went to the Roundhouse', *Daily Mail*, June 8, n.p., Production File for *Paradise Now*, Roundhouse 1969, V&A.

Machon, Josephine (2009), *(Syn)aesthetics: Redefining Visceral Performance* (London: Palgrave).

Marowitz, Charles (1973), *Confessions of a Counterfeit Critic* (London: Eyre Methuen).

Nuttall, Jeff (1973), 'The Situation Regarding Performance Art', ACGB 43/42/7, reproduced in *Contemporary Theatre Review* 22.1 (2012): 175–7.

Pearson, Mike (2011), *Mickery Theater: An Imperfect Archaeology* (Amsterdam: Amsterdam University Press).

Rudman, Michael (1973), 'Edinburgh Traverse, Now and Then', in Sheridan Morley (ed.), *Theatre 72: Plays, Players, Playwrights, Opera, Ballet* (London: Hutchinson): 123–31.

Shank, Theodore (1975), 'The Pip Simmons Group: Commemorating the Nazi Concentration Camps', *The Drama Review* 19 (4): 41–6.

Simmons, Pip (1970), *Superman, New Short Plays 3* (London: Methuen).

Simmons, Pip (2000), interviewed by Jill Evans, Theatre & Performance Department, Victoria & Albert Museum.

Stefanova, Kalina (2013), *Who Keeps the Score on the London Stage?* (Abingdon: Routledge).

Stuart, Chris (1978), '*Woyzeck* in Cardiff', *Plays & Players*, February.

Tan, Ed and Henry Schoenmakers (1984), '"Good Guy Bad Guy": Effects in Political Theatre' *The Semiotics of Drama and Theatre: New Perspectives in the Theory of Drama and Theatre* in Herta Schmid and Aloysius van Kesteren (eds) (Amsterdam: John Benjamins Publishing): 467–509.

Time Out (1971), 'Guide to Underground Theatre', Theatre Survey no.1, *Theatre Quarterly* 1: 61–4.

Wardle, Irving (1971), Review of *Do It!*, *The Times*, 20 August.

White, Gareth (2013), *Audience Participation in Theatre: Aesthetics of the Invitation* (London: Palgrave).

Chapter 7

Ansorge, Peter (1975), *Disrupting the Spectacle: Five Years of Experimental and Fringe Theatre in Britain* (London: Pitman Publishing).

Arts Council of Great Britain Archive in Victoria and Albert Museum, London (1968), Drama Panel minutes, 126th meeting, 6 December, ACGB 43/3/1.

Arts Council of Great Britain Archive in Victoria and Albert Museum,

London (1971), Hugh Willatt, Letter to John Fox, 24 September, ACGB 41/78/2

Arts Council of Great Britain Archive in Victoria and Albert Museum, London (1972), John Fox, Letter to Nick Barter, 1 October, ACGB 41/78/2.

Arts Council of Great Britain Archive in Victoria and Albert Museum, London (1973), Nick Barter, Internal ACGB memo, 11 January, ACGB 41/78/3.

Arts Council of Great Britain Archive in Victoria and Albert Museum, London (1976a), John Fox report on *Island of the Lost World* and related correspondence, August, ACGB 34/163/1.

Arts Council of Great Britain Archive in Victoria and Albert Museum, London (1976b), Correspondence from Welfare State, ACGB 34/163/1.

Arts Council of Great Britain Archive in Victoria and Albert Museum, London (1976c), Letter from Peter Kiddle to Clive Tempest, 12 August, ACGB 34/163/1.

Arts Council of Great Britain Archive in Victoria and Albert Museum, London (1976d), Clive Tempest, Internal ACGB memo, 24 March, ACGB 34/163/1.

Arts Council of Great Britain Archive in Victoria and Albert Museum, London (1978), Luc Mishalle, Letter to Tony Field, 24 April, ACGB 34/163/4.

Arts Council of Great Britain Archive in Victoria and Albert Museum, London (1979), John Fox, Note accompanying letter from Galactic Holdings, 30 August, ACGB 34/163/4

Bishop, Claire (ed.) (2006), *Participation, Documents of Contemporary Art* (London: MIT Press).

Bishop, Claire (2012), 'Participation and Spectacle, Where are we Now?', in Nato Thompson (ed.), *Living as Form, Socially Engaged Art from 1991–2011* (New York: MIT Press).

Brook, James, Chris Carlsson and Nancy J. Peters (eds) (1998), *Reclaiming San Francisco: History, Politics, Culture* (San Francisco: City Lights).

Coult, Tony (1976), *Plays and Players* (May): 20–3.

Coult, Tony and Baz Kershaw (1983), *Engineers of the Imagination, The Welfare State Handbook* (London: Methuen).

Craig, Sandy (ed.) (1980), *Dreams and Deconstructions, Alternative Theatre in Britain* (Ambergate: Amber Lane).

Davies, Andrew (1987), *Other Theatres: The Development of Alternative and Experimental Theatre in Britain* (London: MacMillan).

DiCenzo, Maria (1996), *The Politics of Alternative Theatre in Britain: The Case of 7:84 (Scotland)* (Cambridge: Cambridge University Press).

Fox, John (2002), *Eyes on Stalks* (London: Methuen).

Hammond, Jonathan 1973), 'A Potted History of the Fringe', *Theatre Quarterly* 3 (12) (October): 37–46.

Hann, Judith, 'The Young Creators', *Yorkshire Post* (n.d., c. late summer 1968); Welfare State archive, University of Bristol Theatre Collection.

Henri, Adrian (1974), *Environments and Happenings* (London: Thames & Hudson).

Hunt, Albert (1976), *Hopes for Great Happenings: Alternatives in Education and Theatre* (London: Eyre Methuen).

Itzin, Catherine (1980), *Stages in the Revolution: Political Theatre in Britain Since 1968* (London: Eyre Methuen).

Kershaw, Baz (1992), *The Politics of Performance – Radical Theatre as Cultural Intervention* (London: Routledge).

Kershaw, Baz (2007), *Theatre Ecology, Environments and Performance Events* (Cambridge: Cambridge University Press).

Kiddle, Catherine (1981), *What Shall We Do with the Children?* (Devon: Spindlewood).

Mason, Bim (1992), *Street Theatre and Other Outdoor Performance* (London: Routledge).

Nuttall, Jeff (1970), *Bomb Culture* (London: Paladin).

Nuttall, Jeff (1979), *Volume 1: Performance Art, Memoirs* (London: John Calder).

Patrick, Martin (2011), 'Performative Tactics and the Choreographic Reinvention of Public Space', *Art & the Public Sphere Journal* 1 (1): 65–84.

Shaughnessy, Nicola (2012), *Applying Performance: Live Art, Socially Engaged Theatre and Affective Practice* (Basingstoke: Palgrave).

Thornber, Robin (1987), 'Town Hall Tattoo', *The Guardian*, 13 July.

Welfare State archive, University of Bristol Theatre Collection (WSTC) (1968), 'Tide is OK for the 30th July Welfare State Archive, University of Bristol Theatre Collection (WSTC), 1968, Devon', Welfare State leaflet, 14/2.

Welfare State archive, University of Bristol Theatre Collection (WSTC) (1970), *Heptonstall* Welfare State leaflet, 14/2.

Welfare State archive, University of Bristol Theatre Collection (WSTC) Bates, Merete (1972), 'The Travels of Lancelot Quail', *Guardian*, 3 August, 12/1.

Welfare State archive, University of Bristol Theatre Collection (WSTC) Nairn, Ian (1973a), 'Civic Magician– the Best Thing Since the First Division', *Sunday Times*, 3 June, 12/1.

Welfare State archive, University of Bristol Theatre Collection (WSTC) Thornber, Robin (1973b), 'Welfare State', *The Guardian,* 24 May, 12/1.

Welfare State archive, University of Bristol Theatre Collection (WSTC) Kiddle, Peter (1973c), typed notes dated 20 September, 12/1.

Welfare State archive, University of Bristol Theatre Collection (WSTC) (1973d), Welfare State policy document, financial statement and company report, 12/1.

Welfare State archive, University of Bristol Theatre Collection (WSTC) (1974), 'The Welfare States: A Report on the Future', 1 July, 12/1.

Welfare State archive, University of Bristol Theatre Collection (WSTC) Fox,

John (1975a), 'Welfare State 1973–75', typed notes, signed John Fox Autumn 1975, Burnley Lancs., 1 October, 12/1.

Welfare State archive, University of Bristol Theatre Collection (WSTC) (1975b), 'The Welfare State Internal and External Environment', 12/1.

Welfare State archive, University of Bristol Theatre Collection (WSTC) (1976), Welfare State policy statement and Arts Council grant application, 15 August, 12/1.

Welfare State archive, University of Bristol Theatre Collection (WSTC) Fox, John (1978a), undated typed document, c. 1978, 12/1.

Welfare State archive, University of Bristol Theatre Collection (WSTC) Theodore Shank, (1978b), *San Francisco Theatre Magazine*, 12/1.

Welfare State (1972), *The Welfare State Manifesto* (Burnley: Welfare State).

Welfare State (1978), *The Tenth Anniversary of Welfare State* (Burnley: Welfare State).

White, Michael (1988), 'Resources for a Journey of Hope: The Work of Welfare State International', *New Theatre Quarterly* 4 (15): 195–208.

Whiteley, Gillian (2006), *Radical Mayhem: Welfare State International and its Followers*, Exhibition Catalogue, MidPennine Gallery, Burnley, 26 April–7 June.

Whiteley, Gillian (2010), 'New Age Radicalism and the Social Imagination: Welfare State International in the Seventies', in Laurel Forster and Sue Harper (eds), *British Culture and Society in the 1970s: The Lost Decade* (Newcastle upon Tyne: Cambridge Scholars Press): 35–50.

Whiteley, Gillian (2011), 'Sewing the "Subversive Thread of Imagination": Jeff Nuttall, Bomb Culture and the Radical Potential of Affect', *The Sixties: A Journal of History, Politics, and Culture* 4 (2) (Winter): 109–133.

Whiteley, Gillian, author's unpublished interviews with John Fox, 2006, 2014.

John Fox and Sue Gill's, www.deadgoodguides.com

Unfinished Histories project (a research resource on alternative theatre 1968–88, includes interviews with Tony Coult and Albert Hunt), www.unfinishedhistories.com

Welfare State International, www.welfare-state.org

Chapter 8

Anderson, David and David Maclennan (1987), *Roadworks: Song Lyrics for Wildcat* (Glasgow: Third Eye Centre).

Arts Council of Great Britain Archives, Victoria and Albert Museum, London (1971), John McGrath letter to Nick Barter, 20 September ACGB 43/43/2.

Arts Council of Great Britain Archives, Victoria and Albert Museum, London (1972a), John McGrath letter to ACGB, 31 January, ACGB 34/168/1.

Arts Council of Great Britain Archives, Victoria and Albert Museum, London (1972b), Nick Barter Show Report on *The Ballygombeen Bequest,* 18 October, ACGB 34/168/2.

Arts Council of Great Britain Archives, Victoria and Albert Museum, London (1972c), Lt. General Sir Harry Tuzo letter, ACGB 98/112.

Arts Council of Great Britain Archives, Victoria and Albert Museum, London (1972d), Minutes of 198th meeting of Council, 29 March, ACGB 36/1.

Arts Council of Great Britain Archives, Victoria and Albert Museum, London (1972e), Minutes of 11th meeting of Experimental Drama Committee, 7 May, ACGB 43/43/4.

Arts Council of Great Britain Archives, Victoria and Albert Museum, London (1972f), Minutes of 199th meeting of Council, 26 April, ACGB 36/1.

Arts Council of Great Britain Archives, Victoria and Albert Museum, London (1972g), Minutes of 202nd meeting of Council, 26 July, ACGB 36/1.

Arts Council of Great Britain Archives, Victoria and Albert Museum, London (1972h), Minutes of 203rd meeting of Council, 27 September, ACGB 36/1.

Arts Council of Great Britain Archives, Victoria and Albert Museum, London (1972i), Minutes of 204th meeting of Council, 25 October, ACGB 36/1.

Arts Council of Great Britain Archives, Victoria and Albert Museum, London (1973a), Minutes of 208th meeting of Council, 28 February, ACGB 36/1.

Arts Council of Great Britain Archives, Victoria and Albert Museum, London (1973b), Minutes of 210th (25 April), 211th (30 May), 214th (26 September) and 215th (31 October) meetings of Council, ACGB 36/1.

Arts Council of Great Britain Archives, Victoria and Albert Museum, London (1974), Minutes of 226th meeting of Council, 30 October, ACGB 36/1.

Arts Council of Great Britain Archives, Victoria and Albert Museum, London (1975), Minutes of 229th (29 January) and 232nd (30 April) meeting of Council, 29 January, ACGB 36/1.

Arts Council of Great Britain Archives, Victoria and Albert Museum, London (1976), Minutes of 232nd (30 April) and 240th meeting of Council, 30 April, ACGB 36/1.

Arts Council of Great Britain Archives, Victoria and Albert Museum, London (1978), Anton Gill internal memo, August, ACGB 38/9/19.

Bourdieu, Pierre (2010), *Distinction : A Social Critique of the Judgement of Taste* (London: Routledge).

Bull, John (2005), 'Serjeant Musgrave Dances to a Different Tune', in David Bradby and Susanna Capon (eds), *Freedom's Pioneer: John McGrath's Work in Theatre, Film and Television* (Exeter: University of Exeter Press): 39–54.

Craig, Sandy (ed.) (1980), *Dreams and Deconstructions: Alternative Theatre in Britain* (London: Amber Lane Press).

DiCenzo, Maria (2002), *The Politics of Alternative Theatre in Britain, 1968–1990: The Case of 7:84 (Scotland)* (Cambridge: Cambridge University Press).

Edgar, David (1988), *The Second Time as Farce: Reflections on the Drama of Mean Times* (London: Lawrence and Wishart).

Gooch, Steve (1945), *All Together Now: An Alternative View of Theatre and the Community* (London: Methuen).

Holdsworth, Nadine (1997), 'Good Nights Out: Activating the Audience with 7:84 (England)', *New Theatre Quarterly* 13 (49): 29–40.

Itzin, Catherine (1980), *Stages in the Revolution: Political Theatre in Britain Since 1968* (London: Eyre Methuen).

Kershaw, Baz (2002), *The Politics of Performance* (London: Routledge).

MacLennan, Elizabeth (1990), *The Moon Belongs to Everyone: Making Theatre with 7:84* (London: Methuen).

McGrath, John (1975) 'Better a Bad Night in Bootle', *Theatre Quarterly* 19: 39–54.

McGrath, John (1981), *A Good Night Out* (London: Methuen).

McGrath, John (1985), 'Popular Theatre and the Changing Perspective of the Eighties', *New Theatre Quarterly* 1 (4): 390–9.

McGrath, John (1990), *The Bone Won't Break: On Theatre and Hope in Hard Times* (London: Methuen).

McGrath, John (1996), *Six Pack: Plays for Scotland* (Edinburgh: Polygon).

McGrath, John (2002), *Naked Thoughts that Roam About: Reflections on Theatre, 1958–2001*, edited by Nadine Holdsworth (London:Nick Hern).

McGrath, John (2005), *Plays for England*, selected and introduced by Nadine Holdsworth (Exeter: University of Exeter Press).

Megson, Christopher (2012), *Modern British Playwriting. The 1970s: Voices, Documents, New Interpretations* (London: Methuen Drama).

Nairn, Tom (1977), *The Break-Up of Britain: Crisis and Neo-Liberalism* (London: New Left Books).

Norton, Alex (2011), 'My Father and I Fought Like Cat and Dog' (Interview, *Glasgow Herald*, 14 February).

NOTES ON CONTRIBUTORS

John Bull is Professor of Drama at the University of Lincoln, UK, and Emeritus Professor of Film and Theatre at the University of Reading, UK. He has published widely on modern and contemporary British and European drama and post-Restoration theatre, including: *New British Political Dramatists* (1984), *Stage Right: Crisis and Recovery in British Contemporary Mainstream Theatre* (1994) and *Vanbrugh and Farquhar* (1998). More recent publications include: chapters and articles on the Berliner Ensemble and on works by British playwrights, including Howard Brenton, David Edgar, David Hare, Anthony Neilson, Joe Orton, Tom Stoppard and Arnold Wesker. He also recently worked with Graham Saunders on the five-year AHRC-funded project 'Giving Voice to the Nation: The Arts Council of Great Britain and the Development of Theatre and Performance in Britain 1945–1995'.

Kate Dorney is Senior Lecturer in Modern & Contemporary Performance at the University of Manchester, UK. She publishes on many aspects of theatre and performance, including on modern and contemporary British theatre practice, curation and documentation and theatre history. Her publications include: *The Changing Language of Modern English Drama 1945–2009* (2009), *Played in Britain: Modern Theatre in 100 Plays* (2010; co-author with Frances Gray), and *The Glory of the Garden: The Arts Council and Regional Theatre* (2010; co-editor with Ros Merkin) and the journal *Studies in Theatre and Performance*. She was previously curator of modern and contemporary performance at the Victoria and Albert Museum, UK, where she oversaw the acquisition and development of key contemporary performance collections.

Bill McDonnell is Senior Lecturer in Theatre and Performance at the University of Sheffield, UK. He joined the university in 2002 after twenty-five years as a professional theatre worker. He has published primarily on British and Irish political and activist theatres of the twentieth century, and is the author of *Social Impact in UK Theatre* (2005) and *Theatres of the Troubles: Theatre, Resistance and Liberation in Ireland* (2008). He is currently working on a study of theatre in community development.

Chris Megson is Reader in Drama and Theatre at Royal Holloway College, University of London. He has published widely on post-war British theatre, documentary/verbatim performance and contemporary playwriting. His publications include *Get Real: Documentary Theatre Past and Present* (2009; co-editor with Alison Forsyth) and *Decades of Modern British Playwriting: The 1970s* (2012).

David Pattie is Professor of Drama and Popular Music at the University of Chester, UK. He has published on contemporary theatre and drama, popular music, Samuel Beckett, Scottish theatre and popular culture. His books include: *Samuel Beckett* (2004) and *Rock Music and Performance* (2007).

Grant Peterson is a Lecturer in Theatre at Brunel University, UK. He has published work on a diverse range of subjects, including British alternative theatre history, dance, gender, sexuality and digital research methodologies. He also has experience as a performer in theatre, musical theatre, television and commercials, and has worked in numerous venues throughout Los Angeles and Southern California.

Gillian Whiteley is Senior Lecturer in Critical and Historical Studies at Loughborough University, UK. Her research focuses on interdisciplinary practices and cultural production within radical socio-political contexts from the 1960s through to contemporary practice. Recent publications include: *Junk: Art and the Politics of Trash* (2010) and '[Schm]alchemy: Magical Sites and Mischievous Objects – Episodes in a Performative Inquiry into the Transformative and Disruptive Potency of Stuff', in *Body, Space & Technology Journal* (2016). She is a member of the improvising performance/live art group Alchemy/Schmalchemy.

INDEX

This index covers alternative and fringe theatre in all chapters, primarily by other headings. Terms are indexed in full, or by commonly known abbreviation.

Index

Black Power movement 86
Black Theatre Co-Op 91
Black Theatre of Brixton (was Dark and
    Light Theatre Company) 70, 71,
    88, 89
Black Theatre Workshop 89
Bleak House 99
Blood Red Roses 271
Bloody Sunday 36
Blow-Up 24
bonfire events 235–6, 246
Boon, Richard 185
Borderline Theatre 269, 271
Bouncing Back with Benyon 65
Boyd-Carpenter, John 31–2
Boylan, John 103
Bradford College of Art Theatre Group
    58
Bradford, David 264–5
Bradford Festival 68, 116
Brecht, Bertolt 128–9
Brenton, Howard 20, 59–60, 174–5,
    258–9
    aesthetics and 181–2
    Anne Boleyn 192–3
    Christie in Love 175, 182
    Fruit 183–5, 190–2
    In Extremis 192–3
    social work and 59
    Weapons of Happiness 44
Brighton Combination (later
    Combination) 18, 55, 59, 69,
    121, 125
*British Alternative Theatre Directory,
    The* 50
Brook, Peter 121, 206
Brown, Ian 209
Bryant, Julian 89–90
Bryden, Ronald 163
Bubble Theatre 106
building workers' strike 37–8
Bull, John 19, 153–4, 173, 182, 260
Burnley, Claire (Muldoon) 122–3, 127
bus 75

cabaret 163
Cabaret Show 163
Café, Rebecca 7
Caliban Lives 89–90

Callaghan, James 35, 46
Cambridge Footlights 9–10, 25
Camden Festivals 113
Cameron, Shirley 116, 117
Campaign for Homosexual Equality
    (CHE) 96
Campbell, Ken 76–8
Carib Theatre Company 91
Caribbean Cultural International 89
Carnaby Street 23
carnival 224
Carr, Robert 37
Carry on Matron 7
CAST (Cartoon Archetypal Slogan
    Theatre) 18, 80, 122, 123–4, 125,
    130, 132–3, 256
    Aunt Maud 125, 139, 144
    class factors 80, 121, 124–6, 127–8,
        132, 137–8
    Come In Hilda Muggins 125
    Confessions of a Socialist 126–7, 134,
        140, 141, 142
    creative control 121, 130
    festivals 125
    funding and 130–2, 133, 135, 136–7
    Goodbye Union Jack 134
    Harold Muggins 144
    Harold Muggins Is a Martyr 125
    John D. Muggins 121, 124
    Mr Oligarchy's Circus 124
    Muggins' Awakening 138–9
    Overdose 126
    recognition and 143–5
    Return of Sam the Man 130
    Sam the Man 126
    scope 121–2, 127
    thinking against 128–9
    Three for the Road 126, 133–4
    Trials of Horatio Muggins 124,
        129–30
    What Happens Next? 127, 135,
        142–3
Castle, Barbara 32
Cathy Come Home 28
Caute, David 127–8
ceilidh 268
Centre 42 255
Chapter Arts 200, 210, 212–13, 214, 215
Cheeseman, Peter 257–8

participation and 226–7, 235–6,
238–9, 240, 246, 248
pay and 241
professional–amateur bonds 232
registered as Galactic Holdings Ltd
241
SCAB 229
scope 223–6, 227, 228–30, 231, 232,
233, 235, 237–8
Shipyard Tales 240
site-specificity 223, 225, 229, 232–3,
234–6, 238–40, 244
Town Hall Tattoo 239
transport and 241–2
Travels of Lancelot Quail 232
Vigil of Icarus 245
vigils 231–2
Wesker, Arnold 255
Westbrook, Mike 148, 230–1
West London Theatre Workshop
(WLTW) 62–4
What Happened to Blake? 190, 191
What Happens Next? 127, 135, 142–3
What's Going On Here? 63
Whistling at Milestones 65
White, Gareth 196
White, Michael 225
White Heather Club, The 268
Whitney, Ray 135
Wildcat 256, 271
Will Spoor Mime Theatre 69
Wilson, Derek 165
Wilson, Harold 3, 15, 16, 30, 32–3, 41,
42–3
class factors 14–16
devaluation of pound 30–1
housing and 30
legacy 16
Wilson, Snoo 167–8
Winter of Discontent 46

Wintle, Justin 75
wire-walking 72–3
Woman's Work Is Never Done, A 81, 93
women and feminism 39, 40, 92–3, 114,
151–2
collective working 95
festival 71
lighting and staging 162
MR 93, 94–5
pay and 39
Pirate Jenny 65, 96
Red Ladder 81, 93
sexual factors 40, 149, 186–7, 202
success and 40
Women's Company 93–4
Women's Theatre Company 94
WSTG 92, 93
see also gender factors
Women's Company 93–4
Women's Festival 71
Women's Liberation (WL) movement
39, 92
Women's Street Theatre Group (WSTG)
51, 92, 93
Women's Theatre Company 94
working men's clubs 84, 255
World Cup 1966 22
World Cup 1970 32–3
Woyzeck 212–13, 214, 215
Wyndham's Theatre 85

Year 1967, The 129–30
Yippies (Youth International Party) 202–3
Yobbo Nowt 263
Yoko Ono 69
York Arts Centre 70
Yorkshire Gnomes 51, 115, 120
Young, B. A. 102

Z Cars 252